Violence,
and Bloodlines

Violence, Veils and Bloodlines

Reporting from War Zones

LOUIS J. SALOME

March 19, 2011
To Amy, a fellow
Crusader and now
a fellow reader.
Lou Salome

McFarland & Company, Inc., Publishers

Jefferson, North Carolina, and London

LIBRARY OF CONGRESS CATALOGUING-IN-PUBLICATION DATA

Salome, Louis J., 1941–
    Violence, veils and bloodlines : reporting from war zones / Louis
J. Salome.
      p.   cm.
    Includes index.

    ISBN 978-0-7864-4659-9
    softcover : 50# alkaline paper

    1. Military history, Modern — 20th century.   2. Military history,
Modern — 21st century.   3. World politics —1945–1989.   4. World
politics —1989–   5. Nationalism.   6. Tribes — Political activity.
7. Ethnic conflict.   8. Social conflict.   9. Salome, Louis J., 1941–
Travel.   10. Journalists — United States — Biography.   I. Title.
    D858.S25   2010
    909.82'5 — dc22   2009053550

British Library cataloguing data are available

Cover images: gas fields of Hassi Messaoud (photograph by
Louis J. Salome, 1997); ©2009 Shutterstock

Manufactured in the United States of America

McFarland & Company, Inc., Publishers
  Box 611, Jefferson, North Carolina 28640
   www.mcfarlandpub.com

To my family,
and to all the tribes that
talk to others, trying to understand

Contents

Acknowledgments

Some of the information on which this book is based was accumulated through my entire life. But the understanding required was only lately realized.

The lately part comes first because without the work and travel that journalism provided there would have been no book. Without the interviews and observed conduct and tribal conflicts among peoples, there would have been at best an internal and unspoken understanding that comes from the continuous but ordinary reflection on a life. Reflection alone would have been an insufficient route to understanding roots, religion and tribe, and probably would not have triggered the broader process.

Mixed in with the reflection and the journey are the immediate aiders and abettors, each of whom was essential in a different way. Most authors cite family first and now I understand the reason. Encouragement, support and tolerance are the words often used to describe the role of family in the creation of a book. For those contributions I thank my wife, Pat, and our children, Margaret, Mary and Andrew.

Others are equally easy to thank because of the help they offered.

Betsy Willeford, a former colleague and continuing friend, for her encouragement and unceasing willingness to provide editing skill, knowledge and advice.

The Rev. Alam Alam, a wise, spiritual and worldly man, a son of Maarrat-Saidnaya, Syria, and an admirer of the United States and its freedoms, for conveying a rare understanding of his native country and home town, its people and religious institutions.

Randa Alam of Maarrat-Saidnaya, the daughter of Father Alam and Salima Alam and an astute guide and translator, for introducing me to many relatives and residents in Maarrat-Saidnaya and for shepherding me through the many marvels of Damascus.

The Palm Beach Post library, notably its former director, Sammy Alzofon, for research that far exceeded my expectations or their obligations.

Paul and Karen Dale for the use of their cabin on the shores of Lucas Pond in Northwood, New Hampshire, where, secluded and without a television or a car, I wrote the first draft of this book during the four seasons of 2004.

Rick McKay, former photo editor at the Cox Newspapers' Washington Bureau, for having the foresight to save the bureau's photo archive, including most of the many hundreds of photos I took while working overseas. And to Pete Cross, Mark Edelson and Ray Graham of The *Palm Beach Post* Photo Department for ferreting out a few photos that I shot in Afghanistan and Somalia.

John Hockenberry and Doug Struck, friends and professional journalists of the first order, for their interest and encouragement.

Ed Gleason, a professor of American and Irish literature at St. Anselm College in Manchester, New Hampshire, and a friend for 50 interrupted years, for reading the manuscript and insisting that I find a publisher posthaste.

Diane Monti, a former English teacher, a neighbor and an even better friend now that she has proofread the manuscript, and liked it.

Grace Peirce and her computer wizardry, without which the maps would not be where they are and the stories would be less understood.

Kathy Lockwood, a new friend and author, who tipped me to a publisher that, she said, would probably like my book. She was right.

Thanks also to Jim Trupin for his encouragement, and his effort.

Collective thanks to all the nameless people I met from Belfast to Kabul who, wittingly or not, revealed the intricacies of their worlds. And to all those at home and abroad who listened to my stories as they accumulated and as I thought and talked my way through what was happening in the world that I met and that met me.

Finally, special thanks to the source of it all, my grandparents, John and Mary (Shaheen) Monsour, who were among the vanguard from Maarrat-Saidnaya, and Louis and Mary (Ghazale) Salome, all of whom ventured into a strange new world and thrived. And to my parents, Abraham Louis Salome and Rose (Monsour) Salome, for giving me the opportunity to understand what was happening at home and away. Without all of their journeys, I would not have had mine.

"For everything I relate, I have seen; and although I may have been deceived in what I saw, I shall certainly not deceive you in the telling of it."

From a letter to Henri Marie Beyle, the French author known as Stendhal

Preface

The question was simple: Would I prefer to be a political reporter in Washington or move to Jerusalem as the Middle East correspondent for Atlanta-based Cox Newspapers? The answer was simple, too. It was like asking whether I wanted to continue to stare into a mirror at home or, as things turned out, see the world from both sides of a rolling picture window.

After decades of keeping *The Miami* (Florida) *News* alive, Cox decided in late 1988 to let the ink run dry. My job as the paper's editorial page editor, always rewarding and almost always satisfying, was ending.

To Jerusalem I would go for four years, followed by five in London. From those hubs, I reported from the mysterious and fractious Middle East, throughout Europe and parts of Central Asia into North and East Africa and later from Afghanistan and Pakistan.

Timing and experiences, old and new, combined to unveil tribal behavior so universal that it seems for sure like an identity stamp impressed on bodies and souls.

As a reporter and editor, I always felt like a naked outsider. That role suited my personality, but in darker moods seemed to wrap me in the robe of a professional voyeur. Reporting from Belfast to Kabul, my role didn't change, although the full meaning of what I observed was transformed. My family background, I learned over time, enriched and enlightened my understanding of the behavior that I saw through my reporter's lens from tribe to tribe on three continents.

After three months in Washington, where I observed Middle Eastern tribal leaders, American political chiefs and journalists tickle each other and the world with smiles, false promises and even lies, my wife, Pat, and I left for the lands of Abraham.

Before our personal possessions had reached Jerusalem, where tribal behavior is as visible as temples, mosques, churches and police reports, I was

1

off to Iran to report on the death of the Ayatollah Khomeini. Within weeks Lebanon was my destination, followed by a lengthy journey to Moscow, Leningrad and Ukraine, where I wrote about Jews fleeing the dying Soviet Union.

So it went across the world where I reported for more than nine years. My senses were bombarded with bloody divisions that swelled from families, clans and tribes to broader ethnic, religious, language, cultural and territorial faults, leaving survivors wondering why and how former friends and neighbors could become deadly enemies. On the flip side of all these divisions are, of course, unions just as numerous.

In some regions, abuse and oppression reached to the largest and most basic tribal fissure of all — gender.

The more borders I crossed, the better I understood tribalism's universal nature, the behavior that I viewed outside the rolling picture window. On the other side of the window, my own background came into clearer focus and sharpened my understanding of tribalism in the world's behavioral chain.

At first I was unaware that my own background could help me understand what I was reporting. But when similar patterns of behavior rose in bold relief from tribe to tribe, I realized that my own family experiences were an aid, not a hindrance, to comprehending what I was seeing and hearing.

But not until a young Macedonian-born Albanian man asked, "Mr. Lou, what's your blood?" did I realize what people want to know when they ask a visitor, "Where you from?" They don't want to know where you were born, where you live, or the color and script on your passport. They want to know your grandfather's — always your father's father's — origin, your tribe and ethnicity, religion, ancestral language and territorial roots, all the characteristics that, they think, will identify you as friend or foe.

Laced with voices, faces and events that are usually vaguely known and even less understood, the tribal stories are rich with detail that flows from desperation:

- An aging couple huddles with a grandchild amid sandbags in a hut a scant yard or two from their tiny flower and vegetable gardens.
- An elderly woman waits for death while lying in a rain-drenched dugout at a refugee camp.
- A child stricken with diarrhea vomits at the feet of his rigid and famine-stricken mother who bears no milk to save her son.
- Families frozen in terror at the mere thought of missiles laden with poison gas pulverizing their homes and suffocating its occupants.
- Children with guns in hand and others with bullets in their bodies; a man who, dressed in unmatched dignity, talks of surviving years of solitary confinement and nearly three decades of imprisonment

because he fought for freedom in a tribal clash that pitted the weak against the more powerful; a lone survivor tells of his extended family being slaughtered in a religious, political and territorial conflict; in the name of God and religion, the more powerful kill the weak and rejoice because, they are convinced, that truth, beauty and righteousness are theirs exclusively.

Travel, on its own terms, removes a person from himself and opens a path for information and understanding to journey from eye to mind and back again. Add a journalist's life and work and the paths multiply, widen and lengthen.

Without the luck of the assignments, I would not have traveled from Belfast to Kabul to witness the innate and universal power of roots, religion, tribalism and blood. At the same time, the family and culture brought to the United States by my grandparents, sifted down to me and then leavened by my own education and life, added richness and credibility to the tribal realities that I witnessed, and to the narrative.

Readers, I feel certain, will scramble to confirm or deny their own tribal behavior. They will also be surprised, perhaps shocked, at how often they see and hear tribal behavior in their midst.

<hr />

Some of the names in this book have been changed to protect people who live in dangerous places. In Chapter 13, however, only my family name has been changed.

ONE

Faces, Faiths, Tongues and Blood

The first question was always the same: "Where you from?" Sometimes I answered "Lapland," casting a mental wink toward my seventh-grade geography teacher then laughing to myself at the absurdity of my tribal joke.

At other times I would say Sweden or Norway as I recalled reporting on the Ayatollah Khomeini's funeral in Iran with two tall, fair-skinned Norwegian journalists. They were mistaken for Americans while I was taken as some sort of Iranian tribal cousin.

To stretch the inquisition and force more pointed questions, I would sometimes say that I hailed from Millville, Massachusetts; Woonsocket, Rhode Island; New England or Miami. Even when I introduced myself as an American correspondent with Cox Newspapers in Atlanta, my interrogators weren't satisfied: "Where you from?" they repeated, emphasizing the word from and raising their voices when my answers fell short of their expectations.

In Aberdeen and Belfast and all across the Eurasian expanse to Afghanistan and Pakistan; in North and East Africa, the Middle East and Persian Gulf region, tribal chiefs, political figures, religious worthies and unworthies, killers, hostage-takers, desperate refugees, hotel clerks, cooks, taxi drivers, translators, life-saving aid workers, soldiers, police, arms dealers and women weeping for dead children asked, "Where you FROM?"

The question says more about the questioner than the questioned. Few asked where I called home or even where I was born, unless they thought I was born in their world or in the lairs of their ancient tribal enemies. They really wanted to know my roots, my religion, my tribe, whether I spoke their language, and by extension whether I liked their culture and supported their status in the world. My answers would determine whether they would trust me with their truths.

People of the deserts, steppes and littorals, of the mountains, valleys and islands were eager to fill a slot in their cultural lock boxes with a simple answer that would tell them all they needed to know about me. By my answer they would judge me, probably for all time or at least until they learned more about me as an individual. Most often we didn't get to know each other well enough as individuals because I trudged from war to war, crisis to crisis, during my nine-plus years as a foreign correspondent.

For almost half that time I was based in Jerusalem, a city that suffocates under the religion and religiosity of three major faiths. When I wasn't in the city that Christians, Jews and Muslims bless more for themselves separately than for each other, I ranged across landscapes that were no less tribal.

Mere days after I arrived in Jerusalem I learned that "Where you from?" means, "What's your tribe?" "What's your religion?" as if Islam, Judaism and Christianity were the only religions in the world. Wherever it is asked, the question cuts two ways: It binds and it divides. Which of the two prevails depends on where you sit and the answer to the question.

Everywhere I went the question came up because I have Mediterranean features and don't look like the tall, blond Hollywood version of an American. My waning Massachusetts accent altered by twangs from other languages and dialects acquired in my travels added to the mystery. Often I was accused of not even sounding like an American, so eager were people to put me in a slot they could more easily judge and understand. My Slavic, Semitic, Latin and Nordic friends refused to be tricked and thrown off course by the simple answer that I was an American. They knew better. They could tell by looking at me that it wasn't that simple. They wanted to identify a friend, or an enemy, a person they could or couldn't trust.

But I seldom answered the question they wanted answered unless they asked me pointedly. I was not eager to help them put me in one of their identity boxes that locked out individuality and sealed in generalizations. Because of an inadequate vocabulary or because they wanted to be subtle and inoffensive in their search for generalizations, my inquisitors usually couldn't figure out how to frame the question to get the answer they sought. So they simply repeated it, each time shouting "Where you from?" a little louder and shouting the word "from" loudest of all. They behaved something like an American speaking loudly to a foreigner who knows little English in the belief that turning up the volume will force understanding from the ear to the brain.

Most of the time, I began my part of the dialogue by saying simply that I was from America. When that didn't satisfy the questioner, who was searching for something much deeper, I strung out my American connections this way: I was born in Woonsocket, Rhode Island, grew up in Millville, Massachusetts, went to college in Massachusetts, which is in New England, a small region in the northeastern United States. This tactic usually produced more frustration than enlightenment or even sharper questions.

In Europe, mainly on the continent, when I introduced myself as Lou Salomé, a knowing smile often was my reward. Many an inquisitor asked, "Do you know who Lou Salomé was?" Nietzsche's lover, I answered, following their line of thought. This was always an entertaining twist to the usual line of inquiry. Louise von Salomé, an attractive Russian-born woman of German descent, was Friedrich Nietzsche's real or would-be lover as well as an object of desire for many other men of her time. That Lou Salomé, no tribal cousin for sure, was also a friend and colleague of Sigmund Freud and a psychologist and psychotherapist in her own right. But Nietzsche, not I, remains her tether to history.

The names of my father and grandfather were an occasional point of interest among those trying to nail down my origins.

A female security officer at the airport in Tel Aviv, where the questioning of departing passengers was routine, once asked about my father's name in an attempt to expose the heritage that she probably suspected would match my appearance. My father's name was Abraham, Ibrahim among Arabs, a name that works wonders among Jews and Arabs. But Abraham was of no defining help to her.

"What's your grandfather's name?" the security officer asked, reaching back a generation. "Which one?" I answered. That was my trick answer. "Wait a minute," she responded, leaving to discuss this heavy security matter with her boss. "You can go," she said upon her return, without uttering another word. Her boss probably figured that I couldn't possibly be a problem if I didn't know which grandfather counted for both. His conclusion was right, but for the wrong reason. My answer was a cultural curveball, because in the Middle East only one grandfather counts; the paternal grandfather holds all the sperm. Your mother's father is strictly second rate in that part of the world.

On a few occasions, such as at the airport in Djibouti, the former French colony on the Horn of Africa, inquisitors quickly narrowed the question to, "Where's your grandfather from?" I was in a hurry and the airport workers were holding my passport, so I omitted the grandfather distinctions and answered quickly. "Syria," I said, my tone dripping with, "And what are you going to do about it?"

The sharpest tribal question that I received came from Diamant, a translator and guide whom I had hired in Skopje, Macedonia. Born in Macedonia, Diamant was in his early 20s. But he was an ethnic Albanian, and in his mind, body and soul he would always be an Albanian, not a Macedonian, although I thought he most certainly would never live in neighboring Albania, Europe's poorest country. Albania was so deprived it was the only country where I ever saw a pig on a leash, although many peoples elsewhere had no pigs.

My translator spoke the Slavic tongue of Macedonia, and he spoke Albanian, too. He said he was a Muslim, but not to his marrow, not the kind who would fit comfortably in Iran or Saudi Arabia. We were traveling from Macedonia to Albania on a reporting trip. It was August 19, 1995, and we were crossing the border where autos were required to drive through a depression in the road that was filled with dirty water and mud. The object was to cleanse the underside of vehicles, an impossible chore as I saw it, so mirrors at the end of long poles could detect any bomb. Before crossing the border, passengers were required to wash their boots in a pan filled with dirty water, as if one of the countries were cleaner or less tainted than the other, which seemed an absurdity of a high order.

Cleared to go, we pulled away from the local version of a car wash and entered Albania. My translator quickly turned inquisitor. "Mr. Lou," he said, "Where you from?" He knew that I was an American because we had discussed this before. Now, in his mind, he was searching for soul not surface. He wanted to learn what was beneath my skin because he believed that if he knew that, he would know where I stood on tribal issues that were important to him and therefore what he should think of me.

My answers at first were the usual ones: America, New England, etc. Impatient, he cut me short.

"Mr. Lou," he said, "What's your blood?"

I raised my eyebrows, smiled and mumbled holy shit under my breath. Give this kid an "A," I thought. No one had ever put the question exactly that way to me before and no one has since, but this was the real and proper translation of "Where you from?" For most of the world, the tribe is where life begins and often ends. Tribe means the corps a person can count on to help in times of difficulty. Forget about individuality, education or the effects of where you have lived and with whom. Heritage, religion, language, race, ethnicity, soul, history — blood, if you will — are what matter. I stopped playing around because I thought his question deserved a direct answer, although I knew my answer would probably deceive him even if he thought it did not.

What little light there was near the border of Macedonia and Albania flicked on around me: This was the real question people wanted to ask when they said, "Where you from?" I knew what they wanted generally, but the specifics escaped me until my ethnic–Albanian friend from Macedonia asked me the question that people the world over want to know about everyone they meet. What's your blood?

After I explained that my grandparents had gone to the United States from Syria almost a hundred years earlier and settled in Rhode Island, this young man of Albanian descent who lived in Macedonia didn't ask another question. Syria, roots, was what he was after. I don't know exactly what that meant to him, and maybe it was a cipher that he wouldn't admit, but he seemed to have his answer to all the personal questions he could ever think to ask about me.

———

All the principal traits that people apply to identify themselves and separate themselves from others I call tribalism. This elastic circle of union and separation literally begins with family, clan and tribe. These basic alliances naturally include language, religion and sects within religions, culture and all that implies, ethnicity, race, gender, region and territory, wealth, power and national interests. Those are all tribal traits. They are all — especially religion, tribal blood ties and flags representing saints, sinners and nations — the eggs of war, to paraphrase the French writer Guy de Maupassant.

Wherever war and mayhem thrive, tribalism — now often couched under the rubric of national interest — rules. That's what you see when you strain the alphabet soup of wars from Algeria to Bosnia to Iran and Iraq, to Lebanon, and Somalia, Israel and Palestine, Tadjikistan, Afghanistan, Rwanda and Northern Ireland. Tribes usually resist shedding their views of history. In that way, tribes can use their same views over and over to rekindle the flames of tribal hatred. Outsiders, with their own interests to feed, are always willing to pour more fuel on the pyre.

Tribal unity prevails almost uniformly in the smaller circles of families and clans but surely not always in the larger orbits. When you share pastry and tea with a poor Lebanese family in the middle of a war and the father asks, "Do you like our food?" he is really asking, "Do you like our culture? Do you like us, our tribe, better than you like our tribal enemy?"

Some alliances that seem to defy logic are made along larger tribal fault lines. Trying to divine which alliances will crumble and which new ones will deepen and strengthen and why is a lifetime job, especially in the Middle East. The word Byzantine, used to describe an indiscernible labyrinth of political and social behavior, wasn't coined in Lapland.

Westerners, especially Americans, prefer to think in a more linear and naive fashion: For example, all Shiite Muslims think and act alike whether they live in Iran, Iraq or Azerbaijan; all Kurds will always stick together against a common foe; Arabs always will oppose non–Arabs, such as Iranians. But life and the competing interests of religions, ethnic groups, nations and rulers are too complicated for such simplicity.

At the same time, two old saws generally, but not always, hold true among people in the Middle East as they often do among tribes elsewhere: Many alliances are formed and broken according to the rule, the cliché, that,

"The enemy of my enemy is my friend." When conditions change, so do enemies and friends.

The second rule, which is tribal to the core and often quoted, goes something like this: Me against my brother, me and my brother against our cousin and then the circle widens slowly until it becomes, under great stress, all regional tribes against any foreigner. In other words, loyalty stretches throughout the extended family and tribes to include ethnic, religious, language and most other tribal ties almost without end until the line is drawn at foreign tribes. When foreign tribes enter the fray, they will not receive permanent visas.

American officials have been fond of saying that foreign fighters have infiltrated Iraq to boost the insurgency there. Whatever truth there is in that line of thinking, the language is essentially propaganda aimed at deceiving the American public. In Iraq's sectarian, regional and ethnic tribal conflict, American, British and other Western troops were considered the foreign fighters.

To these two maxims I would add a third: "Every man for himself." This explains why expected tribal alliances do not always hold, but it doesn't destroy the dominant, "What's your blood?" principle that governs tribal loyalties and actions.

These maxims don't fit snugly and may seem contradictory, yet they are real and can coexist simultaneously. That's the reason comprehending tribal politics is so difficult. If you're looking for one overarching tribal theme in the Middle East, it would be this: The tribal circle with all of its real and potential contradictions extends to region. Right or wrong, foreigners in large numbers or as occupiers will never be welcome there in the long run. At the same time, individual visitors are accorded great, perhaps unmatched, hospitality throughout the region. Hospitality is, in fact, a tribal obligation. It is a cultural sin of great magnitude if a person or family fails to provide food, drink and comfort no matter how meager their resources. But don't plan on staying too long.

Referring to Israel's presence, an intelligent Palestinian, not a religious extremist by any means, once said to me that although it took almost 100 years, the Arabs and others in the region threw the Crusaders out of Jerusalem. He wasn't affected by a khamseen, which in Arabic means 50, and which is one of those brutally hot and sultry desert days when the temperature reaches 50 degrees Centigrade or about 127 degrees Fahrenheit. That was his history, his tribe, talking and revealing another characteristic of the region: No one forgets any slight. This view of Arab/Muslim dominance and persistence also displays another regional characteristic: a selective view of history. The Arabs prefer to forget the centuries-long Ottoman Turk domination of the region that ended after World War I, and the region's earlier history when Jewish kingdoms competed with those of other tribes for regional power. Of the Turks, the Arabs would say, at least they were Muslims; as for the old Jewish kingdoms, well, that was very long ago.

On more than one occasion young Palestinian Muslim men became visibly saddened and their faces pale when they asked if I was a Muslim and I said, "no, my family is Christian." Their color returned a little when I brought the conversation back around and said that my grandparents had gone to the United States from Syria almost a hundred years earlier. Their reaction laid bare the scale of competing tribal traits and interests in the region.

Lebanon, unfortunately for all Lebanese, is a classic example of unifying and competing tribal interests. Differing Sunni and Shiite Muslims, Maronite Christians who like to consider themselves French or even Phoenician, Palestinian refugees and Druze, who are Arabs but not Muslims or Christians, all battled over historic slights and for power during the civil wars of the 1970s, 1980s and early 1990s. The blood prizes were religious, economic, political. When Syria, with its historic ties to Lebanon, Israel, Iran, the United States and France all plunged into the quagmire in attempts to further their own interests, Lebanon burned ever more deeply.

The Syrian-Iranian alliance demonstrates how the usual tribal rules can be broken when other, stronger tribal interests prevail. In broad tribal terms, an Iran-Syria alliance is more of a mismatch than a match. Syria is an Arab country and a majority of its people are Sunni Muslims, Islam's largest and most powerful sect. For a few years in the latter half of the twentieth century, Syria and Egypt, which is predominantly Sunni and the most populous Arab country, built a political union. But Syria's secular government has for decades been controlled by the Assad family which belongs to the Alawite sect, a minority branch of Islam's Shiite sect.

Iran, however, has a fundamentalist Shiite Islamic government. Iranians are an Indo-European, not a Semitic, people. Shiites are Islam's largest minority, but a minority nonetheless. To say that establishment Sunnis and Shiites do not normally mix well is to say that Irish republican Catholics and Protestant British unionists in Northern Ireland don't love each other.

Syria and Iran are brought closer on a sectarian level because the Assad family's small Alawite sect is closer religiously to Iran's Shiite population than to the majority Sunnis in Syria. At the same time, the Assad political network is more balanced than Iran's and includes members of the Sunni majority as well as members of Christian sects.

On a political level, the Iran-Syria alliance is a smoother blend because their two governments have shared common enemies — Iraq and Israel — and interests. Iran fought a long war against Saddam Hussein's Iraq, while Syria and Iraq have long been divided along Arab political/ideological lines. Iran gave military and economic help to its deprived Shiite brothers of South Lebanon, where women still follow the tribal codes and walk three steps behind men. A major reason for Iran's support was to counter the Israelis: Syria supported that same cause and aided Iran's efforts to build the Hezbollah fundamentalist Shiite movement in South Lebanon.

Syria, of course, was directly and indirectly engaged in fighting the Israelis in Lebanon after Israel's 1982 invasion. Later still, when Israeli troops remained in South Lebanon backing their Lebanese Christian proxies, Syria indirectly fought Israel through the Lebanese Shiites that Iran also supported. So, Lebanon remained a periodic punching bag in Middle East power politics.

On nationalistic paper, Syria and Iraq should have been allies, leaving the Indo-European Iranians as the odd-tribe out. Like the Assad family in Syria, the late Saddam Hussein led a secular, not an Islamic fundamentalist, government. But deep political, personal and sectarian differences blocked a Syrian-Iraqi alliance. Other Arab strongmen, Sunnis by sect, considered Saddam Hussein a threat to their power. But for various reasons, those dictators could not at first completely sever the tribal bond to a fellow Sunni Arab. Besides, the other Arab dictators considered a secular Arab leader as less of a threat than Iran's Shiite fundamentalists, at least until Saddam Hussein invaded Kuwait in 1990.

Saddam Hussein and his family of Sunni cohorts controlled Iraq and subjugated its majority Shiite population and large Kurdish minority almost exclusively through his extended family from its narrow tribal base in the village of Tikrit. Here again one family and one tribe ruled.

For weird tribal alliances it is tough to top Iran's pals in the 1970s and 1980s. Under the shah, Iran and Israel were allies during the Cold War in part because Iraq was the enemy of both. But after the Ayatollah Khomeini and his band of Shiite fundamentalist mullahs deposed the shah, Iran saw Israel as its bitter enemy and Syria, an enemy of Israel and Iraq, as its friend. So Syria and Israel, enemies of each other, have both been allies of Iran, but at different times and under different circumstances.

The most reliable absolute in the tangled tribal allegiances and divisions of the Middle East and South Asia is that there is none. If all of this appears convoluted and almost unfathomable, one reason is because the tribes and the reasons for their conflicts and shifting alliances are unfamiliar to most Americans and other Westerners.

Afghanistan's clans and tribes, save for the Afghan Communists, fought the Soviet Union throughout the 1980s. Even in that hard war against a common enemy, the Afghan tribes did not fight under a common command. They fought separately, divided literally among tribes that split along ethnic and language lines, and Islamic leanings. When the defeated Soviets withdrew, stung by U.S. military aid to the Afghan tribes through Pakistan's intelligence agencies, the Afghan tribes turned against each other in a destructive civil war that produced the wildly extremist Taliban, the Students of Islam. The Taliban warred against women and children as well as against their military and political rivals on just about all tribal terms.

Although Israel is comprised of Jewish tribes and subtribes from throughout the world, in the Middle East Israel is a tribe unto itself. When Israel tries to play the regional game of the enemy of my enemy is my friend, it makes short-term gains that may buy time and confuse its enemies, but is usually less successful in the longer term. Israel has been successful when it deals directly with its enemies, such as Egypt and Jordan, with whom it has peace treaties thanks to American money and military assistance. The Israelis, when they plunge into the Byzantine game, play what is usually called their minority card, sometimes called their Muslim card. When Israel plays that card, it tries to split non–Arab Muslims from its Arab Muslim enemies.

Israel's attempt, with the Reagan administration's backing, to set up a friendly Christian regime in Lebanon in the 1980s was a disaster that took Israel more than 20 years to undo and which still simmers for the Arabs. That the Christian phalange militias were as brutal as those of any other Lebanese tribe wasn't the only point. The Israelis were looking for a counterweight to hostile tribes in Lebanon, including the Palestinian refugees there. They backed the wrong tribe in Lebanon and probably always will because they can't win by backing proxies on that turf if all the other tribes allied against them. When the time came for the Maronite Christians, who like to accent their Francophile ties and their long-faded Lebanese Phoenician genealogy, to tie the knot with Israel, their leaders couldn't do it. They could not separate themselves from their Lebanese tribal cousins, although Israel and the Lebanese Christians shared common enemies in Lebanon.

Although the Ayatollah Khomeini is long buried, the mullahs who succeeded him in Iran retain a vitriolic hatred of Israel. This is partly because Israel, along with the United States, backed the shah, whose secret police imprisoned and killed thousands of Iranians, among whom were Shiite fundamentalists.

When the shah dumped the Iraqi Kurds in the mid–1970s, with the complicity of the United States, Israel had been backing the Kurds and the shah because the Israelis and the shah shared a common enemy: Saddam Hussein. That didn't work well either. Ask the shah. Ask the Kurds. Ask Israel. Ask Henry Kissinger. With Saddam Hussein gone from the scene and Iraq riven by tribal rivalries and still a potential quagmire, Khomeini and his descendants sat on their religious throne in Tehran for more than thirty years.

Israel's latest Muslim ace in the hole is Turkey, also a U.S. ally and a member of NATO. Turkey, as the Ottoman Empire, ruled the Middle East for centuries. A large country, Turkey sits atop the rest of the Middle East like a lid on a large pot and controls much of the region's water supply. Most Turks are Sunni Muslims, but with a strong strain of Sufi Islamic traditions and practices, a curious mixture of warrior brotherhoods, poets, mystics, love and tolerance. Its government is secular and real control rests in the hands of generals. Sometimes shaky, the Turkish-Israeli alliance seems to be holding.

Western tribal alliances and conflicts can be just as complex, but usually they don't seem so because the players are more familiar, the policies are our own and we trust our propaganda and nuanced language more. We may even think we know enough to take sides in familiar fights. Some conflicts appear more linear than others, but a closer look shows their complexities.

Everyone knows that the Protestant and Catholic tribes, may their gods bless them all, have fought for centuries in Northern Ireland. It's not all of the Catholics and it's not all of the Protestants although sometimes it appeared that way. Their cooling conflict is more than a tribal fight about religion. It is thoroughly cultural, linguistic, ethnic, political and territorial, imperial, and centers as much on history — Britain's long and brutal rule over Ireland — as it does on the fact that most of the Irish are Catholics and most of the British unionists in Northern Ireland are Protestants.

Coleridge's warning about religious fanaticism applies to members of all sects, not only to Christians. "He who begins by loving Christianity better than Truth will proceed by loving his own sect or church better than Christianity, and end by loving himself better than all," the poet said. To the great extent that his admonition has been ignored throughout the world, religious tribalism has given birth to wholesale death and unyielding hatred.

Tribal conflicts — whether singly or in combination, about language, religion, race, gender, ethnicity, power and land, national interest or any other aspect of tribal chauvinism — are driven by fundamentalist extremism, which need not be sectarian but in which religion usually plays a part. Sometimes the extremism gestates on the fringes before it bursts to the dominant center. At other times extremist tribal themes are generated by governments or the powerful center. In the Balkans and Iran, for example, it was the power of the historic center stirred by dominant figures that dictated public behavior. Individuals and minority views are silenced or drowned out by the sweep of broad passion. Anyone in strong disagreement gets killed, flees or joins in to survive.

Americans remember fundamentalist Iran for its masses gathered in the countless tens of thousands to shout "Death to America" while the believers beat themselves in a frenzy of rage and religion. What I remember is talking

sanely with many Iranians in the midst of funeral proceedings for the Ayatollah Khomeini. They asked about America and U.S. government policy,
but they were not threatening. Yet when the crowd grew into the thousands
and the "Death to America" chants began, the sanity disappeared. The people who had been talking rationally joined with the crowd to wail and shout
and beat their breasts. They had no choice, with the religious police, the army
and the crowd watching. The crowd had taken over from the individual and
the human dynamic was instantly transformed. This could happen anywhere,
I thought, if government power and popular emotions are allowed to run
amok.

Many tribal forces, not just one or two, may determine alliances and
betrayals and result in a contradictory picture that often is difficult for outsiders to see clearly. So it's a mistake to believe that all Shiite Muslims, those
in Iran and Iraq, for example, share the same views about the role of religion
in the state, or that all Orthodox Christians automatically will unite on all
tribal issues. Some tribal beliefs are stronger than others, and some threats
are more personal to one tribe than to others.

Russia publicly supported Serbia in the Balkans wars. Both are historically Christian Orthodox countries, but Russia's Orthodoxy was newly redis-
covered after the fall of communism and a weakened Russia was not about
to fight to defend Serbia when NATO bombs rained on Belgrade. A few years
earlier and the Russians, the Soviets, might have behaved far differently. And
so, too, the United States and Western Europe.

Minority tribes in the Middle East and East and North Africa, and to a
lesser extent Eastern Europe, deal with their status in different ways, depending on their size. If they are small, like the Circassians in Syria and Jordan,
Christian Copts in Egypt or ancient but obscure religious sects such as the
Yazidis in Iraq, they try to stay under the radar of the ruling tribe. For them,
almost any glare brings the boot. They adapt, compromise and try to avoid
calling attention to themselves, although even those actions don't always save
their blood. Their objective is to survive, to shield themselves from persecution by governments and dominant tribes that periodically must instill fear
and flex their power to stay on top. Members of these minority tribes occasionally deny their heritage to strangers to avoid being seen as troublemak-
ers. At the same time, large minority tribes and even tribes that are a numerical
majority but lack political, military and economic power often rebel and
threaten the ruling tribe.

The Kurds in Iraq, Turkey and Iran are examples of large minority tribes
that frequently rise up, try to act like their oppressors by engaging in shifting alliances in their struggle for freedom before they get outmaneuvered and
overpowered by the controlling tribe. Majority Shiite Muslims in Lebanon,

poor and forever suppressed by once-dominant Christians and minority Sunni Muslims, made their strike for gold during the long Lebanese wars of the 1970s, 1980s and early 1990s. The Party of God — Hezballah — eventually succeeded, with the intentional help of Iran and Syria, and the unintentional aid of Israel and the United States.

In many countries, minority tribes are referred to by the word ethnic followed by a hyphen, as the ethnic–Albanians in Macedonia and Kosovo, the ethnic–Syrians of southeastern Turkey and the ethnic–Tadjik and ethnic–Uzbek tribes of Afghanistan. In countries like those, nothing melts in the pot because there is no real pot. The hyphen has real meaning. It is used to distinguish members of a minority tribe who live in one country but, in the opinion of other tribes, don't really belong there. They are singled out for a hyphen because the majority tribe believes the hyphenated minorities belong in a neighboring country that usually bears their name, such as Tadjikistan for Afghanistan's ethnic–Tadjiks and Uzbekistan for Afghanistan's ethnic–Uzbeks. Hyphenated tribes, if they are large enough, usually spend all their waking hours fighting for their rights, sometimes politically, sometimes with arms. If they are too small to fight back, they go quietly into the mix without ever blending in.

In all my years of working abroad I never heard anyone, except foreign government officials, refer to the United States as the United States. America is the name people from most other tribes use, although I was careful with officious British customs officials to say that I was from the United States. If I told a customs official at London's Heathrow Airport that I was an American, he might respond, as some have, "North or South America? There's more than one country in America, you know." That's how people behave when their empire disappears.

Outsiders, by and large, know much more about America and Americans than Americans know about Arabs, Russians, Poles, Bosnians, or even about Israel and Israelis. I sat in classrooms in Normandy, France, where middle-school students studied D-Day and the American-led invasion of Europe during World War II with the interest of American students trying to master computer science. The French boys and girls could trace in great detail the march of American GIs through their land. The records of a Dutch Catholic priest remain the best source anywhere of information on American GIs who were killed or unaccounted for fighting in Western Europe during World War II.

When I first visited my own family members in Syria I found that they knew the names and relationships of all their principal relatives in the United

States, most of whom are dead. But my knowledge of those relatives in Syria, some of whom are first cousins, was almost zero. One man, a second cousin who lives in the family village, recalled how, after his family had heard of my father's death, he postponed his wedding in 1964, and later had only a church ceremony with no reception.

The people I met while working and traveling generally have a good bead on America. That view can be skewed some, but not entirely, because it is shaped heavily by the exercise of American power in their country or region.

From the outside, America is a magnet because of its military power, wealth, size, opportunity to study and make money, and for its freedom. Of those, I believe, political freedom is the least understood because most other tribes know little about it. The freedom to work, study, own a business, make money and perhaps become rich is well understood because that prospect exists elsewhere, although the opportunities are fewer. Because of its size, wealth and freedom, America offers greater opportunities for success.

But the full meaning of political freedom is more difficult for many outside tribes to grasp. In countries where ruling tribes suppress other tribes for many reasons, a person learns to have political conversations under a tree in a park. True stories of husbands and wives squealing on each other in Communist East Germany, Romania and throughout the old Soviet Eastern bloc offer a hint of the difficulty that people from suppressed societies have in understanding freedom of speech and other democratic exercises. Go to America, work hard, make money, keep quiet, maybe return to the native country before the kids become teenagers in order to avoid drugs, street crime and sex in the cities. This view of America still prevails in other tribal lands.

The outsiders' view of America is more pink than rosy as it once was. But few foreigners would turn down the opportunity to move to New York, Chicago or San Francisco. There is a real fear of crime and drugs and sexual permissiveness, and the harm those aspects of American culture can do to families. Drug abuse, to be sure, exists at various levels throughout the world. But to the rest of world, crack-cocaine America is the global drug capital. Sexual repression is almost as much of a problem in the Arab Middle East as is the wholesale commercialization of sex in the United States, although Middle Easterners would never admit that.

In the dim light of a Cairo club, I watched with great amusement as two young Saudi princes, apparently making their debut on the town and on the barley, consumed several bottles of whiskey during hours of galloping delirium while continuously throwing fists full of money at fully clothed dancers who did nothing but toss their long hair around and swivel their heads. The young Saudis won the money-tossing competition with two Libyan business-men who cried oil when they ran out of cash. By the time the featured belly-dancer reached the stage, the Saudis were dead drunk and vomiting on their zippers as they stumbled to the men's room. Hanging on the shoulders of their minders, the princes left for their limo before the best belly-dancer I ever saw anywhere heaved and shook her way on stage.

Criticism of the American people is rare among tribes in the Middle East and Africa, more common among tribes in Europe. But in the Middle East, I found no shortage of criticism leveled against U.S. government policy. At the core of this criticism, the Arab tribes will tell you, is the failure of the U.S. government to follow fair and balanced policies in the Palestinian-Israeli conflict.

Members of Afghanistan's various tribes know few details of the running Israeli-Palestinian conflict. But when they watch the BBC and/or Middle East networks showing Palestinians being attacked by Israeli forces, the picture they see shows America and Israel on the same team and Muslims on the other side. If they know about the Palestinian suicide bombers, either they don't let on or they consider it a fair response to the Israeli occupation of Palestinian territories. But that's only the most obvious point of criticism by outside tribes. Beyond Israel and Palestine, America and the West are targeted for their exploitation of the region, specifically, for trying to control its oil resources. The acquisitive, imperialistic nature of Western culture is also widely suspect. This contrasts sharply with today's tribal cultures that by nature are more closed and protective of their heritage and traditional way of life.

Some Middle Eastern and North African countries want to modernize, and have to some degree, but on their own terms. They want to acquire the tools of technology to modernize, but without having to surrender their cus-toms and religious norms to an alien culture. At their roots, those tribes know that to modernize wholesale on Western terms would be to sacrifice their cul-tures. No matter what others think of their traditions, this is not a trade they wish to make. More open societies would benefit more people in those lands, but even those who are suppressed by ruling elites believe, as many have told me often, that change must come by their own hands.

Even in some Western societies, a person's tribe contains a person's essen-tial identity. In America people say that "Blood is thicker than water." Or "You have to take care of your own." Or "Keep it inside the family," and "Don't wash your dirty linen in public." If you pay close attention, you will be surprised at how often you hear the words "blood" and "tribe" and "fam-ily" mentioned in a tribal context.

Class lines are fading in Britain, but still a person's accent gives away his region, education level, social and economic status. When I lived in London from 1993 to 1998, the tabloids there still published headlines about frogs and krauts if they believed they could stir up the blokes sufficiently to sell a few more papers. Ask an East Londoner what he thinks of Yorkshiremen and he's likely to laugh and say, "They all have short arms and deep pockets." Put Scots, Welsh, English and Irish in a pub after hours and duck. But let another country threaten Britain, and the old Angles, Saxons, Normans, Picts, Scots and Welsh become one.

Class, wealth and education, as well as race, gender, religion, refugee status, language and region are tribal zones in the West. Westerners, especially Americans, like to believe that all citizens of their countries are equal, but anyone who sits in court or seeks health care but can't get insurance knows better.

Even globalization is a tribal matter. Globalization, which is nothing more than triumphant post–Cold War capitalism on steroids, is one of the most important tribal dividers on the map today although it is obscured by meaningless nation-state power acronyms and silly jargon. Globalization is the wealthy countries taking advantage of the poorer peoples masked by the cliché that a rising tide raises all boats. Problem is the money goes into yachts for the few, not even rafts for the many.

Money tends to be the great leveler in the United States, as well as the great divider. Race, ethnic background, gender, education and career remain great tribal fault lines in America.

These days the West's main tribal motivator is economic, the acquisition of wealth at the expense of others on the grounds that everyone has the same opportunity, which is not so. What the United States and the West can't get by bullying, they try to buy. They can buy political leaders, as the Bush administration did in Iraq, but in the long run it is impossible to buy the street. Globalization is a marketing word coined to paint exploitation as opportunity. Poor people yearn for a better life, but not for foreign exploitation that destroys native cultures and shifts the bulk of a country's natural wealth to foreign tribes.

I've heard Western aid workers in Afghanistan condemn the use of the word primitive as judgmental because it suggests that materially advanced nations belong on a higher plane of human values than countries where camels and donkeys draw water from wells by walking in circles. Tribal contrasts are highlighted, not blurred, when materially advanced countries seek to suck up the wealth and resources of poorer countries, no matter what label they give to the latest shell game in which wealthy tribes again conquer poorer tribes under the guise of spreading democracy and civilization, as if civilization belongs to one tribe, one kind of culture, only.

Two years into the 21st century, not long after I had returned to the United States from London, I met a young Haitian man who was carting groceries to customers' cars in Palm Beach Gardens, Florida. We talked in English at first. As we walked to my car, I spoke a little French, knowing that a smile awaited me because language sunders barriers, opens doors: "What's your name? How are you? How old are you?" I said to him in French. The man was surprised to hear someone who was not a member of his tribe speak a language that is closely related to his native Creole.

"Where you from?" the man inquired. "Here, the United States," I answered, thinking the question strange because most of the time I speak decent American English.

"No, No," the man answered. "Where are you FROM?"

TWO

Across the River and
Into an Iraqi War

"That is not Iraq. That is Kurdistan," said Tariq, a Kurdish guide, pointing across the Tigris River to Iraq from the Syrian border crossing near Malakia. We were about to cross the Tigris on our way to Zakho in northern Iraq during the abortive March 1991 Kurdish uprising against Saddam Hussein's Iraq.

After we scrambled up the east bank of the broad and muddy Tigris River, Sherco, a Kurdish fighter who doubled as a tribal folk singer to pass the time, led us to a flat worn spot on the dirt road that was free of bomb craters. Sherco didn't know the territory so he feared land mines astride the beaten path. With a nod toward his cohort Nammo, who was wrapped in bullets and ready to shoot or be shot, Sherco said we would be safe there in the gathering night until other Kurds arrived to drive us to the nearby city of Zakho, a little deeper in northern Iraq.

Soon we were clapping and singing chorus to Sherco's lead, in effect baying at the three-quarter moon as we sat in a circle around a gas lamp under a clear, starry Middle Eastern sky: Martin Nangle, an Irish free-lance photographer working for a wire service out of London, two Kurds from Germany who were with a German woman — radio reporters, they said, although they carried no equipment — and I. This was a beautiful moment — the river racing high behind us, the ceiling of stars, the ancient tribal exhortations — especially so if you didn't think about the land mines around us and the slaughter building to the south.

Six months earlier I had walked across the Euphrates River in northern Syria. A trickle then, the great Euphrates was blocked by Turkey in the mountains upstream to fill dams as part of an elaborate hydroelectric scheme that provided Turkey with more power than ever over the Tigris and Euphrates waters and could also deprive Syria and Iraq of more water than ever. Within six months I had crossed two rivers that nourished early Western Civilization as did no others. From the beginning of recorded time in the West, an almost infinite number of warriors, immigrants, traders, refugees and others who advanced and restrained human progress had crossed those waters. Although I was and would remain ill with a severe case of diarrhea and unsure of the war that rumbled in the distance as I joined with Sherco and Nammo singing songs that I didn't know, I was impressed to be crossing those same waters, trodding those same paths.

"Oh, my love, I am always thinking of you, but I must go to fight," Sherco sang in Kurdish, recalling the powerful oral tradition of the tough mountain tribes. Born in the Iraqi Kurdish town of Sulaimanya, Sherco was a pesh merga, the honored name of a Kurdish mountain warrior. He and Nammo bore all the instruments of their profession: a turban and scarf, pantaloons, wide, sash-like wasteband, rifle with bayonet, bandoleer, 10-inch knife and two grenades hanging from the belt. Sherco, 26, spoke English well. Short, stocky, handsome, filled with the purpose of someone in his mid-twenties and sure of the historical mission of his people, Sherco said that he had lived in Turkey, Iran and Syria in the previous five years, fighting for Kurdish rights in his wider Kurdistan. If the Kurds have a cultural mantra, it is to fight. Sherco explained that pesh merga means, "Man who is facing death." The Kurds have left enough blood in their mountains and villages to make it ignorant and foolish to quarrel with that definition.

Artillery fire boomed to the south and east as we sang and waited. Columns of weary and ragged Iraqi soldiers, from Sunni Arab tribes who had given up the fight, trudged by. Guarded by Kurdish fighters, they were being taken across the Tigris to Syria probably to be drained of military intelligence. Egyptian nationals, such as Majdi, Farid and Talit, were fleeing the Kurdish uprising from Zakho and heading home. They were running from what we had come to witness, the Kurdish rebellion against Saddam Hussein immediately after the Persian Gulf war in March 1991. In little more than a week, that rebellion and Saddam Hussein's counterattack would turn Martin Nangle and me into refugees along with our Iraqi Kurdish hosts. Because of the Gulf war and the truce that followed, this was also an American story, maybe the end game to the unfinished war. Ultimately, it became another international story of brutality and betrayal in Kurdistan. Again the Kurds were buried at the bottom of the tribal heap.

Encouraged, along with the Shiites in southern Iraq, to revolt by then-President George H. W. Bush, the Iraqi Kurds began their uprising on March 7. Despite early successes, by the end of March the Kurds who hadn't been killed by Saddam's helicopters and tanks were in full and baleful retreat to Iran and Turkey in one of the largest refugee flights in the memory of any-

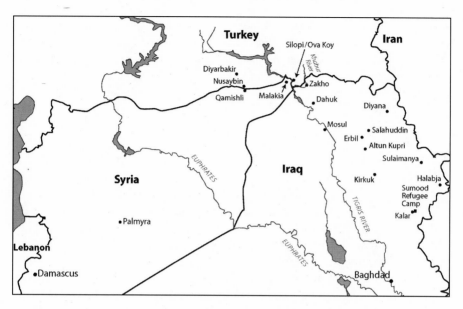

Iraqi Kurdistan, where Kurds lived and often died under Saddam Hussein's boot, and where I entered a war zone from Syria and fled through Turkey.

one anywhere. Bush the Elder ignored his own words urging the Kurds to revolt; the United States did not help the Shiites or the Kurds or stop the Iraqi army from putting lethal helicopter gunships into the air thereby killing any chance the tribal rebellions had of succeeding.

When our rescue vehicle came later that night, I gave Sherco my business card which carried the address of the Cox Newspapers Washington Bureau. I was based in Jerusalem, but it was always unwise when traveling in the Middle East to carry any material that could trace me to Israel. A couple of years later, I received a letter from Sherco, postmarked in Damascus, which he had sent to my Washington office. He asked for help to reach the United States. That wasn't the first, or the last, time that interesting people I had met and who had helped me in difficult circumstances sought my help in this way. I was never in a position to help them, which always made me feel selfish and dishonorable, as if I had let them and myself down.

According to international maps, we were in Iraq, an artificial nation-state of various incongruous ethnic, sectarian, linguistic and cultural tribes created by Britain in 1932, after World War I and the breakup of the Ottoman Empire. But Sherco and Nammo knew this wasn't Iraq. We were in their Kurdistan, the land of the Kurds, they emphasized. They were Kurds, Iraqi Kurds, but never simply Iraqis. Linguistically and religiously diverse, Kurds are an Indo-European people, more like Iranians than Arabs, primarily Sunni Muslims by religion, and they are mostly secular, not fanatical, and by appearances barely mainstream Muslims.

A large minority in Iraq, Kurds are the second largest ethnic group in that country, but they are not Arabs. They are composed of many tribes who speak many different dialects of their Indo-European language. Though ethnically Kurds throughout the region are the same, in many other ways they are as different and divided as are the Arabs.

Fractious, rebellious and an exploited collection of tough mountain fighters and urban professionals, the Iraqi Kurds had killed each other fighting for and against their greatest scourge, Saddam Hussein. Outgunned, outwitted and sold out by traitors, they didn't just lose; usually, they were slaughtered. They were brutalized by Saddam Hussein's chemical weapons and slaughterhouse tactics that states supposedly more sophisticated ignored and even exploited. Many of those sophisticated states, including the United States, sold Saddam Hussein the lethal weapons that he used to kill Kurds as well as the Ayatollah Khomeini's Iranians.

In the land called Iraqi Kurdistan I would witness a large-scale tribal war. For less than a month, a mainly Sunni Muslim Arab army commanded by Saddam Hussein and his extended family from a single village would rampage against Iraqi Kurds. Tribes of nation-states that had contributed to the immediate conditions leading to the Kurdish uprising and Saddam Hussein's counterattack watched in self-righteous indignation but did nothing to stop the slaughter.

When the Kurds had their own chance to beat up less fortunate tribes, they did so in typical tribal fashion, such as against the Armenians in Turkey early in the twentieth century. They have tried regional and international alliances, including several with the United States, and always been betrayed by the self-interest of their supposed allies. Huge oil deposits gurgle in Iraqi Kurdistan. But first Britain and France and then Saddam Hussein stole the oil and the Kurds were left with their mountains, villages, traitors and betrayers. Even Turkey, no friend of the Kurds, took a small percentage of the oil in the interest of self-serving international deal-making.

The land of the Kurds, Kurdistan, is not limited to Iraq. Kurdistan stretches into Iran, Syria, Turkey and Azerbaijan. About 25 million Kurds exist in the world, but it's impossible to make anywhere near an accurate tally. Everywhere they are a minority. After the Arabs, Turks and Iranians, the Kurds are the largest tribe in the region. Like many countries in the Middle East, and like Somalia, Bosnia, Algeria and Afghanistan, Iraq is a land where many ethnic groups and sects, in some cases speaking many languages or dialects, live and often war against each other. In Iraq the Assyrians, Chaldeans, Nestorians, Turkoman and other smaller tribes should not be confused with the Kurds, with the Arab Sunni or Arab Shiite Muslims, with the so-called Marsh Arabs in southern Iraq, with Shiite Muslims from Iran or with the many sub-tribes within those groups. These large tribes, while not noted for absolute internal unity, adhere to each other more tightly than they do to the Iraqi state. For more than 30 years, the Iraqi state was ruled by the extended family of Saddam Hussein from the village of Tikrit and anyone else who could be cowed or bought.

When we crossed the Tigris on March 25, 1991, to meet Sherco and Nammo, the Kurds were heady from their recent triumphs. They had captured city after city, town after town, in Iraqi Kurdistan from Saddam Hussein's bedraggled northern forces. The question was, could the Kurds keep their gains? And that question depended on the answers to other questions: Would Saddam Hussein crush the Shiites in the south and turn his full attention to the Kurds? Would the U.S.–led coalition come to the aid of the Kurds by preventing Saddam Hussein from deploying helicopters, the use of which didn't violate the February 28 truce that ended the first Gulf war? As we traveled slowly from Zakho south to the front at Altun Kupri between Erbil and Kirkuk, the outcome became clear to us: The Iraqi Kurdish tribes were doomed if they didn't receive U.S. aid and if Saddam Hussein's helicopters took to the air.

A light infantry, the Kurds were no match for helicopter gunships, tanks and rockets. Most of the captured artillery, mortars and tanks they showed off to visitors didn't work and the Kurds lacked the means to repair them. The journey south was like a visit into the romantic imagination of a people schooled to fight but who couldn't see through the fog to the slaughter that awaited them. When the haze cleared, thousands of Kurds had been killed and many thousands more walked, ran and drove in mass panic over mountain roads to Turkey and Iran with all the possessions they could carrry. I saw a calf stuffed against the rear window of a Volkswagen Passat filled with fleeing Kurds, clothing and small furniture. When the Iraqi Kurds were in full flight, Martin Nangle and I, along with 14 other journalists, joined them. We had been in Kurdistan a week without being able to send stories, photos or videotape chronicling the approaching doom and the embarrassment that would bring to the United States and the Bush administration. We had to tell their story and we had to get out alive to do so.

———

My journey to Kurdistan began in Cyprus on March 14. From Tel Aviv I flew to Nicosia where an agency operated by a former British journalist was arranging for Kurds to help me and other journalists enter Kurdistan. When those arrangements fell through, I flew to Damascus to try my luck there. In

Damascus I met Martin Nangle, who had the same objective: Find a way into Kurdistan as quickly as possible to learn the fate of the Kurds, Saddam Hussein and American policy and promises. Nangle and I traveled and worked together from that time until we escaped from Iraq through Turkey and returned to Syria during the first week of April. Nangle was one of the brave ones when our group of 16 journalists fled Iraq. He had tried to swim to freedom and for help across the Khabur River from Iraq to Turkey but was turned back by gunfire from a Turkish border post. When we finally reached the Turkish shore the following day, Nangle said, "The last time I came here I was photographing refugees. This time I am one." That was probably the most accurate post-mortem of the day.

The Kurds rose up on March 5, just a week after the truce that ended the Gulf war and about three weeks after President Bush's February 15 call for "the Iraqi military and the Iraqi people to take matters into their own hands." The Shiites in southern Iraq rebelled immediately after the cease-fire. Two weeks later the Shiites, lacking outside help, were crushed. The Iraqi army was moving north en masse and its counterattacks against the Kurds were sharp, fast. Time was running out to reach Kurdistan before events there would make the journey impossible.

After doing some background work in Damascus, Nangle and I arranged to fly from Damascus to Qamishli in northeastern Syria on the border with Turkey and about 30 miles from Syria's border with Iraq. From there, we believed, we could cross the Tigris into Iraqi Kurdistan. When the flight fell through, we hired a driver and made the trip by car on March 25, 1991. During our long but fascinating journey east-northeast through the Syrian Desert, Nangle and I gazed in awe at the ruins of the glorious Roman city of Palmyra, now called Tadmor. We stopped at a small storefront restaurant by the roadside in Tadmor for a lunch of chicken kabobs, french fries and salad. From Tadmor we rode through the rich oil and gas fields around Deir Izzor and over the mighty Euphrates, which by this time was flowing wide and free again. That was the easiest journey we would make in the next week and a half. The flight to Qamishli would have cost $17.88. The hired car cost me $127.50. Easterners are, indeed, better bargainers.

Largely Kurdish, Qamishli proved to be our lucky city, although one might argue about whether the luck was good or bad. Qamishli was a staging area for some Kurds operating in Iraq, and we met one of their two top leaders at the Medina Shebab Hotel there. Jalal Talibani headed the Patriotic Union of Kurdistan. Talibani and his old rival, Massoud Barzani, led a new front of six Iraqi Kurdish parties.

Barzani, who would later lead Iraqi Kurdistan, and Talibani, who was to become president of Bush the Younger's Iraq, were Kurds from vastly different tribes. Talibani and Barzani, whom we would meet later in the Kurdish city of Salahuddin just before the Kurdish revolt turned into a rout, were at various times allies and enemies of Saddam Hussein and Iran. Both were mostly used and abused by Saddam Hussein and his allied tribes, and by the Iranians. At this point Talibani and Barzani were allies, but they were not cut from the same turban. A pesh merga from his turban to the bottom of his pantaloons, Barzani led the mountain Kurds and the Kurdistan Democratic Party. He was a son of the combative Mullah Mustafa Barzani, whom the shah of Iran and Henry Kissinger's U.S. government abandoned in 1975. In his suit, tie and sweater, the older, portly Talibani said he was a soldier. Funny looking soldier, I thought. Probably in the same army as Kissinger and Britain's Foreign Secretary Douglas Hurd. Talibani's support came mostly from urban Kurds, not from the mountain tribes, and that was evident.

Talibani gave no hint of the debacle that was a week away. He didn't want to. If he hadn't seen it coming, his vision was not that of a leader but of a self-centered political figure who refused to let reality interfere with a dream. "The genie is out of the bottle," he said of the Kurdish revolt. "It's impossible to bring it back into the bottle." About that Talibani was dead-on. The revolt had spread among Christians and some Sunni Arabs in the pro-government northern city of Mosul, and Talibani chronicled Kurdish successes throughout their home grounds. He did speak of the difficulty of organizing a popular army, of feeding and supplying the Kurds in the face of the U.N. embargo against all of Iraq and Saddam Hussein's embargo aimed at the Kurds. But Talibani said nothing about the Shiite failures. And he insisted that Kurdish fighters had plenty of arms which they had taken from Iraqi soldiers during the recent fighting. The Kurds needed anti-aircraft weapons, food and medicine, Talibani said, but there was no hint of the disaster that awaited if Iraqi helicopters and tanks moved into Kurdistan from the south, as they were doing.

From the moment we reached Zakho, it was evident that the Kurds lacked the weapons necessary to fend off an Iraqi helicopter and tank attack. It was Talibani and his people who had arranged for Sherco and Nammo to meet us on the Iraqi side of the Tigris and for other Kurds to take us to Zakho. Syrians in Qamishli helped Nangle and me to reach the Tigris. War, after all, must be chronicled when it's in your interest, and just in case your side wins.

For a moment on the night of March 25, Nangle and I felt like Kurds and thought we would be lucky to get out of Qamishli alive. Our hotel room there cost $5 for one night, and that was $5 too much. We were awakened in the middle of the cold darkness by huge licks and crackles of flames leaping through the hallway outside our room. My immediate thought was that the building was going up, and down, in flames. But the blaze, which we could hear and see through a window over the door, was under control shortly after we rushed into the hall of the ramshackle building that looked like it couldn't house too many people let alone survive a fire inside. Drugs being cooked in the hall, I thought, as I returned to my room to sleep, fitfully. The next day our Syrian and Kurdish connections came through. No friend of Saddam Hussein's Iraq, Syria wasn't throwing up obstacles to journalists wishing to enter Kurdistan. Quite the opposite. We were never treated better than in the office of a Syrian official who had a color spectrum of telephones on his desk, phones that, surprisingly, reached around the world.

In a city where it was impossible to call across the street, Nangle called his wife in Ireland and I called my wife in Massachusetts and my office in Washington. We were headed for Iraq. We left our heavy gear in an office, where it remained until we picked it up on April 3, when we called our wives and offices again to say that we were safely out of Iraq and Turkey.

Local officials in Qamishli arranged for transportation to ferry Nangle and me, along with the two Kurds from Germany and their German female companion, to the Tigris. I bought two dozen oranges, some nuts, raisins and grapes and four large bottles of water before we left for the river crossing. A little food and water carried on the shoulder might be all the nourishment that would cross our palates in the war zone where we were headed. Unfortunately, the bottles flew from my lap and exploded on the floor of our army-green vehicle as we hurtled along and hit a large hole on a rough dirt trail to the river. I was angry because I had been ill with diarrhea for several days, and knew that I would miss the water desperately. Except for the hospitality of Kurds in Zakho and Dahuk and morsels of chicken and a couple of beers at a hotel in Erbil, the oranges, grapes, raisins and nuts were nearly all Nangle and I would eat for the next week. The raisins and two of the oranges lasted until we reached the Khabur River on the Iraqi-Turkish border a week later, where we took fire from the Iraqis on one side and Turks on the other.

Nangle and I crossed the Tigris at a point in Syria called Malakia in a leaking rowboat with half a horsepower engine. The small man who guided the boat also bailed water and we helped him. At the same time, we felt like the Dutch at the dikes, trying to plug small holes in the boat's bottom with our fingers. The river flowed about half an inch below the side of the boat. I know because I stared hard at the water and the side of the boat because I can't swim. My strategy of sinking to the river bottom and walking to the closer shore is not something I wanted to test. Not then and not later, when we were forced to flee across the Khabur River from Iraq into Turkey on a raft made of four large inner tubes and orange crate staves, bound by brown television antenna wire circa 1955, and gas pipe tubing. From beginning to end and on several occasions in between, our mission to report on the fate of the Kurds was filled with dread. For more than a week, we felt like refugees, which in Iraq and elsewhere, I came to learn, is the lowest social status in the world next to being a slave or a prisoner in solitary confinement.

At that time, Kurds controlled the road from the Tigris all the way to Zakho and well south deep into Iraqi Kurdistan. In a few days, that control would shift to the Iraqi army. The Kurds would be in full flight to Iraq's borders with Turkey and Iran by then, and Nangle and I, along with 14 other journalists in our group, would be on that same flight path.

After Sherco and Nammo handed us to our new Kurdish hosts near the banks of the Tigris, we found Zakho roiling with pesh merga, wild talk of triumph, even concern that the West might save Saddam to preserve Iraq's territorial integrity if it appeared the Kurds would defeat the Iraqi army. The city of 50,000 was also filled with the fear that if Saddam Hussein again used napalm, phosphorus, sarin gas or other chemical weapons or threw up helicopters bristling with firepower, the Kurds would be doomed again. Right then we knew there was no chance of a Kurdish victory because the West would again leave the Kurds to die. These sneaker-fighters knew they needed the United States and the international coalition that drove the Iraqi army from Kuwait to compel Saddam Hussein to keep his helicopters on the ground. They must have known, but wouldn't admit, that their rifles, machine guns and rocket-propelled grenades couldn't stop helicopters and tanks. And the Kurds knew the wrecked artillery pieces and tanks they controlled were useless, although they pretended otherwise. The romance of fighting for freedom was like a blanket covering Zakho, but it was threadbare and offered no protection against fear, panic and helicopter gunships that in days exploded throughout Iraqi Kurdistan.

On the night of March 26, we slept on mattresses that lined the floor of a beautiful villa in Zakho. I slept poorly, in constant intestinal distress and shivering with fever. Neither my condition nor that of the Kurds would improve. The house lacked running water. Even the chairs had disappeared. But our hosts accommodated us in typical Middle East fashion, making the best of what little they had. After a breakfast of laban (yoghurt), hummus, bread and tea, we watched scenes typical of war zones everywhere: Testosterone mixed with fear created a brew of bravado racing blindly toward disaster. Men preened on the streets with sure-to-lose weapons slung over their shoulders and an edginess in their eyes. Boys of 14 or younger strutted like their fathers while doctors with meager resources saved lives by amputating limbs. It was the women who struggled to find food and shelter for their children and elderly men and women.

From that moment, it was apparent, and it would become even more obvious in Dahuk, Erbil and at the front near Altun Kupri outside of Kirkuk, that the Kurds were doomed. We had to reach the front to be sure that appearances were real. Then we had to escape from Iraq to inform the world of how the great powers that saved Kuwait's oil were sacrificing the Kurds as they had the Shiites in the south to maintain the integrity of Iraq so that great Satan, Saddam Hussein, would have a country to rule and so Iraq's oil would be safe until the United States and Britain decided to take it. Once we knew that the rebellion had failed, we had to escape as quickly as we could because we had no means to report the story from inside Iraq.

—⚬⚬⚬—

Amidst a complete breakdown of normal life, a mini-bus load of journalists left Dahuk at 4 P.M. on March 27. A four-man CNN crew hired the bus to haul its equipment. Nangle and I jumped aboard. We were bound for Erbil and as close to the front line as we could get. The trek normally takes about six hours. It took us a mere 16. Traveling in the dark on dirt roads through the lush green hills, our driver lost his way. He didn't find it until dawn, when the rising sun became our compass. We took the dirt roads to avoid Iraqi army troops. Twice, as we wandered lost and disoriented in the middle of the night, the fan belt broke on our mini-bus. And twice our driver told us to wait as he wandered off into the darkness. We waited, immobilized and defenseless, not knowing where we were or who might shoot first and count the bodies later. Twice our driver returned with a new fan belt or something similar. Where our loyal driver found fan belts in the Kurdistan hills remains a mystery. But I have learned never to be surprised by the resourcefulness of poor but brave people determined to trudge on in a fight they could not win. No matter where I have traveled, guides and drivers have never let me down. We were so lost on this trip that at one moment we were headed toward the Sunni stronghold of Mosul, straight into the turrets of Iraqi tanks, when CNN cameraman Mike Raye spied the tanks on the road through his night-vision camera. We made a U-turn faster than Raye could say "tanks," avoiding the Iraqi soldiers. Then we became lost again driving in the opposite direction.

Not once was I harmed while working overseas, mainly because I learned to trust the people I hired to work with me. Those were drivers, translators, fixers who understood journalism and knew local politics and personalities. Robbery or worse would have been easy, but only once was I robbed. That was by a uniformed guard at the airport in Tashkent, Uzbekistan, in October 1992. Pierre Rousselin, who worked for the Paris daily *Le Figaro*, asked to borrow $10 to pay the airport exit fee. I pulled $20 from my wallet to pay for both of us and stuck my wallet under my heavy coat into my rear pocket. We were in a large, heaving crowd waiting for a plane that already was hours late, jockeying for position to grab a seat when there were no seat assignments. In a few moments I reached back to make sure my wallet was safe. It was safely in someone else's hands. Someone had been watching us and instinct told me that it was one of the guards. I went to the security station and told a guard what had happened. All I want is my wallet back, I said, with all my credit cards and identification papers. Forget the money. A few minutes later, a security guard approached and pointed to a support pillar in the center of the large room. Despite the crush of people, no one was standing near the pillar. My wallet, with only the money missing, was propped against the base of the pillar. I didn't offer a reward because I figured the guard already had a tidy profit for the day, a couple of hundred dollars, a few months' pay.

———

Trucks filled with refugees fleeing Mosul arrived in Erbil when we finally did at 8 A.M. on March 28, 16 hours after we had left Dahuk on our midnight express mini-bus. Off we went to the nearby town of Salahuddin to interview Massoud Barzani, whose father's fighting pedigree is unmatched in modern Kurdish history. Here was a pesh merga, and he knew it. A small man, Barzani didn't act small. In his red and white turban and full regalia, with a sidearm on his hip, Barzani gave us his version of the fate that awaited Iraq's Kurds. Even his story was terribly wrong. "There is a danger of losing Kirkuk," Barzani said, "but even if the government takes it, we will retake it." Within three days, the government took Kirkuk, Altun Kupri, Erbil, Dahuk and Zakho. A disaster. We saw it coming and we saw it happen. If Talabani and Barzani thought that we could help their cause, they were terribly wrong on that score, too, because none of us could communicate with the outside world.

Barzani also pleaded for help. He knew the Kurds would be doomed if the West allowed Saddam Hussein to fly his helicopter gunships. To ease the fears of the West, Barzani wanted the world to know that the Kurds weren't interested in breaking up Iraq. Iraq could stay as one, he said, even with Saddam Hussein. The Kurds wanted only freedom and autonomy in Kurdistan, not separation, he said. We couldn't tell the world what Barzani wanted the world to know. What Barzani, his pesh merga and the Iraqi Kurds received was another lesson in moral vacuity from the West and another whipping from Saddam Hussein.

Unmatched as mountain guerrillas, the tough, brave pesh merga could not stand against the superior firepower of a modern army. History, too, had abandoned them in the snowy mountains and narrow passes of their victorious past. If the odds against them weren't heavy enough, another tribe in the region's baffling array of alliances and betrayals faced the Kurds: the Mujahedin Khalq, Iranians who supported Saddam Hussein during Iraq's war in the 1980s against the Ayatollah Khomeini's Iran. On Thursday March 29, the bad news was drifting north from oil-drenched Kirkuk, where Saddam Hussein's army had retaken control. The streets of Erbil were filled with warped displays of courage, empty cheers and panic. The war was moving north at top speed. The Kurds would fight as long as they could. Then they would flee.

A young woman dressed entirely in black wept as she spoke on an Erbil street: "We are afraid from Saddam. We are afraid of his picture," she said, the palpable heat of the coming disaster fresh in the air and reddening her face. "Every day he kills our young men. We want to save our mothers, brothers, our children. If he comes here, we will go to Iran. We do not stay here. He wants to kill Iraq people, Arabs and Kurds." Nearby, Ahmad Abdullah appealed for American help, but his voice couldn't be heard: "The Kurdish people have love in our hearts for all the American people, especially your leader, Bush. We need help now, not later." In a few hours, lamentation on the battlefield and in the streets changed to, "Where Bush? Where Bush?"

On March 29, Good Friday on the Western Christian calendar, about 500 fighters massed on the edge of Erbil, ready that night and the next morning to make what would be the Kurds' last stand in Altun Kupri between Erbil and Kirkuk. Erbil was suffocating in bedlam. Rifles were fired wildly in the air and loudspeakers urged fighters to the front. Some in the ragtag army went to the front in buses covered with mud, Kurdish camouflage. Their cause appeared hopeless. It was. The Kurdish force included a young man in a gray pin-striped suit, a gray sweater and maroon loafers. He carried a Kalashnikov. Jailan, a 25-year-old veteran female fighter, the only woman I saw on the battlefield, took up her position in the grass, mud and oncoming darkness at Altun Kupri. "All of them are my brothers," Jailan said, as Iraqi army artillery crashed over our heads and to our flanks. After the battle, I saw the muddied man in the gray suit, but now he had added some legitimate tribal regalia, the cummerbund-like sash of a pesh merga. I never saw the woman again. Nangle and I watched the shooting for a few hours before it grew clear that the Kurds would lose and we might catch flak if not a direct hit as a reward for sticking around to chronicle the disaster.

The Kurds had chosen to join the battle at night in an attempt to negate the use of Iraqi helicopters. But they never crept close enough to use their rocket-propelled grenades against the Iraqi tanks and had no answer to Iraqi artillery and cannon fire. When the shells started dropping closer, landing in a shrinking circle around us, Nangle and I convinced ourselves that we weren't Kurds and that we would learn little more and risk more than necessary by staying. We looked at each other and said, as if with one voice, "Let's get the hell outta here." So we hitched a ride back to Erbil where we spent the rest of the night and prepared to flee Iraq the next day, the day before Easter.

A CNN crew of four stayed and moved closer to the front with their night-vision camera and sound gear. Nangle and I thought that was slightly insane, but a ringside seat at a battlefront is a prime ticket in the audio/video world, even though it would be a couple of days at least before the crew could escape and ship its film from Iraq. We saw the CNN crew on Saturday, March 30, in Erbil. They were neither excited nor depressed. They had done their job. As disaster sped toward them, Kurdish gunmen in Erbil fired tracer bullets wildly into the air, a superficial sign of celebration; a real sign of defeat. Their own bullets rained down upon them, as if Saddam Hussein's weren't enough. We knew their firing was a sure sign that the Kurds were about to die on another funeral pyre. We preferred not to go with them.

Most of Saturday March 30 passed before we could find transportation to flee north from Erbil. The city was much quieter than the previous day, a brief lull as the mass exodus was building. Within hours Kurds, again in the role of refugees, would jam the treacherous mountain roads to Iran and Turkey. We were aiming for the border crossing to Syria, where we had entered Iraq only five days earlier, although the Iranian border was closer. Our information was that the best way out was the rough ride east and then north through the mountains to Dahuk. By the time we reached Zakho, the Iraqi army had sealed the crossing to Syria. So we struck out for the Khabur River where we could cross to Turkey. In the more than 21 hours it took us to travel over pinched mountain roads clogged with deep mud, boulders and fallen branches, riding at various times in ordinary cars, Toyota Land Cruisers, a 10-wheel dump truck, a mini-bus and an army truck, our tribe of 16 assorted journalists was always on the lookout for signs of Iraqi soldiers and helicopters.

If we hadn't stayed ahead of the Iraqis, we probably would never have reached Turkey. We were in desperate shape, but we had money, the means to buy our escape, and we were on the job. The Kurds weren't so fortunate. Accustomed to being gassed, shot and buried alive by Saddam Hussein's killers, old women and old men, children and pesh mergas of all ages carried all they could on their backs or in small cars and cart-like trucks, if they were able to find gasoline. Individually and as a people, the Iraqi Kurds were fleeing to survive with scant means to do so.

We decided to stick together, all 16 of us, ornery and irascible as any 16 individuals could be. That plan lasted only a few minutes — which is predictable when more than two journalists decide on a common objective — before seven in our group went off to find transportation on their own in Erbil. All 16 of us met up again, more or less accidentally, high in the mountains in the Kurdish village and pesh merga post of Diyana. There, we all climbed into a 10-wheel Scania dump truck for the long run to the border. In Erbil, before we reached Diyana, the remaining nine of us needed two large vehicles for our bodies and equipment. Fear grew among us as panic rose among the Kurds during the nearly eight hours it took the nine of us to find two vehicles large enough for the journey. While I and a few others waited for transportation at a hotel, a member of our group pointed to a pesh merga who had a car and told me that if we didn't get out of Erbil soon, he would ask the man to look at his rifle, then take the gun and the man's car and vamoose. "I've done that before, you know," our colleague said, mentioning a rash act in another war zone. "Let me know when you get ready to do that," I answered, thinking of the mayhem that would ensue. "I don't want to be around when you do it."

Our search to locate and gas up two Toyota Land Cruisers lasted from 8 A.M. until 4 P.M. Before we could leave the hotel whose owner, we were told, had long ago fled to Las Vegas, one of the drivers insisted on going to tell his wife that he wouldn't be home that night. His goodbye kiss took 30 minutes. Our second Land Cruiser was soon wrecked in a crash at the large square near our hotel. We found another Land Cruiser quickly, but that one was declared unfit for travel. Then, Eureka, out of nowhere appeared another Land Cruiser, this one fit for the job. We were off, finally, on a trip to the mountain redoubt of Diyana, a trip filled with stops to cool the radiators, fill extra tanks with gas and satisfy pesh merga paperwork as we sped from tribal zone to tribal zone. We actually were required to obtain pesh merga approval to use the mountain route at night, which we finally received from some of Barzani's men. Two armed pesh merga dangled from the rear of the car loaded with CNN gear when I realized that we didn't have an armed guard in our vehicle. When I pointed that out to our driver, he said, "Keep going."

As we were about to leave Erbil, our driver said the tires on his Land Cruiser needed air. He said this after he and his vehicle had waited hours for the second vehicle to reach our hotel. We never pumped up the tires. On the way to Diyana, our vehicle became separated from the second Land Cruiser when we went looking for some food in a village. We never found food, but we did find the other car quickly. We were stopped by pesh merga repeatedly on the road to Diyana. They kept requesting permission slips to continue on the road. We're fleeing, trying to get out before the Iraqi army reaches us, not going to a wedding, we shouted. We kept stopping for gas because we could only get small amounts at each stop. A group of pesh merga said we wouldn't be allowed to travel beyond Diyana that night. "Forget that," we argued and shouted, "we're going all the way through." The chief pesh merga looked at the paper that Barzani's people had given us and said that it was up to us: We could risk the narrow, muddy and blocked mountain road and wing it or we could stay and risk waking up to be greeted by unsmiling Iraqi army troops.

We argued again in Diyana. The pesh merga there said our four-wheel-drive Land Cruisers would never make it through the mountains. We needed trucks, large trucks, they said, because the mountain road was blocked in places, washed out in others while sporadic gunfights were breaking out in some spots. Besides, the road was a road in name only. It was really only a rough trail that ran along steep cliffs above raging rivers. Later, after we reached the mud, boulders and tree limbs in the road, we were happy the pesh merga had forced us out of our Land Cruisers and into a dump truck. As we argued at the pesh merga base in Diyana, Barzani's fighters tried to stall us by serving tea, cheese and bread, in an upstairs room, probably in the hope that we would fall asleep there. We would have none of their strategy, if a little of their fare. In 30 minutes, we told the pesh merga, we will leave in our cars or in other vehicles if we can find them. We vowed not to spend the night in Diyana because the Iraqi army and the flood of refugees were close behind. By this time, the seven journalists who had split from the group of 16 earlier in the day in Erbil showed up in a small car that was lucky to have reached Diyana and would have been a pigeon on the higher mountain route. Now the group was 16 strong again, if strong is the correct word.

About 30 minutes after our warning that it was Dahuk or bust that night, a young man appeared in a large dump truck with a heavy canvas that covered the bed like a blanket. We were off, with a pesh merga riding in front with two of us and the driver, and everyone else, including five other pesh merga, in the truck bed with the canvas cover for warmth. The pesh merga riding in the cab was a gray beard, but everyone over 35 often looks like 65 in this part of the world. It was 10:30 on Saturday night, March 30, when we pulled out of Diyana to begin another leg of the hellish mountain journey that was just as rough as the pesh merga had described.

The 10-wheeler was home for another 16 hours before we reached Zakho, still a mini-bus, a military truck and a short march away from the Khabur River. At the river bank we hid next to a pesh merga post and dodged Iraqi rockets and artillery fire. Turkish soldiers across the river saw every moving figure in Iraq as a Kurd who should be shot or otherwise kept from entering Turkey, where the Iraqi Kurds' Turkish cousins were waging a civil war. When dawn came on a cold, drizzly Easter Sunday, I was in the bed of the truck, having moved there to give someone else a chance to enjoy the cab and to better grasp just how close to the edge of every precipice we were traveling. Despite its huge tires and great weight, the truck was barely able to negotiate the deep mud and debris on the trail. At the same time, the size of the truck added to our difficulties because the margin for error between the muddy and sometimes washed out road and the abyss was mere inches. Our driver became ill at one point from the stress of constantly using two shift levels, creeping along cautiously and hoping the road wouldn't just give way as we rolled along on the edge of steep cliffs. At one point, our driver became so ill that he asked for relief. Azzem, a Jordanian cameraman for a Swiss television company, offered to drive. No problem, Azzem said, he had experience driving large trucks like this one. Azzem drove for a few miles while our ill driver managed to stay upright long enough to help do the shifting. Our driver went behind the wheel again when we reached a particularly bad spot in the road. That's when Azzem smiled at me and said, "You know, I never drove a truck like this before." I smiled back and said, "I'm glad you didn't tell me that before." We stumbled on a small pesh merga camp in the mountains. Our driver stopped so he could stretch out in the cab while we ate bread and sipped water from a stream. We were cold and our shoes and boots were filled with mud from the worst 60 minutes of our trip.

North of Diyana we became stuck in deep mud on a particularly narrow section of the road. Two huge boulders and many smaller ones blocked the trail. A rock and mud slide apparently had caused the damage. We had no choice but to break off large limbs from nearby trees and use them as levers to move the boulders. Then we had to pile large rocks in the mud to give the tires traction. This road construction job took 45 minutes before we were able to inch our way through the mud without fishtailing over the high cliff that overlooked a river raging from late winter and early spring rains and melting snow. While we were working, the pesh merga who had been sitting in the cab with Azzem and me smiled broadly as he showed us a 16-inch fish he had caught. Our friend and protector had slipped down the cliff to the river far below and caught the fish with his bare hands. He threw his catch on the dashboard, and there it stayed and decayed for half a day before he took his food home. Our driver was, literally, a life-saver. At one point, he slid the huge truck over a mountain stream which flooded a culvert that might have disappeared at any moment. As soon as we freed ourselves from the mud we had to take a sharp left over a long bridge. No bridge in these parts, especially under these conditions, is reliable. We saw hundreds of refugees of all ages trudging through the mountains, heading for Iran or to Dahuk and on to Turkey.

Outside of Dahuk the refugee flood grew. It was like watching tributaries flow into the mother stream. The refugees talked of fleeing from Iraqi helicopter and artillery attacks and napalm bombs. "Where Bush?" they shouted as we drove by the trudging mobs, heads down, their backs bent with all they could carry. "Bush caused the war," they shouted. People on foot, in cars, taxis and trucks and riding tractors, leading cows, sheep, donkeys and goats, carrying bedding and anything else they could, all fleeing from the Dahuk area. A man in a wheelchair struggled to keep up with pesh merga warriors carrying babies.

Dahuk and Zakho were expected to be hammered in hours. Like the Kurds, we were on the wrong side of the battlelines and we all had little time to avoid the rockets and shells that make only the broadest of tribal distinctions. In war, as in any tribal conflict, individuals become invisible, except to their families when they are killed.

We were still rumbling over the mountains, about eight hours from Zakho, at dawn March 31, Easter Sunday. I lifted the canvas on the truck bed near the cab where I had nestled to take a peek at the dying night. This was not encouraging. A heavy mist slapped my face in the raw cold as we bounced on. Pale slices of light squirmed to sneak past huge, low dark and gray clouds. A good moment to use the word ominous. No matter where else I might have been on this day, I probably would not have been inside a church. Still, there was something metaphysical and spiritual about the atmosphere. We were 16 journalists from other worlds who really didn't know each other, but we were turned into refugees fleeing a tribal war in another world with a driver we didn't know but had to trust.

At 2 P.M. on Sunday March 31, we rejoiced at the sight of Zakho. We felt good about our chances of escape until our driver, emotionally spent, refused to take us farther. He said that a part that held the fan belt in place was broken and he didn't want to damage his 10-wheeler by continuing on. We were in no position to argue. The driver took his $400 and left us, again, looking for transportation.

Total panic engulfed Zakho. Good luck, and money, came to our aid. The driver of a blue mini-bus we spotted on the street agreed to take us to the Tigris and the crossing to Syria. But a few miles from the river our luck turned sour. A flat tire, and no spare, put our mini-bus out of service about five miles short of the border. Kurds driving a military truck warned us not to try for the Tigris because Iraqi soldiers already had sealed the crossing to Syria. Forever helpful, those same Kurds who were fleeing for their own lives agreed to drive all 16 of us closer to the Khabur River, which forms the Turkish-Iraqi border. Then we hauled ourselves and our gear about a mile to the Khabur.

With the river in sight, we were greeted by long-range Iraqi artillery apparently aiming for a border post occupied by Kurds who were firing back. We could see the Iraqi helicopters, but we couldn't see them firing. In the late afternoon of March 31, we took cover behind damaged and abandoned cinder block buildings for about an hour as rockets pummeled the Iraqi and Turkish sides of the Khabur and killed fish in the middle just beyond where we were ducking and hoping. Heads between our knees, crouching at the base of one of the buildings, we refused a Kurdish offer to take shelter at their anti-aircraft post. It didn't make sense to hide with the target at which the Iraqis were aiming. The pesh merga also said they would lead us to the Tigris crossing to Syria just beyond a hill, but we thought that would have been punching our ticket to disaster because other Kurds had told us shortly before that the Iraqi army had already sealed that crossing. Besides, small arms and heavy weapons fire grew closer, louder, which made Turkey seem like the right direction for us.

But the Turks despise the Kurds, especially those who live in Turkey and belong to a loose conglomeration of clans that fight for tribal and national rights under the banner of the Kurdistan Workers Party, called the PKK. The war between the PKK and the Turks was a wholly different tribal clash from the one we were trying to leave behind in Iraq. The PKK are not pesh merga. They fancied themselves as socialists, Marxist-Leninist even, and train their fighters in doctrine akin to what Che Guevara might have been doing in Bolivia in the 1960s. Five months after we escaped from Iraq, I spent a couple of days at a PKK training camp in Yanta, Lebanon, near the Syrian border, and watched men and women being trained to fight in their civil uprising in Turkey. The PKK fighters seemed an anachronism in every way, although for a time they raised a lot of hell in Turkey and the Turks punished them way beyond the pale for doing so. The Turks punished the Iraqi Kurds as well on the principle that they might help their brothers and sisters in Turkey. The Turks, after all, were one tribe and the Kurds were another tribe and never the twain shall meet. If you lived in Turkey, you had better be a Turk even if you weren't.

The Turks didn't want anyone of any tribe, least of all a Kurd in disguise, to sneak across the border. They made that clear to us when we were hiding in the reeds on the Iraqi side of the Khabur. When one member of our journalism tribe wrote in Turkish on a large white sheet that we were Western journalists and we were coming across the river, Turkish soldiers across the river answered in the uniquely subtle way of people trained to kill: "Come and we'll shoot you." Not one of us said, "What do you think they mean by that?" Right on the edge of our potential escape hatch, we had a problem every bit as serious as the one closing in from behind.

Saddam Hussein's counterattack against the Iraqi Kurds was so quick and crushing, and the West's response so flaccid, that Turkey ironically was forced to shelter thousands of Iraqi Kurds in makeshift refugee camps, at least for a time.

The pesh merga left their border post and took their blankets and automatic rifles into the reeds and briars on the Iraqi side of the river to spend the night. They invited us to join the 13 of them. We joined the pesh merga at 2 A.M. on April 1, when we left our position on a higher more rocky area above the bank and sloshed through water and mud and climbed over, through and around tall reeds, thorny bushes and trees to reach our night camp. There we persuaded the Kurds not to reveal our position by shooting at targets they couldn't hit. They promised to die for us if necessary. For us, we thought, surrender would be preferable to a Kurdish shootout with the Iraqis. But for the Kurds, surrender would have meant sure execution. Our Kurdish friends gave us blankets to spread over the mud and reeds and to keep warm. Around this time I shared the last of my small stash of raisins. It was a short, cold and dismal night. We were wet from the knees down because we had to wade through the flats to reach the river bank.

Shooting continued through the night. Sleep was left to the Turks on the opposite bank. A man in our group sobbed quietly, briefly, but there was no panic, no fear so great that we lost our ability to reason. Before we reached the mud and reeds we had discussed swimming across the Khabur. Nearly everyone backed that strategy at the beginning, but not I. "Go ahead," I urged them all, "then send help for me. I'll take my chances with the Iraqis because I can't swim half a stroke." "Don't worry," some of my colleagues said, "we'll help you." "You'll have a tough enough time helping yourselves," I answered. "When we get out of this," one CNN crew member said to me more in humor than in anger, "I'm going to get you swimming lessons at the 'Y.'"

Some in the group wanted to swim the river that night, but I argued against it for several reasons: The river, fast-moving and high, was probably heavily mined on both banks and we had no more idea than did the fish or snakes where the mines were. We didn't know the best place to enter the river, where exactly the hostile Turks were or where we would hit the opposite bank. And it was night. The Turks would shoot at the first sighting or sound and search the bodies for tribal affiliation later. Eight of the 16 journalists wanted to swim for it when our discussions began. When it came down to getting in the water more than 12 hours later, four agreed to go. The rest of us would gamble that the Iraqis wouldn't reach us before our pals sent help from Turkey.

I awoke from a light sleep at 6:30 A.M. on Monday, April 1. The joke was on us. Iraqi helicopters forced us to stay in our den of reeds throughout the day. In the early days of spring, a warmer, drying sun was a poor excuse for a heat lamp, but it helped. Day or night, the pesh merga said, they wouldn't swim to Turkey. They knew that they would be shot on sight. Our pesh merga friends advised us to wait until dark before going into the river so neither the Iraqis nor the Turks would see us. They also suggested that we wait for a raft that was due to pass at 7 P.M. We had no faith in that possibility, as the Kurds had said that bread would be delivered the previous night. But if the bread man left the bakery, he never reached us. Late in the day, the pesh merga slipped from the reeds and headed for the mountains to the east.

After devising and altering escape plans throughout the day, we finally stuck to one. Jim Hill, a CNN reporter from the New York office, and Rich Brooks, a CNN sound man working out of London, said they were strong swimmers and would go. Xavier Gauthier with the Paris national daily *Le Figaro* said he would join them. Gauthier had reported from the area of Turkey we were trying to reach and we learned later, to our good fortune, that previously he had interviewed the governor of that province. That was, in our minds, the most fortuitous interview anyone had ever conducted, at least up to that time. Nangle, an avowed good swimmer himself and a man of quiet courage, said he would make the swimmers a foursome.

Just before we put our plan into action we shared a little beef jerky and water before I gave my last two oranges to two of the swimmers. At 5:45 on the afternoon of April 1, with dusk creeping in but with enough light for the Turks to see us but perhaps not the Iraqis from their helicopters, we stumbled along the river bank to an open beach where the Turks could see us. On our dash toward the open beach, the earth gave way as I stepped right beside a rotting log. This sinkhole will swallow me, I thought as I fell. But as my left leg plunged into the hole I swung my right leg over the log, as if I were leaping on a horse that was wearing a very hard and pain-inducing saddle. The log held and I scrambled, aching, to solid ground.

On the beach, Hélène de Costa of International French Radio, a tough reporter and the only woman in the group, and Yves Heller of the Paris national daily *Le Monde*, held up a large white sheet on which Costa Sakellarion had written in Turkish, "Journalists American." Sakellarion, a Greek freelance photographer who held dual Greek-American citizenship and had hiked for three-and-half days over the mountains from Turkey to reach the Kurdish debacle in Iraq, wrote a note in Turkish and gave it to one of the swimmers to show the Turks. The note explained our plight and sought further help. Turkish soldiers answered by asking how many we were. At one point during our shouting back and forth the soldiers said that if we tried to cross they would shoot us. At 6:15 we all came out of the woods near the beach and shouted our identities. We were from many tribes, tribes within tribes in fact: We were from France, Ireland, Greece, Jordan, Germany, the United States and Switzerland. Not one of us was a Kurd so we had a chance with the Turks.

I counted 12 to 15 shots when our four swimmers entered the river. The nearest Turkish village was Ova Koy. The Turks shot in a wide circle around Jim Hill and Xavier Gauthier, the first swimmers to enter the river. As the

Turks fired, Gauthier shouted, "Don't shoot, you idiots." I hoped that the Turks didn't understand English. Hill later said he was greeted by attempts to force him back into the river. Gauthier wore the low cut shoes that I had bought in Cyprus because he would have drowned trying to swim in his high black gestapo boots, yet he needed shoes when he hit the shore. The soldiers shot over their heads and in circles around Hill and Gauthier, but Hill made it almost straight across and Gauthier landed a little farther downstream. The Turks got more serious with Rich Brooks and Nangle. Two men the Turks thought they could handle; four they didn't want to try, Kurds or no Kurds. Immediately after they entered the river, the circle of bullets tightened on Nangle and Brooks. The Turks shouted and shot in a language anyone would have understood. Brooks and Nangle swam back to the Iraqi shore.

Gauthier and Hill spent the night and early the next morning trying to get help for the remaining 14 of us still in Iraqi Kurdistan. Efforts to get help from the French and American governments were futile. Hill and Gauthier said they were told to work with local Turks because we were in a restricted area and there was little the diplomats could do. Finally, Gauthier reached the governor of the Turkish province, the man he had interviewed a few months before. The governor took charge and arranged for our rescue. We spent the night sleeping in two large clusters for warmth on blankets spread over mud on the river bank. Fourteen well-placed bullets, or one wild rocket, could have taken care of us. When we woke around dawn, I noted Mike Raye's lightness of being as we waited for help: Referring to two other members in our group, Raye said, "I woke up last night with Sasha's elbow in one rib and Costa's in another rib and I said to myself, 'I'm not going through this one more night. I want someone more curvy.'" But Xavier Gauthier and Jim Hill came through. Another night in the Khabur mud waiting for help or bullets wasn't in our future.

The previous afternoon, just before Gauthier and Hill swam for help, the Iraqi army had overwhelmed Zakho, crushing the Kurdish rebellion and sending tens of thousands more Kurds in a panicky flight deep into the mountains towards Iraq's borders with Turkey and Iran. We were lucky. Shortly after dawn the next morning, April 2, we would be in Turkey, free to reenter Iraq another time.

Iraqi soldiers were edging closer to the border and to us when Jim Hill shouted from the Turkish bank of the Khabur. I looked at my watch. It was 10:30 P.M. on April 1. Hill's voice faded into the night just after his words fell on our ears. Hill said that he and Gauthier had found a way out for us, but weren't sure exactly when that would be. All day and night we waited. Nothing. At 6:15 the next morning, two Turks in undershorts and T-shirts, one of whom wore a blue blazer, came to our rescue with a raft cobbled together from large inner tubes and thin pieces of wood that looked like staves from orange crates, all unconvincingly lashed together by old brown television antenna wire and hoses that looked like they were made for gas stoves. Our enthusiastic rescuers even brought water. We met them with even more enthusiasm. Guiding and pulling the raft as they swam, needing help from some passengers as they struggled against the fast current, the Turks hauled us across in two groups of seven. Our tribes had escaped, but our pesh merga friends and their families were just beginning another long trek into hell and back.

The Turks were our friends now. That happened quickly, unexpectedly. They took us first to a small room away from the river where we huddled around a stove to warm and dry, wring out clothes and enjoy hot tea before we piled into two military vehicles and traveled to the town of Silopi. There, we ate a breakfast of olives, eggs, cheese, stacks of bread, tea and bottled water. And we toasted the Turks. That was the first meal we had eaten in many days. I had exhausted my supply of Imodium, which I had shared with Nangle, days before when we arrived in Erbil, and I was still suffering from unrelenting intestinal distress. Just by crossing the Khabur my chances of recovery increased many fold. From Silopi the Turks took us to an army base near the town of Khabur, where we filled out papers and had our photos taken. We signed forms that described what had happened and were taken to a courthouse to sign papers which said that we had entered Turkey illegally. We'll sign anything, I thought, just let us get out of here. The Turkish government paid our fines, although I never learned the amount. Taxis brought us to Nusaybin, across from Qamishli, Syria. From a hotel in Nusaybin we told the world of the disaster that had befallen the Kurds and U.S. policy in the aftermath of the Gulf war.

Smart, courageous and committed, Xavier Gauthier went on to report about the Bosnian wars. Perhaps he came too close to uncovering some of the worst evils at work there, or thought he had. On May 19, 1996, Gauthier was found hanging under mysterious circumstances in his holiday home in Menorca, Spain, while on sabbatical to write about Bosnia. He was 35.

Exactly a year after our flight into Turkey I returned to Iraq. Saddam Hussein's post–Gulf war counterattack against the Iraqi Kurds was over by then. Most of the Iraqi Kurds had returned from Turkey and Iran to their homes in northern Iraq, but Saddam Hussein continued to pummel and harass the Kurds with no need for rationalizations. Turkish Kurds were no better off than their Iraqi brothers and sisters. At this time, the Turkish army assaulted Kurdish PKK rebels throughout southeastern Anatolia.

For three days I camped at a restored caravanserai in the large Kurdish city of Diyarbakir in southeastern Turkey. Ramadan was in full swing, which is anything but the right word for the Islamic holy month. Because it was Ramadan, I was the only guest in the old hotel that had served caravans for hundreds of years from its post near the old city gate beyond which the ancient Silk Road passed on its way to the Syrian border and eastward to Iraq. Although the sparse hotel staff fasted during daylight hours, cooks and waiters happily served me sustaining meals anytime I wished, further testimony to the hospitality of the region and its people.

My job in Diyarbakir was to hire a car and driver for a high speed trip to the Khabur River bridge at the Iraqi-Turkish border. Three days after I began my search, I settled into the passenger seat with a driver I knew nothing about but trusted fully. We sped through Kurdish towns that Turkish forces had devastated only days before, passing Turkish army checkpoints by simply saying "basin," the Turkish word for journalist. The race was on to beat the Turkish army to the next Kurdish town, the next battle zone, so the Turks could not block my path to Iraq.

This time I walked into northern Iraq from Turkey on a bridge over the Khabur River, not far from where I had fled from Iraq with colleagues on a raft twelve months earlier. My leisurely walk over the bridge compelled me to recall, but not yearn for, the leaky little boat that carried me from Syria across the Tigris into the Iraqi abyss a year earlier. But this second journey along narrow, muddy roads through the mountains of Iraqi Kurdistan, across rivers on rafts pulled by cables, ropes and wiry little men, all of us enveloped in fear and every Kurd idle but armed and ready to fight just about anyone, also focused the mind.

After I crossed the bridge into Iraqi Kurdistan, local Kurdish connections helped me find a driver with a good car, which meant one that the driver could fix easily when it broke down, which it surely would. With Salaam Khalid, I learned again why the Kurds are so perplexing. Khalid was my driver in March and April 1992, but not my translator. He spoke little English, and some of his actions needed a cultural translation. When Khalid, trying to display his power, wasn't laughing and taking aim at a legless man trying to wiggle across a dirt street, he was picking flowers from the roadside to show that his esthetic sense had not been eroded by war.

For four years, Khalid said, he suffered from the same tooth ache. On March 28, 1992, Khalid decided to quit suffering. He pulled to the side of a street in Erbil, turned the ignition off, pointed to his tooth and to the second floor of a nearby building and then dashed into the building. Fifteen minutes later, Khalid returned, acting as if he had seen Allah. Someone pulled the old tooth, string, doorknob trick on him and his aching tooth ached no longer. Khalid smiled through a filthy once-white rag stuffed in his mouth to stop the bleeding. All for one dollar. Two hours later we found a place where Khalid could enjoy a bowl of potato soup, bread and two Pepsis.

In late March of 1992, I found the Iraqi Kurds preparing to elect their own government in an autonomous zone that no one really wanted except the Kurds. I also found that the Kurds were being squeezed to the point of desperation by the U.N. economic boycott against Iraq, by Saddam Hussein's brutal internal economic boycott that deprived Iraqi Kurds of food and fuel, and by Turkey's free-wheeling air attacks against the Iraqi Kurds under the guise of flushing out Turkish Kurds hiding in Iraq. I also found representatives of the U.S.–led coalition chafing because the West refused to confront its NATO ally Turkey about its attacks in northern Iraq.

Turkey was taking advantage of the power vacuum in northern Iraq, I was told repeatedly by Western representatives, to punish Kurds in general. The United States refused to challenge Turkey for fear of losing permission to use the air base at Incirlik to maintain the no-fly zone in northern Iraq. Top generals refused to pass to the policy-makers in the Pentagon and the White House information gathered first-hand by officers on the ground in northern Iraq. The result, predictably, was a policy void of reality, almost always a recipe for failure, and certainly one that sacrifices lives and principle on the altar of expediency and what the policy-makers believe are larger, but less human, interests. In other words, the weakest always pay the heaviest price. That's true at all levels of tribal life, within families and nation-states.

—————

On April 1, 1992, I met the Yazidis in their village of Ribebi near Dahuk in northern Iraq. The religion of the Yazidis dates to dim antiquity, and in their presence I felt the weight of the ancients.

Transported in time by the Yazidis and their gods, I felt antiquity even more than I felt it in the Syrian town of Ma'alula, where the people still speak ancient Aramaic, the language that sounds in its ritual-like intonations like a combination of Arabic and Hebrew and which was widely spoken in the region when Jesus Christ gave birth to one of the world's largest sectarian tribes about 2,000 years ago.

Yazidis are believed to number about 250,000 in Iraq. Those in Iraq say there may be 150,000 Yazidis combined in Georgia, Armenia and Azerbaijan, 50,000 in Germany and a totally unknown number in Turkey, where they are suppressed. The Yazidis in Iraq are religious and ethnic outsiders, a tiny minority within a minority. They are lower on the Iraqi tribal totem pole than the Assyrians, Chaldeans, Nestorians and Turkoman, lower even than other small denominations or ethnic groups with origins in times long-forgotten, even in this land where blurred memory can be more important than the transparent now. Kurdish speakers, the Yazidis consider themselves the original Kurds descended directly from the first Indo-European Kurdish tribes. Yet even the mainstream Kurds have persecuted them because the Yazidis are not Muslims and are on the thin edge of mainstream Kurdish culture.

Saddam Hussein tried to deny the Yazidis their religion and their Kurdish heritage by proclaiming them Arabs. His proclamation didn't stick for a minute, and for that the Yazidis paid the usual price. In 1979, a Yazidi religious leader published a book about his people and their religion. Saddam Hussein's henchmen, in a book-burning Iraqi style, collected the books and destroyed them. Still unhappy that the Yazidis remained the Yazidis, Iraqi forces uprooted them from their villages in 1983, and transported them to the more mainstream Kurdish strongholds of Zakho and Sulaimanya. A year before I met them, the Yazidis had fled in an 11-day walk to Iraq's border with Iran after Saddam Hussein crushed the post–Gulf War Kurdish rebellion, which sent all Iraqi Kurds running for their lives. Riven as are all Iraqi Kurds by betrayals in their own ranks and manipulation from outside, the Yazidis had recently ostracized another religious leader who, for personal convenience, agreed with the Iraqi government's contention that Yazidis are Arabs.

Tenets of the Yazidi religion are passed down orally and are not written. Yazidis practice a Mithraic religion related to Zoroastrianism, the religion of ancient Persia that sees the world through a stark prism of good and evil.

Many of their main religious tenets are conveyed through women which, in the powerfully patriarchal Middle East, probably is another reason for the Yazidis' difficulties. Yazidi men and women, unlike those of most other regional tribes, also usually dance together at major festivals.

This female lineage probably explains why Yazidi women in Ribebi warmly embraced two female students from the University of London who were doing a study of the Yazidi religion and culture. Their meeting was like an advertisement for worldwide sisterhood. The Yazidis have less than most Kurds, but like poor people everywhere they gave us, strangers, all they had. They shared at breakfast more than they could spare, and made me feel poorer in the process. Eggs, cheese, tea, bread, olives, everything they had and could not spare we ate. We dined in a sparsely appointed room with an overhead fan, three photos of prominent Yazidis on one wall and a small mirror on another wall. A mountain scene with deer, painted roughly in green and brown, hung from a wall. The room also contained a clock and a television covered by a cloth trimmed in beige and black lace. A radio-tape player was on top of the television, completing the modern technological presence in the Yazidis' ancient world.

In Dahuk I had met the two doctoral students — Maria O'Shea and Christine Allison — from the University of London's School of Oriental and

African Studies, Dr. Philip Kreyenbroek, a professor of modern Iranian languages at the university, and Oric L'vov Basirov, a lecturer in archeology at the same school. One of the women planned to stay six months with the Yazidis to gather information for her doctoral dissertation, while the other woman planned to stay only a month. The professor and the two students feared that a journalist might frighten the Yazidis into silence or even animosity. When I assured them that I would only watch and listen and not intrude, they agreed to let me go along. Thrilled at the invitation, I kept my promise, but regrettably let more mundane obligations persuade me to reject a Yazidi invitation to visit one of their sacred shrines in a cave near the mountain village of Atrush southeast of Dahuk. That failure to visit the shrine, truly a once-in-a-lifetime opportunity, remains one of my greatest regrets.

To peek at the Yazidis is to glance into the recesses of a part of ancient life that still breathes. As with many religions and cultures, the Yazidis combine their own practices with others found in more dominant religions such as Judaism, Christianity and, more recently, Islam. Adaptation has helped them survive as various conquerors and people of other religions swept through the region. They pray three times a day, for example, but always facing the direction of the sun. They believe that Mecca is holy to all believers, not only to Muslims. The Yazidis celebrate major festivals in spring, summer and autumn. They color eggs to represent the renewal of life and place flowers over doorways in their villages. Sometimes they are referred to, falsely, as devil worshippers because of their emphasis on the duality of good and evil. They kill a bull at their annual autumn festival to signify renewal and to honor Mithra, their chief deity, because they believe that Mithra killed the devil who had killed a sacred bull and all other living things.

Yazidi women, unusually expressive with foreigners, wore long skirts with toga-like sashes draped from one arm to the opposite shoulder. They also wore white pillbox hats wrapped with white cloth. The women did not wear veils. The men wore their hair long and sported mustaches that turn down around the mouth. Pir Khader Sulaiman, a short, thin man, wore a red and white turban and a pesh merga outfit with long, baggy pants when we met. Pir is a religious title. Pir Khader, as he was called, was an important religious leader who represented one of the eight princely families in the tribe. A man identified as Sheikh Ali wore a long downward-turning mustache, a red and white turban and a lock of hair curled under his headdress to his forehead.

Among the Yazidis, Iraqi Kurd and Iraqi Arab sects and cultures, I found an illogical but not uncommon example of conflict based on power and tribal differences: Kurds, whom mainstream Iraqi Arab Sunni Muslims consider akin to Islamic heretics, persecute Yazidis — who are Kurds themselves — for not being Muslims at all. Iraqi Arabs — Sunnis and Shiites — persecute or sneer at the Yazidis for being neither Arabs nor Muslims. The Yazidis, in short, barely survive at the bottom of the Iraqi tribal ladder.

∞∞

Sumood Refugee Camp, March 27, 1992 — Three men whispered to me: "Would you like to meet a boy who escaped Al Anfal?" "Absolutely," I answered.

Al Anfal was the code name for Saddam Hussein's 1988 slaughterhouse campaign against the Kurds.

Saddam Hussein created Al Anfal to justify removing from the land and killing as many Iraqi Kurds as possible. He delegated well: his relatives, religious brothers and frightened people seeking favors or merely to survive killed for him. In Arabic Al Anfal means the spoils or the booty of war. Saddam Hussein and his propagandists claimed that Al Anfal was justified by a section of the Koran that permits Muslims to fight and kill infidels and destroy all of their property. The Kurds believed that Saddam Hussein's Sunni Arab henchmen warped the Koran. As an outsider, I believed that Saddam Hussein made sport of killing Kurds.

Between 50,000 and 100,000 Iraqi Kurds were rounded up and slaughtered from February to September of 1988, in the killing fields, villages and burial pits of Iraq, according to Middle East Watch, a division of the international organization Human Rights Watch. At the time of my visit, few details were known to outsiders about Saddam Hussein's campaign to wipe out Iraq's Kurds, which Middle East Watch later called war crimes, crimes against humanity and genocide.

The three men led me to the safety of a small walled compound where curly haired Taimur Abdullah was hiding. A cluster of pesh mergas, Taimur's cohorts now, gathered around to hear the story he told through a translator. Almost four years after he and his family had been abducted, bused to burial pits and trenches in the desert near the Saudi border, shot to death or shot and left for dead, the 16-year-old Taimur was hiding because he feared that Iraqi soldiers would return to finish the job. His sad eyes rimmed in red, Taimur told his story in great detail.

Nearly four years earlier, Taimur said, he, his mother and three sisters were captured by Iraqi soldiers after they had fled from fighting near their home in the village of Kolajo. After almost a month as prisoners, Taimur said, he and his family were taken by bus to burial pits near Iraq's border with Saudi Arabia. In all, Taimur said, about 30 busloads of Iraqi Kurds were taken to the Saudi border. About 50 people were in each bus, just enough to fill one of the waist-high pits where Iraqi soldiers shot the Kurds and later used bulldozers to bury them.

His father didn't make the day-long bus trip to doom, Taimur said, because his father had been taken away separately with other men when the rest of the family was captured. Taimur said that he never saw his father again.

After Taimur and his family, along with others in their bus, were dumped into a pit at night, the Iraqi soldiers "began shooting at us and a bullet came to me in the left shoulder," Taimur said: "I begged a soldier not to kill me. The soldier was about to cry, but an officer was next to the soldier so the soldier shot at me again and hit me in the lower back. The soldier didn't want to shoot me, but if he didn't, the officer would have shot the soldier."

Taimur said he saw his mother and sisters shot to death in the pit. Only Taimur and a young girl, who both feigned death, were left breathing in the pile of bodies when the shooting stopped. When the soldiers moved away from the pits to await the bulldozers that would bury the dead, and the living, if any, Taimur said, he escaped by crawling and then walking out from among the dead. Taimur believed, as did the pesh merga listening to him, that he was the only person who survived the killing pits. The young girl was too petrified to crawl out with him.

Dogs chased Taimur part of the two-and-a-half-hour walk from the pits to a bedouin desert camp. The trailing dogs finally scattered when they tired of dodging the rocks that Taimur threw at them. Lacking the means to treat Taimur's wounds, the bedouins fed Taimur bread and yoghurt for three days until they could take him secretly to an Iraqi Arab town for medical treatment. For two-and-a-half years, Taimur lived in the town. Dressed in Arab clothing, he put aside his Kurdish language for Arabic until others helped him locate relatives of his mother.

When I found him living with an uncle, or more accurately when he found me, Taimur had signed up as a pesh merga in the Sumood camp, although he would rather have been a doctor than a warrior. His back wound still pained and he lived fearfully in an open territorial prison where the Iraqi army punished the Kurds by allowing them to enter Mosul to purchase food and gasoline only to steal the provisions when the Kurds tried to return home with their hard-earned goods.

Throughout the region, the Iraqi Kurds were rebuilding from the effects of Al Anfal and of Saddam Hussein's continuous assaults on their right to live in their land. In one Kurdish town, Saddam Hussein's economic stranglehold was so tight that cars were lined up for three miles to buy gasoline. Their journey took two days. Piles of rocks that had once been villages lined the roads of Iraqi Kurdistan. A one-room stone house was all that remained in more than one village. Spring planting was vital, so where there weren't enough donkeys to pull the plows, men and women plowed by hand. Whole families, poor, simple, hard-working people, were on their knees planting seeds in the stony fields.

Glancing over the rubble of former villages, the bedrock of rural Kurdish life, and looking sadly over the remaining homes of mud, tin, hay and stone, an old man, an Iraqi Kurd, said of Saddam Hussein's tribal war, "Only the cemeteries were left alone. Only the cemeteries were left alive."

THREE

Jerusalem's Soured Milk and Honey

"Are you a Muslim, a Christian or a Jew?" an Israeli police officer asked me with apparent neutral fervor at the central police station in Jerusalem. Is this some sort of trick question I wondered, the answer to which would damn me forever in two-thirds of the holy land of Christians, Jews and Muslims? Here I was reporting on what locally was considered an act of war — vandalism to my leased car — and the central question was not what had happened but to whom do I pray. The question puzzled and angered me. I had been in Jerusalem only a few weeks when three windows were smashed in my leased car while I was interviewing Palestinians in the West Bank city of Hebron. If I reported the vandalism and received the proper document from police, the Israeli government would compensate the rental car company for an act of war.

Each time I stammered and appeared puzzled by what any God had to do with vandalism, the officer repeated the question. This went on for several minutes before I, unwilling to make a sectarian statement, made a nationalistic one instead when I blurted: "I'm an American." Frustrated and disgusted, the officer surrendered and jotted something on the document before handing it to me. The rental car company was pleased. No one there asked about my religion.

Months later in Jerusalem, a small-caliber projectile pierced a rear side window of my car and a jacket was stolen from the rear seat. This time I trudged to the local police substation to obtain another war-damage document. "Are you a Christian, a Muslim or a Jew?" the police officer said, asking the tribal question again. This time I was ready. "Suppose I'm a Buddhist, a Hindu, a Shinto, a Zoroastrian or a Sikh?" I asked him. "No, no. That's all there is," the officer said with regional surety, referring to C, M and J. I said nothing more. The officer broke the silence by scratching out some information on the document, which again pleased the rental car agency.

Near the end of the first Gulf war in 1991, my leased car was fire-bombed on a main street in Palestinian East Jerusalem. Its sin? Bearing a yellow license plate that indicated the car's tribe; it was rented from an agency in Israel. A blue plate would have linked the car to the West Bank, which would have raised tribal

suspicions among Israelis. Israeli police called the rental agency, which towed the
damaged car. No one asked my religion and no documents exchanged hands.

Sleep was flirting with me when the first siren pierced the Jerusalem
night. I pushed on the light switch to check my watch. On a clear day from
my rented house in the hillside Ramot Eshkol neighborhood I could see the
Mediterranean coast. That night, Friday, January 18, 1991, all I could see was
a people's fear.

The time was 2:06 A.M., the moment when Israelis, Palestinians and
everyone else in the historic city were told that the first Iraqi missiles had thudded into the Jewish nation. A state of emergency was in effect. The first Persian Gulf War was here, a complicated tribal conflict masked by an Iraqi
invasion of Kuwait and global dependence on oil.

An air raid siren's shriek carries fear, visions of bombs and death, a
swelling emptiness in the stomach. But the queasy feelings quickly lost their
immobilizing effect because we were all expecting the sirens, the Scud missiles and the war. The urgency of work and its piggy-backed adrenalin focus
mind and body away from fear, towards action.

I rolled out of bed as the siren sounded and jotted the time in a notebook. Dressing with my left hand and making notes with my right, I recorded
the times of subsequent alarms: 2:10, then 2:11 stretching to 2:12. At 2:16, Israel
Radio reported what I and thousands of others already knew: The sirens of
war had been sounded in Jerusalem. A voice told listeners to go to their sealed
rooms and listen for further instructions, which the radio passed on at 2:30
A.M.

The war had started a few hours earlier when the U.S.–led coalition, a
real international coalition unlike the propaganda shell of 2003, began bom-
barding Iraq. An Iraqi missile assault against Israel was as expected as the sun
rising over Baghdad on its way toward Jerusalem's sectarian shrines, holy to
Christian, Jewish and Muslim tribes.

Saddam Hussein, a secular Sunni Muslim, and a murderous one at that,
was trying to provoke an Israeli military response. If the Israelis retaliated,
the allied coalition that included many Arab nations probably would have
unraveled and the war against Iraq could have spiraled into a wider and more
devastating Arab-Israeli conflict. Israel's fear of a chemical attack was an added
Iraqi weapon, as was the possibility that the Scuds would damage key Israeli
military installations. Even if Israel held its fire, which would be most difficult
for Yitzhak Shamir, then Israel's prime minister and an old pre-state terrorist, to do, Saddam Hussein would get a few free shots at the Jewish tribes in
retaliation for Israel's destruction of an Iraqi nuclear reactor in 1981. In the
end, Shamir yielded to intense U.S. pressure and Israel sat out the war, allow-

ing the American coalition to finally quiet the Scuds and punish Saddam Hussein's military.

When the war began, Israeli citizens had no inkling about what Iraq would send their way or how Shamir and his government would react. A few days before the war, large numbers of Israelis fasted and prayed for peace at their sacred Western Wall in Jerusalem. Some ultra–Orthodox Jews, who don't believe in the State of Israel to begin with, fled the country. Most Israelis hunkered down. When the sirens wailed, they would grab their gas masks and rush to their sealed rooms.

My bag of background material and notebooks had been packed and ready for days. The gas mask that Israeli officials had issued to foreign correspondents was on the rear seat of my car. I kept the mask handy but never wore it because months of gathering background information about Iraq's military capabilities convinced me that Saddam Hussein lacked the capacity to deliver chemical weapons on Scud missiles. There was, however, only one certain way, a risky and distasteful one, to be certain of that and the Israelis were taking no chances.

As I headed to the special wartime press center at the Jerusalem Hilton Hotel, I stopped to pick up a hitchhiker. If the young man were trying to flee the city, or the country, I figured that he would have found a faster, more efficient, way. I guessed that the siren had summoned the nervous hitchhiker to a job related to the emergency of war, so in a loose sense our reasons for being alone on a Jerusalem street in the middle of the night were the same.

After I dropped the man off at an intersection near the city center, I sped to the hotel. Along the way, I noticed the man's black skullcap, which Israelis call a kipa, on the passenger side of the front seat. His kipa must have fallen as the man left my car. I wondered whether he would be upset by the loss of his religious headcovering at a moment of such great danger and drama. I thought about trying to find him, but I had no idea who the man was or where he worked. If his lost kipa was bad karma, to use a term from a non–Abrahamic tribe farther east, the results would be out of my hands, and his.

Fearful and grim, Israelis had awaited the shrieking messengers of war for weeks. Now, in mid–January, members of the Jewish tribes from all over the world, even some religious novices fresh from reborn Russia, were ready, at least physically. Their gas masks were on hand, their sealed rooms supplied for survival. Even bomb shelters, useless and probably lethal in a gas attack, were aired out.

An Iraqi gas attack, with all its historical tribal baggage, is what nervous Israelis feared the most. Frightened but also energized by the uncertainties of war, members of the Palestinian tribes, their various Christian and Muslim sects and political factions, also awaited the whistling Scuds, but for different reasons and with little protection. Few Palestinians had gas masks and all of them would quickly be sealed from the alleys and streets of their own land by a curfew that their Israeli occupiers would impose.

Iraq was ground zero of the blitzkrieg to come during the first Persian Gulf War in January and February of 1991. Backed by the United Nations and led by U.S. armed forces, the onslaught was called Desert Storm. Generals and political leaders love simple code names that ooze military ferocity and invincibility because codes give soldiers purpose and focus, while adding false courage. Flashy code names also give civilians back home a fresh logo to root for, something like cheering for the local team: the Hurricanes, Wildcats, Fighting Irish, Tigers, Trojans. Or Crusaders.

On one side, the war was a global gathering of almost 40 disparate nation-states. Nearly a dozen of those tribes were controlled by Middle Eastern dictators who feared regional turmoil and a loss of power if Iraq and its own dictator Saddam Hussein were not checked. Oddly, those Arab states and Israel were on the same side, although silently and for different reasons, in this war. But most of those nation-states, notably the world's greatest powers, were united by the need to protect and preserve for themselves the Middle East's oil. To attach to their battle standards a more noble and less venal purpose, those tribes proclaimed that they were upholding the notion, which is usually selectively applied, that stronger states must never be allowed to invade weaker states with impunity — especially where oil is involved. The principle that invaders must be stopped is dusted off and polished when the interests of powerful states are threatened, as they were when Saddam Hussein invaded the neighboring oil fiefdom of Kuwait on August 2, 1990.

If Iraq could get away with invading Kuwait, maybe Saddam Hussein or some other power-mad dictator could escape with invading the largest oil drum of all, Saudi Arabia, thereby drastically reducing the global oil supply and the wealth it produces.

The war was fought over oil, and secondarily to free Kuwait from Iraqi control and punish Saddam Hussein, once a U.S. and Western ally, for misreading the U.S. reaction to his folly. In short, all members of the coalition, East and West, shared a common enemy — Saddam Hussein — if not the same reason for opposing him. Although temporary, the awkward alliances brought U.S. and other Western forces into a region, notably to Saudi Arabia, where they were anathema on religious grounds. The regional welcome mat was transparently thin. After the war ended, the continued presence of U.S. forces in Saudi Arabia, Islam's geographic and spiritual core, contributed heavily to the rise of religious extremists such as Osama bin Laden and their war against the Saudi royal family and its "infidel" allies.

Northern Israel and Tel Aviv, with its vital military posts, were the targets of the first bomb-like Scuds that took less than ten minutes to strike after they were launched in western Iraq. The warning time was five minutes or less.

News flowed quickly into the Jerusalem press center. Judging from the first reports, the Scuds apparently carried only conventional warheads. But no one was absolutely sure of that. There were injuries, but they were few and not severe. One of the first Scuds struck a building in the Holon industrial area near Ben Gurion International Airport off the main Tel Aviv-Jerusalem road. With its sprawling commercial and military installations, the airport itself was probably a main target of the notoriously inaccurate Scuds. Other missiles exploded in central Tel Aviv, and a Tel Aviv hospital was taking in the injured. Israeli military officials warned reporters, especially those working for television, not to reveal the exact locations of Scud strikes. Instant reporting of exact strike locations would help the Iraqis readjust and improve their aims, which would put the airport and other prime targets in greater danger from the wobbly Scuds, the Israeli military brass argued with good reason.

I was at the press center in the Jerusalem Hilton with John Hockenberry, then a reporter with National Public Radio, trying to pinpoint the Scud strikes before we dashed toward Tel Aviv. We wanted to drive fast and directly to where the Scuds had landed rather than blindly head toward Tel Aviv while scanning the night sky for flames.

After spending about an hour gathering specific information about the strikes, Hockenberry and I decided that we had enough detail to head out in my leased Subaru sedan. We wanted to see for ourselves the extent of the damage, and whether the Scuds carried poison gas. Still enveloped in the pre-dawn darkness, we looked for fires lighting the sky on the way toward the Holon textile factory. Foot to the floor, I wound the engine of my small car to its grinding limits. The road to Tel Aviv was open and empty. But an unbroken necklace of headlights was bouncing up the hills toward Jerusalem and what the occupants probably thought would be safe haven, safer no doubt than Tel Aviv with all of its fat military targets.

About six miles from the airport, Hockenberry and I spotted flames roaring from a building just off the highway. This was the Holon industrial area. Close enough to hear the crackling, I stopped the car near the textile factory. Mask-less, Hockenberry and I looked at each other, shrugged and smiled in silence; "Mustn't be any gas, we're still breathing," we said with our smiles. Rami Weizman, the factory's night guard, was alone when we arrived. Emergency crews hadn't arrived yet. Weizman described two booms in the air and then a blast on the ground about 2:30 A.M. No one had been injured and Weizman, pointing to his gas mask security blanket, said he was unafraid.

Flames from rolls of ignited textiles shot through the factory roof as we talked. Shortly after Hockenberry and I arrived, emergency crews showed up to extinguish the fire and deal with the chemical fallout that didn't exist. Wearing gas masks and totally enveloped in white suits, the workers looked like giant white insects from an alien world.

From the Holon factory, Hockenberry and I drove to areas of Tel Aviv where other Scuds had slammed into buildings. Seven people were slightly hurt in the Ezra neighborhood, but the missiles carried no chemical weapons.

On and off for the next 18 days, we sped around central Israel, speaking with frightened and defiant Israelis, counting the Scud attacks and the casualties, assessing the damage, and making sure we arranged nighttime escape routes so we wouldn't be trapped in our Tel Aviv hotel when the sirens sounded.

Driving was easy because the streets were eerily empty. Traffic signals lost their purpose. The final tally showed that Iraq had fired 39 Scuds in 18 separate attacks; the last four Scuds struck harmlessly in the Israeli-occupied West Bank. Saddam Hussein, it turned out, was probably unable, rather than unwilling, to deliver chemical weapons on Scud warheads. After the last Scud attack, Israeli officials reported that altogether two Israelis had been killed directly by the missiles and 12 others died of suffocation in sealed rooms or from stress. Another 228 Israelis were injured, most lightly and without counting the psychological scars. Property damage was estimated at $200 million. As far as I could determine, no Palestinians in the West Bank or Gaza were killed or injured in the attacks.

Iraq's attacks against Israel, Israel's treatment of the Palestinians during the war, and the Palestinian reactions to the Scud assaults lay bare the tribal side of the Israeli-Palestinian conflict. That decades-old war is rooted in the sticky sands of religion, ethnicity, culture, land and language, topped by the usual heavy doses of foreign intervention. What could be more tribal than a Jewish state? An Islamic state, such as Iran or Pakistan? Palestinian Muslim fundamentalists who believe that a Jewish state is anathema on Islamic land? Palestinian Muslims and Christians who want their land back because they don't understand why they should have lost their homes due mainly to what German Nazis and their European cohorts did to Jews in the 1930s and 1940s, and because the United States and other Western powers did so little to help European Jews at that time?

The 1991 Gulf war exposes many reasons why the Israeli-Palestinian conflict continues and even deepens. Political and military occupation and its daily humiliation lead to land expropriation and repression which provoke stone-throwing, rioting and shootings; violent resistance brings curfews, the destruction of homes and olive groves, large scale arrests and detentions without charges or convictions; harsher punishments bring suicide bombers attacking civilians and that in turn leads to tank and missile attacks against the blind religious fundamentalists, secular militants and civilians. The West winces and shudders when suicide bombers shred the flesh of children, women, old men and soldiers, vicious and incomprehensible attacks to be sure that reveal a broad gap in understanding. When the retaliation comes to suicide bombings, it seems easier to understand. With each attack and counterattack the causes of the fear and loathing are buried deeper and deeper under the broken bones and shortened lives.

Wider expands the circle, fear and hatred thickening and spreading with each action and reaction. Too many Israeli extremists, put the government on that list, want more Palestinian land. Outgunned and controlled by the Israelis, and in many ways betrayed by their own leaders, many Palestinians fight back, determined not only to end the occupation but, in their minds trained on history, to regain all of Palestine. Terror spreads on both sides: Everyday state terrorism aimed at a total population versus individuals who deliberately kill themselves to kill soldiers and civilians, often without distinction.

As of January 10, 1991, during what is known as the first Palestinian uprising, or Intifadeh, Israeli officials said, they had 10,785 Palestinians in administrative detention or prison. Of those, 1,442 were being held without charges or verdicts; 3,955 had already been tried and sentenced; 1,375 had been arrested and would be charged and sent to trial; 4,013 had been arrested, charged and were in the midst of court proceedings. Repression and arrests breed more freedom-fighters, more real terrorists, more excuses to take more land.

Iraq's Scuds exposed the depths of the fear and the fighting in Israel, the West Bank and the Gaza Strip. The fears of many Israelis remained rooted in World War II and the Nazi extermination and concentration camps. The Holocaust is, to varying degrees, exploited by some Israeli politicians. Israelis know this far better than do Americans and many object strongly to such denigration of that colossal slaughter. But among Israeli civilians, the widespread fear of an Iraqi gas attack was real and raw in 1991, as much because of Jewish history in Europe as it was because in the 1980s, Saddam Hussein had used poison gas against Iraqi Kurds and Iranians in the Iran-Iraq war.

I have seen the crumbled stone homes of Iraqi Kurds that Saddam Hussein's forces leveled in Halabja. I have watched Iraqi Kurdish women slave to draw life from the rocky and poisoned soil next to their flattened homes while their fathers, husbands, brothers and sons strutted aimlessly nearby, wrapped in their tribal warrior uniforms and girdled in bullets ready to be fed into their shouldered assault rifles. That Iraqi Kurdish picture is a universal one, another form of tribalism: women groveling to sustain life; men poised to cause death. Saddam Hussein was America's pal in the 1980s because he was the chief antagonist of the Islamic Iranian state, then America's main enemy in the Middle East. The West, too, knows how to apply the Byzantine standard of the region: the enemy of my enemy is my friend.

Jews in Israel come from all over the world, from Europe, the Middle East, North, East and South Africa, Asia, Australia, North and South America. But it is the European experience and fear of a repeat that drove most of them to Israel and that permeates the country. But that is no solace to the Palestinians: While Jews flowed into the Palestine that became Israel, Palestinians were driven from their homes or fled. About 750,000 Palestinians who had lived in Jaffa, Haifa, Ramla, the Galilee in 1948, live under Israeli occupation inside and outside of refugee camps, even inside and outside of refugee camps in Jordan, Lebanon and Syria. Many thousands more Palestinians were displaced as a result of the 1967 war. The broad Palestinian diaspora is now one of the world's largest. One of the ironies of the first Gulf war is that some of Saddam Hussein's imprecise Scuds struck Tel Aviv neighborhoods occupied by poor Jews from Iraq.

When Israelis lined up for gas masks, acquired kits to seal rooms against gas attacks, bought bottled water, sugar, flour, batteries, rice, tuna, tuna and more tuna, many were reminded constantly of Birkenau, Auschwitz, Treblinka, Dachau and on, and on. To highlight the historical references, some Israelis pointed fingers at Germany for supplying Saddam Hussein with the materials to make chemical weapons. When the German minister for economic cooperation visited Jerusalem during the war, he was greeted with placards that said, "Germany gassed wrong," "The German Gas Company. We specialize in Humanicides serving Iraq and Libya," "Russian Scuds modified by Germans into Iraqi Scums."

No one pointed a finger at the United States, but someone should have. During the long Iran-Iraq war of the 1980s, the United States backed Saddam Hussein against Iran's Islamic leader, the Ayatollah Khomeini. American policy was geared to stop Khomeini and his throbbing radical Islamic regime at any cost. Even in death and the American occupation of his country, Saddam Hussein has proven that the American decision was a costly one. Khomeini is dead, too, but his fundamentalist regime prays on.

On the fifth night of the Gulf war in Israel, the conductor and violinist Zubin Mehta gave American comedian Jackie Mason a gas mask when he introduced Mason to an audience at the Tel Aviv Hilton. Before Mehta could finish saying to Mason, "Whether you know or learn how to put this on, may it never happen that this mask is ever put on again in Israel," a siren sounded again and the crowd fled to the hotel's sixth floor, which was sealed against a gas attack. The sealed floor seemed anything but impenetrable, although it served as a psychological shield for the people huddled there.

Every time a siren sounded, hotel guests, their gas masks locked on their faces, rushed to the sealed sixth floor. The drill was repeated so often that I learned to identify the faceless people — who looked like bipeds with long black insect-like snouts — by their shoes, shirts, dresses and pants. Identification versatility, I called it, flexibility and minor ingenuity learned under the threat of missile, and maybe chemical, attack.

The average Israeli in the Tel Aviv area was wounded more by fright and the disabling uncertainty of when and where the Scuds would hit than by actual injuries and damage caused by the missiles. But fear wounds, too, scarring the mind and thickening suspicions. After a Scud attack, I saw a man lying on the ground in Tel Aviv, his head resting in a crooked fashion against a metal clothesline post, weeping like a child, apparently in shock. A Scud had slammed between a performing arts center and a gymnasium, leaving a crater 25 feet across and 15 feet deep. The damage was heavy, but good fortune dictated that neither the man nor anyone else was physically injured. To everyone's relief, the Scud carried no gas. But residents, prepared for the worst, clutched their gas masks in their sealed rooms just in case.

After a particularly severe attack in Tel Aviv on January 22, when 70 people were injured and 20 houses damaged, a terrified school teacher stammered and told me, "In the night when the sun goes down, nobody goes out. You don't know what is coming."

Palestinians, too, suffered from the war, internationally because of their political support for Iraq and in their own homes, because of Israel's long curfew, where the Palestinians breathed and worked. A few days after terrified Israelis stared blankly eastward into the unrevealing Tel Aviv night after a Scud attack, a 42-year-old Palestinian woman hunkered down in a refugee camp near the West Bank city of Ramallah. She was living like a squatter in two large tents provided by the U.N. with her 12 children and an extended family that totaled 18. No one in the family was working, no one had a gas mask or a sealed tent. Israeli soldiers had earlier destroyed the family house because one of the woman's sons had been active in the Palestinian uprising against the occupation, and the area had been under an Israeli-imposed curfew for more than a week. "We live one day at a time," the woman said. "Today we will cook the rest of what we have."

Under curfew, the West Bank was off-limits to journalists, but Hockenberry and I managed to wiggle into a refugee camp near Nablus, skirting Israeli troops and barriers along the way. We wanted to find out how the war and the curfew were affecting the Palestinians, not that editors or the world were clammering to know. In the camp, as in most of the West Bank and Gaza, no one had a gas mask, and the curfew made it difficult for people to obtain food in their own land. The Palestinians weren't working and they weren't starving. But they were running low on food, and on February 4, 1991, the U.N. appealed to major donors to feed 1.5 million Palestinians. Rice, flour, canned or fresh meat, beans and milk of any kind were badly needed.

A family of four I visited in the Balata refugee camp had some food in the refrigerator and pantry, but not much. On February 5, 1991, the U.N. had just delivered milk. A few vegetables, a little meat, eggs, stale and frozen bread, ketchup, beans and eggplant would last a few more days of dietary dining.

A 28-year-old Palestinian man in a refugee camp near Ramallah described the curfew this way: "We are in a big prison here anyway. It doesn't make any difference if we get arrested in the street during curfew. They (Israeli soldiers) go house to house to get us." Of course getting arrested did make a difference, and Palestinian kids didn't want to get arrested; that's the reason they dashed like world-class sprinters through the streets in the early morning to find fresh bread. But the man's sense of being in a big prison in his own land was echoed by Roman Catholic Bernadette Devlin McAliskey in British controlled Northern Ireland and the ethnic–Albanian rebel Adem Demaci in Serb-dominated Kosovo when I interviewed them in later years. Occupation and the dominion of one people over another have a universal way of turning homes into prisons, teenagers into guerrillas and once-oppressed people into oppressors.

As long as Israel was an occupier, the curfew could be justified because the Palestinians were cheering for Saddam Hussein on the combat cliché that people who share an enemy become friends. Israel did not want to face Scuds arriving by air and a possible full-scale rebellion on the ground by Palestinians. There again the fear of a Fifth Column is rooted in the Israeli occupation.

Israel also had to be concerned about its borders with Syria, Lebanon and Jordan, although Syria — which then controlled Lebanon, was a member of the U.S.–led anti–Iraq coalition and opposed and feared Saddam Hussein — was not about to cause trouble. Jordan was in such a bind that the late King Hussein felt forced to dance carefully with Saddam Hussein. Iraq and Jordan shared a long border and Jordan was dependent on Iraqi oil. Israel expressed a legitimate fear in the tense climate of the time that Iraq might use Jordan as a highway to Israel, although that would have been at least as suicidal as Saddam Hussein's invasion of Kuwait.

The late Yasser Arafat, then leader of the Palestine Liberation Organization, had openly lined up with Saddam Hussein, a move that seemed as puzzling as it was impolitic and self-defeating. Perhaps Arafat had to repay Saddam Hussein for aid Hussein gave Arafat when the PLO and its leader were fighting for their lives in Lebanon during the 1970s and early 1980s. Unlike the Arab dictators who opposed Saddam Hussein because they feared his destablizing effect on the region and on their regimes, the Palestinians had no state and no reason to fear Iraq.

A Palestinian man at a camp near Ramallah explained the pro-Iraq position this way: "It's like you are in a river drowning and a branch sticks out and you grab the branch to save yourself. You don't look to see how strong the branch is or what kind of tree it is. You only want to save yourself." Title his discourse blind desperation, because the Palestinians knew that the branch belonged to Saddam Hussein's beleaguered Iraq and they should have known that Saddam could never save them. But the Palestinians were willing to cheer any damage done to Israel by anyone.

A woman in the same camp explained the Palestinian position in these words: "Of course the children cheer the Scuds. We are happy because some people are standing with us. We're like in a zoo. All the West countries are putting Israel on their shoulders no matter what Israel does, but for us we are not human beings. No one cares about us." A decade later, the woman could have been speaking in support of Osama bin Laden. Her words, too, were cries of desperation.

The American-led coalition wanted to keep Israel out of the fray so the coalition would hold together and the war wouldn't widen and get out of control. That's the main reason the United States sent Patriot anti-missile missiles to Israel and the reason U.S. diplomats strained to calm Israeli leaders and convince them not to retaliate after the Scud attacks. But to the Palestinians, the Patriot missiles were another example of U.S. aid going to Israel, while Arabs and Muslims, which meant them and the Iraqis, were targets of the West.

Israel's failure to provide Palestinians with gas masks and its rationalizations for not doing so were typical of the way Israel treated the Palestinians, whose land and resources Israel policed, administered and continued to absorb at the time.

In October 1990, before the war began, it was apparent that few Palestinians would receive gas masks. The Israeli message was always murky and contradictory. At one moment, Israel said it was buying masks to distribute to the Palestinians; at another moment, an Israeli general said that Israel would sell masks to Palestinians but couldn't afford to give them for free. By the end of the war, the appearances of neglect turned into reality. A few Palestinians who lived in and around Jerusalem or worked there received masks well before the war began, but the vast majority of Palestinians never received them. Judging from the results, Israel never planned to give all or many of the Palestinians gas masks. But there were always strong elements of contradiction and confusion in Israel's messages.

On one occasion, Israeli officials said, about 173,000 masks were in storage and ready for distribution. But before and during the war, various Israeli officials created a rhetorical game with the gas masks, making it clear that the Palestinians would never receive them: the masks were too expensive; there weren't enough masks anyway; Israel has its priorities; Iraq wouldn't strike the West Bank or Gaza (although no Israeli ever explained how it would come to pass that chemicals could differentiate between peoples and borders or why the Israeli settlers in the occupied territories weren't short of masks). It would also take time to distribute masks to the Palestinians, Israeli officials said, and relief workers in the West Bank and Gaza would be the first to receive masks. On and on the excuses went.

On January 14, 1991, Israel's High Court of Justice ordered that gas masks be distributed to Palestinians in the West Bank and Gaza. Twenty days later, on February 3, Israeli Brig. Gen. Freddy Zack said it would take months to distribute gas masks to the Palestinians. Besides, Zack said, the Palestinians wouldn't need masks if Saddam Hussein weren't threatening Israel. So Zack asked the Palestinians to take physical risks for what the madman of Iraq was doing. Zack spoke after the 10th Scud attack against Israel, but the missiles kept coming. By February 25, 1991, nine more Scuds were fired at Israel. By February 9, the daytime curfew had been lifted against Palestinians who worked in Israel because the Israelis needed them.

Most Palestinians never touched a gas mask.

On February 28, as Israelis began to celebrate the holiday of Purim, Etty Feinstein, an Israeli bank clerk, said with a broad smile, "No more war, no more sealed rooms. I'm happy, and it's a holiday, too."

An old man, an Italian pilgrim, stumbled up the worn and uneven limestone steps in Jerusalem's walled Old City. He carried a large wood cross almost twice his height on a frail right shoulder as he plodded, mesmerized, over the rough stones. The man, who appeared to be in his seventies, was leading other pilgrims towards the Via Dolorosa, the path that Christians believe Jesus took on his way to death on the cross.

This 2,000-year-old image was as alive as were the pilgrims, as real as were the Rosary beads they carried to mark the stops that their faith says Jesus made along the route. This was a pilgrimage that the old man apparently felt personally compelled to complete without help. It was his religious mission, his Hajj, his Mecca, his Western Wall. If he died along the way, he would have died happily, falling in what he believed were Jesus' footsteps frozen in the limestone, although the actual or supposed sites in most cases are buried many feet below the current walkways.

Christian pilgrims, mostly Europeans, frequently walk and pray on the same route. Along the way, they buy religious items from Palestinian merchants. The business of religion is especially big in Jerusalem, where Christian, Islamic and Jewish tribes compete and contest for religious supremacy amid implicit and explicit claims that the God of each is a superior God. When there is violence and tourism falls off, so does the business of religion, in Jerusalem and all over Israel and the West Bank. God is always busy in Jerusalem, being asked to damn enemies and bless friends. I never heard any of the believers question how a just and merciful God, or gods, could take sides in such a puerile human way.

This pilgrimage was particularly bizarre. The old man and his followers walked blindly into, around and through a mass of Israeli and Palestinian women demonstrating for peace and past platoons of Israeli security forces trying to corral the female demonstrators. The Women in Black, as those peace campaigners were known, were trying to march to the top of a small hill that, to Jews and Muslims, is every bit a match in historical and religious importance as the Via Dolorosa is to Christians. The women were shouting and praying and demanding that Israeli border police let them through to the top of what Jews call the Temple Mount and what Muslims call Haram es-Sharif, the Noble Enclosure. But the Israeli guns and uniforms would have none of it.

The Women in Black were protesting the killing of 17 Palestinians by Israeli police atop Haram es-Sharif on October 8, 1990. The blood was still warm when the women marched. Emotions ran as high as the shouts of the women and the police were loud. Noise from the confrontation thundered and echoed along the narrow stone streets and walls of the Old City. Students and teachers at a Jewish school — its mere presence in that neighborhood a provocation to Palestinians even at less tense moments — added to the surreal quality of the confrontational mismatch when they handed cold drinks and cookies to the police. Their guns a quick hand movement away from ready, aim, fire, the quasi-military border police drank and nibbled between shouts and counter shouts. Into this melee walked the Christian pilgrims, apparently oblivious to the confrontation and the reasons for it.

From a niche carved into a wall that allows a pedestrian to duck into and avoid being smashed by car or donkey cart — or by a crush of demonstrators or soldiers — racing along the narrow street, I watched the pilgrims, police and peace-seekers engage in a weird tribal, sectarian, ethnic and political dance. By most outside standards, the scene would be considered positively nutty. By Jerusalem standards, it was fairly routine. I remember watching the bizarre scene and thinking that somebody was crazy here and I wasn't the one, a claim I cannot always make. Tribalism in its many forms had run amok in a small space where God and related religions, if not universal spirituality, were supposed to reign. In the end, the pilgrims fulfilled their mission, the Women in Black were stymied and no one was killed on that day of protest. But by then the 17 Palestinians who had been killed only hours before had been laid to rest, no more to participate in or witness Jerusalem's tribal extremism.

As quick as a government wink, Israeli officials moved to paper over the murders of the 17 Palestinians by blaming the Palestinians themselves for their own deaths. Less than three weeks after the killings, a government panel appointed by then–Prime Minister Yitzhak Shamir reported that Israeli police had acted in self-defense and to protect Jewish worshippers at the Western Wall from stones thrown by Palestinians. The report also blamed Jerusalem police for failing to prevent the rioting and for some indiscriminate shooting. In case anyone missed the point, the government-appointed investigators said that Palestinians invited the violence by shouting from mosque loudspeakers, "God is the Greatest," "Holy War," and "Slaughter the Jews."

Nine months later, in July 1991, an Israeli judge contradicted the government's findings. A police error, not Palestinians stoning Jewish worshippers, triggered the clash that resulted in Israeli police killing the 17 Palestinians, the judge reported. Police, the judge said, used "improper" behavior when they unnecessarily fired live ammunition and rubber bullets to quell the disturbance. The clash was ignited, the judge said, when a tear-gas canister accidentally fell to the ground and rolled toward a group of Palestinian women near a mosque on Haram es-Sharif. That incident escalated into Palestinians screaming and throwing stones, after which Israeli police began their indiscriminate, lethal shooting. Most of the Jewish worshippers had fled from the Western Wall by the time the Palestinians began hurling stones over the wall, the judge said.

By the time the Israeli judge reported his findings, the killings were more than nine months old. One more footnote in the conflict, the story was largely dead and buried and the Palestinians were saddled with another legend about how they killed themselves with Israeli bullets. To that fable the Palestinians would add this factual footnote: The Israeli bullets, in one manner or another, were supplied by America.

───◦◦◦───

Jerusalem itself, notably the walled Old City, is a metaphor for the tribal nature of the larger conflict. With its serpentine streets and subterranean history, the Old City is a labyrinth of ethnic, sectarian, linguistic, political and cultural diversity, tension and conflict. A magical and sometimes demonic mix of antiquity, exotic orientalism and modernity, its unforgiving stone streets, walkways and walls are wedged into a small space. A little more than half a mile square, the Old City is much larger when you walk atop its high walls, through all its alleys and secret passages, into its hidden tranquil courtyards laden with fountains and trees that, believe it or not, shut out the near-ubiquitous smells and riotous street noise of craven commerce. The Old City grows larger when you descend layer by layer into its basements where Romans roamed and those of many faiths worshipped and then followed their conflicted natures and went off to kill or be killed, usually in the names of their gods or other tribal banners.

Christians, Jews and Muslims of all shades and intensities; Israelis, Palestinians, Armenians, Copts, Ethiopians and others mingle warily in the Old City. They cross historic dividing lines on tip-toes, but they know each other too well to be missed in the crossing. The Old City itself is an enclave in the larger city that lies outside its 16th century walls.

Tribal lines — ethnic, sectarian, cultural and linguistic — split the Old City itself, which is divided into four sections: The Armenian Quarter, the Christian Quarter, the Jewish Quarter and the Muslim Quarter. That's raw tribalism spelled out on a map and on the ground. The Armenians are mostly Orthodox Christians. They aren't Arabs or Israelis; they aren't Palestinians and their language is not Semitic; they aren't Muslims or Jews, Catholics or Protestants. Neutrality is essential for the small Armenian population to survive in the Old City.

Physically separate from the Armenian enclave, the Christian Quarter is a mixture of Palestinians, mostly Christians of various Eastern and Western sects, and Christians of various other ethnic and language groups.

The Jewish Quarter is, as the name suggests, Jewish, and that can mean Jews from various parts of the world who practice different forms of Judaism; some don't even support the State of Israel.

The Muslim Quarter is populated mainly by Palestinians of the Sunni persuasion, Islam's core sect. Generally the labels mean what they say, although Palestinians, regardless of religion, and Armenians mingle openly. Most Jews and Palestinians who pass through the quarters of the Old City do so with little socializing. What business takes place between Jews and Palestinians is usually transacted on the side.

Physical, linear, differences in the quarters reflect the cultural separation among the peoples. The Jewish Quarter is new, clean and its construction and architectural style are Israeli. Except for the ultra–Orthodox Jews, in dress and manner the people who live in the Jewish Quarter look more like

Westerners, mainly Eastern Europeans, than Middle Easterners. Shops appear more Western in their organized orderliness and cleanliness, although there are exceptions.

Exotic orientalism swells throughout most of the other quarters. The unruly din of the open market rules. Age-old and chaotic in its airy jumble of shops, the large commercial sections of the Christian and Muslim quarters amount to an ancient shopping mall without central heating or cooling and, to outsiders, seeming without order. Children and adults pushing carts filled with produce and trinkets shout and wiggle through tiny spaces in the human mass where moments before one wafer-thin human could not wedge. Fields of spices in open burlap bags lure visitors as they have for centuries. Open stalls and shops that surprise in their eclectic offerings, fruit and vegetable stands, butcher shops with sides of lamb and goat meat hanging in less than tantalizing fashion in front of and behind windows all add to the Oriental reality and mystique of the Old City and the region.

Beneath it all, on their own rough-hewn limestone streets, lie the ghosts of Greeks, Romans and Byzantines, and of countless indigenous peoples who lived, prayed, fought and died in the name of tribe and god.

If the sectarian nature of the conflict can be isolated from its other tribal aspects, the lines can be most sharply drawn in the Old City. Sites considered most sacred to Christianity, Islam and Judaism stand wall by limestone wall in historical and contemporary angst. The Western Wall, believed to be the remnant of an outer courtyard-like barrier of the Second Jewish Temple that was destroyed more than 1900 years ago, is Judaism's most sacred site. The Wall is the most powerful place of prayer for Jews. If a third Jewish temple is ever built, it is supposed to be on top of the Wall, an area that Jews call the Temple Mount.

Muslims call that same 40-acre area Haram es-Sharif, which in Arabic means the Noble Enclosure. The Western Wall remnant helps to support part of the Temple Mount/Haram es-Sharif. Al-Aqsa Mosque, Islam's third holiest site, rests within the Noble Enclosure, along with the Dome of the Rock, a magnificent gilded domed building on the walls of which brilliant blue mosaics shine in Jerusalem's fervent and forever sun. Muslims believe that Muhammed ascended to heaven from the site where the Dome of the Rock stands. If that's not a powerful enough symbol, the Dome of the Rock was supposedly built around the rock where Abraham — considered the father of Judaism, Christianity and Islam and still an omnipresent and powerful, if shadowy, figure in the region — supposedly bound his son, Isaac, to be sacrificed. Not far away, on streets that pass through the Muslim and Christian quarters, is the area that Christians believe marks the path that Jesus took 2,000 years ago to his death and resurrection, which is the foundation of

Christianity, at the site now called the Church of the Holy Sepulcher. Various competing Christian denominations routinely squabble for control of that ground.

All of this, along with lesser but still magnetic holy places and sacred symbols, is too much competing religious baggage for any small place to bear. Perhaps the greatest wonder is that the Old City still stands. In Hebrew, Jerusalem means City of Peace. Arabs call Jerusalem Al Quds, which means The Holy. In Dante's world, Hell is located under Jerusalem, extending to the Earth's core. Great poet or not, Dante would be stoned by all sects in today's Jerusalem. To members of the tiny Samaritan sect, an ancient offshoot of Judaism, the "chosen place of God, the navel of the Earth," is Mount Gerizim, near the West Bank Palestinian city of Nablus on the ancient road to Damascus. Take that, Dante. Take that, Jerusalem.

After the 1948 war in which Israel won its independence, the Old City was governed, with a heavy, injudicious hand, by Jordan. But in the 1967 Six-Day War, Israel gained control of the Old City, the West Bank and Syria's Golan Heights. After that war, the run-down Jewish Quarter in Jerusalem's Old City was restored and beautified.

My first visit to the Old City was in 1988, at night, before I began work full-time in the Middle East. At the time, I was the editorial page editor of *The Miami* (Florida) *News.*

When the din of daily commerce dies with dusk, Jerusalem's Old City grows ghostly in its dim lighting. At such moments, the shadowy alleys and walls are transformed into a hard-to-read blueprint of real and atmospheric intrigue found in any naturally divisive medieval compound.

The Old City was nearly empty when I first visited. An occasional passer-by looked like a specter in the shadowy light. I probably looked the same to others. The metal doors of shops were slammed shut and padlocked tightly against the stone slabs.

At night the Old City reminds me of paintings of grim walled-in 17th century East London wrapped in a smoke-filled fog, if an Oriental casbah can look like a Western European city. Only Israeli border police, who by any other name are soldiers, were about. They were positioned at key junctions as I walked silently through the Old City from the Damascus Gate to the Jaffa Gate. Be careful, the soldiers warned me, but against what they did not say. The only people I saw with weapons were the soldiers. Solitude was my friend.

My last visit to the Old City was in 1999. That was also at night, but not as late as on my first visit. No one warned me to be careful this time. The walled city was almost empty on that night, too. Israeli soldiers were again the most visible people as all the shop-owners had gone home. Amid the noisy shouts and bargaining of daytime commerce, the Old City is hip to hip with people. Israeli soldiers seem less noticeable in the daytime crowds, but even then they cluster at key corners, in control.

Since its occupation of the Old City and the West Bank in 1967, Israel has expanded the borders of the metropolitan city of Jerusalem in order to increase the Israeli population and diminish Palestinian influence in the Palestinian eastern sector of the city. Israel is counting on the tribal maxim that there is strength in numbers, and more muscular political claims, too. Israel has matched this tactic of taking Palestinian land around Jerusalem with its larger strategy of expropriating more Palestinian land throughout the West Bank under the guise of increasing its security and bargaining power.

As the intensity of the conflict ebbs and flows, Israel adds settlers in the West Bank. Beyond the talk of security buffer zones and more land to house more people is the religious and right-wing premise that the West Bank is part of Eretz Yisrael, Greater Israel, the biblical kingdom of Israel.

Another version of religious fundamentalism was at work then. The Likud Party, the political voice of Ariel Sharon, Menachem Begin and Yitzhak Shamir, does not hide its belief that the West Bank — Judea and Samaria to them — belongs to Israel by biblical divine right. Except in the minds of extreme fundamentalists, the Gaza Strip does not fit that mold.

As Israel expanded its settlements in the West Bank during the early 1990s, I spent many weeks documenting, with photos, shipments of mobile homes to the settlements from companies in Florida and Georgia. Palestinian laborers helped to build many of those settlements, assisting Israel in the taking of Palestinian land. The irony wasn't lost on the Palestinians. Their immediate need for work and food superseded their desire to protect themselves and their land.

Sharon was at that time minister for construction and housing. His job was to claim more Palestinian land by moving Israelis into new settlements and simply taking the territory. This was an Israeli version of squatters' rights applied only to them, although Sharon was taking land that belonged to others, legal sophistry about missing or flawed land deeds aside. One way or another, directly or indirectly, Israel was using American money to buy mobile homes from American companies to help confiscate Palestinian land. Israelis knew this; so did Palestinians. American officials knew it, too. But the American public had no clue. This was a major international political story, not a feel-good story about Florida and Georgia businesses thriving in the global market.

One of the most frightening experiences I had, more frightening than any in Iraq, Algeria, Somalia, Lebanon or any other war zone, occurred on a hilltop near the Palestinian village of A-Ram just off the main road from Jerusalem to Ramallah and Nablus. I was trying to reach a new Israeli settlement that was being built on Palestinian land. My objective was to document Israel's use of its occupation to acquire more Palestinian territory and other resources, such as water.

In my leased Subaru, I began driving up a rocky path that looked like it might lead to the settlement. The road, and my car, hugged a cliff on my left as I drove slowly up the rocky hill. After the path turned sharply to the right and narrowed, it disappeared beneath large rocks that blocked my path as the hill grew steeper. I was forced to stop. Here I was in the Holy Land or thereabouts, but this was not the road to heaven, I thought, as I contemplated my next move. After I decided to back slowly down the hill, my car kept sliding because the rocks slid behind the tires when I applied the brakes. The rocks acted like a sled, preventing the tires from gripping the earth so my car kept moving. I was forced to inch my way down, releasing the foot brakes lightly hoping to roll only inches at a time. When I applied the brakes after rolling an inch or two, the car slid a foot or more against the loose rocks.

To coin a phrase, I was caught in a limestone crevice, between rocks under my tires and larger rocks at the bottom of the cliff, and I was scared. I could easily have lost control and, if I did, it would be goodbye car and goodbye me flying over the cliff. What a way to go, I thought, trying to back a leased car down a deserted hill with no one to chronicle that what had happened was not as stupid as it would have appeared. But I had driven the car up the hill and I felt that it was my responsibility to roll it down.

As I backed down toward the corner just below where the large rocks had blocked the path, the car kept sliding straight but slowly. I backed up with my left foot dragging on the rocks and half my body out the door. I was ready to jump if the car went straight over the cliff instead of turning and staying on the narrow path. With my right foot, I gently released and applied the brakes to creep around the corner inch by inch. The outcome was up to me. I couldn't sit back and rely on Somali tribesmen, Iraqi Kurds, Lebanese Druze or Bosnian Muslims who knew the local terrain. My situation seemed more dangerous than later putt-putting across the Tigris River in Iraq aboard a tiny, leaking rowboat or kneeling on a flimsy raft propelled slowly across the Khabur River in northern Iraq by an old Turkish man wearing a T-shirt, undershorts and a blue blazer. And, remember, I don't know how to swim.

Hold your nerve, I repeated to myself as I dangled from the car, which slid slowly toward the cliff and inched its way around the corner. Don't panic and jump from the car unless you have to, I repeated. It seemed like an entire afternoon passed before I turned the corner and rolled straight down the rocky trail. A short time later, I found an easier way to approach the settlement where hard-up Palestinian workers were hammering away on homes that were swallowing their land.

In the United States, the Palestinian-Israeli conflict is usually presented as the Arabs and Jews fighting again as they have for centuries. In such a context, Americans can convince themselves that seeking peace is a fool's mission and that they can't possibly understand the ancient quarrel. But the conflict is not age-old. At most it is less than a century old, and was triggered in earnest by the German Nazi-led Holocaust against European Jews from which came the successful war for Israel's independence in 1948. That's when the Palestinians were driven into exile, into land then controlled by Jordan and Egypt, which is the West Bank and Gaza, and into neighboring countries. And that's the real origin of the conflict that has deepened with subsequent wars and violent Palestinian reactions to Israel's continued occupation and taking of more Palestinian land.

Israel's withdrawal from Gaza, which is most often described as a hellhole, should have helped to cool the conflict, although attacks against Israel by Islamic militants in Gaza and harsh Israeli reprisals make "cool" the wrong word. Israeli settlements in Gaza were a negotiating tool, and now the government has played that card. But Israel's expropriation of more Palestinian land around Jerusalem and elsewhere in the West Bank, and increasing Islamic fundamentalism and violence among Palestinians will do nothing to settle the conflict.

In the early 1990s, I wrote a story about Israeli soldiers shooting to death two unarmed Palestinian brothers for hurling stones at vehicles traveling on the Jerusalem-Nablus road. The brothers were about 20 years old and lived in the neighborhood near where they and other Palestinians were throwing the stones during the first Palestinian uprising against the Israeli occupation. The brothers were shot to death, executed really, when they easily could have been captured, charged and tried in court for throwing stones at motorists. The Israeli army had apparently decided to teach the Palestinians a lesson by killing the brothers.

Throwing stones can be deadly. Any security force, occupiers or not, would try to stop this activity, which was widespread at the time in the West Bank and Gaza. But stone-throwing is not the same as firing rubber bullets or live ammunition, which the brothers didn't have but which the Israeli soldiers did.

After meticulously surveying the scene where the brothers were killed, counting the scores of bullet holes in the wall of a building outside of which the brothers were shot, talking with local residents and Israeli authorities, and examining the house from which the soldiers illuminated the area to better spot and shoot their prey, I wrote a detailed story about the murders.

Two unarmed brothers killed on the same night, when they easily could have been arrested, by soldiers who fight for a cause that purports to be based on a higher moral plane than their enemy's was news. I couldn't imagine that too many American brothers, well-armed and engaged in combat, were killed on the same night fighting in World War II.

Years later a professional librarian at one of the newspapers where I worked when I wrote the story searched for the article in accessible newspaper archives throughout the country. Maybe some U.S. newspapers did publish that story, but the librarian couldn't find one. One desk editor on duty at the time I wrote the article told me later that there was nothing unusual about two brothers being shot to death on the same night in such circumstances. To me that is shorthand for saying the editor didn't want to publish a story critical of Israel's conduct because he didn't want to receive lots of calls and letters from readers and from powerful Israeli and Jewish interests in the United States.

The larger Palestinian tribal story is untold, partly because the Palestinians do a lousy job of telling it and partly because American news organizations are afraid of repercussions if they take the hard road and tell the whole truth. This is another tribal aspect of the conflict that transcends the region.

Neither the Palestinians nor other Arab and Muslim peoples have anywhere near the political firepower in the United States that Israeli and American Jewish interests have. In order to tell the Palestinian story at all, it is often necessary to turn to Israeli civil rights and peace organizations that run against the conventional tide. Palestinian voices that make findings or claims similar to those of Israeli organizations are seldom heard in the United States.

To most Americans, the result is that the face of a Palestinian is that of a faceless suicide bomber or the masked head of a Palestinian gunman and the families and communities that often publicly applaud those individuals. Seldom are Palestinian families shown mourning their youthful dead who committed acts the parents disagreed with. As a rule, few American reporters take the time to learn what Palestinians really think about acts committed by their sons, and sometimes by their daughters. And those who do rarely find receptive editors.

Americans are more readily familiar, or think they are, with the story of Israel than they are with the Palestinian story. They are more familiar with Israeli propaganda told in words Americans understand — the little country that could against out-of-this-world odds — by Israelis who seem more like Americans, by a people who founded Judeo/Christian philosophy, monotheism and their moral codes. The American slate is almost blank when it comes to understanding Islam, Arabs, the story of Christian Arabs or of other minority groups in the Middle East.

One reason for this blank slate is that news organizations usually refuse to publish or broadcast the other sides of the story because they deem it too insignificant to risk alienating the readers and powerful interests they already know. There's room for truth wherever it is found, without forgetting the reasons that Israel was founded where and when it was founded.

Along the main road outside the Palestinian city of Nablus 20 years ago, when the first Palestinian uprising was raging, a young Palestinian man was completely surprised when I told him about the Nazi-led Holocaust against European Jews. He said he had never heard of it. He knew nothing about the events that occurred in Europe immediately before Israel was founded in May 1948. He seemed stunned, but it didn't alter his view that Zionists had no right to take Palestinian homes, land, villages, cities, orange and olive groves, and to continue to occupy their lands and control Palestinian lives.

This kind of conversation was repeated many times during the four years I was based in Jerusalem. When, usually after a long discussion, Palestinian Muslims learned that my ancestry was Syrian, many smiled. But when I said that my family was Christian rather than Muslim, the color left their faces as their jaws dropped. They usually recovered, but slowly.

I was never ill-treated on any side of the great divide. Most Israelis enjoy a free-swinging debate, hard questions and informed opinion, and handle them all much better than do most Americans. Israelis know the rights and wrongs of their actions because they live with the situation, and I've heard many mock the blind obedience of Americans and American policymakers. When Israelis turn to boilerplate propaganda arguments and are challenged by reality, they often just smile and move on.

Officially, the modern Zionist movement began in Europe in the mid–1890s, with the writings of Hungarian born Austrian Theodor Herzl, a very secular Jew. The movement was fueled in the latter part of the 19th century by rampant anti–Semitism toward Jews in Europe, especially in Russia. With his so-called Final Solution and the Holocaust before and during World War II, Hitler unleashed unequalled anti–Semitism in Europe. About six million Jews were slaughtered in the Holocaust. Hitler, his allies and others in countries the Germans conquered killed millions more of various religious and ethnic backgrounds. But six million of one people, more than two-thirds of all the Jews in Europe, killed out of blind hatred qualifies by any standard as a crime against humanity. Every last person of an ethnic or religious group does not have to be killed for the killing to be called genocide. About a third of all the Jews in the world were killed during the Holocaust.

Secular Jews, religious Jews; rich Jews, middle class Jews and poor Jews; entire families of Jews and Jews who denied they were Jews were killed in Europe during the 1930s and 1940s. They were killed in concentration camps, in camps that were like machines or slaughterhouses built solely to murder, by soldiers killing for the führer or the fatherland. Jews were slaughtered by the German army and by the allies and subjects of Hitler's Germany. Europeans — ethnic, religious, linguistic and cultural tribes from practically every nation-state that had been considered an improvement over earlier ethnic marauders — killed, persecuted or shunned Jews. Members of nearly every tribe of Jews wherever they lived in Europe were killed by members of practically every other tribe, no matter what definition of tribalism is used.

Assigning guilt to tribes wholesale is always risky and usually unfair because not all individuals in a large group share responsibility equally for collective action. Indeed, many individuals resist tribal pressure and die for their courage and moral conviction. But blame cannot always be doled out to individuals according to the proper measure of their guilt. The alternatives are silence or the assigning of collective responsibility where it is obvious that mass collaboration occurred.

From the slaughter in Europe, which the world largely ignored until it was over, the state of Israel was born, built on the foundations in Palestine that Herzl's writings helped to lay more than 50 years earlier. Despite their disagreements over strategy, tactics and purpose, secular Jews joined with religious Jews to create the new state with international help. The United States, Britain, Czechoslovakia, the United Nations and its guilt-ridden members, and even the haters and official atheists in the Communist Soviet Union helped give birth to Israel.

Secular Jews acted for survival; religious Jews moved to Israel for religious reasons, even though some of the ultra–Orthodox believe that the state contradicts Judaism's historic lines. The Ashkenazi Jews who fled from Europe were joined by Sephardic Jews from the Middle East and elsewhere in the Mediterranean basin. New Israelis came later from other countries, such as India and Ethiopia. Israel was created as a haven to save Jews from further persecution. Once created, Israel brought in as many people as it could gather to provide roots, to hold the land and, with and after the 1967 war, to expand.

Jewish roots in the area called Palestine were centuries old, biblical, but had withered until the last decade of the nineteenth century with the birth of Zionism. So withered were those roots that countries such as Argentina and Cyprus, along with garden spots such as Uganda, Madagascar and even an area near the Egyptian border called El Arish, were discussed as locations for a possible Jewish state after the Holocaust.

But Jewish history, contemporary politics and the vulnerability of the people in the area pointed to Palestine, which after World War I was a British mandate. The Palestinians, who are not Jordanian bedouins, Lebanese, Egyptians, Syrians, Iraqis or Saudis, were the people who lived in Palestine before and after the disintegration of the Ottoman Empire. Anyway you look at it and regardless of the historical and contemporary justification for a Jewish homeland, the Palestinians would be made to pay for the demonic sins of the Europeans and the failure of the United States and other Western democracies to open their doors during the Holocaust.

Israelis like to claim that the Palestinians never had a state, and therefore were never a separate people. That argument is supposed to mean the Palestinians don't count as a people. They never had a modern nation-state of their own, true, but the Palestinians were and are a separate, indigenous people. Both Israeli claims are irrevelant to the conflict anyway. The Palestinians lived and still live in Palestine. They had homes, farms, shops, orchards, vineyards, families in Palestine, many of which they don't have now. That's all that matters, if you're Palestinian. Some Palestinians, perhaps a million, still live in Israel, up from the roughly 150,000 who remained rooted there after Israel was created. A few of them even serve in the Israeli parliament. But overall they are not treated like citizens equal to their Jewish neighbors.

Israelis and Palestinians, Jews and Arabs, are Semitic cousins. Hebrew and Arabic are Semitic languages. Judaism and Islam are different religions, yet they share a common root through the biblical figure Abraham. Some Palestinians are Christians, which separates them in religious terms from other Palestinians. But there again, Christianity is considered an Abrahamic religion. All of these familial connections somehow make the conflict more, not less, intense.

The Palestinians, too, have historic claims to Palestine, perhaps as descendants of the biblical Philistines, of Phoenician traders, of Aramaic peoples, perhaps descendants of Arabs from the Syrian or Arabian deserts, or maybe a mixture of all those and other tribes. Perhaps the conflict would have burned itself out by now if the Palestinians had accepted the original U.N. partition plan that would have created two states. But that was a lot to ask of a people then, as they were having their land and lives taken because of atrocities committed by others far away.

With their Arab relations as allies, the Palestinians also were affected by what can be called outside intervention that overall has harmed more than helped them. Wars with Israel involving Egypt, Jordan and Syria have cost the Palestinians more land; the West Bank and Jerusalem's Old City and surrounding areas, for example. The Israeli government lashes out at Palestinian terrorists, conveniently forgetting that Jewish terrorists, led by Menachem Begin and Yitzhak Shamir, both of whom became prime ministers, used terrorist tactics to force the British to abandon their mandate and leave Palestine, thus opening the door to the creation of Israel.

The Cold War, an all-encompassing international threat to global war, had a direct effect on the Israeli-Palestinian conflict. The United States and the West supported Israel out of a sense of moral guilt for the Holocaust, for power and a Western anchor in the Middle East, and to check the Soviet threat to the region's oil. With nowhere else to turn and despite their hatred of Soviet atheism, the Arab states looked without a natural amicus to the Soviet Union for arms and financial support to counter U.S. support for Israel. Here again tribes already in conflict were manipulated, in this case willingly so, by foreign intervenors.

If the Israeli-Palestinian conflict proves anything, it is that violence, deceit, religious extremism, demonization and occupation breed more lies and hatred. In all the worst ways, each side becomes like the other; Israelis and Palestinians are more aware of this than are outsiders.

Out of the corner of my right eye I saw a hefty chunk of concrete grow larger as it flew toward my windshield in the dusk that absorbed the daylight. Oh shit, I thought, here it comes and here I go. At the least, I expected to be picking glass from my hair, skin and teeth, perhaps using plastic from the dashboard as a toothpick.

I blinked and flinched as the stony missile thudded against the windshield at a sharp angle and ricocheted to my left. I kept driving, headed more than 3,600 years into the past. Saved by the laws of physics, I thought. The concrete must have struck the slightly curved windshield at its strongest point and the angle must have been just sharp enough to diminish the impact. Otherwise, the concrete would probably have landed in my lap or on my head and my car might have landed in a ditch, or worse.

Driving north from Jerusalem, I was outside of Ramallah in the Palestinian West Bank where the road narrows on a corner and buildings hug the asphalt. This was a ready spot to ambush any car bearing yellow Israeli license tags rather than the blue tags that signaled a West Bank residency. This was all very predictable, if not always expected, part of a mindless reaction to a symbol that is very modern, very ancient and very tribal.

My destination on that Monday night, April 9, 1990, was Mount Gerizim near the West Bank city of Nablus. Mount Gerizim is the spiritual home of the ancient Samaritan sect, an offshoot of Judaism. The Samaritans, who are linked to Western Christian memories mainly through the New Testament story about the Good Samaritan who helped an injured man by a roadside, were celebrating their 3,646th Passover, a sacrificial ritual that commemorates the exodus of Jews from Egypt to their Promised Land. The Samaritans have celebrated 20 more Passovers since my visit.

I was headed to the mountain to watch the dwindling number of Samaritans — an estimated 550 in the world then and maybe 600 to 700 or so now, nearly every last one of them in Israel and the West Bank — slaughter, roast and feast on 34 sheep.

Their ritual took place amid contemporary conflict that put the Samaritans squarely in the middle even if they were bit players. They are a tiny tribe in a land where every sect, ethnic group, family and individual is viewed as being on one side or another no matter what a person says or does. A year later, when I visited the ancient Yazidis in Northern Iraq, a pre–Roman Zoroastrian religion almost as old as the mountains and caves where they live and worship, I thought of the Samaritans. The Yazidis, small in number but more numerous than the Samaritans, were trying to keep their balance and stay alive in the midst of Iraq's tribal conflicts.

Whatever anyone thinks of religion in general, its power, mystique and abuses, the older the rituals the more fascinating they are as examples of human behavior that in many ways change slowly or very little. As an outsider, I feel able to observe these ancient practices with detachment, without the burden of worship, expectation or specific belief.

My fascination comes from a desire to imagine what the ancients were like when they conducted similar rituals more than 3,500 years ago and how those rituals and worshippers may have changed or stayed the same. There is no longer, if there ever was, purity of race or ethnic groups; neither is there purity of religion no matter what the faithful believe. But that only adds to the fascination because newer religions develop by adopting beliefs and practices from their predecessors and the older religions also evolve in order to survive at all, even if only as minority cults. It has been, I always thought, a great privilege to have observed these almost timeless practices; it is like having a powerful telescope that permits a narrow and seemingly unbroken peek into a world that stretches from the ancients to the present. In my mind, I was going to listen to 3,500-year-old words mouthed by 3,500-year-old voices. Reality TV permits no such observations.

At exactly 6:55 P.M. by my watch, on that Monday night, the high priest of the Samaritan sect climbed three four-foot-high stone steps and began to pray, I was told, in ancient Hebrew. The moment was deemed perfect because it was, as required by the ritual, "between the light and the dark." Within two minutes, as the bearded, robed High Priest Yusef Abu Al-Hasan recited the commanding sacrificial words from the Samaritans' Scripture, several men strode along a narrow ditch and slit the throats of 34 sheep that were being held in place to be slaughtered on the ground. Their life blood pumped out like water from a pressurized tap, the sheep died quickly. The earth soaked up their blood. Better sheep than people, I thought. The slaughter of animals for food takes place all over the world every day. Most people never see those deaths. Most see butchered meat in open-air stalls, groceries or supermarkets because that's the way we do things now, and that's expected.

The slaughter of animals in the Samaritan fashion, as part of an ancient religious ritual, occurs less frequently now, and very few people see it when it does. Watching any living being die is not something I would normally go out of my way to see. But this was different. This was a piece of ancient human history that remained alive.

Six more priests and other male members of the sect, their faces framed half in the approaching darkness and half in the orange-red of flames leaping from deep ovens, prayed fervently for almost two-and-a-half hours during the sacrificial ritual and the meal preparation that followed. After the sheep were slaughtered, worshippers embraced, kissed and smeared blood from the animals across their foreheads in another piece of the ancient tradition. This sight is not readily witnessed at your local grocery, yet I watched with detachment and disbelief, bemused and blinking, intent on capturing the details.

As the butchering process continued, members fed huge fires blazing in concrete and stone ovens five feet wide and dug about eight feet into the ground. The Samaritans were stoking old-style giant barbecues. Only when the ovens reached an acceptable temperature were the animals placed inside to roast. The ovens were then covered so the flames were snuffed out, but the heat was deemed high enough to cook the meat slowly. Over the centuries, the entire process had been well-tested. To an outsider, it looked like a grandmother fingering salt into a stew and then tasting it to determine whether more was needed. "This is beautiful," said a smiling 17-year-old Nagla Masilyah Cohen, looking more like a teenager from Tel Aviv than from the Palestinian city of Nablus. "We don't talk about this as a strange thing because we do it every year."

Most members returned to their nearby homes in the darkness until the meat was cooked and ready to be eaten. About midnight the Samaritans returned to the roasting pits to eat and mark the completion of the ritual sacrifice and Passover meal.

A little more than half of the Samaritans lived in their isolated Kiryat Luza settlement near Mount Gerizim in the Palestinian West Bank. The remainder lived in a settlement in Holon, Israel, where one of the first Iraqi Scud missiles struck a textile factory as the guns sounded to begin the first Persian Gulf War.

The Samaritans are trapped like tiny animals in the Israel-Palestinian conflict. Those huddled at the base of Mount Gerizim used to live in Nablus, then a focal point of the Palestinian uprising, but they were compelled to move because most Palestinians consider them to be Jews and Israelis, or at least more sympathetic to the Israelis than to the Palestinians. Yet the Samaritans in the West Bank, who believe that many of their Palestinian neighbors once were Samaritans, appeared to be more Palestinian than Israeli, while the Samaritans in Holon appeared to be more Israeli than Palestinian. "We are Palestinian Samaritans who live in Palestine," said Nagla Masiliyah Cohen. Her friend, Rifka Atef Cohen, then 18, agreed.

Members of minority sects in the Middle East often comply with the rules of the majority around them. It's called survival. The Druze, an Arab people who are not Muslims but practice a secret religion, as well as the Yazidis in Northern Iraq, are good examples of that survival technique. Druze live in parts of Israel, Lebanon, Jordan and Syria according to live and let live pacts. Fierce fighters, Druze even serve in the Israeli army. As long as they are left alone, the Druze, who believe in reincarnation, usually cause no problems for the majorities and the national rulers where they live.

Religious cousins of Judaism, the Samaritans are believed to have split with Judaism in the 6th century A.D. They share several, but not all, customs and beliefs with Jews. Samaritans claim to be descendants of the 10 ancient northern tribes of Israel, but they deny ever having been deported to Assyria in ancient times. Jews, however, believe the Samaritans were imported into the West Bank, into the biblical land of Samaria, from ancient Cutha, by the Assyrians who conquered the northern Kingdom of Israel in 722 B.C. Samaritans believe divine revelation ended with Moses, their only prophet, and their sacred scripture is rooted in the first five books of the Old Testament, known by the Greek term Pentateuch and which Jews call the Torah.

During the early Christian era, when there were far fewer people in the region, the Samaritans, the good ones and the bad, numbered well over a million. Persecutions and forced conversions, first to Christianity and later to Islam, reduced their numbers to fewer than 200 during World War I. Since then they have slowly been increasing. But they remain a tiny tribe lost in a convoluted tribal conflict laced with sectarian, ethnic, linguistic and cultural differences now embedded in territorial disputes and inflamed by foreign intervention. They are a telling footnote in a relatively small region known through the centuries for waves of tribal conquest and subjugation.

FOUR

Lebanon's Cedars of Mayhem

"Your accent sounds like you learned your Arabic in Jerusalem," said the leader of a Lebanese Islamic fundamentalist group that was believed to be holding Western hostages, including American journalist Terry Anderson. This was in September 1991, in the waning weeks of the hostage crisis. I was in the mountains of eastern Lebanon with the hope that my timing would bring me luck and an interview with Anderson and others just before they were freed. The man's statement was a test. Astute and well-informed, Hussein Musawi knew that a large majority of Western journalists working in the Middle East were based in Jerusalem, in Israel. He also could tell, I figured, that my Arabic accent was closer to that spoken by people along the Lebanese-Syrian border than to that of Palestinians in Jerusalem. But he wanted to see how I answered the question. I looked him straight in the eye and in a mixture of Arabic and English told him that I learned my Arabic from my grandparents who moved to America almost 100 years earlier from Syria. "And you can tell that," I said with emphasis—adding that my Arabic was leavened with a New England accent because by grandparents had settled in Rhode Island. I never said a word about Jerusalem. Musawi smiled but said nothing more. I passed the test.

When political leaders—democrats or dictators—raise the flag of fear or sect, and pound the propaganda drums to demonize those they wish to kill, when bombs and missiles pound cities and villages and people in them, when armies overrun other armies, war becomes the ultimate in mob rule. Individuals can't be separated from the evil whole, which makes it easier to justify killing. But when individuals meet, separate from the pressures of culture and tribe, a different psychology often comes into play and good, rather than evil, often results.

Abdo Saade, a Lebanese Christian who lived in Damascus, told me the following story on March 18, 1991, when the civil war in Lebanon was in its death throes: "Once I met a man in Lebanon with the same last name as mine. The man was a Muslim. We liked each other and were friendly. Then, after the Israeli invasion of Lebanon in 1982, I approached an Israeli checkpoint leading to Beirut and I was angry for needing Israeli permission to enter my own city. The Israeli at the checkpoint asked for my papers. I showed them and the Israeli said, 'OK, cousin, go ahead.' The Israeli was named David Saade."

Like blinking bright neon, the light from a full Mediterranean moon shimmered across the rolling waves that punched the *Santa Maria*. Except for the rakish and imperiling moonbeam, we were in complete darkness on the old Roman lake, a fast fifteen to twenty minutes west of the blacked-out Lebanese port of Jounieh.

The captain said that French and Syrian warships were patrolling harmlessly in the area, and that U.S. warships cruised farther to the south. A moment before, exactly nineteen minutes in front of midnight by my watch, the captain of the Norwegian-owned twin-hulled catamaran quietly cursed the bright moon and ordered all lights turned off on the boat, sending its 300 or more tense passengers into a hellish, dead darkness with these words: Please turn off all the lights. No cigarette smoking, no radios, no lighting matches, no flashlights, lights or electronic signals of any kind. With the darkness and the electronic silence came the human hush of the graveyard, a sure sign that this was serious.

Turning our sleek, fast boat into a ghost ship was protection against possible artillery fire from the mountains east of Beirut. Without lights or electronic signals, it would be more difficult for artillery gunners to home in, the captain said. If we were unfortunate enough to be struck, it would be more by bad luck than good aim. The artillery gunners were taking a break and the area around the port of Jounieh just north of Beirut was quiet as the catamaran sliced through the sea at 34 knots. From these same waters six years earlier, U.S. warships shelled Lebanese Muslim and Syrian positions which ultimately brought a noisy death-knell to the Reagan administration's misadventure in Lebanon.

If the guns in the mountains remained silent, the captain said, we would dash into the port and unload almost as quickly as four people could roll out of a taxi and pay the fare. But if the firing resumed, we might just make a U-turn, run outside the range of the artillery and wait a while, or speed and dodge our way into the shelter of the port, depending on how close we were to the dock when the firing started again. How the captain would make that decision remained his secret.

Lebanon's thin lifeline to the outside world, the *Santa Maria* was aptly named. On August 18, 1989, we were churning uncertainly into an uncertain world, the latest phase of ethnic, religious, political, economic and regional tribal wars that for more than 15 years made Lebanon synonymous with fratricide, hostage-taking and all-around chaos. As with so many civil conflicts, foreign invasions and interventions added tribes and grievances to the poisonous brew, deepening wounds and punishing the local tribes most severely.

Most of the *Santa Maria's* passengers were Maronite Christians heading home to be with their families after doing business in Europe or trying to arrange permanent refuge there. One by one they criticized Syria for the bombardment and the United States for abandoning Lebanon. George, 27, was a dress designer returning from a show in Rome to be with his wife, three-month-old daughter and his parents. Better for Syria and its Lebanese allies to level Beirut, said George, because then Syrian forces might leave a city that no longer existed. Otherwise, he said, with the sardonic wit of a war-battered cynic, a Beirut that was only damaged might be rebuilt so it could be bombed again in two years.

With his crew of five working and whispering in the wheelhouse barely lighted by instrument panels and moonglow, the young Norwegian captain was making only his sixth 127-mile run from Cyprus to Lebanon, his first under such tense conditions. In that sense, we were, so to speak, uncomfortably in the same boat. The *Santa Maria* had been making the run for only three months, and the captain was as alert as the moment and his relative inexperience demanded. His assurances that the boat had excellent equipment to detect incoming fire raised both confidence and concern. Another captain was on board training for the possibility that two captains would be aboard on later trips. That, too, was both a reassurance and a worry. One captain or two, it matters not at all if an artillery shell has your name on it.

Less than 24 hours earlier, the *Santa Maria* had encountered heavy fire while docked in Jounieh, a bit of recent history that made passengers wonder whether Lebanon really was worth a visit this time. On a return trip to Cyprus earlier the same day, the *Santa Maria* was chased from the dock at Jounieh by shells that, as one passenger later described it, "burst like rain." About 300 passengers had disembarked at Jounieh that time, but the boat had not reloaded when the captain suddenly ordered the gangplank raised, extinguished all lights and signals and ran back to sea with only eight returning passengers aboard. Another 300 or so passengers were left at the dock to dodge the shells. The boat waited for three hours out of range of the artillery. When the shelling continued, the captain returned to Larnaca, Cyprus, with only the eight passengers and his crew.

Before the lights went out and the cigarettes were snuffed as we sped toward the dock, the trip seemed more like a Caribbean cruise than a speedboat dash into a war zone. We weren't far from Cyprus' waters when a gambler's dream was announced on the public address system. "We wish to inform passengers that the American poker table is open in the VIP section," a man announced over the public address system. Fitting, I thought — an American game in a VIP section — that people who would shortly be gambling with their lives dancing around the land mines on terra firma first should risk a little money in further anonymity on the open sea. "What else do you want me to do, die?" a Lebanese would say. A beautiful 25-year-old woman actually said that a couple of days later as she sunned herself at Faraya, a mountain resort about 30 miles northeast of Beirut. Rita was simply taking a normal weekend break from Beirut and the war.

A Lebanese croupier ran the poker table with Monacan, or perhaps Lebanese, skill. His brother was a steward who operated the boat's food and drinks concession. The croupier took a cut for the house from each pot, and jumped in when a body was needed to fill a game. Just like the old days when I was a kid in the Fifties, I thought. I recalled how Big Louie, my grandfather, in his waning gambling days ran a poker game in a small, smoky back room where a green-shaded bulb lighted a round, slightly wobbly green-felt-covered table in Millville, Mass. Out front, balls clicked on a couple of pool tables. Cheap small silver painters' pails posing as spittoons caught dead cigars and cigarettes back then. Lacking legitimate back-room flavor and failing to keep up with advances in the cuspidorial arena, the *Santa Maria* cut spittoons from its decor.

Big Louie, who was born knowing when to hold 'em on the Syrian side of the Lebanon mountains in what was, in 1892, all called Syria under Ottoman hegemony, looked at his opening cards for free. He didn't ante, which was the house's cut, and the reason he seldom lost. It was his house; he ran the game, paid for the heat and electricity, supplied what passed for bonhomie, and he played nearly every hand. When another player was needed to fill a game, my father usually jumped in. One or more of my uncles often played, too. On weekend nights, I managed and played on the pool tables while the town's luminaries and literati played draw poker or five-card stud on that stable land-locked ship. Too bad for me there were no pool tables on the *Santa Maria*, although the balls might have been a little hard to pocket on the rolling sea.

When we docked at Jounieh, the passengers literally jogged through the exit into a new steel and glass terminal that was braced with sand bags. As we left the boat, other passengers were loaded in double-time for the return trip. As many as 1,000 people lined up to buy tickets for each trip to Cyprus. The *Santa Maria* held 333 passengers. We left the terminal through a narrow domed walkway surrounded so high with sandbags that it looked like an elongated igloo. Within minutes the lights were out again and the ghost ship vanished from the dock. With another reporter, I flagged a taxi and headed to a hotel in Jounieh where we would spend the nights trying to fall asleep to the music of shells whistling overhead and plunging into the sea, killing fish instead of people.

If nothing else, this was an appropriate welcome to Lebanon at that moment, where the tribes, sects and nations were still clashing, Lebanese hid like rats hunted in the night, the air was foul with uncollected garbage, roads were pulverized asphalt, buildings looked like concrete skeletons and the beautiful people of Beirut fled to a mountain resort on weekends for a breather from the pressures of war that ignored the calendar.

Another phase in Lebanon's seemingly unending wars had begun only days before I had reached Beirut for the first time. Syrian artillery gunners, backing Druze, Muslim Shiites, Palestinian fighters and Syrian special forces, were lobbing round after round of shells from the mountains 15 miles east of Beirut into the capital city and neighboring coastal areas. Night after night the pounding went on. The Maronite Christian militia, formerly the extreme right-wing phalangist fighters and now, for public relations purposes, called the Lebanese Forces, retaliated along the front line near the battered but once delightful mountain town of Souk el-Gharb, which in Arabic means the western market.

The Lebanese Forces militia was joined by a unit called the Lebanese Army, which represented the Christian government that was then marginally in charge of very little. Israeli troops had shot their way around the area seven years earlier on their way to besiege and batter Beirut. A year after that, U.S. warships pounded Souk el-Gharb trying to save the weak Maronite Christian government from Muslim rivals, which convinced the Muslims that Ronald Reagan's America was an enemy of Islam and not an honest broker in attempting to drain the Lebanese quagmire. Ultimately, that conclusion killed 241 Marines in their Beirut barracks. In 1989, Souk el-Gharb was being freshly etched in crimson in Lebanon's war history.

The armies and militias that controlled slices of Lebanon at this time showed the breadth of the tribal fighting. Numerous tribes, believers, ethnic groups and nations were still carving up the tiny country as they had been for fourteen years. Language was a dividing line in Lebanon, too. Most Lebanese Christians spoke French and Arabic, and many also spoke English. Invading Israelis spoke Hebrew and many spoke Arabic as well. For most of Lebanon, Arabic was the dominant language. Lebanon had no more than 3.5 million people. But it had some 17 officially recognized religious sects which do not always live by the Golden Rule.

Most of the people in Lebanon said they were Lebanese, but very few acted as if they were. Otherwise, why would there have been a civil war? The bloodshed wasn't all caused by Palestinians, Israelis, Syrians and Iranians, although they bear a heavy share of responsibility. Those who believed they were Lebanese had their own discrete definitions of what that meant and their fragments were all that mattered. Above all they were Druze, Shiite Muslims, Maronite Christians, Sunni Muslims, Greek Catholics or tribal variations of the above; their principal Lebanese connection seemed to be that they lived in a place called Lebanon.

If Caesar were to have divided Lebanon at that moment, he would have needed both hands and maybe his toes: Parts of the country were controlled by Syrian forces, Lebanese Maronite Christians, Druze, Israelis and their Lebanese Christian surrogates, Sunni Muslims, Shiite Muslims, the Iranian-backed Hezballah militia of Shiite Muslims and a U.N. force. Refugee camps for Palestinians, who were mostly Sunni Muslims although some were Christians, remained in place, and a Palestinian force under Damascus-based Abu Musa fought under Syrian control. Lebanese Christians remained divided among sects, families and tribal chiefs.

Syria was then and remains controlled by the Assad family and its small Alawite sect of Shiite-related Muslims, although a majority of Syrians are Sunni Muslims. As a counterweight to its Syrian foe, Saddam Hussein's Iraq funneled weapons to French-backed Michel Aoun's Lebanese government forces, further evidence of convenient alliances that confuse outsiders but are as constant in the region as the desert sun. Although Iraq was controlled by Saddam Hussein's personal Sunni Muslim tribal band, a majority of the people in Iraq are Shiite Muslims. In 1982, when Israel invaded Lebanon and after years of civil war had been intensified by Syrian intervention, countless private militias, criminal thugs and sectarian gangs roamed Beirut.

Lebanon became synonymous with hell on Earth, although that term connotes some kind of arbitrary extraterrestrial judgment that exonerates humans of culpability. Humanity slowly ran amok in Lebanon, and constant killing — civil warfare fertilized by outsiders — was the blind driver. What happened in Lebanon happened in Bosnia, Somalia, Afghanistan, Rwanda. Change the speakers, and the words of confusion and lament that I heard in the Lebanese town of Faitroun were exactly the same as those I heard later in Sarajevo. In Bosnia, Catholic Croats, Bosnian Muslims and Christian Orthodox Serbs used to live together until Croat nationalists in Zagreb and Serb nationalists in Belgrade decided to herd Bosnian Muslims into death prisons and execution pits and set Bosnia ablaze with the aim of dividing the charred ruins among Croats and Serbs.

After 14 years of brotherly killing and invasions, Salam surveyed the bomb damage in the Lebanese town of Faitroun and said in earnest, "We are good friends. We used to live together, Muslims, Druze and Christians. We never thought about religion. We were just friends. Most of the people in

Lebanon never think about religion. Now we don't know what's going on."
A few years later, Bosnian Muslims said much the same in Sarajevo. Salam
was a Muslim who became a Christian because her husband was. They were
planning to flee Lebanon when we talked, no longer able to understand or
bridge the sectarian divides that trapped them.

What happened in Lebanon and its sister killing fields can happen anywhere. Once killing becomes a way of life and replaces civil order, killing
becomes the essence of life itself. Individuals kill, not causes or ethnic groups,
nations or races. When the killing starts, it becomes easier to kill again and
to justify it. Vengeance it's called, and vengeance is always justified by the
avengers. Slowly order and civil society disintegrate and the killers, whether
they are gangsters, militias or armies, take control. I use the words killing and
killers to pin the responsibility on individuals where it belongs. To use the
words soldiers, armies and war gives collective legitimacy and lessens individual responsibility. Governments, sects and tribes and their armies are
responsible for giving the orders under flag, patriotism, God and cause, but
if individuals didn't kill, there would be no carnage. When individuals kill,
humanity evaporates. The enemy is demonized as a group and killing becomes
unquestionably easier, more justified, blind. When law and order disintegrate, the killing usually doesn't stop until there is annihilation, subjugation
or all the killers become exhausted and can't even recall what started it all.
For more than 15 years, this was Lebanon's portrait.

In August of 1989, 13-year-old boys fondling Kalashnikovs and sport-
ing the kill-or-be-killed moves of their fathers were being raised in Beirut's
new generation of killers. In the mountains east of Beirut a 24-year-old man
in an army uniform and laden with weapons said he had been waging war
since he was 12. War was his school. The man was blind in one eye. With the
other, he saw only the need to fight and kill.

Beirut was as good a symbol of grinding, corrosive destruction as one
could find short of the London blitz, a Dresden-style carpet bombing, or
Hiroshima. What civil and sectarian wars left standing foreign tribes had
destroyed. Beirut wasn't flattened, although probably not for want of trying.
Worse, it was plundered, raped, tortured, made to suffer and left to die. But
it didn't die and it won't. Buildings in the city of more than half a million
people looked like a collection of giant, fractured faces with missing teeth,
broken jaws and smashed cheekbones, black eyes and missing eyes and mul-
tiple lacerations, most of them deep. The rest was black and blue and bleeding. By all accounts, life in Beirut during the civil wars and foreign invasions,
hostage-taking, gangster battles and massacres was unmitigated hell. I was
not upset to have missed its worst moments. Beirut is the only city where I
saw signs on overpasses and bridges banning tanks. The signs had nothing to

do with traffic control or a sudden appearance of law and order. They were put up to save the structures from collapsing because the probability of tanks rampaging through the city was too real.

With Syrian troops controlling large sections of the country, I was concerned that Lebanese would look at my name and face and ask, "Where you from?" If I were pinned down, I wasn't about to say that my family had gone from Syria to the United States in the early part of the 20th century. For the longest time, no one asked. And I volunteered nothing. I had seen the name Salome and its variations in other parts of Lebanon, so I felt no discomfort. My guess was that no one asked because they thought they knew. At the same time, the Lebanese had more pressing problems than to worry about an American reporter's identity. They had seen everyone except an Inuit rampage through their country, so one foreigner's identity mattered little to them as long as the fighting dragged on. As they ran from the shelling, most Lebanese also had little time to socialize. I interviewed families in blacked-out and collapsing apartment buildings and in small towns under siege. But I didn't meet people in large groups where a curious person in the rear might ask what he thought would be a wise-guy question: "Where you from?"

At a Lebanese base in Souk el-Gharb, a colonel in the Christian militia surprised me and asked my origin. His question defied ducking. Somewhere near Beirut, I answered, with insufficient conviction. "No," he said, "you won't find the name Louis John Salome around Beirut." "Well," I countered, "probably from the mountains east of Beirut; I'm not sure." His look told me that he didn't believe that story either, although it's close enough to be true. We both knew that, so he gave up acting like an immigration officer to talk about the pending Syrian bombardment, a subject closer to his survival instinct.

By that time, nearly the only Americans left in Lebanon were hostages. The Reagan administration's misguided and bungled attempt to back Israel's ill-conceived and disastrous effort to prop up a Christian government in Lebanon had been a miserable failure, as anyone outside of Washington and Jerusalem could have predicted ahead of time. To punctuate Reagan's policy failure, 241 U.S. Marines were killed when a suicide bomber crashed into their barracks at the edge of Beirut's international airport. The Palestinian Liberation Organization's excesses helped trigger the first of the civil wars in 1975, and by now its leaders had been sent sailing from Beirut and Tripoli.

The Iranian influence was entrenched in the south and in the Beqaa Valley with the creation of Hezballah (the Party of God), thanks in part to Israel's invasion in 1982, and its occupation of South Lebanon. With its Lebanese Christian surrogates, Israel would maintain its self-imposed security zone in South Lebanon until the late spring of 2000. More than 1,500 Israelis were killed in Lebanon from the time of Israel's first incursion in 1978, until the last troops left the south. It is a testament to collective bad memory and some form of national desperation that Ariel Sharon, the chief architect of Israel's disaster in Lebanon, later became Israel's prime minister. Then again, if Richard Nixon were to find his way back and run again for president of the United States, he might win on the grounds that he got a bad rap the first time around.

Syria had returned to Lebanon in force in June 1976. Under the guise of halting the civil war, Syria at that time backed one Christian militia's claim to control the country, although that alliance was like loose putty and wouldn't hold. By the summer of 1989, Syrian forces controlled large swaths of Lebanon. In the latter decades of the Turkish Ottoman Empire, the lands of Lebanon, Syria, Jordan and Palestine had been grouped together in a region the Ottomans called Greater Syria. After World War I, Syria and Lebanon became French mandates, and Lebanon became independent in 1943.

As alliances shifted with illogical suddenness almost by the hour, and armies and militias moved in, out and through Lebanon, nothing much changed in Souk el-Gharb except the names on the uniforms and the origins of the artillery shells. Once a beautiful mountain town of about 10,000 people, lush gardens and orchards less than fifteen miles southeast of Beirut, the town overlooked a wide valley, which apparently increased its strategic value. Israeli troops moved through the surrounding area on their way to besiege Beirut in 1982. After the Israelis had come and gone back to hunker down in South Lebanon, Lebanese Christian militias took over. In August 1989, the Christian phalange/Lebanese Forces were holding on against Syrian artillery and Palestinian, Shiite and Druze infantry. The town's showcase Haggar Hotel, a Lebanese militia headquarters in 1989, had seen all the occupiers, like a citadel on the west bank of the Euphrates watching invading armies crisscrossing the mighty river through the centuries. All roads still led to the Haggar, but the hotel was a military base and the roads were dust and rock, the asphalt pulverized by tanks and armored personnel carriers, mortars, rockets and fatherless artillery unseen and unheard until it screamed and struck.

Khalil drove me to Souk el-Gharb in his old baby-blue Mercedes, a perfect juxtaposition of perceived opulence and real decay. Lebanon, after all, was an open depot for sturdy Mercedes stolen from Europe. Khalil drove faster than he thought bullets could fly, ignoring lanes, median strips and other cars. To drive otherwise would be to invite gunmen seeking to sharpen their aims, he explained.

All the buildings in Souk el-Gharb were heavily damaged and many were destroyed. At most 20 civilians were left in the town, fortifying their small bunkers awaiting the next bombardment. Old men and women with tiny vegetable gardens stood steadfast in collapsed houses, refusing to leave because this was where they were born; they had no other refuge and they preferred to die at home. Three generations living in what looked like a poor man's bunker, defiant, cheerful, unbroken. Just like in Azerbaijan, Bosnia, Iraq and the Soviet Union, here was another example of those with the least sharing the most.

All I wanted was an interview when I knocked on the door of what turned out to be Toufik's ruins. What I received was an afternoon of sweets, tea and coffee, humorous conversation from intelligent, educated people who spoke Arabic, English and French, and an invitation to stay the night. I had to return to Beirut to file a story, so I apologized and didn't stay. But this is another of my great regrets, like not swinging by Bukhara when I was in Samarkand to see if I could find the emir of Bukhara's viper pits, and missing Lahore while I was in Pakistan.

Toufik and his wife, Alice, lived in quarters so tight there was barely enough space for a visitor to sit at the table. But they made room. The poorest always do. They lived with their two sons, their pregnant daughter-in-law, and their eighteen-month-old grandson, who was tucked behind us in an alcove darkened into perpetual night by cement blocks and sandbags. When I looked at the sleeping boy all I could see was a coffin waiting for an artillery shell fired by someone far off who because of distance felt exempt from personal responsibility for killing. The matriarch would not have argued if the family decided to seek another bunker elsewhere. But the numbers were against her. The family had lived in the town for 40 years and leaving was considered akin to treason.

Everyone laughed when Alice flexed her thin wrinkled right bicep after I asked why the family stayed in the rubble and in the gunsights. She feared for her grandson's future, but she shielded her fear with humor. More realistically, one of her sons said, "No one lives here; we survive." Exhaustion was winning, said the other son, "All we want is the peace."

Besides the Lebanese militia, Toufik's neighbors were people such as Khalil, 70. Khalil wasn't sure whether he would live or die in Souk el-Gharb, but he was certain that he wouldn't leave. His large house surrounded by vegetable gardens and fruit trees had been pared to two eight by twelve-foot rooms with no windows. The rooms were shaped like large beehive ovens and looked, appropriately enough, like bomb shelters. Along the walkway leading to his quarters, Khalil was growing five small pepper plants. Next to them, in a special garden spot, he tended prized parsley. Small rocks surrounded the garden, which was only three and a half feet in diameter. The rocks weren't intended to protect the garden from visitors because usually there were no visitors. And they certainly were no barrier to bullets let alone

artillery shells. But esthetics has its place, even in tiny gardens in a shooting
gallery.

After I turned down an invitation to spend the night in Souk el-Gharb,
I returned to my hotel in Jounieh, a few artillery lobs north of Beirut. There
I filed a story and tossed in my sleep beneath the alternate hymns and rhymes
of off-target artillery shells whose noise alone spread terror before they expired
with the fish in the Mediterranean.

The last phase of Lebanon's wars had 14 more bloody months to run when
an Italian journalist and I knocked on the door of Maronite Bishop Nasral-
lah Butros Sfeir's offices in the Beirut suburb of Bekerke in August 1989. The
most powerful figure in the Maronite church, Sfeir had been its patriarch for
three years when we met. The Maronites are an Eastern Rite of the Roman
Catholic Church. The Maronite patriarchate was created in 686 A.D., and
Maronites are the largest Christian sect in Lebanon, but not the only one.
Greek Catholics, also called Melkites and like the Maronites also in union
with Rome, Greek Orthodox and some Protestant denominations are other
Christian sects in Lebanon. Maronites recognize the pope's authority and are
the most Latinized of all the Eastern churches in union with Rome.

If I hadn't been with an Italian journalist, I probably would never have
met Sfeir, now a cardinal in the Catholic Church. The patriarch was news in
Italy; two months earlier he had met the pope, and he talked regularly with
the papal nuncio in Lebanon. It was a good guess that the pope would agree
with whatever the patriarch suggested when it came to Lebanon.

As much as any Lebanese sect, the Maronites, their powerful families if
not their religious leaders, were critical kindling to the start of the fighting
in 1975. They were Israeli allies and vicious killers of Palestinians and other
Muslims, and they took punishment in return. If the fighting were to stop,
the Maronites would have to step back and down. When Lebanon became
independent in 1943, the Maronites were the largest religious tribe in the
country and for the next four decades a power-sharing agreement with the
Sunni and Shiite Muslims centralized wealth and political power in the hands
of brutal and repressive Maronite tribal leaders and their militias. As the population shifted in favor of the largely dispossessed Shiites, power and wealth
did not.

After a decade and a half of fighting with insiders and outsiders, the
Lebanese, all of them, suffered the most. Although Maronite Gen. Michel
Aoun warred against Syria and its Lebanese Muslim allies in August of 1989,
the Maronite power structure finally realized that the political arrangement
had to be changed to reflect demographic and political realities and to stop

the killing. The Maronite patriarch's conciliatory comments concerning Lebanese Muslims reflected this shift, and changes in the political/sectarian arrangements to reflect population shifts came in October 1989, with the Taif Agreement.

Aoun held out for a year after that before Syrian forces bombarded the presidential palace at Baabda, Aoun's citadel. That effectively ended the broader civil war, although Aoun fought with a Maronite rival and two Shiite factions battled each other. Syria ended up policing Beirut and much of Lebanon, and Shiite Hezballah fighters continued to resist Israeli forces and their Lebanese surrogates in the south. Syria retained heavy-handed control of its neighbor for another decade and a half, the political, military and economic advantages too great to surrender easily.

We met the patriarch in a huge, ornate room that, I presumed, was designed to reflect his religious stature, although I have always been puzzled by religious leaders who display wealth and power while many of their followers are so lacking and the founders of their religions are noted for material poverty. Others believe that trappings radiate power and stature and attract adulation; all I see is the gap.

Believers and influential political figures would be properly impressed, I suppose, by such a huge banquet-like room ringed with 40 large high-backed wood chairs draped in a red silk-like material. Such ornate displays are part of Middle Eastern culture. A beautiful chandelier shone brightly on two large magnificent Oriental rugs that filled the floor. At the far end of the room the largest chair of all was reserved for the spiritual leader of a sect that carried its own heavy weight and responsibility in national religious and political circles. The concept of the greeting room with chairs lining the walls is typically Arabic. But this room was anything but typical in size.

Befitting the occasion and his political message, Sfeir didn't sit in the largest chair when he entered the room. He sat next to it, in one of the 40 smaller chairs, to be closer to his visitors. A small man with sharp eyes, the patriarch wore a simple white cassock free of colorful robes or other adorning signs of his position.

Like the members of so many other Lebanese tribes, including a growing number of his own people, Sfeir realized that the country and its people were exhausted by war that had to end for the country to breathe again. He talked openly and avoided the obscurantist throat-clearing that diplomats favor to duck questions. Sfeir acknowledged implicitly that the Maronites had their chance to rule during the civil war and failed miserably in pulling Lebanon together, although he spread the blame for that to include foreign interveners. How could he deny the role of Maronite and other Christian militias in the slaughter of many hundreds, maybe more than 1,000, Palestinian children, women and old men in the Sabra and Chatila refugee camps, massacres carried out with a wink and a nod from Israeli forces that controlled the camps from the outside?

Sfeir was one of the few Lebanese I met who didn't castigate the United States for pulling out of Lebanon after 241 Marines were killed in a suicide bomb attack, or for entering the country with a multinational force to bolster the Maronite government of Amin Gemayel. He couldn't damn the United States too much because Ronald Reagan sent U.S. troops, planes and ships to join French, Italian and British forces in support of Gemayel's Maronite regime, which is precisely what led to Muslim attacks against the multinational force.

The patriarch was conciliatory toward Muslims in general; he knew that political power in Lebanon had to be more fairly shared for the fighting to end. That meant that the Maronites, all of their powerful families, would have to yield more power and influence to the Sunni and Shiite Muslims, and to the Druze, who are Arabs but who practice their own secret religion. From Lebanon's independence in 1943, the Druze never shared in the National Covenant under which the country was ruled, with the Maronites lodged firmly at the top.

The Christian government that Michel Aoun represented wanted Syrian troops out of Lebanon. Aoun's supporters fought on, but other Lebanese realized that Syrian troops were staying and that if peace were to dawn, it would have to come with Syria disarming the militias, all but Iranian-backed Hezballah in the south, of course.

Without peace, Christian East Beirut and Muslim West Beirut would remain divided by metal ship containers and tires piled fifteen-to-twenty feet high along the Green Line. Lebanese such as Suad Wahbe, her two children and her mother would be forced to continue to flee from artillery shells every night. During the daytime, when the shelling usually stopped, Wahbe and her family lived on the third floor of a heavily damaged building. At dusk, just before the shelling started, they fled to the ground floor seeking greater protection from the weakening concrete high above.

Only the Iranians, Israelis and Syrians — outsiders in Lebanon — would have quarreled with Sfeir's words. The patriarch knew the foreigners wouldn't be leaving; there was no international support for his position. The foreigners and their allies in Lebanon could ignore him, and they did. But for the Maronites, his own people, and for the integrity of Lebanon, his words echoed with truth.

In a clear signal designed to bring the Christians and Muslims together, Sfeir said, "There have been many mistakes in Lebanon, and all the Lebanese have made them. The Christians have responsibility, too. All the Muslims are not radical. There are a few. Most of the Muslims are good and we are able to live with them in cooperation." In another plea for a united Lebanon, Sfeir said, "We are against an Islamic republic. We cannot live in an Islamic republic. We are in a democratic system, enjoying liberty. There is reason to believe this country can exist and continue. We don't want a Christian republic either. We want room for all religions."

When we interviewed Sfeir, 16 foreign hostages, half of whom were Americans, were still being held in secret Lebanese dungeons. U.S. Marine Lt. Colonel William Higgins, who had been kidnapped on February 17, 1988, had been executed on July 31, 1989. We didn't discuss the hostages with the patriarch, because we figured that he knew no more about their condition or when they might be released than we did. At the time, any signs that hostage-taking had exhausted its political value were known only to the abductors. Two years later, those signs were seeping into the public domain with increasing frequency. When I returned to Lebanon in September 1991, nine hostages were still held, five of whom were Americans. By December 4, of that year, seven of the nine, and all of the Americans, would be free.

I pulled out of still-suffering Lebanon the same way I had entered, aboard the ghost ship *Santa Maria*. With 300 other passengers, I rushed to board the catamaran so we could leave the dock before the shelling started. The engines strained hard in total darkness for about 20 minutes. When the ship reached the open sea out of range of artillery shells, the lights went on, the passengers exhaled audibly, like the boat shifting gears; the poker game began and a small piece of Lebanon moved safely to Cyprus.

My departure came after a slight hitch that a flexible gatekeeper corrected. Another lesson in the unpredictability of Middle East customs was thrown in free of charge. My ticket said the boat was to leave at midnight on a Thursday. Because I misinterpreted the departure date, I arrived at the dock before midnight on Wednesday. The young Lebanese man taking the tickets pointed out that I had arrived a day early, midnight Thursday being the end of the day on Thursday, not Wednesday. Still, he said, there was a chance that I could board.

Trying to find a ride back to the hotel in the middle of what would soon be a thunderous night was not on my schedule. Within a short time the ticket-taker said there was room on the boat and I could board. To show my thanks, I discreetly offered the man $20. No, the man said, he couldn't accept my generosity. He was just doing his job. In a region where baksheesh, bribes and healthy tips are as routine as no thank you, I was surprised that the young man wouldn't accept an after-the-fact thank you note. This was not, after all, an upfront bribe, like slipping a maitre d' $20 for a table to avoid waiting in a chic Miami or New York restaurant. When to tip, how and how much is an art that I always found difficult to master. The acceptable custom varies from place to place, people to people. A healthy thank-you tip is usually, but not always, easy to give. An advance for a service to come is routine. The problems often lie in between. To offer at the wrong time can be insulting; not to offer at the right moment can also be insulting.

—❈—

When I returned to Beirut in September 1991, this time flying in from Cairo with another reporter, the civil war was over but its scars were still tender. Beirut remained a spectral city. Traffic lights were alien; motorists drove anywhere there were no craters. Whole concrete floors were hanging like shades inside buildings. Pungent odors of rotting garbage and open sewers made breathing a test, and electric wires sagged like overcooked spaghetti from ruined building to ruined building.

Beirutis referred to areas of destruction according to which sect, tribe or nation did the damage and when. Here it was the Druze; there it was Israelis; nearby it was Syrians. In a light-hearted and convincing promotional blitz, the blue billboards of the Shahba company said, "What is common between our boards and CIA agents? They're everywhere."

Syria controlled most of Lebanon and suppressed all the militias except for Iranian-backed Hezballah which fought the Israelis and their Christian puppets in the south. Five Western hostages had been released in 1990, two were freed in August 1991. That left nine still in captivity in September 1991, when strong signals were flowing from Iran and within Lebanon that more hostages would be out soon and that the tactic of hostage-taking, its perceived political capital having diminished in value, was being scrapped.

In the more than two years since the Ayatollah Khomeini's death, power had shifted to more pragmatic hands in Iran and tugs from those hands were being felt by the Iranian-backed abductors in Lebanon. Confident that the end was near, my purpose was to see whether I could meet with some of the hostages before they were released. To do so required meeting Lebanese Shiite leaders who, if they chose, would be able to get me underground where the hostages were being held. The opportunity to talk with the powerful and complex Lebanese Shiite leadership was not a frequent one. Under the softening circumstances, I thought there was little risk involved while the possibility of a fascinating story was good. I was right about the risk but wrong about getting the story.

"So, you want to meet with Terry Anderson?" Abu Mahdi asked with a loud, mocking laugh, apparently amused by the tantalizing prospect of bringing Anderson company. "Sure," Abu Mahdi said, adding a sardonic smile to his answer. "We can take you to see Terry Anderson," the local wit said, as we were about to meet with a man who, if he wished, probably could have arranged for us to see Anderson or one of the other hostages. A colleague, from her position three paces behind me as required by Abu Mahdi and his culture, and I laughed with Abu Mahdi and his friends. We had little choice. "Well, we just want to interview him," we answered. "We'd prefer not to stay." They laughed again. So did we, although with more restraint.

Lebanon's tribal wars were not confined to Lebanon. When the first foreign hostages were taken in 1984, the conflict took a new twist. It became, in one part, a militant Shiite Muslim war against the world. From January 17, 1984, when the first foreigner was abducted, until June 17, 1992, when the last two kidnap victims were released, various Shiite Muslim factions and other, smaller organizations with motives unknown kidnapped 98 foreigners. The radical Shiite rage against Israel, the United States, Westerners and foreigners in general was palpable and essentially tribal-based in that it was fundamentally and deeply sectarian and cultural. It was a war against the Western tribes, taken out on individuals who were handy and who would draw enough attention to the Islamic cause to make a powerful and long-lasting global statement.

Hundreds, maybe thousands, of Lebanese were also kidnapped by rival sects, militias and factions. Most of those were probably killed, and few received any attention outside of their families. Most of the organizations that kidnapped Westerners acted independently of each other although under the common umbrella of the Shiite Hezballah movement. Other groups operated under more than one name to shield the real kidnappers.

Eighteen of the 98 foreigners kidnapped were Americans, including one Indian who was a U.S. resident alien. Fifteen French citizens and fourteen British were abducted. Citizens from 17 other nations were also kidnapped in what became a sweeping orgy of tribal vengeance against real and imagined offenses committed by other tribes. Of those kidnapped, ten were executed. Other foreigners, such as Malcolm Kerr, the acting president of the University of Beirut, were simply murdered rather than abducted. Terry Anderson, the bureau chief for the Associated Press in Beirut, was kidnapped on March 16, 1985. Anderson was finally released on December 4, 1991. He was held longer than any other hostage. When two Germans were released on June 17, 1992, after being held for more than three years, the extremist Iranian and Lebanese Shiite kidnapping war against the world had ended. But Osama bin Laden's fundamentalist Sunni Muslim war against the United States was beginning to flower in another land.

Despite what governments and some publications would like their publics to believe, the Lebanese Shiite community is not monolithic, although the nuances seldom escape the dark shade cast by militant leaders and their masses.

To learn more about Shiism, I and another reporter arranged to meet with three Shiite leaders in September 1991. The men, two secular leaders and one cleric, showed the different sectarian, cultural and political hues of Shiism in Lebanon. We were also interested in interviewing a foreign hostage or two before they were released which, as it turned out, was as imminent as we expected. Our hosts were not interested in helping us; to do so would have been to admit what they denied. But we did learn more about the divisions among Lebanese Shiites and their militias, their strong but fluid ties to Iran and Syria, and their fierce and ultimately successful campaign to drive Israeli forces from South Lebanon.

First we traveled to Baalbek in northeastern Lebanon's fertile Beqaa Valley, where two of the men lived. Baalbek and the Beqaa were strongholds of the Iranian-backed Lebanese Shiite group called Hezballah. Those who operated in the Beqaa did so with the blessing of Syria, which was the area's military god. Iranian militants sent money and weapons to the area through Syria.

Large footprints of numerous ancient tribes remain in Baalbek. Named after the Phoenician god Baal, Baalbek is a citadel of awesome Roman ruins. Carvings of grapes, wheat and poppies above the door of the Temple of Bacchus are the classic symbols of the city. Massive ruins of the temples of Jupiter and Venus crowd the acropolis, which housed the largest religious center in the Roman Empire. In Hellenistic times, the city was called Heliopolis, or sun city.

With its mammoth hilltop ruins of antiquity, warming Mediterranean sun and the exoticism of the Arab world, Baalbek is an irresistible magnet in the Orient. For the first time since the fighting began in 1975, Lebanese from outside the Beqaa were traveling in large numbers to Baalbek to enjoy its sensuous atmosphere. Stands overflowing with vegetables leaned against butcher shops with fresh and not-so-fresh lamb and chicken. Large but simple woodframed structures groaned under the weight of fruit of prosaic and exotic varieties next door to bakeries with tempting sweets and warm, luscious breads. Lamb roasted over open fires with vegetables as sweet company, all waiting to be sprinkled with spices that could be eaten with just about anything.

First to belly up, first served. Hordes of customers pushed their way through the crowds and the aromas to the man with the cash register in his pocket to pay up. One minute you feel as if you're in heaven; the next seems far from it. In Baalbek you could buy ground lamb at a butcher shop, take it next door to the baker who would add dough and make and bake 75 delicious meat pies, all for $6, of which 50 percent was a tip. The meal was consumed at an airy, old hotel nearby, which provided fresh vegetables and drinks.

All in the warm glow of the ancient world, and the shifting shadows of the modern one.

Syrian secret police and soldiers patrolled Baalbek's streets. But Hezballah controlled its soul. Flags and faces of sects, causes and nations flew over the city and stuck to its walls in unmistakable tribal statements. The glue holding Hezballah together was clear and strong, its tribal messages transparent: America and Israel were enemies of Islam and Israel had to be removed from South Lebanon. Hezballah posters displayed Stars of David next to helmets, representing Israeli soldiers, with jagged edges that looked like sharks' teeth. Muslim faithful were exhorted to liberate the Dome of the Rock, a principal Islamic shrine in Jerusalem. All the messages were similar to those I saw in Tehran when the Ayatollah Khomeini died two years earlier. His message lived, if with variations.

In Arabic Hezballah means The Party of God. In any language, Hezballah in Lebanon was created, with the help of Khomeini and his hardline Shiite mullahs in Iran, and with the cooperation of Syria after Israel's full-scale invasion of Lebanon in 1982.

Driving his tomato-red BMW, Abu Mahdi accompanied us to the home of Hussein Musawi in the Beqaa village of Nabi Sheet near the border with Syria. Abu Mahdi was security of the informal but certain kind. His handy automatic handgun let us know that he wasn't just a handsome chauffeur. Abu Mahdi liked to use his weapon. Later, as we left the area, Abu Mahdi pulled over to fire for fun at a flock of soaring and beautiful heron-like birds. "Remember, you are here," another man said in a rising but whispered warning when he suspected that I might question Abu Mahdi's target practice.

On the way to Musawi's home, we drove past the fortress-like building where we believed some of the hostages were being held. Whenever we left our car, our escorts insisted that my female colleague walk three steps behind me. When she moved closer than three paces, our escorts reminded my colleague of their social, religious and tribal customs, one of which is that women must walk three paces behind a man in public. This was somewhat humorous to me at the time, although not everyone in the group grasped the humor.

Neither Musawi nor others we interviewed at his house would answer the questions of my colleague. When she asked a question, silence was their answer. So I repeated every question that she asked, and our hosts answered the questions as if my colleague weren't there. This behavior, while cultural, also reflects aspects of a gender conflict that is not limited to the Middle East or to Islam, although the lines are more sharply drawn in those citadels of male domination.

A man of many faces in Lebanese Shiite circles, all of them clever and knowing, Musawi was influential, powerful and increasingly militant. Typical of Lebanese political and sectarian leaders, he was not afraid to make new alliances as situations demanded.

A former schoolteacher, Musawi had been vice president of the Shiite Amal militia until 1982, when he was bounced after clashing with Nabih Berri, a lawyer and Amal's chief. Berri's Shiism was more personal, pragmatic and geared to survival in Lebanon than it was to Islamic fundamentalism. Musawi was more militant. Like Khomeini he favored the establishment of Islamic republics in Lebanon and beyond, and his goal was to drive the Israelis from South Lebanon and Jerusalem.

The Amal militia grew out of the Lebanese Shiite Movement of the Deprived, founded by Iranian-born Imam Mousa Sadr, a fascinating man of wide appeal inside and outside Lebanese Shiism. Sadr's movement was religious but centrist, a mixture of secular leaders such as Berri and Musawi and clerics who thought that Lebanese Shiites, the poorest of Lebanon's sects, could accept a Lebanese state if they had a fair share of economic and political power. Sadr disappeared and was probably murdered on a trip to Libya in 1978. His disappearance remains an abiding and magnetic mystery in the region. The wars had already started when Sadr was taken, but I always believed that if he had lived, they would not have lasted as long or been as punishing. Perhaps that's why he was killed. Libyan agents are usually blamed for killing Sadr. But if Libyans squeezed the trigger, my guess has always been that Iranians paid for the gun and the bullets. More than any other person, Sadr was an obstacle to Khomeini's plans for Lebanon, its Shiites and the creation of Hezballah.

After he left Amal in 1982, Musawi formed his own militia, Islamic Amal, which he based in the Beqaa Valley. The new name suggests exactly what the group was, a more fundamentalist and universalist Shiite movement rooted in Khomeini's Iran and focusing beyond Lebanon to Israel. More militant and determined to drive the Israelis from South Lebanon, Islamic Amal linked up with Hezballah immediately or perhaps even became a founding member of Hezballah, which also sprung up in 1982, after Israel's invasion, when members of Iran's Revolutionary Guard filtered into Lebanon through Syria.

Islamic Jihad for the Liberation of Palestine was a kidnap group and a spin-off from Musawi's Islamic Amal. Islamic Jihad for the Liberation of Palestine was believed to have kidnapped four Americans, one of whom was a U.S. resident alien. Two of those men remained hostages in September 1991. When we met with Musawi, he was a leading Hezballah policy-maker, tightly aligned with Syria and the post–Khomeini pragmatists in Iran. Their new strategy was to release all foreign hostages, take no more and concentrate on driving the Israelis from South Lebanon.

Musawi's evolution as a militant Shiite leader was related to Israel's invasion of Lebanon and to the fact that a cousin, Hussein Yousef Musawi, was serving a life sentence in Kuwait for a series of bombing attacks there against the U.S. and French embassies and the Kuwaiti government in 1983. The kidnappings in Lebanon began as a way of gaining leverage to force the release of the prisoners in Kuwait.

A picture of Khomeini transposed against the Dome of the Rock in Jerusalem was prominently displayed in the reception room where I and another reporter met Musawi. The strategic message accompanying the picture, as if words were needed, said, "Quds (the Arabic name, Holy, for Jerusalem) belongs to the Muslims and must be returned to them." A large fan whirred overhead and eight tan chairs and a couch ringed the room in typical Arab fashion. We were offered coffee, tea and large amounts of fruit before we were tested with a couple of questions about our origins, tribes and purpose. We passed.

One of the few, if not the only, non-clerical members of Hezballah's leadership, Musawi wore a dark blue suit and a dark shirt and could have passed for a college professor. He wasn't alone when we talked; one young man wore a khaki-colored uniform that said Casual Force and NAF NAF (a French clothing brand). But if there was any attempt to intimidate, it was light.

A trim man with a neatly cropped beard and penetrating dark brown eyes, Musawi was clear about the need to release the hostages. But he was very unclear about what his role might be in such a process, although diplomats and international aide workers in Lebanon believed that he was pivotal in arranging the release of American hostage Robert Polhill in August 1990.

Israel's invasion of Lebanon in 1982 and its continued presence in South Lebanon angered Musawi. The United States was the enemy of Muslims, Musawi believed, because in the mid–1980s, under Ronald Reagan, U.S. forces attacked Muslim militias in support of the Israel-backed Maronite government in Lebanon. Musawi wasn't any happier with George H. W. Bush in power than he was with Reagan in the White House. "Bush's history is to deceive Hezballah," Musawi said. "Bush is concerned only with Israel and this is wrong. This is not to the benefit of the American people."

Musawi's militance about opposing Israel and the United States and his feelings that America has treated Muslims unfairly were widely shared among Muslims and many non–Muslims in the Middle East. His denunciations of Israeli and U.S. conduct and policies toward Muslims made Musawi and his associates, philosophically at least, forerunners of Osama bin Laden and Al-Qaida. Although Musawi and Hezballah belong to Islam's minority Shiite sect and bin Laden is a Sunni Muslim, they are linked philosophically by the thick cord of Islamic fundamentalism.

Whatever one thinks of fundamentalist Shiite Islam and its goals, the men behind it then followed a consistent sectarian and cultural logic that was swelled by political, social and economic inequities. They were determined, smart, steely and often ruthless. But they were not born angry. They are Islam's suppressed people, and that is more a fault of Islam and other regional tribes than of Westerners or anyone else. In Shiite Iran many were harshly suppressed by the shah, who for 25 years was one of America's and the West's favorite royal rulers in the Middle East. To America and the West, the Cold War came first; nothing else came later. Maronite Christian tribes and their brutal militias led other sects in suppressing Lebanon's Shiites in every way possible. When Israel invaded Lebanon to oust the Palestinian Liberation Organization and tried to create an allied Maronite government, the Israelis automatically bought the Shiites as more bitter enemies than they had been. With the Lebanese Shiites came Khomeini's Hezballah.

Nabih Berri met us in the marble-floored office of his beautiful and well-guarded hillside home south of Sidon. From the garden outside his house, we could see outposts in Israel's self-imposed security zone in South Lebanon. A shifting survivor par excellence in Lebanon's warring tribal jungle, Berri's Shiite Amal militia fought for and against the Palestinians and with and against the Druze, another powerful tribe and militia of Arabs who practice a secret religion and aren't Muslims. Although both are Shiite-based, Amal and Hezballah did not always fight on the same side of Mount Lebanon.

A lawyer born of Lebanese parents in Sierra Leone, educated in Lebanon and Paris, Berri lived in the Detroit area from 1976 to 1978. He would be at home in Paris, Damascus, London, New York or Detroit. He returned to Lebanon to lead Amal after Imam Mousa Sadr's disappearance in Libya. Once a mentor of sorts to Hussein Musawi, it would be a mistake to regard Berri as just another Shiite Muslim clone, meaning an Islamic radical. He appeared to be equal parts Shiite and Lebanese, and wholly a survivor.

Only a picture of Iman Mousa Sadr, the founder of the Lebanese Shiite Movement of the Deprived and Amal, decorated Berri's office. There was no space for the Ayatollah Khomeini, which means that Berri probably did not carry a plan for an Islamic republic in his briefcase. In 1992, he became the speaker of the Lebanese parliament, an equal part with Sunnis and Christians in the three-headed Lebanese executive.

Berri, too, said the hostage-taking era was over. He called it "useless," but admitted that its conclusion would be difficult to reach because it involved Iran and its supporters in Lebanon, along with Israel and the United States. Amal held the remains of two Israeli soldiers, Berri said. If Israel released 28 women whom it held in the El Kiam prison in South Lebanon, he said, Amal would allow the Red Cross to see the bodies of the two Israeli soldiers.

A consistent ally of Syria, but never of fundamentalist Iran, Berri accepted Damascus' military and political role in Lebanon essentially because it ensured his survival. But like nearly all Lebanese at this point, except for Israel's Christian surrogates in the security zone, Berri insisted that Israel leave the south, which he called "the Israeli finger in the Lebanese stomach."

The third leading Lebanese Shiite figure we interviewed, but certainly not the last of their line, was Sheikh Subhi al-Tufeileh, an unbending hardliner who at the time was losing ground to pragmatists in Iran, Syria and in Hezballah itself. Hussein Musawi and Tufeileh showed how complex and varied Hezballah could be. They agreed on their goals but differed widely on how to reach them. That distinction put Musawi in line with the ascendant pragmatists and pushed Tufeileh to the outside with the hardliners. Through clenched teeth, Tufeileh mouthed the party line about the need to release the foreign hostages, but his heart wasn't in it. He said Iran would not benefit if the hostages were released.

During the late 1980s through 1991, when more pragmatic leaders held power in Iran following Khomeini's death, Tufeileh was Hezballah's general-secretary. He lost ground after the pragmatists' line became dominant in Tehran, Damascus and in Lebanon's Beqaa Valley, although he remained on Hezballah's general council. Tufeileh even opposed the agreement that ended Lebanon's civil war and kept Syria's heavy boot on Lebanon's neck. That deal, he said, was orchestrated by other Arab states and the United States. He was not interested in participating in the Lebanese government. An Islamic republic was more to his taste, and he wanted to take a more principled and less pragmatic Islamic road to reach his goal.

A heavy set man who wore the trappings of a Shiite cleric, Tufeileh met us in a large anteroom of his house in the Beqaa Valley. A young man carrying a machinegun and wearing a bulletproof vest stood guard outside. If anyone doubted where Tufeileh stood, two pictures of Khomeini framed on the wall removed the doubts. In one of them, Khomeini's right hand was extended along with these words: "The hands of the Americans and other superpowers are plunged to the hilt in the blood of our youth. We will combat them to the last drop of our blood because we are warriors." A photograph of Ali Khameini, Khomeini's staunch spiritual successor in Iran, but apparently not the man calling the shots for Iran in Lebanon, also was hanging from the wall.

Tufeileh was gracious, calm. He answered our questions without being accusatory or intimidating, although I don't think that we asked all the right questions. On the small finger of his left hand he wore a silver ring with a light blue stone. On the small finger of his right hand he wore a silver ring with a red stone. Thick black glasses framed his eyes over a black beard. A traditional white turban signaled his clerical role, as did a black robe over a white shirt and a gray waistcoat. Tufeileh was far different from Berri in just about every respect. With Musawi, who was not a cleric, Tufeileh shared a beard and common goals. Their objectives might be the same, but their tactics and strategies were different enough to obscure the similarities of their goals. It would have been a mistake to be fooled by the obscurity.

Tufeileh never asked, "Where you from?" To him, our questions gave us away. At the end of our conversation, as we continued to press Tufeileh about the imminent release of the hostages who would soon come out through Syria, I asked in a joking manner, "When should we go to Damascus?" His answer, which we took as his end of the joke, was, "You are more American than the Americans."

FIVE

Gender War Unveiled
in Afghanistan

Right behind two other Western reporters, a man and a woman, I was dash-
ing through the desert from the chaotic cemetery compound where the remains of
the Ayatollah Ruhollah Khomeini, Iran's revered Shiite Islamic leader, were being
buried. We were rushing in hopes of catching one of the first army helicopters to
leave for Tehran 25 miles away so we could file our stories.

The woman reporter was fully garbed in a black chador, just like most Iran-
ian women in Khomeini's fundamentalist Islamic state. As she ran and we
approached the helicopters, breezes blew the chador slightly away from the reporter's
head, so that a few strands of hair were visible. An angry young soldier ran up to
the reporter and reached to pull the chador so that it would cover the little hair
that was showing.

"Don't touch me, you're not my husband," the reporter shouted, pulling away
from and trumping the soldier, who appeared to be in his late teens. The soldier
backed away. Calmly, the reporter tucked the exposed strands of hair under her
chador. Well-prepared and quick-witted, the reporter used the religious and tribal
rules governing the behavior of women, and men, in an Islamic society to her
advantage. Her Iranian sisters might have done the same.

The young mother glanced at me and my camera in that oblique, magnetic way, highlighting her bold bright eyes that shouted in silence: Look at
me, I am real. I am worthy of being seen. I am not invisible.

When I attempted to take a photograph, the woman shook her head and
shied away: Eye contact had obvious limits, but a photo seemed infinite. I
handed the camera to my translator, Eymal, then walked off so he could take
a photo furtively. By the time Eymal aimed and clicked, the woman had tilted
her large brown eyes downward, humbling the angle of her pride. But the
woman still did not cover her face.

It was the Afghan New Year and we were at the Shuhada Salain (Inno-

cent Martyrs) Cemetery in the neighborhood of old Kabul called Shasheed.
There, several women felt secure enough to show their faces in public for the
first time in almost six years. The long midnight of the Taliban's fanatical brutality and gender war was giving way to a new dawn. Slowly, women were
shedding their burqas, those personal prison cells that stripped women of
their identities. The traditional burqa represented the Taliban's public subjugation of Afghan women. The coming freedom to choose the burqa or to
reject it would bring other choices as well.

Naw Roz the Afghans call it. It's the advent of a new year. An ancient
rite of spring and symbol of fertility, Naw Roz also represents the freedom to
grow, smile, walk to a cemetery for a picnic and a children's carnival and have
a little fun celebrating other Afghan traditions.

The date was March 21, 2002, on the modern calendar, year 1423 on
the Muslim lunar calendar. To most religious, ethnic and linguistic tribes, this
was Year One in the annals of post–Taliban Afghanistan. This was the first
time since the Taliban took control of Kabul on September 26, 1996, that
Afghans were allowed to celebrate Naw Roz, an ancient festival familiar in
principle if not in name to people of the region. Naw Roz predates Islam and
is too old to have a finite age. The Taliban wanted no part of joy, so the religious extremists banned Naw Roz as unIslamic and unworthy, similar to the
way Iran's fundamentalist Shiite mullahs deny that country's glorious Persian
past because it, too, predates Islam. Part of the Naw Roz festivities honor Ali,
the fourth caliph, from whom sprung Islam's Shiite sect. To the Taliban, Pashtun tribesmen who belonged to their own far-right wing of the larger Sunni
sect of Islam, the Shiite connection was probably another reason to ban Naw
Roz celebrations.

For Afghans, especially women, the revival of New Year celebrations
offered the first taste of freedom in five-and-a-half years. The Taliban, which
means Students of Islam, had compelled Afghan women who went out in public to wear the burqa, hooded gowns so enveloping that only a wearer's shoes
were exposed to the outside world. The sensation of imprisonment was real:
Women looked at the world through small openings that resembled prison
bars. For Afghan women, peripheral vision did not exist.

Even at that Naw Roz moment, most women still feared that walking in
public without a burqa and without a supportive government edict would
jeopardize them with Taliban sympathizers who secretly stalked Kabul's streets.
The new U.S.–backed government, which lacked widespread support and
control over the country, was reluctant to issue an edict permitting women
to shed their burqas. The government was afraid to arouse the opposition of

super-orthodox believers. Most men and women were tip-toeing around the burqa question.

The communal picnic at the Shuhada Salain Cemetery by the lake that used to be the sanctuary of Afghan kings is one tradition of Naw Roz. First, pray for the dead at the cemetery, and then honor the living with food and a little fun, a traditional juxtaposition of respecting the past while enjoying the moment.

As some women furtively shed their burqas, vendors sold potatoes, chick peas, bread and fruit to the thousands of people who gathered on the hillside above the lake. Cheerful girls and boys rode in four wood bucket seats that were part of a hand-made wood ferris wheel all of eight-feet high and pulled and shoved all day long by weary old men. Six wood seats attached to wood poles that moved around a rotating center pole entertained other children. The motors were other men who breathed hard and heaved, taking turns one after the other, pushing in circles. Danish, age ten, her sister, Ramallah, nine, and their brother, Matiullah, three-and-a-half, reached down from their wood seats on the circular swing, trying to pick up a plastic chip from the dirt. A child who snagged the chip won two free rides on the swing. The simplicity with which children can be entertained is often lost but it is universal.

With picnics and prayers, paeans to Mother Nature and miniature carnivals and events that resembled county fairs without neon, glitter or deafening noise, the people of Kabul smiled again in public. Better than any outsiders, they knew what the Taliban had stolen.

Near the cemetery, at the Shashaheed Shrine which is dedicated to a former king, women gathered to celebrate the new year. They went alone. Men were not allowed. Yet almost all of the women wore their burqas. A group of women who appeared to be in their twenties said before they entered the shrine that they were waiting for a statement of support from the new government before they would show their faces in public. For those women, it was as if the Taliban remained in power, their murderous ferocity still dominating Afghan society, still attacking the female psyche.

Elsewhere, the Taliban's psychological grip was slipping.

The largest New Year's event in Kabul unfolded at the 15,000-seat athletic stadium. Nearly every structure in the capital had been heavily damaged during the fighting. The stadium was no exception. Its infield had been blood-stained, concrete in its grandstand cracked and broken off in large chunks by artillery. The New Year's parades, speeches, displays of traditional forms of Afghan labor and entertainment were an attempt to eradicate the Taliban past and revive other aspects of the country's culture. Around the infield, where the Taliban had executed alleged criminals at soccer games, the people of the plains north of Kabul bravely presented a float that mocked the Taliban who had leveled their villages.

Anjilah stood in the midst of what often seemed like delirium at the packed stadium. Her burqa was off; her face blazed like the sun that brightened the scene. "Enough is enough. I feel terribly happy," said Anjilah, 24. A doctor's assistant, Anjilah said that she had removed her burqa 20 days earlier after nearly six years of public anonymity. "The burqa was a cage for me," she said. "When I see my friends, I encourage them to take off their burqas and some of them do."

Many more men than women were in the stadium that day, but the women who were there wanted to be hidden no longer. A woman, who my translator said was a lieutenant colonel in the old Afghan Communist army, was driven into the stadium after she parachuted to the earth but missed the stadium infield. The large crowd cheered wildly as she marched around the infield waving the Afghan national flag.

Naw Roz traditionally is a three-day festival; the opening celebration, called Farmers' Day, celebrates nature in a universal way. Animals were paraded around the running track and the Agriculture Ministry distributed brochures detailing how to raise the best crops and animals, as if the farmers had forgotten. Heads high and spinning, hands clapping vigorously, male dancers twirled and leaped in circles as they performed the traditional Afghan dance called the Atan. In a show of tolerance, even non–Muslims marched. Loud cheers greeted doves of peace that were released in the stadium. A few drummers and buglers added to the festivities that were as simple at times as farmers marching with shovels.

After I had interviewed Anjilah and other women at the Kabul stadium, my interpreter pointed to an area of the infield and told this story: The Taliban had accused a young man of killing another young man and brought the accused to the stadium to be executed, although no evidence had been presented to prove the man's guilt. When the time came for the execution, the Taliban brought forth the mother of the dead man; the woman promptly slit the throat of the accused in front of the crowd. The Taliban tribe was expert at making victims of the living as well as the dead.

Brutal teachers, the Taliban executed about 25 people in the stadium, survivors said. The Minister for the Prevention of Vice and the Promotion of Virtue would announce an interesting soccer match; when fans showed up, the minister made certain that executioners appeared to dispatch an accused criminal or two. The dead were displayed as a warning to all the spectators of what would await them if they ran afoul of the Students of Islam. The matches proceeded in a distinctly somber mood. Soccer hooliganism never sprouted from Taliban soil.

News of the Taliban's gender war dribbled to the outside world. If the Taliban had been welcomed at first for snuffing out the civil war, the fanatics soon poisoned their greeting. Afghans who expected a return to pre-war conditions were mistaken. Mullah Omar and his cohorts sucked dry what joy remained in Afghan life. Women, they decided, would have no public face.

Tribal conflicts of many kinds had battered Afghanistan for almost 30 years. When the Soviet Union failed to control the country using its Afghan puppets, the Soviet nation-state invaded its southern neighbor at the end of 1979. The Afghan tribes fought back fiercely from their mountain hideouts. But their alliances were loose and seldom unified. Some of the tribes fought under Islamic banners; others flew their ethnicity and language loyalties higher up the tribal pole than their religious beliefs. By funneling U.S. money and weapons into Afghanistan, Pakistan's intelligence services entered the fray on the side of the Afghan tribes, ultimately nourishing the Taliban. Pakistan, where many brothers, sisters and cousins of the Afghan tribes lived, had its own nation-state interests. The Pakistanis wanted to control more land to bulk up against India, its much larger rival. The main American interest was to thwart and severely wound the Soviets in the global Cold War conflict.

After the Soviets fled in defeat in 1989, the Afghan tribes turned on each other full bore, resuming the internal strife that began in the mid–1970s and demonstrating once more that war is easier to start than to stop. From the vicious civil war of the early 1990s, which leveled swaths of Kabul and the countryside and had just about destroyed Afghanistan as a functioning society and nation-state, rose the Taliban.

Before the U.S.–led invasion in search of Osama bin Laden also put the Taliban to flight, Afghan women had become the targets of the broadest of all tribal conflicts: Gender war. Using their triumph in war and their extreme religious beliefs as cudgels, the men of the Taliban subjugated women almost totally.

Women were not allowed to teach school, although some did in secret underground classes. Girls were not allowed to attend schools, except secretly. Nearly all jobs were closed to women. Even widows were not allowed to work to support their families. The Taliban continued to permit women to work as doctors and nurses, but with restrictions and only because men were not allowed to care for women. Then there were the burqas.

Women as Targets

Stooped but much younger than she looked, Khunum swept the floor of Habibia, the first high school built in Afghanistan and once a national centerpiece. Walls had been blown away, windows were wide open spaces, their glass ground back to dirt; doors were memories and the floor would have benefited more from replacement than sweeping. Forty-five going on 65, Khunum was sweeping the area near a walkway that led, through huge openings that once were windows of glass, to a soccer field behind the building. The predominately boys' school in West Kabul, built in 1903, was supported in its early years by American money. A plaque near the front door showed a U.S. insignia in the form of a chevron, four stars, two hands clasped, and the words "United States of America." The school was scheduled to open in a week, and certain matters had to be attended to. Only to an outsider did it appear ludicrous for a woman to be sweeping the floor of a structural skeleton that had been used for target practice by warring ethnic and religious militias. When repairing a building is out of your hands and out of the question, you sweep.

Unbroken by the Taliban, two younger women who worked in the office strolled by the sweeper. They were puzzling over how the school was going to open without desks, without chairs, without paper, without just about everything except students, and with almost enough teachers eager to start again.

Afghan women survived the Taliban using different stratagems. Some were among the millions of Afghans who fled with their families to Pakistan, Iran or wherever a door opened. Millions more became prisoners in their homes, in their burqas. Many older women mocked and defied the Taliban and survived because their wrinkles and bent spines made them invisible. A few teachers bundled their courage and minds underground to show little girls that they could still learn. By the time the Taliban had been toppled by U.S. attacks near the end of 2001, most 12-year-old girls had never attended school. The education of 21-year-old girls had stopped when they were 15. The Taliban forced most of the boys to join its army or attend hard-line religious schools.

When we met on March 14, 2002, Khunum, the school sweeper, did not wear a burqa, not in the school or on the street. Why should she imprison herself then when she had defied the Taliban for more than five years? She dismissed the Taliban with a wave of the hand. "I was once threatened by the Taliban," Khunum said, "I didn't pay attention. I am old. No one will look at me." People age prematurely in societies rent by poverty and war. At the doorsteps of the few restaurants that were operating in Kabul at the time, bowed old women begged for coins, wearing ragged burqas because their long blue garments were in better condition than the clothing underneath.

Feeling free and optimistic, the young office workers at the school shed their burqas while working. But the street was another matter. There they

Innocent Faces, Uncertain Futures: With the Taliban in power, Afghan children like these, especially the girls, were barred from school. Even the boys were forced at an early age to attend fundamentalist religious schools before they became soldiers. This photograph was taken in 2002, at the Kabul Zoo, where most of the animals had been killed during the Afghan civil war and subsequent Taliban rule (photograph by the author, © Cox Newspapers Inc.).

feared male retaliation, as the ghosts of the Taliban lived on. In a short time, said Rahisa and Belqis, both 25 when we met, they and many other women would be brave enough to walk in public with their faces showing. Their courage would be nurtured, the women said, by the acquisition of clothing good enough to be seen on the dusty streets of Kabul. Urban Afghan women were noted for being stylish and for at least keeping up appearances. The Taliban never extinguished the desire among many Afghan women to look attractive in public.

The Sultan Razai girls' school, in the same west end of Kabul, hadn't seen students in ten years. More holes than walls, it was almost totally destroyed. But the students and teachers said that walls did not make classes, people did.

Outside the school, a girl named Tamona, who wore a lilac head scarf and a black and white skirt, said that she had never before attended a regular school. She learned to read and write at an underground school during the Taliban years, which corresponded roughly to what would have been her first years in school. To enter the Sultan Razai school, Tamona had to pass a qualifying exam in order to begin the second grade. She was twelve.

Nearby, a 40-year-old teacher named Gul laughed at the inconsistency of wearing a head scarf on the school grounds while carrying her blue burqa to wear later on the street. But her job as a teacher was no joke. A teacher by profession and instinct, she told me, "We have to teach, although we have nothing. We have no chairs, no desks, no windows, but we have to teach. We have no choice. We have done this work before and we will do it again."

Imprisoned by Poverty

If desperation had a name, it would be Nasima.

With her husband, their four children, some bread, rice and beans, Nasima lived as a squatter in Kabul, a victim of Afghanistan's generation and a half of warfare. The burqa was not her concern because she seldom left her squatter's quarters — two bedrooms, a toilet and a small stone room where she cooked over a metal and stone pit. The family slept on mattresses over stone-cold floors. They had no furniture. The entire second story of the mud-brick house, which once had eight rooms, in Kabul's Karte Char quarter had been destroyed. Her roof was the shaky floor of the second story. She had no electricity and drew water by hand from a well. Most of the family's living was done in a small courtyard outside the cooking area. Nasima was 30 but looked 50 in her white headscarf and long brown and red dress that she wore over tan pants.

Nasima had never known life without conflict. She was the skeletal form of an Afghan woman battered by war and poverty, scourges that consume women, children and old people. Worn out and weary, she was a target with a bull's-eye on her back of war in general and gender war in particular.

More Afghan women lived as Nasima and her family did than in any other condition that I saw. No matter what their age, women in Nasima's state had been blinded by Afghanistan's long period of darkness. Her choices were few, her role narrower than ever, her restrictions many. Her first house in Kabul's Old Town had been destroyed during ethnic and religious fighting more than a decade before we talked. Her furniture had been burned or looted. She had lived as a squatter since 1992. The scene reminded me of Sarajevo in the mid–1990s, when Bosnian Muslims, Bosnian Croats and Bosnian Serbs took refuge anywhere they could, which usually was in someone else's bombed and abandoned house.

On the street outside the small space that Nasima called home, children played as children do. A vendor pushed a cart containing the heads of two water buffaloes, their stomachs and entrails out of place beside their heads. Buffalo brain, I was told, is prized.

The New Woman

Another version of the Afghan woman sat confidently on the second floor of a building in the center of Kabul. She wore black fish-net stockings. That's right, black fish-net stockings. A large gold ring glittered on her left hand. Her nails were painted a silvery white. A black head scarf covered her shoulders and fell gracefully over a long dark green dress. This was the outfit she wore in the safety of indoors. Outdoors, she still feared the Taliban mentality and stuck with her burqa, although she planned to shed it shortly. No beggar in a tattered burqa, she was 30 but looked younger. With a degree in literature, Suray was, indeed, unusual for this time and place, but she was not a species unseen in Afghanistan's history.

With help from CARE International, Suray shortly before we met had started an organization to teach women vocational education skills. Ambitious in all the right ways, she ran an organization called The Voice of Women. Her office, while not lavish, showed her ambition to teach, and to learn: A large desk and chair, two sofas, a long table, six smaller tables and four small chairs. She was ready for business, ready to bring in more women to learn vocational skills.

With a puny budget of $3,509 for cloth and salaries, Suray put 50 women to work in their homes making white scarves and charcoal gray dresses, school uniforms for girls. Their work and their product excited the women, who each earned $2.30 daily. Now Suray was begging for more money. From a business standpoint, the Taliban had been her inadvertent allies because international non-government organizations were eager to help women during the oppressive Taliban years when Afghan women's groups were few and worked underground. With the Taliban on the run, more women's groups were springing up openly and competing for limited aid dollars from more wary donors.

Like most of the women in Kabul, rich or poor, educated or not, Suray remembered the day when the Taliban conquered the city: "The last time I walked on the street without a burqa was September 26, 1996." She and I talked on March 2, 2002.

The Face and Voice of Afghan Women

Tired and afraid, Jamila had every reason to be. She was, as much as anyone, a symbol of Afghan women whom the Taliban silenced. She was also the public face and the voice of emerging Afghan women. After the Taliban were ousted, Jamila was the first woman to appear on Afghan state television; hers was also the first woman's voice to be heard on state radio. She read the news on radio and television twice weekly for an hour each time.

Shortly before we talked, also on March 2, 2002, Jamila had started a woman's magazine, a shiny ten-page periodical called *Malalai* after the Afghan woman who fought British invaders in the early 1880s. She also directed an association of Afghan women in the media, a rather thin corps. Five-hundred copies were published of her magazine's first edition, at a cost of $1,500. The money came from a French non–governmental aid organization. With considerable overstatement, she called the publication a scientific, social and literary magazine. All such labels are relative in poor countries, but she had to start somewhere.

The risks that Jamila, 36, was taking would have made any man or woman weary and fearful: "Sometimes my friends tell me to be more careful. They say there are still Al-Qaida in Kabul city." She wore a head scarf when she read the news on television. Yet Jamila was still too frightened to show her face on the street. "I am afraid because I was the first woman whose voice was heard in the media and there were Taliban still near Kabul," she said, recalling the lingering effects of the Taliban's reign of terror. "But some Afghan men called me to say how I did a great job."

With her husband and their five children, Jamila lived in a two-bedroom apartment that also had a kitchen and a bathroom. Her telephone didn't work, but most Afghan women would have been happy to switch places. "Sometimes I get so tired I can't eat. I go to sleep without eating," she said, with the weary look of someone who has been working too hard and sleeping too little.

Jamila was passionate about boosting the fortunes of her Afghan sisters. She yearned for women in the United States and Europe to cast an eye eastward and to help. Education was the primary need of Afghan women, she said, followed closely by freedom: "The freedom of their ideas and the freedom to have the right to take part in social affairs." Little of the freedom that she was talking about existed in Afghanistan or in most other countries in her neighborhood.

Echoing the message of her magazine, a plea the Taliban's gender warriors never heard, Jamila said, "The woman is a human being and she has the right to do what she wants. My intention through this magazine is to call attention to the rights of women to the political parties, to all the things that Afghan women need. I want this magazine to be sent to different countries all over the world. I want the people of the world to understand what is going on for Afghan women."

The reason Jamila wanted the rest of the world to possess her eyes, to see Afghanistan as she saw it, was because she couldn't be sure of support from the fathers and grandfathers, husbands, sons and brothers or of the religious leaders and tribal chiefs in her own land.

The Healers

Babies, badly undernourished, were wailing and their confused mothers were pleading for milk to feed their children. Dr. Freba, 26, was angry, desperate, frustrated and begging, all at once. "Why don't you help us!" she said, by exclamation more than interrogation. The United States and the West, she meant, not me personally. Dr. Freba had survived the Taliban's near-total subjugation of women because the Taliban had allowed women to practice medicine so other women could receive medical care. The poverty and ignorance of the people at the refugee camp were as great as the camp itself was desolate on the rim of the great Turkestan steppe near the city of Mazar-ash-Sharif in northern Afghanistan. Along with another Afghan woman doctor and an Afghan male doctor, Dr. Freba worked at the camp's Sakhi clinic, which was operated by the fearless and courageous French aid organization called Medecins Sans Frontieres (Doctors Without Borders).

Woeful conditions among the camp refugees sprouted from entrenched religious rules of conduct, restrictive tribal traditions, civil war, invasion and lesser forms of international meddling. Afghan religious and tribal codes stretched back centuries. They didn't begin with the Taliban although the Taliban drove the stake of fear, ignorance and religious fanaticism deeper in a shorter time than had any other indigenous Afghan group in modern memory. Here as elsewhere, women, children and the elderly suffered the most when war, poverty and ignorance ruled.

Dr. Freba, who wore a black dress, no burqa and no head covering when we met at the clinic, said that some women didn't even know enough to nurse their babies immediately after birth, which was hard to believe but true. Knowledge of proper hygiene, Dr. Freba said, was as foreign to the women in the camp as were American faces.

Just as the education of girls and women can do much to elevate overall knowledge in a society, ignorance among women has a sharply negative effect. With their war against girls and women, the Taliban were determined to breed only ignorance. Nurses and doctors were the only women who could work under the Taliban, but they functioned with restrictions that were themselves the products and tools of ignorance. In 1992, during the height of the civil war but before the rise of the Taliban, 250 women graduated from Kabul

University Medical School. Only 150 men graduated that year, because the men had to join the national army, which was controlled by whatever tribal clique posed as the government, before they could enter medical school. Because of earlier Taliban dictates, 2002 was the first time in four years that women were allowed to enter medical school at Balkh University in Mazar-ash-Sharif. By that time, the Taliban had been ousted and most of its members and their beards had melted back into the deserts of Afghan society.

Asma, 32, was another lucky woman. Also a doctor, she had been allowed to practice her profession under the Taliban. With a bemused look, she recounted how the Taliban required female and male doctors to enter and leave rooms by separate doors. The better to cool sexual passions among professionals trying to save lives. Dr. Asma had been a doctor for six years with Medecins Sans Frontieres when we spoke on April 3, 2002. She had just been promoted to head the organization's mother and child health care and nutrition program for Balkh Province in northern Afghanistan.

High death rates from disease and malnourishment among Afghan children were almost obscured because of their severity. Dr. Asma said that 25 percent of Afghan children did not live to the age of five. That figure, she said, was one of the highest in the world. A 1998 U.N. study backed her up, reporting that 257 of every 1,000 Afghan children did not see five summers. Conditions in Afghanistan were much more severe than even in the developing world, where the same U.N. study reported that 97 children out of 1,000 died before the age of five. The normal child mortality rate should be under one percent, another Afghan doctor said. Even the newborn mortality rate in Afghanistan was two-and-a-half times that of developing nations.

Diarrhea, pneumonia, acute respiratory infections, malnutrition, all were child killers, said Dr. Asma, who wore a white head scarf and a long denim coat when we began talking. She removed the scarf as we talked. Twenty-eight or twenty-nine of every 400 children were severely malnourished, she said. The remainder were moderately malnourished. Disease, brain damage and death flourished in such an environment. "In our clinics, we don't know when our children die because their parents don't come back to see us," said Dr. Amiri, Dr. Asma's male colleague.

Young mothers and grandmothers, nearly all wearing white burqas, clogged the Sakhi Clinic seeking food and medical care. Umid's aunt, who was raising the infant boy, brought him to be weighed so doctors could determine just how malnourished he was. Umid's mother died in childbirth and his father was in Iran. A month old at the time I took his photograph and all eyes, Umid's body barely filled a woman's hand. He weighed 3.96 pounds at birth; a month later, he weighed only 4.6 pounds. Umid was a poster child for the society's weakest members and for the ignorance of Taliban tribal and sectarian policies and practices that punished everyone, including healthy adult males even if they didn't know it.

Afghanistan Mon Amour

When two other American journalists and I arrived at the defense ministry office in Mazar-ash-Sharif, a stronghold of ethnic–Uzbeks, everyone was rushing to the auditorium at Balkh University. The last man to turn out the lights invited us to join the crowd, to see the premiere of the first movie shown anywhere in the entire country since the Taliban more than five years earlier had banned any kind of entertainment except public executions at specially arranged soccer matches, and denied women identity outside their homes. We were lucky, the kind of luck that often greets persistence. The movie allowed us a peek into Afghan society — pre–Taliban, pre–civil war, pre–Soviet war — that we might never have seen if we had arrived at the defense ministry five minutes later after a day-and a-half trip from Kabul. With a correspondent and photographer from *The Dallas Morning News* and our translator, driver and local expert whom journalists call a fixer, I saw a film version of Afghan society before war and fanaticism sent creativity and civility into exile. The contrast between the country's past as artistically presented and its raw and gnawing present was stunning.

Academic leaders, local political figures and the movie's director, all in suitcoats and ties, gave grand speeches exhorting Afghans to reclaim their rich cultural heritage from the creative desert. Five Jordanian soldiers, part of a team assigned to guard the local hospital, listened from the front row as a man sang verses and read prayers. The prayer readings and the showing of the film indicated to me that Afghanistan's strong religious tradition, minus the fierce fanaticism, could coexist with a local form of secular creativity.

In the grand tradition of premieres, the film director cut a ribbon and the curtain rose in the wedge of another Afghan counter-revolution, this one in a cinematic cocoon in northern Afghanistan. The standing-room-only crowd was buzzing with excitement. This was more than just a national movie premiere, which alone was worthy of celebration, and the hundreds of men and women who filled the auditorium at Balkh University knew it. For sure this was Afghanistan's first major social, intellectual, educational and cinematic exchange since the Taliban torture had started, and maybe its most daring film since the mid–1970s.

Not one woman in the hall wore the imprisoning burqa. Although the Taliban were out of power and on the run, nearly all the women on the city streets outside still wore white burqas. White is the traditional color of Mazar-ash-Sharif, unlike in Kabul where the traditional color is blue.

The movie, titled *Chapandaz* after the name given to Afghan horsemen who play the traditional game called "Buzkashi," was made in Uzbekistan with Afghan actors. The sound was poor, the acting was not what might be called Shakespearean in quality, and the picture was as grainy as a reel-to-reel pirated film from the West in the 1930s. But all that was irrelevant. That the film existed at all was a triumph of Afghan creativity, culture and persistence. It was a cog-like step toward reviving the variety in Afghan social and cultural traditions that tribal wars, an invasion and religious fanaticism crushed but did not quite kill.

Here in black and white was the Afghan version of a classic story of romance and tragedy in which a young woman was torn between her duty to her father and her love of her father's enemy. In that part of the world, it is taboo for a child, especially a daughter, to challenge a father's authority or question one's duty toward a parent. The film unveiled a creator's view of an Afghanistan that most of the outside world never knew existed. On the screen was a freer, more open Afghanistan that predated the country's immolation. With its mix of Uzbek, Pashtun, Tadjik and other tribes, Mazar-ash-Sharif is traditionally one of Afghanistan's least conservative cities. And the audience, in a university setting, was an elite one. Still, the film offered a glimpse of the society that educated, urban Afghans remembered and wanted to revive. That was the Afghanistan the audience cheered on the afternoon of March 31, 2002, while on the street outside the fresh wounds of Taliban repression remained visible.

Unintentionally, perhaps, the film and the university setting highlighted the cycles of change in Afghan society. Before its national fabric was shredded by conflict, Afghanistan's often warring tribes flitted through periods of tolerance, liberalism and reaction. How Afghans dressed, practiced Islam and conducted their business had very much been left up to individuals, families, tribes and standards established in the different regions of the country. Periodically, when the religious rules were relaxed too much for the rule-makers to stomach, the society would swing in the only other direction it knew, a stricter observance of Islamic and tribal standards. Women — how they dressed, behaved and worked — usually bore the brunt of the repression because the men make the rules. The Taliban took repression and the gender aspect of tribal conflicts to new lows.

Despite its universal human theme lodged in Afghan traditions, the movie also highlighted the ever-present clash between conservative rural areas and the more liberal cities. I couldn't imagine the film being shown in an Afghan village, not in the 1960s and not in the 21st century.

Originating on the open steppes in the north of Afghanistan and in Uzbekistan, the fast and furious game of Buzkashi can be played by countless riders on beautiful horses sometimes representing numerous teams led by tribal chiefs called khans. Each rider's goal is to seize a water-logged carcass of a calf or lamb, toss it over his saddle or pin it between his leg and the horse then haul the carcass to opposite ends of the field, around goalposts you might say, in order to score points. Teammates try to protect the rider who is carrying the carcass while every rider from all the other teams attacks the horseman with the carcass so another rider can grab the prize and run with it. The city version of the game has a time limit and a well-defined playing area. On the open steppe, however, the field has no boundaries and the game can last for days and days in a circus atmosphere that involves entire tribes.

Play is rough, often extremely violent. Horses rear and bite their rivals while riders whip horses and other riders. A colorful crush of rearing horses, teeth and hooves flashing, their riders whipping wildly reminded me of a medieval painting depicting ferocious horsemen in a mad dash from Hell. No wonder the game is seen as a metaphor for Afghan politics, in which individuals and tribes are pitted against one another in constantly shifting alliances.

In the movie, the young woman has a choice that goes beyond her usual role, a choice that is rare not only in Afghanistan, but in most traditional societies. She makes her choice, but it's not the traditional one. She loves a Chapandaz who is her father's rival, and rejects the rider whom her father has chosen for her. The woman and her lover meet secretly in the woods. The audience applauded. When next the lovers meet, the chosen rider gives the young woman a pair of earrings, which she wears home. A great hush blanketed the audience after the woman's mother tells her that if her father learns of the liaison, he will kill his daughter. This is too close to reality to merit applause. But it is acceptable precisely because it is real and it is art.

Defying her father, the smitten young woman rushes to her fallen lover in a secret house where he was taken after he had been badly injured in a riding accident. The accident happened because the horse of the woman's lover had been poisoned by a professional assassin whom the girl's father had hired. The audience again applauded the young woman's decision to stand by her man, whatever the consequences. Humor, not easily identifiable in Afghanistan, made its way into the film. Viewers laughed loudly when the man hired to poison the lover's horse fell into the oats after he planted the poison. The simple opportunity to see the game of Buzkashi played in a movie aroused the viewers to cheer and applaud.

Most of the violence in the film is pertinent to the story. Some activity concerned Afghan atmospherics, which are important to maintain cultural integrity and because of the groundbreaking nature of the film. A camel fight and a cock fight, for example, are often part of the scene that surrounds a

Buzkashi match. Afghans expect to see such activity in an honest film. No one walked out and no one in the audience hissed at the scene in a hashish club, where a woman was dancing and gyrating alone and six men were swaying nearby, all apparently under the influence. But when my translator whispered, "That's a hashish club," he appeared embarrassed. With all the poppies grown in Afghanistan, I figured that the scene was probably supposed to be in an opium den, but I didn't press the point. This part of the movie reminded me of the time in Kabul when a government official, a leading drug-fighting figure, casually offered me a small ball of opium. "Eat this and you'll be drunk until tomorrow," he said. "No thanks," I answered, "I like my chances better sober." One of my Afghan aides took an agate-sized ball of the swirled brown and black opium, but we never discussed its use or effects.

Destruction, Afghan Style

The Taliban emerged directly from the chaos of civil war and indirectly from the heart and history of Afghan society, not from its fringes. With help from Saudi Arabia's and Pakistan's Sunni extremists, the Taliban's bearded and zealous mullahs established a radical Sunni Islamic state of exceptional harshness. But the objective of creating an Islamic state was not foreign to Afghanistan, although Sufism, a more moderate brand of Islam, has deep roots among Afghans. The Students of Islam filled the expanding sinkholes in Afghanistan's political, social and economic structure. Their imposition of order was not entirely unwelcome at first. Only when their fanaticism became evident did opposition begin to swell against them.

Besides the Taliban's gender war, just about every other form of tribal warfare rocked the Afghan people in the last quarter of the 20th century. Ethnic and language groups and ideologies fought each other, with various shades of sectarianism at least a subliminal part of the explosive mix. The Soviet invasion countered militarily by the United States and Pakistan provided the foreign intervention that whipped up and deepened the internal tribal strife. Sunni Saudi Arabia and Shiite Iran injected competing sectarian ideologies. In the more distant past, the Russian tsars and British colonialists vied for influence in Afghanistan; Britain fought three rather disastrous wars there. Go back far enough and different Afghan tribes were fighting Alexander the Great.

Afghan history is also marked by conflicts among and within the country's tribes and ethnic groups. Brief periods of tolerance were usually followed by religious backlashes aimed at a laxity of obedience to Islamic codes and tribal traditions. More liberal urban behavior regularly butts against tight tribal and religious codes that flourish in more remote areas.

More than a million Afghans were believed killed during the 25 years of fighting that began in the mid–1970s. As many as six million Afghans fled to Pakistan, Iran, Uzbekistan, Tadjikistan and other countries combined.

Billions of dollars worth of American arms went through Pakistan to the more than half-dozen Afghan Islamic and tribal guerrilla groups that fought for nine years to oust the Soviet army. Washington paid little attention to the arms, such as Stinger surface-to-air missiles, that Pakistan kept or to which Afghan organizations the Pakistanis sent American arms. Which web of mujahedin fighters — Islamic-based or ethno-centric — would lead Afghanistan after the war against the Soviets ended never seems to have caught Washington's ear or eye. The U.S. objective was simply to make sure the Soviet Union was bled white. Washington again found Afghanistan on the map long after the Taliban and Osama bin Laden hooked up.

The long war to oust the Soviet army was the yeast that gave rise to bin Laden and his al Qaida (The Base) organization of Islamic fighters. Any gun was welcome in that war. But when that conflict ended, bin Laden and Pakistan hung around Afghanistan, while the Afghan tribes kept fighting each other. From this meddlesome and incendiary mixture rose the flaming quackery called the Taliban and their war against women. Only after the September 11, 2001, attacks did the United States offer the Taliban and bin Laden its undivided military attention.

SIX

The Bumpy Tribal Road from Moscow to Tel Aviv

Shortly after I arrived in Jerusalem from Miami, via Washington, London and Paris, I traveled to Bethlehem for a routine story. As I was leaving the town, I decided to stop by the Church of the Nativity to see what that was all about. The church was built by the Crusaders about 1,000 years after the birth of Jesus Christ, and Christians believe the building covers the cave where Jesus was born. As I was gawking in the basement surrounded by burning candles and objects deemed holy, an Israeli tour guide entered with two American couples. "This is where all our problems began," the guide said.

About a year later I attended the wedding of a Palestinian Christian couple in Jerusalem. The men were seated on one side of the reception area, and the women were on the opposite side, as is customary. We were discussing the first Intifadeh, the Palestinian uprising against Israeli occupation, when an elderly man interjected: "The Jews killed my God and we will never forgive them for that."

When the Soviet security guard tried to yank the camera from my hands and snap its strap from my neck, I sensed that things weren't going my way. He tugged and I pulled back in a little hand dance that I hadn't counted on when I entered the train depot. Our standoff wouldn't last, I knew, because this was his turf and reinforcements were coming his way, not mine.

Joined by several right-hand men and left-hand men, the guard insisted, with the firmness of those in a position to give orders and be obeyed, that I say hello to his boss in the depot, a man who, no joke, identified himself as Igor. This was Igor's den and I was from an alien tribe. In an earlier era, I probably would have vanished for a while, like the victim of a bad magician. But this was a lighter time; Soviet communism and the Cold War were expiring.

When Igor suggested that we walk to a nearby building to meet his boss, a large man with eyebrows so bushy and thick he looked more like Leonid Brezhnev than Brezhnev himself, I knew my fortunes were slipping further. It was time to anticipate the lines of questioning and plumb for new negotiating techniques.

I had flown from Moscow southwest to L'vov in the western Ukraine during the late spring of 1990, seeking Jews who planned to drive to Israel. I wanted to ride with them because I thought that would be a terrific story. My search proved unsuccessful, but the unfolding story touched many tribes across the Soviet Union. Hundreds of thousands of Jews from throughout the massive Soviet empire, which shortly would be in ruins, were taking the opportunity to say *dasvedanya*, goodbye in Russian. This was a story rooted in history, in religion and its lack, in culture, language and nationality — literally in tribe or what might loosely be called exiled sons and daughters returning to the tribal bosom.

What religion was left in those Soviet Jews was faint indeed, separated as they were from their spiritual past by 70 years of communism's forced unbelief. Even their Jewish identity had been watered down. But some were learning Hebrew and trying to revive their Jewish past while they waited to leave. A great many of them were economic emigrants happy to inject a little Judaism where there was little or none. Others hoped simply to seize the opportunity to leave the crumbling empire that was never warm and cozy to them under the tsars or the Communists. As communism disintegrated to be replaced by a political vacuum and woeful economic times, fears of civil war, soaring Russian nationalism and renewed anti–Semitism ballooned. Given the Jews' tribal history in Russia and elsewhere in the Soviet empire — periodic nationalist pogroms under the tsars, the leading role of Jews during the Communist revolution and now a possible backlash as communism withered and died — those fears were not unjustified. Uncertainty hovered like the omnipresent brooding skies that blanket the Soviet empire, and that was sufficient to convince many Jews from Tadjikistan to the Ukraine to leave while they could.

The end of Soviet communism meant the end of an empire and a state of many tribes dominated by Russians. The conquered tribes were about to rise again, from Central Asia to Ukraine and the Baltic states, on the ashes of empire. Historians, I believe, will view the sweeping changes that followed the Soviet disintegration as one of the great migrations and evolutions in history, in a land that has known many.

Huge still, the new Russian state also began to suffer the effects of tribal eruptions within its own borders, notably in Chechenia, Dagestan, Ossetia

Knocking on Israel's door: As many as 2,000 people gathered almost daily outside the Israeli consulate at the Dutch Embassy in Moscow in 1990, when this photograph was taken. Their mission: Leave the dying Soviet Union for the Jewish state (photograph by the author, © Cox Newspapers Inc.).

and other areas of the Caucasus region. With its suffocating linguistic, cultural, ethnic and sectarian nationality, Russia soon began struggling to keep together what the various Caucasus tribes wanted to shrink further. The powerful centrifugal force of the imperial dissolution also threw into the crosshairs of the resurgent tribes millions of Russians who lived in the new nation-states beyond the borders of redesigned Russia.

Jews were only a part of the tribal migration that was sweeping across Europe and Asia. With their new-found language, religion and perhaps nationality, Soviet Jews were to join another tribal state in a land alien to them in most respects. The re-emerging Jews who, with Israeli help, lined up to leave from throughout the dying Soviet empire gave Israel a chance to build a more positive relationship with Russia and the empire's other successor states, most of which in Central Asia were at least nominally Muslim. The new Russia would play a lesser role in the Middle East. No longer would it be, as the Soviet Union was for so long, an effective Arab counterweight to the U.S.–Israel alliance.

While Israel was beefing up its population with Soviet Jews, Saudi Arabia and Iran were trying to strengthen their rival brands of Islam with the fresh Muslim blood of Central Asia, where Islam is rooted in moderate Sufi traditions and behavior. Strains of Sufism exist among followers of both Sunni and Shiite sects, but Sufism itself is more a set of practices for abiding by Islam's core beliefs rather than a separate sect. The Saudis, Iranians and Kuwaitis were shipping millions of Korans and many more millions of dollars into the newly minted Muslim states of Uzbekistan, Tadjikistan, Kyrgyzstan, Turkmenistan and Kazakhstan. From the Saudi standpoint, if the new Central Asian states were to be truly Muslim, they should wear the conservative, even reactionary, Saudi brand of Sunni Islam. The Iranians saw it differently; to them Shiites were the true Muslims. Turkey, a large secular Sunni Muslim state where Sufi beliefs and practices are strong, also has a major economic and strategic stake in the region.

Later in the 1990s, Israel joined the competition in Central Asia, making for a parallel contest but no clash with usual rivals Iran and Saudi Arabia, which wanted to revive Islam and reconvert the Muslims where they were. The Israelis on one side and the Saudis, Iranians and Kuwaitis on the other sides were like rival sectarian and ethnic caravans plodding past the same sand dunes seeking different cargo. Each side appeared to ignore the other because their tribal goals were more different than similar. The Israeli objective was to fly Jews from the region to Tel Aviv. Beyond that Israel used the official links built to ease the Jewish exodus to forge economic, commercial, scientific and agricultural relations with those essentially Muslim countries in Central Asia. Friendly ties between Israel and countries in the region would nullify those tribes on the sectarian front as well, at least for a time.

The vast majority of Jews who were banging on the Soviet Union's exit doors preferred to go to the United States. But most were not allowed to land immediately at a U.S. port. Israel's portals were beckoning, its officials eager to swell the country's population with returning tribesmen and women to combat other tribes, such as Palestinians and neighboring Arab nations, and to expand Israeli settlements in the occupied territories. For their part, about one million emigrants were happy to take the route to Tel Aviv, at least as a first step. There they could sell what possessions they brought out, including Russian Orthodox icons held dear by still other tribes. The Israelis, meanwhile, believed that if they could force-feed the new immigrants Hebrew and Judaism, Zionism would follow without a hiccup.

The idea of driving from the Soviet Union to Israel was brilliant, I thought. From my base in Jerusalem I wrote about a former Jewish Refusenik who said that he drove a new Volvo 3,500 miles from Moscow to Israel. That's when I thought about trying to make the trip with Jews emigrating from

Russia or any other part of the old empire. As I roamed Moscow, Leningrad (now St. Petersburg again) and L'vov for almost a month, I found many people who said they planned to drive to Israel, but they had no idea when they would be permitted to leave. Approval could take months, or perhaps never come at all, so all I could manage were promises but never a solid connection. Short of becoming a Soviet or Russian citizen myself and hanging around to hook up with a motorist heading to Israel, I realized that my plan lacked high promise. After more than three weeks of trying and getting a little hungrier by the day, I glimpsed my good fortune: At least I could leave and no longer have to watch and listen to the Russians plunge deeper into depression over their loss of power and prestige in the world.

My search took me to L'vov, a city of beautiful parks and Eastern and Central European baroque-style buildings, and about 800,000 people. L'vov is recognized by UNESCO for its architectural beauty that rivals Prague, Budapest and Polish cities such as Krakow. The sky in L'vov seemed a little bluer, the atmosphere less grim and the buildings less bulky and bleak than in other points to the vast east. A commercial and cultural hub, L'vov was an appropriate place for me to follow the tribal trail. It is next to Poland, near the Carpathian Mountains, and not far from Romania and Moldova. During its 750-year history, L'vov has been under the domination of Poles, Russians, Germans, Swedes and Austro-Hungarian emperors. Eclectic in ethnic, linguistic and sectarian terms, L'vov is the city's Russian name. It goes now by its Ukrainian name, L'viv or Lviv, as Ukraine became independent in 1991. The city has also been known by its Polish name of Lwow and its German name, Lemberg. Jews have thrived and suffered greatly in L'vov and all its guises, and when I visited in 1990, freedom's door was springing open to them again.

The drive through the Ukrainian countryside from the airport to the city was like wandering through a pre–World War II tableau: Horse-drawn carts, small black motorcycles with sidecars, cows being tended individually beside the road, men with scythes cutting tall grass in the fields, men, women and children hoeing and planting, people wearing dark clothes that looked much too large. If I had been born anywhere in what Western Europeans call the East, I thought, my first conscious act would have been to flee west or south. Jewish leaders in Moscow told me that many in L'vov's large and resurgent Jewish community were planning to leave for Israel, south and sort of semi-West. So I took my chances.

After I connected with local Jews, my guide/translator led me to the L'vov train depot to see for myself evidence of the baggage bound for Israel. When I entered the depot, I was on my own, carrying only a small shoulder bag with a camera and notebooks inside. As I strolled around the depot, trying to look as much as possible as if I belonged in the neighborhood, I casually checked the addresses on baggage, most of them bundled crates and strapped trunks. I noted that most of the crates were about six-feet long, four-feet wide and three-feet high. Scores of the pieces, maybe 60 percent, had Tel Aviv or Jerusalem written on them in large, bold letters. From what I was told, the baggage would be shipped to Budapest by rail and then flown to Israel.

First, I gathered this information in my head before deciding that a few photographs would be worth more than pictures in my mind. At that point, I felt it was worth the risk. Cautiously, I removed my small aim-and-shoot camera, draped the strap around my neck and began to aim and click as surreptitiously as I could. Faster than I could fill the frame and center the baggage in the lens, Igor's men descended.

"Nyet, nyet," they shouted. "Nyet, nyet," I answered, resisting their attempts to pull the camera from my hands while demonstrating part of my vast Russian vocabulary. Their attention focused on the camera, not on where they might pummel me. The men didn't wear uniforms or bear identification. I assumed they were KGB agents, or secret police, but they could have been customs officers, border police or railroad police, although I would not have known the difference if there was any.

We pulled, yanked and shouted for a few minutes before we reached a standoff. That's when the agents took me to a small office at the far end of the depot where Igor presided. A relatively young man, no older than 40 I thought, Igor spoke English well enough, but in a stilted manner that reveals textbook knowledge but a distinct lack of conversational experience on the streets of New York. Igor couldn't tell a Boston from a London accent.

Who was I and why was I taking photos in the train depot? Igor asked. Igor seemed satisfied with my passport, newspaper credentials and explanation of my purpose. Once he saw my U.S. passport, Igor didn't ask, "Where you from?" which immediately endeared him to me. But he wanted to know how I found the depot. For a reporter, this was easy to answer, without giving away my guide. I'm a reporter, a journalist, that's what I do, I told Igor, I find people and places and write about them. A local man would have been in much greater distress than I if the security men had caught him bringing a foreign journalist to the depot.

No photographs were allowed in the depot, Igor said, insisting that since this was still the Soviet Union, he made the rules. He was certain that I couldn't take photographs at train depots in the United States. In that case, he asked, why should I be free to take them in L'vov? There I had him, and I embellished the truth with a big fib. "I can take photographs of anything and anyone anywhere in the United States," I said with great conviction.

"Anything. Anyone. Anywhere." I repeated those words several times in different contexts. "The United States is a free country," I said. Igor was on uncertain ground here. He didn't have the knowledge to contradict me. He fell back on the Soviet rules of the moment; I was happy that we were having this tame discussion in the middle of 1990, instead of a few years earlier when no Soviet citizen would have dared to openly mock Raisa Gorbachev's expensive Western clothes as some were at that very moment.

Igor was an underling. He lacked the power to decide my fate on his own. Come with me, Igor said, and we went from the train depot to a blocky featureless building a ten-minute walk away. My translator/guide was standing outside the depot when we left. As I walked beside but slightly behind Igor so Igor couldn't see, I flapped my hands backwards and forwards as I dangled my arms by my sides. I was signaling my guide, who had started to follow us, to take off fast. He caught on, peeled off and disappeared.

After we reached the building, I waited in a small anteroom with a young woman clerk when Igor went to fetch his boss. There I decided to react to my inquisitors, rather than come out swinging, which proved a good strategy. My thoughts centered on how I would free myself from this corner that seemed to be getting smaller. In the anteroom I prepared my case. Igor said that the top man was out of the office, but the deputy would be happy to interrogate me. We went into a small bare room that had only a table and a couple of chairs. That's where I met Brezhnev's spitting image, whose name I never learned. He didn't threaten me, but he was insistent and we went over the same ground that I had with Igor at the depot. Neither of us budged: My inquisitor said that by not asking permission to take photographs I had broken the rules, the same rules that would apply in the United States. I repeated my false claim of invincibility in the United States, and that's where we stood until I saw and seized a way out.

Looking Igor's Brezhnev straight in the eye, my body language as straight and unflinching as my stare, I said that as a journalist I was only acting as I would have in the United States and elsewhere, but if I had known the rules in the Soviet Union I would have requested permission to take photographs at the depot. If I broke the rules, I added, I was sorry, but I didn't do so intentionally. Those were face-saving words for us both: For him my words served as an apology and an admission that I had acted improperly; for me those words were a conditional apology without an admission that I had done anything wrong. I had stumbled on a strategy that would prove useful in other tight spots.

Brezhnev's lookalike and I both smiled. Squirming from our mutual corners, we shook hands, both happy and free to go on to other business. I don't think that he wanted me around anymore than I wanted to be with him. I asked for permission to shoot more photographs at the depot. The boss checked my passport, visa and hotel pass, left the room briefly and returned with a nod and a smile. Again I praised the calendar, happy that I was in Gorbachev's Perestroika years, and that Gorbachev's era was ending on the plus side for me. The entire confrontation took no more than two hours. As Igor walked me back to the depot, he said that with my accent I didn't sound like an American. He appeared shocked when I explained the phenomenon of regional accents in the United States.

From the moment he told me that photos were taboo in the depot, Igor said he wanted to ask me a "delicate" question. I could not guess his keen interest. As we walked back to the depot, this was his moment to whisper the question, as if the answer might be super-secret. "Why are you so interested in this story?" Igor asked. "The mass emigration and changes in the Soviet Union were news and readers, especially Jews, in the United States were interested in the story," I answered easily enough. Besides, I was based in Jerusalem, and this was an extension of the Israeli and Middle Eastern story, too. I told Igor that all this was more obvious than delicate, although the story had major

Ready to go: After my peace treaty with Soviet security at the railroad depot in L'vov, workers boosted me atop crated luggage bound for Tel Aviv in 1990, the better to snap the photographs that two hours earlier were deemed objectionable (photograph by the author, © Cox Newspapers Inc.).

implications in the Arab-Israeli conflict. The next surprise was on me. When I returned to the train depot, Igor and his colleagues helped me climb on top of large, sturdy pieces of baggage so I could take better photos of all the trunks and crates that were bound for Israel. In the evening, I found my smiling translator and continued to search, without success, for anyone who would be driving to Jerusalem.

Even at midnight as we rumbled and swayed through the invisible landscape between Moscow and what was then Leningrad, a train ride offered rare glimpses into Soviet society. Rocking toward Leningrad, Simon and I talked most of the night about the future of what soon would no longer be Soviet society. Simon, 42, and I each had a bunk in a first-class compartment, which cost me $259. That price included a return flight to Moscow, a one-night stay at an Intourist hotel and a taxi from the train station to the hotel. I was in berth number 10, car 11 of the number 10 train northbound, which left Moscow shortly after midnight on May 27, 1990. Come 8:15 A.M., we were due in Leningrad. We pulled out of Leningradsky station on time but arrived in Leningrad only 40 minutes late. By Soviet standards, the train was decent: The compartment was clean, but the toilets were filthy.

Simon was depressed, but he was not alone. So were millions of other Soviet citizens. His reasons were partly personal. An artist-designer with ties to a sociology institute, Simon spent several years conceiving and illustrating future living conditions in the Soviet Union. First, he created concepts of what future disasters might be and how Soviet citizens might be protected from them. Second, he theorized about future relations and cooperation among peoples. He drew a picture of a machine with people moving and wheels turning that represented human cooperation and progress. I copied his drawing in my notebook, sketched it so clumsily that his schemes would never have worked if anyone followed my blueprint. If everyone worked together, he said, everyone would benefit. But Simon's realm was imploding, a development that was welcome probably because it was overdue, and depressing because his world of 42 years was disappearing.

For several hours, well into the darkest moments of the morning, we talked about the systematic mental depression that was cascading over the people in the Soviet Union. "It's the most destroyed society because of the ideology," he said. "I feel fear. I would like to spend the next 10 or 15 years somewhere else, not here." Half Jewish, Simon said he would like to move to the United States where a cousin already lived. Just before he tired of talking, Simon said that he didn't believe he would fit well into the Israeli glove, but that he probably would try.

Known for their grim and sardonic view of life shaped by conflict, climate and oppression, the Russians were adding another layer to their thick coat of depression. The collapse of their state in the global spotlight hit hard, leaving them no excuses and few useful monuments to Soviet superiority.

Leningrad, where I met with several Jewish Refuseniks, proved to be all I expected and more: An old beauty in tattered clothes and chipped gold jewelry, short of food, depressed, falling deeply in love with all things American as the Soviet world crumbled, dicey and a little dangerous in its accelerating decay and want, its showcase buildings showing all the ill effects of 70 years of material decline. In my Intourist hotel room, where I conducted several interviews that I had lined up from Moscow, I was greeted by a television tape of the Boston Celtics playing the N.Y. Knicks in a playoff game and the announcer shouting, "NBA: grosta fantastika." My Russian vocabulary expanded instantly. A young man later struck up a conversation with me at a hot-air balloon show, filled with American adventurers and promoters, on the banks of the Neva River. Then, exactly as I had been warned, the man followed me, with larceny in his footsteps. But I lost him with a tactic devised on the spot: I crossed the street in a crowd, walked back in the opposite direction then recrossed the street to come up behind the man; I could see him but he couldn't see me as I returned safely to the hotel.

In Moscow, Leningrad and L'vov, the people praised everything American and denounced all that was Communist. Boirow, a Moscow engineer, asked for a cigarette when we sat to talk. "I don't smoke," I said, but I gave him a pack of Marlboros that I had brought, against my better judgment, to entice taxi drivers to stop for me on the street. American cigarettes were the best currency on Moscow's streets and sidewalks. The best way, sometimes the only way, to convince a cabbie to stop in Moscow was to wave a pack of American cigarettes. Then their brakes always worked. After I gave him the cigarettes, Boirow smiled, made the sign of the cross on his chest, kissed the cigarette package and promised not to blow smoke in my face. I felt guilty for advancing his addiction. When I asked what he thought of America, Boirow put his right hand high over his head. As for the Soviet Union, he lowered his hand down around his ankles. This depression was so deep, widespread and discomforting that I found myself playing amateur psychologist and trying to raise the spirits of many of the people I met. All people want, I learned everywhere I traveled, is a little respect.

Political conditions were uncertain and the economy lower than a curbstone. The ruble was losing value rapidly. The exchange rate on the black market was 15 rubles for $1. The official exchange rate was 6.25 rubles for $1. In an attempt to manufacture foreign currency, hotels that catered to foreigners pegged the value of a dollar at an outrageous 60 cents. A joke that Soviets told was a much better gauge than the exchange rates of how fast the ruble was falling in value: One man asked another as they were going out to eat how much money they should bring. Instead of giving a figure, the second man held his thumb and forefinger two inches apart to indicate the thickness of the wad they would need. The wad thickened daily.

Jews, half–Jews, quarter–Jews and less weren't the only people who wanted out of those circumstances. Ethnic-Germans, ethnic–Armenians and tribal Russians were also lining up to leave. Life was harder than Siberia's frozen earth. When it wasn't raining or snowing, motorists in Moscow removed their windshield wipers so they wouldn't be stolen. At night motorists drove with only their parking lights on, sometimes with no lights at all, to save their batteries, another signal that I was in a poor country. Food, work and money were scarce, persuasive reasons to get in the exit-visa line and wait. At the same time, it was difficult and very expensive to say goodbye. Yevgeny, head of a Hebrew teachers' organization in Moscow, had his Soviet exit and Israeli entry visas and was planning to leave for Israel the following August with his wife and two children. "It's impossible to live here," he said, "There's nothing to eat. You don't understand; we are living in a country of beggars." He wasn't exaggerating.

Before I left for the Soviet Union on this occasion, I was urged to eat heavily at breakfast because I probably would not eat again until the next breakfast. Because I had money I was luckier than most locals. I could break that 24-hour fast if I bought canned food, nuts, crackers and fruit — I remember paying $23 for nine oranges — in a store that took foreign currency. To paraphrase an old military term, a foreign correspondent travels on his stomach. Without food the stories tend to become shorter and less frequent.

Scrambling for bread and boiled eggs in the Soviet Union reminded me of an assignment in Libya eight months earlier. In Moammar Khadafy's Tripoli, not generally acknowledged as a five-star kitchen, I enjoyed my best and most expensive lunch ever on the company. A magnificent seafood buffet with global reach for a mere $75 a person at the Grand Hotel in Tripoli. Sans alcohol, of course. Libya had invited journalists to observe the twentieth anniversary of Khadafy's revolution. To show how much Khadafy liked and trusted the foreign press, each of us was assigned to a cell-sized room on a large ship. Two persons to each cell, the better to guard us all. My cell-mate was a nice Egyptian man with an eye infection. We got on well, my eyes remained clear, and I still remember his tribal lesson: "Remember," he said, "blue and green are the colors of Islamic movements."

One morning I decided to skip a day-long controlled desert tour of

Khadafy's Great Man-Made River project, which was designed to get the journalists out of town and out of sight for the entire day while revealing nothing. By the time I walked off the ship later that same morning, the guards were napping because all the journalists were supposed to be off watching sand grow in the desert. All taxis in the city had been commandeered by the government to serve Khadafy's celebration. As a result, I was forced to hitchhike to the suburbs for pre-arranged interviews with French and Italian diplomats. With little traffic in the suburbs and no taxis answering calls, I was prepared to take the long, long walk back into the city center. But the ever-present secret police saved my soles. A smiling young gun picked me up and drove through the center of a nearly deserted Tripoli at 110 miles per hour in midafternoon. That was my fastest urban taxi ride ever. In an attempt to be courteous to a visitor, my temporary minder dropped me off near the ship. But I made a fast and sharp right turn, shunning the galley's soup, bread, security guards and its prison-like atmosphere in favor of a walk to the Grand Hotel where my palate rolled its eyes in amazement at the lobster, shrimp and crabmeat, and my wallet opened wide.

Breakfast in Moscow was gobble time, if you arrived early: boiled eggs, thick dark bread, small frankfurter-like sausages, cabbage salad, beet bits and carrot shavings. A few restaurant cooperatives were beginning to open, but their hours were irregular and difficult to divine. If I returned to the hotel during the dinner window, I bribed a waitress to serve me a scrawny chicken leg. A bribe was necessary because I was alone rather than with a group. The waitresses hid me in a corner so no one would notice me eating alone.

After several weeks traveling on my stomach this way, my hunger quite naturally expanded in conjunction with the amount of food that I wasn't eating. By the time I flew to L'vov, famished, I was determined to eat on the night I arrived. After I checked into the older of two Intourist hotels at dinner time, I made a forced march directly to the dining room. Time was against me, as well as the fact that I was alone and government hotels at that time served only tour groups; individuals were a Western conspiracy.

I was shooed out of one overcrowded restaurant in the hotel. So I jogged to a larger one which was not busy. That's where I drew a line on the tables. I hadn't eaten the entire day and had one meal the day before that. If I didn't eat right there where the band was playing, the mood seemed bright and many of the tables were empty, I knew that sleep was my only chance of easing hunger pains that night. Tomorrow promised to be another bad eating day. When I entered the dining room I was prepared mentally to be a one-man group, on a reconnaissance mission for a group, or even a tiny subset of a group — I was ready to assume any title, comply with any definition, for vittles.

Both the waiters and waitresses ignored me at first, preferring to drink coffee and smoke in a back room. I found a table that was set for four, with plates already filled with salad, and sat down. Still I was ignored, until I started to eat one of the salads. Then a thick-fingered waiter dashed over with his equivalent of a stop sign. A quick translation: "Grupa! Grupa! Only groups. You are not a group. Get out!" The waiter, of noticeable sinew, pulled hard on my right arm, trying to jerk me out of the chair or pull the chair from the room with me on it. And I wasn't even taking photographs. I resisted, shouting in English as he shouted in Russian. We each knew what the other was saying, without an exact translation. The band played on. By now we were the featured attraction, a Chaplinesque interlude during what was becoming an otherwise sour dining occasion.

When I held my ground, the waiter left in anger, then returned to remove the plate of salad that I had been eating. He carried my precious salad to the waiters' table along a wall. Undaunted, I retrieved the salad, walked back to my table and continued to eat. There was a point to be made here. My anger was rising, but all these physical antics were becoming funny. Maybe I should have laughed out loud, but I didn't. This agent of Intourist hospitality tried again to separate me from my chair. Failing that he picked up my entire table and transported it to the side of the room. There I sat, alone, in the middle of the room, with no table and no food, thinking that maybe my calling in L'vov was to play the part of a stooge.

For a moment, I considered taking a bow, but thought better of that when I remembered that I was a lone visitor from another tribe in the waiter's homeland. But if the waiter could move the table, I could move the chair. Within seconds I picked up my chair, held it behind me as if I were still sitting and carried it to the table where I resumed eating. The waiter then surrendered in that logistical war of attrition. He moved the table back to its original location, brought me two bottles of mineral water and held up four fingers, switching tactics and trying to get the last word. Although I was not a group I could stay, he was indicating, but I must pay for four people because I was sitting at a table for four and eating all those salads.

"Nyet, nyet," I said, digging deeply into my vast Russian vocabulary and refusing on principle to be a real group or to yield to his demand. I held up only one finger. Four, one; four, one, we shouted snappily back and forth with our fingers. Earlier I would have been happy to agree to pay for four meals, but at that point I had to object because of the way I was treated. My waiter did not press his demand, probably because he was reluctant to get into a water fight.

All the salad dishes were mine to eat. But no one would bring more food. In the end, I ate all the salads, but not much of a meal. To continue with the allusion, I sort of won a few battles but lost the war. The bill was 4.35 rubles, or about 70 cents. I gave the waiter 10 rubles, $1.65, which angered him at first because he didn't want to make change. I waved him away when he brought the change. With such a tip, he was no longer an angry old waiter, but a smiling one at least. In the middle of all this, I was really trying to teach the waiter that he could seat fewer than four people at a table for four, perhaps several times in an evening, to make more money and receive more tips. Perhaps much about the lesson was lost in the lack of translation.

The following day I returned for lunch because there was no other handy place to eat or quarrel. A quick study, relatively speaking, the waiter greeted me warmly. He seated me immediately and later showed a couple, deeply in the grasp of love and lust, to my table for four. The food was better, the comic drama was in recess, and my tip made the waiter smile even more broadly than the night before. Gratuities do have a way of smoothing the transition from communism to capitalism. When I left, the waiter urged me to return. Instead, but not reluctantly, I made an easy choice. I took the train west, to Budapest. Years removed now, I would love to return to see the higher prices and built-in gratuities on the menus of Ukraine's L'viv.

Mother Russia was never a soft billowing skirt that sheltered Jews, although in a momentous hiccup Josef Stalin dropped his hatred of Jews long enough to support the creation of Israel in 1948. Like so many other self-serving interventions that punished or rewarded people in the Middle East, Stalin's momentary change of direction was based on international politics and self-interest, in this case a chance to drain British influence in the region where oil bubbled through the sands.

When Jews in Russia weren't being forced to convert to Christianity or be killed back in the 16th century, they were banned from the country altogether. After Poland was partitioned in the late 18th century, Jews were allowed back into Russia so that later they could be persecuted in pogroms and by laws that severely restricted where and how they could live. Under the tsars, repression of the Jews was royal policy. Many were sent to Siberia or killed in organized massacres; others were among the first European Jews to flee to Palestine in the late 1800s and early 1900s.

Karl Marx was Jewish. So were Leon Trotsky and many other leading Bolsheviks. But most Jews in Russia fared poorly under communism, often being punished for their heritage and for being linked to the good Jewish Bolsheviks who tried not to be Jews. Even the Jewish leadership in the Communist Party eventually was thinned dramatically. History reveals that Stalin was a harsh repressor of the Jews, as was Khrushchev, while Brezhnev allowed more than 250,000 Jews to leave from the early 1970s to the early 1980s.

From one to two million Jews — depending on what definition was used and on the number that considered themselves Jews — remained in the Soviet Union in 1990. Those were the people whom Israel wanted to bring home, to rescue, and to add weight to the Jewish state while expanding it further into the occupied Palestinian territories.

While the fear of anti–Semitism was great in 1990, actual incidents of violence were few and those were almost all of an individual rather than a mass nature. Uncertainty was the great prod. When the emigration door did open after having been officially closed since 1979, the anti–Semitism of old proved an ironic obstacle to Jews attempting to leave. During the long Communist era, many Jews sometimes changed their names simply to survive. During slightly better times, Jews changed their names to Russianize their identities, making it easier to enter universities or find better jobs. As a result, their identity papers showed no Jewish connections. When the exit door opened, those people had a hard time walking through it because they had no Jewish identity and it was difficult to have their Jewish names reinstated officially. But the Jews who had plodded on for 70 years without changing their names had a much easier time emigrating. Anger within the Jewish communities thus shifted from those who hadn't changed their names to those who had.

Most of the Jews I met were in reality Russians first. Russia had become their nation and nationality, their tribe and, in a way, their religion. But they were willing to dig for their Jewish roots, for their historic religion, tribal language and traditions, especially if that would banish fear and uncertainty. They had no problem leaving one tribe for their original one in search of a better life and the prospect that their dormant blood lines and traditions would be reborn.

As communism lay dying, no one really knew how many of the hundreds of thousands of Soviet Jews were bona fide members of the tribe that had come to claim them. It was also impossible to know how many had continued to practice Judaism to any degree, but the figure was probably minuscule due to the imposed atheism of communism and despite the efforts by some Jews to practice Judaism in secret. Israel promoted urgent efforts to teach Hebrew and Judaism to Soviet Jews in 1990. From what I observed, those classes were effective, but they reached a small percentage of their intended targets.

For many years the story of Soviet Jews trying to leave was the story of the so-called Refuseniks who were barred from emigrating on the grounds that they possessed state secrets. Perhaps 450 Refuseniks were still in the

Soviet Union in 1990. Fifteen of them had been denied permission to leave since 1978, when the door was first shut to them. When Gorbachev opened the way to wider emigration, many Refuseniks felt they were shoved into the background. The restrictive Soviet emigration law was being debated at this time; the objective was to reform the law to ease departures.

David Mikhalev was one of those fifteen Refuseniks who had been denied an exit visa since 1978. His is one story of old-time religious and ethnic tribalism magnified by the Cold War and the tribalism of nation-states. Depressed but not defeated, Mikhalev talked with me over cheese toasted on small slices of white bread, sliced cucumbers and small pieces of salami-like meat with white bread in a tiny restaurant in Moscow.

Mikhalev, who was 51 in 1990, said he had quit his job at the Central Science Research Institute of Communications in 1975. He had security clearance there. Three years later, in 1978, he applied for an exit visa to go to Israel, where a cousin and friends lived until they left later for Switzerland and then the United States. Israel was the only country where he could go at that time. Instead of receiving permission to leave, Mikhalev said, he was forced to take a salary cut, apparently for making his request. From the time he first applied to emigrate until we talked, Mikhalev said, he was punished for applying to leave. Every year since 1978, Mikhalev sought permission to leave and every year he was denied. "The government says I have state secrets, so they keep me in this country," he said. "That is their game with people. I certainly know I didn't know any secrets. Even if I knew something, 15 years have passed since I left that job. There would be no doubt those secrets had expired by now."

Mikhalev said his work concerned only the theory of wire communications. The ministry of communications used his mathematical calculations to test the reliability of some communication links, he said. "I didn't deal with any secret jobs, only with theory," Mikhalev said. "I published 30 scientific articles, some were translated in English, and all my results were published openly."

After he left his institute post in 1975, Mikhalev worked as a junior science researcher at another government institute dealing with food production. Once he sought permission to emigrate in 1978, Mikhalev said, the government for eight years tried to force him from his job at the food production institute. Finally, in 1986, he quit that job and found another, but only after "very, very great difficulty." That new job, he said, was "far below my professional level, but they pay me a salary that gives me an opportunity to make ends meet." Three months after he took that new, less demanding, job, Mikhalev said, the government tried to get him fired again. "They said I was not a real Soviet person because I had applied for emigration."

When we talked, Mikhalev was working at the Research Institute of Tin Food. "We have such a research institute but we don't have food," he said, laughing. Mikhalev and other Refuseniks established a committee in 1988 to monitor the Soviet emigration office. The government harassed him and the committee for six months before finally leaving him alone. Mikhalev was about to become the chairman of that committee when we shared our snack.

After his 8-year-old daughter became ill with a disease that impaired her growth, Mikhalev and his wife divorced. That allowed his daughter and the girl's mother to emigrate, under a different family name, to the United States where the girl received treatment that she could not obtain in the Soviet Union.

Daily during May of 1990, I met a great mix of Soviet citizens, saw their cities and observed their society, which was opening up as it was falling down. When the question of my own roots came up, most Russians thought that I was from a Turkish or Iranian tribe. If that was fine with them, it was fine with me. As for the Russian Jews, any questions along those lines stopped when they learned that I was based in Jerusalem.

Fledging Jewish societies were organizing to teach Hebrew. Synagogues were opening with help from Israelis seeking religious and political advantage with the reconverted back in Israel. Some Soviet Jews who did not pretend to be at all religious or Zionist were even trying to work peacefully with Palestinians concerning the possible effects of the massive immigration on Palestinians in the West Bank and Gaza Strip.

With the immigration of Soviet Jews, Israel was adding another wing to its own nation-state. To do so, Israel was forced to work from the ground up with about a million fellow tribesmen whose relationship to the tribe had become obscure during the Soviet era. That required teaching a new or forgotten language and reawakening dormant religious beliefs. The combined teaching of Hebrew and Judaism, of language and religion, each a major tribal element, would inject the new immigrants with a fresh ethnicity, a new culture, nationality, even a new religion, in a new nation-state. All together that meant an entirely new or restitched tribal identity.

When the immigrants reached Israel, the process of building a new identity would continue, as it does routinely with other immigrants there. An intense and lengthy course in Hebrew awaited most of the new immigrants. By osmosis the teaching of Hebrew in a greenhouse atmosphere included the teaching of Jewish culture and religion from which was expected to flow a new Jewish-Israeli identity. The older immigrants were, the more difficult it was for them to learn a new language and new ways in a vastly different culture, climate and country. So they would stick together. Many of the new immigrants wanted no part of religious beliefs and practices, Judaic or not, but that certainly didn't exclude them from learning Hebrew and becoming patriotic Israelis.

Two years later, in Uzbekistan, Tadjikistan, Georgia and Azerbaijan, as throughout most of the Central Asia and Caucasus regions, I witnessed the same conversion, or reconversion, process. The number of Jews in those lands was fewer than in Russia and in the old Soviet lands to the west. But the system was similar although the urgency may have been greater because of the fear of ethnic violence where local tribes were already fighting. Potential Israelis were offered tastes of Hebrew and Judaism in Central Asia and the Caucasus while flights were being organized to whisk them to Tel Aviv. Many of those lost tribesmen were pondering whether to seek comfort in their faded Jewishness, to head for America or to stick with the devils they knew.

<hr />

Most of the people I met were eager to talk openly. That alone represented an historic change in Soviet society. Many opportunities to learn about Soviet life unfolded in conversations and as I wandered the streets, met with a KGB officer in a Moscow park where we talked about Sunni and Shiite Muslims competing for power and influence in the emerging Central Asian republics, chatted with cautious, wary, throat-clearing diplomats, flagged taxis by waving Marlboro cigarettes and used the capital's prized subway system with millions of Muscovites.

Those tangential, sometimes incidental, opportunities to learn were in many cases the most unforgettable from a personal standpoint. Yet they cannot be separated from the work that I was doing. Journalism gave me the journey, as the ancient Greeks might have said. If I were not on assignment, I would never have been in the Soviet Union. I certainly would not have visited the Bolshoi, or one of the famous Russian circuses, enjoyed a live theater version of *The Odd Couple*, visited an amusement park where I watched people trying to avoid hitting each other, rather than slam each other, on the bumper cars, or wandered through a crowded flea market where the silence of the humans was so inaudible all I could hear were the leaves rustling.

On one glorious evening I attended a performance of *Giselle* at the Bolshoi. I sat at the end of an aisle, the center aisle, in the seventh row, so close to the stage I swear that I could see the colors of the dancers' eyes and I felt, granted a great deal of artistic license, as if I were dancing myself. After the performance I received an insider's tour of the wonderful building, one of those unmatched benefits of my job, but which is inseparable from the job itself. Most Soviet citizens had no opportunity to enjoy the Bolshoi. It was essentially there to impress foreigners and high-level Soviet officials, and by extension to inform those who couldn't enter that Soviet society remained culturally superior. My translator, who was teaching Hebrew to some of Moscow's Jews, obtained the tickets through her mother who worked at Aeroflot, the Soviet airline. I wished that I had dressed better for the occasion, but I was traveling rather rough because of the work I was doing. Again, I acted as if I belonged. If I didn't meet the dress code, no one seemed to notice. At the Bolshoi, I was not required to explain where I was from or what I was doing.

As difficult as it was to live in the Soviet Union, it was almost as difficult to leave. Invitations from Israelis to Soviet Jews were required before a person could apply for an exit visa. Each invitation was valid for one year. Aspiring emigrants complained at the time that invitations weren't coming fast enough. Yet receiving an Israeli invitation was the easy part. Considerable time was needed to obtain a Soviet exit visa because emigration offices were flooded and the bureaucracy required enough paperwork to pave a road to Tel Aviv. The best strategy was for a person to quit work at least six months before beginning the exit visa process. That would provide the time required to stand in line for long periods, day after day, to obtain all the necessary documents. This strategy was costly, too, and savings were necessary to live on while an emigre waited for an exit visa.

Once an exit visa was obtained, the bureaucratic path became slightly less cluttered and easier to negotiate. Naturally, the Israeli government was quick to grant immigrants entry visas. But Israeli-bound newcomers with several pieces of luggage were forced to deal with Soviet customs, which could get tangled as the costs rose. Direct flights to Israel weren't allowed then, so the Israelis paid for airplane tickets to third countries, such as Finland, Hungary, Poland and Romania. Israel paid the normal prices for the tickets and then charged passengers about $4 at the official exchange rates. Israel also paid the immigrants' fares from third countries to Tel Aviv. Sharp restrictions were placed on the amounts of money and personal possessions that emigrants could take with them, and fees were levied on each piece of luggage. As the value of the ruble was plunging and since rubles could not be taken out of the country, many emigrants used rubles to buy places from others closer to the front of the exit visa lines.

An exit visa cost about $34, which for most emigrants was a month's salary. A person who emigrated to Israel lost his Soviet citizenship and paid $83 for that privilege, or diminution. To leave required papers from employers saying that they had no claims on those departing. If a person was leaving close relatives or former spouses behind, the relatives or former spouses had to sign documents saying that they could survive alone. If an apartment was to be left behind empty, the apartment reverted to the state. If an emigrant's parents were dead, the dearly departing emigrant had to produce death certificates. One man said that he had no death certificates to prove that his mother and father had died. As evidence that his parents had died long ago, the man said, he brought in their bones. No one badgered him about DNA testing.

Outside the Central Synagogue in Moscow, Jews who had lost touch with their traditional religion, language, culture and ethnicity during the Communist era were searching for a path back into the tribal tent. Others gathered on Saturdays at the old synagogue, which was worn from disuse rather than overuse, in hopes of making a connection, any connection, that would lead them from the Soviet Union. Where they went didn't matter, so long as it was somewhere else. There to help them decide were religious and political leaders of an ultra–Orthodox sect from Israel, along with a member of the Likud Party's central committee who was an ally of then-Housing Minister Ariel Sharon.

Fears that the Soviet government might slam shut its exit doors rose in Hebrew classes and in Moscow's main synagogue when the prospective emigrants heard of then–Prime Minister Yitzhak Shamir's remark that a big Israel would be needed to welcome Soviet Jews to their new country. Shamir's comment was interpreted to mean that Israel just might take all or most of the Palestinian West Bank and Gaza Strip. Or that Israel would force the new immigrants to settle in those Palestinian territories that Israel occupied.

Talk like that raised the anxieties of Palestinians and aroused other Arabs. Shamir's words were also hostile to the Soviet Union's historic but fraying Middle East policy. But few in Israel, elsewhere in the Middle East or the United States cared any longer about the Soviet Union's Middle East policy because very soon there would be no Soviet Union and no policy. Gorbachev was forced to react. Soviet Jews should not be allowed to settle in the Palestinian West Bank or the Gaza Strip, he said. Gorbachev's public relations rhetoric, however, was meaningless. One very important reason that Israel wanted, without a whole lot of religious questions asked, all the Soviet immigrants it could get was to boost its population. Inevitably, that would force more Israelis, new immigrants or not, into the West Bank and maybe even Gaza, and no one could then foresee Israel surrendering Gaza. The political and religious competition in Israel for the souls and votes of the new immigrants would be stiff as well.

This wasn't just a story about a lost people returning to their tribe in another grand sweep of history. It was also a critical international political story. The Soviet Union, once a military superpower, soon would be gone. In its place would be Russia and the new nations that would replace the former Soviet republics. The opportunity for Israel to work with the Soviet government, which would essentially become the Russian government, in helping Jews to leave for Tel Aviv gave Israel an opportunity to forge new diplomatic and economic relations with Moscow and other emerging capitals in the region.

A couple of years later, I saw this policy in action first hand in the Caucasus and Central Asia. Israel was preparing and helping Jews to leave Uzbekistan, Tadjikistan, Azerbaijan and Georgia. This grand opportunity allowed the Israeli government to play another of its Muslim cards, to send its eyes and ears to alien soil, to build commercial, scientific, agricultural and other links with the nominally Muslim countries, in another attempt to undermine Muslim solidarity with the Palestinians and Arab states in the Middle East.

—∞∞—

About 200 people attended services in Moscow's Central Synagogue on a Saturday night in mid–May 1990. They were a confused lot. All were searching, some for religion, others weary of living in the diaspora and eager to return to the relative safety of the tribe in Israel. Some yearned to live in the United States or any other friendly shore. Still others were desperate to find a reason to stay where they were.

Without direction from an ultra–Orthodox rabbi from Israel, it appeared that the service could have been conducted by a Mormon and no one would have known the difference or it could have evolved into just a social gathering. Men and women were separated in the ultra–Orthodox service. The women were told to sit in the balcony, separate from the men on the main floor. But the women never caught on, or refused to. They moved constantly down to the main floor and just as constantly were told to return to the balcony where, the men told them, they belonged. Religious orthodoxy, wherever you find it, dominates with rules written by men, which usually mean that women are to be kept in their place.

A young woman, a dentist, illustrated the confusion and the searching that filled the synagogue that Saturday night. Galina was alone. Her entire family was dead. She had no friends in Israel or the United States, and she feared a rise in anti–Semitism at home. Galina wanted to stay in Moscow because she had friends there. But still she went to the synagogue "once in a while." She was trying to figure it all out, to determine where her lost religion might fit into her life and whether leaving would help her do so. "Do you know your religion?" I asked her. "Fifty-fifty," she answered, which I took to mean that the tribe was calling but the sound was still faint.

—∞∞—

After the food fight and final truce at the Intourist hotel in L'vov, I concluded that I might slowly waste away and evolve into a shadow before I succeeded in finding a family of Soviet Jews ready to head for Israel by car. Still, my search was otherwise rich in stories, knowledge and memories. When I waved goodbye to the waiter in L'vov, I knew that I was saying goodbye to the Soviet Union, at least for the moment. The next time I visited Moscow, I was in the ethnic-state of Russia. When I flew to Tashkent, Baku and Tbilisi and drove to Leninabad in Tadjikistan, I entered new nation-states of old tribes, not Soviet republics won by conquest.

Rather than fly from L'vov to Budapest, I decided to sit for an overnight lesson in contemporary Eastern European social affairs. The night train to Budapest took thirteen hours. We arrived about 5 A.M. Budapest time. I slept little, trying to absorb as much about the people and places as I could. Most of the passengers, lacking similar curiosity, insisted on a pillow. What conversations I had were unworthy of note, although that detracts little from the experience. Darkness fell somewhere in Transylvania, an interesting moment when you think about it.

I talked with a Soviet hockey player who had played in the United States, although not in the National Hockey League. Friendly enough, he wore the craggy face of a hockey tough guy, the kind of player you wanted to avoid knocking jaws with fighting for the puck in the corners. Nina, a large jovial Russian telephone operator from way to the east of Moscow, was heading for a vacation in Italy. Here was proof that sometimes the more things change, the more they do change. Feeling certain that she would not see Siberia again, I thought of the musical refrain: How you going to keep her out in the permafrost after she's seen Pisa? The status of Berndt, an East German physicist, forced him to hold most of the passengers in contempt, especially the lowly Russians and Ukrainians around him. An old woman was in the compartment with me. She angled her head slightly sideways and gazed at me, puzzled and unspeaking, seeming to understand nothing except for the need to sleep. Her blank face told me that she had a better chance of figuring things out in the morning.

Traveling across Asia and Europe, there is a feeling that the people, the landscape, the sky, the cities, even life itself become lighter as one moves west. Relativity is never to be totally ignored. So it seemed on this trip. Budapest was a new horizon. I knew nothing about the hotels there, except that I had heard or read an ad for the Budapest Hilton. In the ad, a weary traveler hails a taxi in Budapest and says, "Take me to the Hilton." Such tips should never be forgotten.

Tired and still in my Soviet state of perpetual hunger when I arrived at the train station in Budapest, I hailed a cab in the hazy dawn and, smiling to

myself as I remembered the advertisement, told the driver with great deci-
siveness, "Take me to the Hilton." Hilton was the only Hungarian word that
I knew then and I was sure that the taxi driver would get the idea.

For two days I did nothing but eat and eat again, and watch the French
Open tennis tournament on the television in my room. During a break from
the dining trolley, I took the elevator to the lobby. Instead of going down,
however, the elevator first went up, to the casino, where a young woman
boarded and said, panting and as if she were trying to stay on a personal
schedule: "Sex. You like sex?" Her abruptness made me laugh. I motioned
for her to step back and said, "Let me look at you," which was my idea of a
joke. I think she understood my words, if not their full meaning, because she
stepped back. With a shake of my head I told her to move on, thinking at
the same time that Hungary could do better, much better. Disgusted, she
moved on.

After almost a month in the Soviet Union, and revived by two days in
Budapest, my hunger pains had eased. I flew to Tel Aviv on a plane filled with
Soviet emigrants who thought they were ready to become Jews again and
maybe Israelis. The trip was much shorter and easier than driving would have
been, but nowhere near as instructive or as much fun.

SEVEN

Riding the Rails
and Crossing Borders

A few dozen cheeseburgers, standing at attention like squat soldiers in tan uniforms, were lined up for the Americans. The exercise was more than lunch; it was a cultural statement made by families of different tribes on opposite sides of the Atlantic.

Before the tunnel under the English Channel was opened to the public in 1994, the press and other media were invited to ride on a special trial run of the Chunnel train. Based in London at the time, I drove my rental car aboard the train on the English side. When the train reached France, I drove straight down the left-hand side of the road as if I were still in England. About a mile later I realized my mistake and got things right before a collision woke me.

My first stop in France was at the terminal where passengers who crossed the Channel on a Hovercraft disembarked. Would those passengers later abandon the Hovercraft for the train under the Channel, I wondered? I decided to find out. The first group of passengers who walked off the Hovercraft happened to be a tour group from Mississippi. The cheeseburgers were for them, I was told by the French workers at the terminal, because experience said that Americans would always ask for cheeseburgers over a croissant or fois gras.

At home or abroad, Americans will always reach for a cheeseburger. That ethnic food is an element in their culinary blood. As much as most French detest ketchup as a vegetable, which Ronald Reagan once proclaimed that it was, most Americans love it with their cheeseburgers.

While the French chefs smoothed the culinary and cultural transition for their visitors, cheeseburgers, French fries and ketchup could not bridge the monetary gap. You mean a franc is different from a dollar? How many francs in a dollar, or dollars in a franc? At the time, five francs equaled one dollar. I explained to the visitors that ten francs equalled $2, that 25 francs made $5, and I wrote out several cheat sheets showing the exchange up to 100 francs, or $20. Even with the cheat sheet, the visiting Americans couldn't grasp the idea of a monetary exchange. At

141

home, as many Americans abroad like to point out, there are no exchange rates. I wrote out a few more cheat sheets and vanished. Frankly, I thought, since Americans like to believe in the survival of the fittest, here was a chance to see whether they really meant it.

His face blank from the dull routine and the desert's draining heat, the uniformed Jordanian flipped through the familiar passports. The train travelers were from many tribes in the region. Some, bedraggled and hauling what looked like a lifetime of personal possessions, were fleeing the fighting in Lebanon. Others were ordinary workers and families moving back and forth between Syria and Jordan, wanting more, better or simply different. Slow, steady migration by people seeking work, peace or simply to visit relatives is greater in the region than generally recognized.

One passenger caught the Jordanian's eye because the stranger's blue passport set the American newspaper correspondent apart. But we all seemed content in our own skin, happier still to learn that there would be no raids or other extracurricular activities in the middle of the desert where the Jordanians and Syrians agreed to share a border.

The story this time was not about a current tribal conflict, although tribalism, past and present, rode the train. This time the story was about romance in the form of anachronistic wood railroad cars ambling along on a narrow gauge track and a view of history being revived for a few final toots before the sounds might be swallowed forever by wider tracks and narrower understanding.

With 47 other passengers, I was in Al-Mafraq, Jordan, about 80 miles south of Damascus creeping toward Amman. All we were missing was Lawrence of Arabia, his bedouin allies and their targets, the Turks, for this was the Hejaz Railway still chugging straight out of that era, the early 1900s.

It was February 1, 1990, and the Hejaz train was making one leg of its weekly trip between the two capitals, a service that had resumed the previous September after almost a decade on a side track. I boarded the train at the romantic old stone station in Damascus to ride with history, not to reach Amman in record time or to enjoy a real Middle Eastern version of what others might call Disney World.

With lengthy pit stops along the way and speeds so slow they would embarrass its cousins elsewhere, the Hejaz train took nearly 10 hours to travel 137 miles before it reached the kids who laid coins to be flattened on the tracks in Amman. Our rust-red rambling wreck averaged about 14 miles per hour. More than once I have made that same trip by car in a little more than three hours.

No longer the new and speedy ship of the desert that it was decades earlier, the train looked as old as its years. The wood side panels of the cars separated and slid laterally but not gracefully with the motion of the train. As I watched the train roll into the station in Damascus, it appeared that the side panels of the carriages were of two minds; some of the panels moved forward while others shifted backwards propelled by no visible auto power. As if by magic, or maybe from decades of practice, the panels came together again periodically in a rhythm that pleased the cars, the engineer and the passengers.

Pulled by its yellow and green diesel engine, the train strained to leave Damascus on the narrow tracks that skirted sand dunes and settled temporarily next to towns where some passengers left, others boarded and the remaining stepped away briefly to purchase food and goods at the local souks, or outdoor markets.

Holes in the wood floors appeared slightly unconventional to me, but I was a Hejaz novice. Without the holes, I would have been unable to see the desert sand and tell that the train was still on the tracks as we rolled slowly across the silky looking Jordanian desert with its grainy waves of sand, far different from the basalt rock-and lava-bed desert that links Jordan and Iraq. Heat shimmered off the sand, which was almost as blinding as the direct desert sun itself. The sky flashed its own brightness, a blue so deep and high that Middle Easterners like to believe it goes all the way to heaven, their tribes' heaven, of course.

The train lacked, among other amenities, usable facilities, not that I expected flush toilets. But nature does call, even on antiquated trains sneaking through the desert like a cog railway. After crossing my legs as long as I could without attracting undue attention, I walked to the rear of the train. Here was a real caboose. It was empty. No one was hanging out smoking Marlboros on the deck. Surely, I thought, no one would be strolling in the sand dunes and the mid-day heat. The decision was not difficult: Ease the pain and hope that no one, especially a woman, veiled or unveiled, wandered into the caboose. If a woman had come by, I probably would have leaped into the sand to avoid being arrested and declared an infidel.

After we curved around a large sand dune, I spotted a cluster of men trudging along, bedouins, I presumed, although they had no camels or other animals in tow and there was no camp in sight. The odds of bedouins catching me urinating in the desert from the caboose of a train made of wood that was almost 100 years old and snaking along on narrow gauge tracks were mighty slim, I thought. But I didn't beat the odds. The bedouins had seen it all before, I suspected, and if there was any hooting and hollering, the dunes and the engine drowned them out. One of the highlights of the trip was that no one entered the caboose as I waved to the bedouins.

When we reached the Jordanian side of the desert border, the engineer stopped the train. The expressionless Jordanian official, who had a wrestler's build under a thick mustache, began checking the passports for Jordanian visas, and any irregularities.

My blue passport stood out among the stack of the mostly red documents the officer held. At least the officer wouldn't have to ask, "Where you from?" In my case, the officer probably checked for stamps from countries the Jordanians didn't favor at the time, such as Israel, or a birthplace he might sniff at or question. My passport was "clean" of visas and proper nouns deemed undesirable, so I was relaxed.

After a stop long enough for me to begin counting pebbles in the desert, the officer handed the passports back, one by one, by calling out the names. Mine he saved for last, and he went by the book. "The American? Where's the American?" he asked, holding up my passport, almost as if he were announcing the winner of a prize fight or a lottery. To the Jordanian that was my name, my tribe; The American. There was no more to say, nothing to understand. All eyes turned my way. For a brief mischievious moment I thought about clasping my hands, raising them above my head and bowing to the passengers. But I restrained myself, smiled and nodded, acting normally rather than like a foreign tribesman who now might become an easy target for someone who objected to a stranger in their midst. Still smiling I walked toward the officer who returned my passport. "Thank you," I said, in Arabic. "You're welcome," he answered in kind, and we resumed our tedious journey to Amman.

<hr />

Engineered by Germans, the Hejaz Railway was built by the ruling Ottoman Turks, with contributions from elites in Egypt and Iran, in the early 1900s. No minor engineering feat at the time, the desert track was designed to transport Muslim pilgrims from Damascus almost a thousand miles away to Islam's holiest city of Mecca in Saudi Arabia, to promote trade in the region and to bridle the rebellious Arab tribes along the way. A trip by camel caravan took two months and cost about $80; the train back then took four days and cost about $7.

Hejaz comes from the name of the region in Saudi Arabia through which the railroad passed. When the railway opened in 1908, it reached Medina in Saudi Arabia, but never went farther. During World War I, T. E. Lawrence led the Arab rebellion against Ottoman Turkish rule and the Hejaz trains were often its targets.

At its peak at the start of World War I in 1914, the railway ferried about 300,000 people annually. Many of those were Turkish troops being positioned for battle. Most of the rest were Muslim pilgrims making the annual Hajj to Mecca, which was the main reason the railroad was built. After the tracks were damaged during World War I and the Ottoman Empire fell off the map following the war, the desert sand took command and the train stopped running in Saudi Arabia. It did, however, continue to operate periodically in Jordan and Syria.

Seven of the Belgian-built wood Hejaz cars, four of them for passengers, wiggled behind the diesel engine when the train pulled out of the sturdy Damascus station. From a distance the train looked like a charming toy. Up close it looked more like a red relic than a charm. The rust-colored passenger cars wore rounded roofs, their painted wood faded badly, the metal chipped and corroded.

I bought a first-class ticket, which was first class in name only, although all is relative even on old trains. A one-way ticket cost $4.25. A second-class one-way ticket cost $2.50. Most of the passengers were in second class, although we all had equal rights to the same toilet facilities.

Two passengers and the conductor sat with me in a compartment that had two long high-backed leather bench seats large enough to hold a total of six passengers, although snugly. One of my compartment mates was a middle-aged Lebanese woman fed up with the chaos in her homeland. Carrying large vases she had bought in Damascus, the woman was heading for her new home in Amman.

Across the narrow aisle in another compartment a man began to eat breakfast. He knew the drill; we were embarking on a long day's journey to travel a relatively short distance and he had enough food for a week in case the train broke down amidst the camels and dunes.

The leather in our seats was badly cracked. The windows were frozen in lock positions; they rattled in frames that danced drunkenly as the train wobbled, making at least one passenger thankful that the desert meant sun and not rain. Cardboard, craggy pieces of concrete and sometimes just open air filled the space between the windows and the window frames. The wood walls of the cars served as ash trays, decorated as they were by countless burn marks from cigarettes extinguished there for almost 100 years.

I considered the journey a major success when the windows were still in place as we slowed to a halt in Amman. Warped and cracked now, the wood and metal inside the train were in top shape decades ago. Remember, it was history and the romance of the railroad that mattered here, not convenience or luxury. And, if it were still possible, I would retrace my steps as quickly as I can say Hejaz.

Because of the uneven narrow gauge track, the train rocked up and down and rolled from side to side, creating the sensation that passengers were being mixed in a blender set on low. Still, the 137-mile trip was worth the money, which isn't saying much because of the low fare, and the time, which is saying a lot. Passengers who carried house and home on their backs had much more reason to complain, and they didn't. For them the price was right.

Raucous young men seeking no-frills, no-charge transportation in the city jumped aboard the outside of the train as it ached through Damascus and into the low hills southbound. Most of the land between Damascus and Dera'a, the last stop in Syria, was green, the soil loam-like with a fertility that spelled breadbasket although trees were sparse. Wood poles lay rotting along one section of track, waiting in vain for wires to bring them to life. Black basalt stones, the remnants of ancient volcanoes, littered the earth around Dera'a near where olive trees stood watch over a farmer seeding his field by hand. This was not a scene from a high-speed train in Japan or Germany.

We stopped for an hour next to the souk in Dera'a on the Syrian side of the border before we reached the desert. Many passengers left to buy food at the souk. So did I. One man rushed to make a call on a phone that he had to crank before using. The mud was sloppy and deep. The day's fresh air was filled with the sharp, enticing odors of grilled lamb, onion and tomato kabobs, their juices popping, singing and beckoning on small open pits, waiting to be plopped, dripping juices and all, into warm absorbent Arabic bread.

As I salivated, zephyrs suffocated the souk with the odor of yesterday's dead vegetables, drying up my saliva and sucking away my appetite. Fearing that the mud might pluck the shoes off my feet, I gave up the food quest, choosing shoes and dry ankles over a satisfied stomach and contented psyche. I returned to the train ahead of most of the other passengers who knew the routine, the length of the stopover and the length of the trip.

As others began to pile back into the train, one of my cabin mates, a well-dressed man in his thirties, brought me a hard-boiled egg sandwich in thick, fresh Arabic bread that reminded me of the kind one of my uncles used to deliver to our house every Saturday morning when I was a kid back in Woonsocket and Millville. The man wasn't giving me his own sandwich; he had bought the sandwich and a bottle of water especially for me, a sign of friendship and hospitality. He smiled as he said that I might enjoy something to eat because Amman was farther away in time, if not miles, than perhaps I thought. It was easy to smile back, say thanks, and be especially grateful by the time we reached Amman, very hungry, many hours later.

The stranger with the egg sandwich reminded me of being at the Ayatollah Khomeini's funeral in Iran in June 1989. That difficult time was leavened by talks with individual Iranians who were for a few moments free of and at the same time trapped in their tribal circle.

During the funeral service for Khomeini, before his body was taken for burial in a cemetery compound outside Tehran, I left the safety of a fenced enclosure with two Norwegian journalists to talk with mourners in the crowd. A few of the mourners spoke English and we had a sane discussion about Khomeini and the United States and the future of Iran. Hundreds of people stood by, listening.

It was all very normal, until the crowd around us grew into the thousands, beyond measure really, and the chants went up: "Death to America! Death to America!" People in the crowd began hissing and spitting and beating their chests, including those with whom we were having a civil conversation a few moments earlier. As the numbers and the volume increased, one of the Norwegians turned and said, "I think we better get out of here." "But don't run," I answered. So we backed up, slowly at first, then more quickly, until we reached a small hill which momentarily put a little distance between us and the crowd. At that moment, we turned and walked briskly away and the crowd lost interest in such small prey.

On the last day of that trip to Tehran, I ran out of money. Most of my cash I dumped at the Istiqlal Hotel (the pre–Islamic revolution Hilton) filing stories on an old teletype machine that needed oil and new keys. To file one story of modest length cost $1,000 or more. I left the hotel for the airport about midnight with just enough money for the taxi fare. I arrived at the almost empty airport about 1 A.M., five hours before the scheduled departure. Except for a few workers, only an Iranian doctor who was headed to a medical conference in Los Angeles was in the terminal. The doctor and I talked easily for a couple of hours, until other passengers began drifting in. Then, without saying a word, the doctor said goodbye by simply leaving, as if forever.

Although the doctor and I loitered in the terminal for another couple of hours, our eyes never met again. He couldn't afford to be seen talking with someone from a foreign tribe, especially an American and a journalist, while he was on his way to America. The pressures of the tribal mass, the crowd, would not permit that, and I understood. That was a lesson that I never forgot; always try to separate individuals from the crowd and don't read the crowd as representing all individuals in the group.

These kinds of incidents reveal individual reactions to tribal pressures. Such behavior is universal, not peculiarly Iranian or Middle Eastern. It occurs when individuals feel they must follow powerful tribal engines in any form in order to thrive or simply survive.

Inside Jordan the desert opens up and swallows the land in great chunks. A couple of stone outposts, probably military, greeted us on one side of the tracks. On the other, a stove pipe rose incongruously through the entrance of a bedouin's goat-skin tent. Shepherds, animals, tents and trucks mingled in an odd mixture of old and newer.

As the desert vista spread before us, the train pulled to a dead stop. Large rocks had to be cleared from the tracks. Silently, I was hoping for a bedouin raid, a routine one, nothing too violent and with or without Lawrence, but all I got were rocks.

Stubbles of green were also sprinkled across the tawny sand that is piled occasionally into natural pyramids like some kind of alien formation that could be better interpreted from the air. In some places the distant dunes looked like snowdrifts in the aftermath of a New England blizzard. The train created excitement whether we passed sheep, goats or a bedouin encampment. Old and relatively slow though it was, I figured the train must look like a red comet flashing through the desert, noisy, frightening, foreign. Kids blocked their ears and animals dashed away. Adults just stared as we rolled through the great desert and into Amman, a manufactured capital of colonialism.

Whatever their tribes, the passengers knew that the trip from Damascus to Amman was greater than the miles or hours involved.

Damascus is everything a foreign tribesman would expect in a quintessential Oriental city. The products of traditional arts and crafts, such as gold jewelry, lace, linen, intricately carved lemonwood furniture inlaid with mother of pearl, and Damascene steel are all widely available in the city's busy shops and souks.

With the dawning of each business day, shopkeepers aggressively seek to please Allah and enhance their good fortune with their first sale, usually a bargain at any price.

Shopkeepers in the large Hamiddiyeh Souk, an elongated Oriental version of a shopping mall, can spot members of foreign tribes when they arrive in the country, or so it seems. The style, cut and color of clothes and the manner of stride give visitors away instantly. "Mister, come in. You don't have to buy anything, just look. Sit, have coffee, tea, sweet drink. Just look," shopkeepers say, one after another in an endless stream. But most visitors can't just look. Enter a large shop, have coffee, tea or sweet drink, and you will stay for hours, hooked, looking like an overburdened donkey when you leave.

Syria was a regime tightly held at the time by the now deceased Hafez al-Assad and his minority Alawite tribe. More pictures of Hafez al-Assad decorated Damascus' public places and private homes than there were shops or homes in the city, or so it seemed. After Hafez al-Assad's death, power passed to his son, Bashar. (Even in death, the number of pictures of Hafez al-Assad on public display seems undiminished, although his photos have been joined by his son's.)

Traffic in Damascus whirred in a wild and noisy Middle Eastern way around restaurants where scents and spices pulled a visitor in all directions. But Damascus is a hospital zone compared with Cairo, for example, which is many times larger and as untamed as the upper reaches of the Nile.

The first time I visited Damascus, I thought that I had been thrown into a time machine and driven back four or five decades. A 1949 Studebaker and a 1952 DeSoto greeted me, followed by a '51 Pontiac and a '53 Ford, some in excellent condition, some not; some serving as taxis, others restored and looking like a million dollars.

A bill outside a movie theater advertised the 1956 movie *The Conqueror*, starring John Wayne and Susan Hayward. In many respects being in Damascus then was like stepping into a time warp. In other respects, Damascus existed in its own time, a slowly changing exotic world in which new seeps into old, not old into new. But Damascus isn't a movie set. One of the oldest, maybe the oldest, continuously inhabited places in the world, it is real in every way, including its paradoxes.

Much smaller than Damascus, Amman is wrapped eerily and almost unnaturally in British-style rectitude. Uniformed police keep cars moving quietly in Amman, challenging and thwarting the regional propensity to honk, shout and dash with the order brought by Britain during its post–World War I mandate period and later embraced by Jordan's Hashemite rulers, notably the late King Hussein.

Jordan's Saudi-rooted monarchy is propped up by loyal bedouin tribes that control the military. Damascus remains a frontline Arab state in opposition to Israel, while Jordan, with more than 65 percent of its population rooted in Palestine, now has a peace treaty with Israel.

For all the noise in the souks and streets of Damascus, most Syrians are wary and quiet when it comes to talking politics. They know the rules and they know the size of the ring in which they can play the game before the hovering referee steps in. As long as they do business and don't play at politics, Syrians can make all the noise they want on the street.

Conditions are almost the reverse in Jordan. For all the observant quiet on Amman's streets, the ring within which Jordanians can operate politically without bringing a knock on the door is larger than that in Syria, but it is not boundless. In the minds of the Western tribes, Syria and Jordan are the same because both are Arabic countries. Aren't all Arabs and all Arabic countries the same? The various Syrian and Jordanian tribes do speak the same

Levantine dialect of Arabic and share a common culture. But tribal origins differ in each country, and the number of religious sects, even among Muslims, is more varied in Syria than in Jordan.

⤜⧟⤛

Our old train curved and creeped through the outskirts of Amman and slipped into a tiny corner of the romantic era of rail travel. As we passed through neighborhoods, children scurried back to the tracks behind us. They picked up coins from where they had placed them to see how flattened the metal had become.

Despite differences in tribe and style, tradition and modernism, a universality exists among humans everywhere. Across the globe, people in similar circumstances repeat similar behavior that they have learned on their own. Certain principles that form the basis of human behavior are understood and upheld from tribe to tribe. Everywhere, people ask only for respect and, where cultural differences exist, that their traditions be honored.

Going to the Dogs in Bulgaria

University students were shouting in the streets, packs of starving dogs — howling, fighting and looking for a meal, any meal — roamed downtown Sofia, and the national economy was diving deeper than a buried artifact of the long Ottoman occupation when I landed in Bulgaria in early February 1997. Here was one of the former Communist tribes now on the other side of the nation-state divide and life wasn't going so well.

My first mission was to report on Bulgaria's economic collapse. Later, I was to find a way to reach Belgrade, Yugoslavia, where massive daily street demonstrations were threatening the regime of then-leader and now dead Slobodan Milosevic, the Serb nationalist who more than anyone else helped to trigger the Serb-Orthodox/Croat-Catholic/Bosnian-Muslim tribal wars in Bosnia.

Following my instincts and a trail greased by a little cash, the second assignment took me on a smugglers' train straight into the heart of Belgrade carrying a visa that I couldn't get anywhere else — not in London, Washington or Paris. Only in Sofia.

A fascinating country that seems to have more Roman than Ottoman ruins, Bulgaria was on its economic knees and on the brink of social chaos. Neither the best aspects of free enterprise nor the best instincts of Bulgaria's political and economic leaders flowered in the tumultuous years after communism's collapse.

The British Foreign Office in London warned travelers of strikes, demonstrations, a breakdown of public transportation, robberies, car thefts, drugged food, and shootings and explosions involving rival gangs in Bulgaria. Otherwise, Bulgaria was a welcoming place for tourists. I thought that the warning was a bit exaggerated, but I always think that way about warnings until I see for myself.

Conditions were so bad, Bulgarian officials said, that the Albanian equivalent of the Red Cross had sent Bulgaria $3,000 in humanitarian aid. That's something like Rwanda sending Somalia food aid. Albania was, or had been until Bulgaria's collapse, the poorest country in Europe.

Bulgaria's free-fall was so rapid and penetrating that the local currency, the lev, declined in value by the hour. As soon as they received their pay, workers lined up to convert levs to American dollars or German marks, or bought whatever consumer item they needed or could afford. If they didn't spend or convert their levs, the money evaporated in their pockets. Bulgaria is the only place I ever worked where the cost of lunch during the first two weeks of February 1997 would have bought outright a three-room apartment a few years earlier during the dying days of the Communist era. Of course, I have reported from many other countries where there was no breakfast, lunch or dinner at any price.

The lunch tab for me and my translator at a beautiful hotel that was a restored palace totaled a little more than $30, including the tip. We ate fish and salad, nice but nothing special except for the atmosphere. When the waiter brought the bill he laughed at the absurdity of life as he knew it. For that same amount of money, when values were different, the waiter said, he bought his three-room Sofia apartment in 1988.

Night after night I ate completely alone in a wonderful restaurant behind Bulgaria's parliament building. The restaurant was empty because no one could afford to eat there, although a terrific meal of salad, soup, meat or fish cost less than $10. The only other place where I had eaten so alone for days at a time was at a restored caravanseri in Diyarbakir in southeastern Turkey. That was during the Islamic holy month of Ramadan in March 1992, when I was the old hotel's only guest while I tried to hitch a ride to Iraq.

Around Valentine's Day in 1997, American fast-food restaurants were sprinkled throughout Sofia's new democracy and stumbling free-market economy. A hamburger at McDonald's was priced at less than 7 cents, and a Coke cost 16 cents. A small vegetarian pizza at Pizza Hut cost about 77 cents, a large pizza cost slightly more than $2 and a Pepsi was less than 15 cents. One American dollar bought a chicken sandwich from the smiling Kentucky colonel.

Despite the prices, customers were few. No wonder. Bulgarians on the average earned $15 a month, and state pensions had just been doubled to $6 a month.

"Despair, hunger, misery," is how Kamen, then 21 and a student leader, described conditions as he plotted demonstrations to come. A finance and economics professor at the University of National Economics in Sofia said that Bulgaria hadn't been mired in an economic crisis of this scope since it was freed of the Turkish occupation in 1878. That period included the long, dismal Communist era. Behind it all, the professor said, was official corruption that bilked the country of billions of dollars and failure to reform the economy or the banking system. The result: huge foreign and domestic debts, the devaluation of the lev, and inflation.

The wave of economic decline also swept over the city of Plovdiv, where a central feature is a Roman colisseum in such excellent condition that one can almost hear the roar of ancient audiences. On the streets of Plovdiv I bought small hand-painted pictures of local scenes from old ladies for $1 each. And I overpaid. The women shook my hand and kissed it. I might as well have been doling out money for the World Bank so happy were the people to see an American dollar.

Most Bulgarians were in the same predicament: Their money was almost useless and the cost of goods was rising higher than the sounds of hungry hounds howling in the night, of which I was told to beware.

Back in Sofia, I was walking at midnight from downtown to my hotel near the parliament building when a large pack of famished dogs raced slobbering and fighting on an intersecting street about a quarter mile from where I stood. If they got a whiff of me, I thought, I'm an appetizer for the pack. As I ran toward the hotel, I began looking for walls, trees, cars or trucks to climb in case the dogs, not toy poodles, came my way. The dogs must have been too far away to pick up my scent because they headed through the intersection and never turned in my direction. I jogged double time back to the hotel, where I decided that the Bulgarian picture was clear enough and it was time to find my way to Belgrade.

A Mini-Strip Show with Cheese and Olives

My translator tipped me to a travel agent who knew a sub rosa route to a Yugoslav visa. Sure enough, $100 did the trick. At the appointed time, I picked up the visa at the Yugoslav embassy in Sofia. Soon after, I laid out $25 for a first-class, one-way ticket to Belgrade on the Balkan Express, without Agatha Christie but not without mystery and a little adventure.

Before boarding I stopped at a small shop where for a few pennies I bought dense wheat bread, bottled water, cheese and packaged ham-like meat. I was sure that the dining car wouldn't make the trip. We were an hour late pulling out of Sofia at midday, which was close enough to our scheduled departure time to call it early.

A weird combination of pealing thunder and snow signaled our departure. Eastern European trains bring to mind those grainy pre–World War II films that show peasants in long, heavy black coats dragging all their possessions and lining up in deepening snow to board coal-black trains. Those trains puffed mighty clouds of thick black smoke into a bleak sky that looked as if it sat ominously two feet above the engine before the train chugged slowly from a dilapidated depot.

The roof of my Balkan Express car leaked, the train lumbered like a worn out mule about to balk, the floors were covered with decades of dirt and there was no heat for most of the trip. Dirty white cloth decorated the headrests on stained red velour seats, hardened spittle stained the windows and obscured the view, many passengers carried much more than boxed lunches, and everybody was rushing and pushing to find a seat. But there were functioning toilets, and I didn't have to search for the caboose. Maybe that's the reason I can say that the Balkan Express was near-perfect.

A few minutes after I found my "first-class" compartment, three women joined me. After they laid out their white bread, water, olives, cheese, some kielbasa-like meat that was still pumping blood and, critically, a knife to cut the cheese and the dying meat, the women removed their heavy coats and started to take off their clothes.

This was a novelty. These weren't the Gabor sisters, I'll admit, but they weren't Grandma Moses either. I became defensive immediately, in my own mind, of course. This is my compartment, and I'm staying no matter how much clothing they remove, I said to myself, as I checked my ticket. I was in the right place. It's fine with me if they stay, I thought, but I'm not moving. Later, after they told me that they paid less than $7 for their tickets, I realized they simply popped into the compartment because I was alone and they could have privacy, more or less.

After they stripped down to light short-sleeved shirts, the women broke open the huge overstuffed bags they were carrying, took out one long blue knit jersey after another and began putting them on, layer after layer, before they donned their heavy coats again. They might as well have been traveling in disguise. As there was no heat in the train and it was winter, all those clothes were warming additions. The husband of one of the women joined them, and he repeated the process, first removing his winter coat, then removing a shirt before he piled on a half-dozen men's shirts under his heavy coat.

My traveling companions were smuggling the garments into Yugoslavia,

Serbia really, as Yugoslavia had been pared to Serbia and Montenegro. They were wholesalers, although for a moment I thought I was in the basement of a discount store before the goods were put on shelves. Smuggling is as old as trade itself. This wasn't the first or last time clothing and other goods have been smuggled on the Balkan Express.

One of the women wore five long blue knit jerseys under two sweaters before she strapped on her coat. She rolled the long jerseys around her waist so that she became A-shaped. One of the other women stuffed ten extra outfits under her coat. The third woman rolled up several shirts and stuffed them under a half dozen jerseys and up her back. Her partners helped to flatten out the shirts by punching them after the woman arranged them comfortably. By the time they finished hiding the clothes, the women looked like too-short linebackers for a semi-pro American football team.

The smugglers giggled a lot behind our closed compartment door as the Balkan Express lumbered along at 25 miles per hour, past forests, jagged mountains and barren trees toward the Bulgarian-Yugoslav border.

At the Kalotina border post on the Bulgarian side, a notorious passageway on the Balkans drug trafficking route from Turkey, the women sailed through without a second look. The problem, if there was one, would come on the Yugoslav side, at Dimitrovgrad.

Yugoslav Serb customs officers, including some women, went through the train, checking passports, looking grim but not acting tough. It was impossible to miss my overstuffed friends, but if the customs officials noticed, they let it go and did not confiscate the goods or charge duties. I figured they knew what was going on and said nothing because the Serbs across the border needed the clothes as much as the Bulgarian smugglers needed the money. After we cleared the border, the mules, their ruse a success, removed their gear and placed the clothes back in their large travel bags ready for sale.

As the train swayed through the mountains and across plains, my traveling companions and I had a party and the women explained their game, even though I don't speak Bulgarian and they didn't speak English. Using hand and body language, a form of charades; a map, a dictionary, a pen and pad, the smugglers told their story. My compartment mates wrote their names in my notebook, showed me on a map where they came from and where they were going and, with my specific prompting, wrote down how often they made the trip and how much money they earned.

They bought the clothes in their home town of Stara Zagora, Bulgaria, and sold them in Pirot, Serbia, just across the national border. Twice a week they made that journey. They were entrepreneurs in the new free-wheeling free-market economy. That was their livelihood. When business was good, they earned $125 each on a single trip. During a downturn in the smugglers'

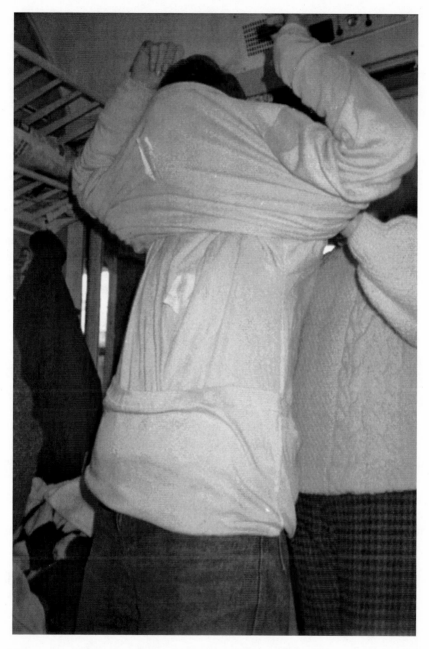

See no smuggling, hear no smuggling: Layers of knitted jerseys disguised a man traveling to Serbia in 1997. Joined on the train by three businesswomen, the quartet would sell their wares after they crossed the border from Bulgaria while I rattled on to Belgrade (photograph by the author, © Cox Newspapers Inc.).

market, they earned $50 each. That sure beat working for a living, in a country where the average monthly income was $15.

Before we reached the border, my new friends and I shared an afternoon meal. We put the two kinds of meat, plus cheese, olives, water, two loaves of bread and knife together and enjoyed a fine lunch. There is nothing like food and drink, even water, to bring people together. By then we members of two very different tribes had become old friends.

A few years earlier, during the Cold War, I probably would never have been allowed into Bulgaria and those smugglers probably would not have dared to be smugglers. But now we even spoke the same language, in a way, an American and four Bulgarians on our way to Yugoslavia where I wasn't supposed to be able to go and where they were headed, shall we say, to do business against the rules. We waved at one another as they left the train and I took photographs, furtively. There went another fleeting moment on a journalist's journey that will never be repeated. I jotted that down as further evidence that on a personal basis, with the pressures and the howling of the tribal crowds out of the picture, people can get along, even with customs officials at remote border posts.

Home Alone: From Skopje to Athens

A new phenomenon — voluntary solitary confinement — rode with me on the old train from Skopje, Macedonia to Athens toward the end of August 1995.

Macedonians, a Slavic tribe with their own ethnic minority sore spots, declared their independence from Yugoslavia in 1991. Like a newborn fawn, Macedonia was being nipped at by neighboring predators, which were trying to bring it down. Soon after Macedonia's declaration of independence, Western nations feared the Balkans' wars would sweep south to engulf Macedonia and involve Greece, a NATO member. Such a development would have been a major political and military complication for NATO.

In this atmosphere, Macedonians were not allowed to travel to Greece because Macedonia and Greece were quarreling over the right to use the word Macedonia. The Greeks, supposedly fearing a Macedonian plot to claim part of northern Greece, said Macedonia was their name and their name only because Philip and his son Alexander said so 2400 years ago. So serious was the dispute that when the newly independent Macedonia joined the United Nations, it was compelled to do so as The Former Yugoslav Republic of Macedonia, not simply as Macedonia. The neighborhood tribal quarrel was more or less resolved later, in 1995, when both countries recognized each other;

Macedonia abandoned the use of the sunburst on its flag and Greece ignored Macedonia's name, for the moment at least.

When the train from Budapest and Belgrade arrived in Skopje, Macedonia's capital, two hours and fifteen minutes late, I felt the makings of a memorable overnight trip to Athens. The conductor, in his T-shirt, slippers and dirty gray slacks, added to my anticipation.

The Macedonians were trusted sufficiently to sell me a basic-fare ticket, for $34.50, but not to take the money for a sleeper. That was the conductor's job. Exquisitely equipped for the job of ticket-seller, the conductor carried no change. A sleeper cost $18 any way you figured it, in Greek drachmas, German marks or U.S. dollars. "Sorry," he said, when I gave him a $20 bill. I nodded and told him that I understood. Keep the change. "Sorry, sorry," he kept repeating, apologizing because the car was old and dirty and the cabin lights didn't work.

Shortly after we pulled out of Skopje in the approaching darkness, a woman stalked the aisles and cabins with a broom. She missed my cabin, and I decided to be well and truly missed. A few minutes after that, the same woman appeared with a baby-sized pillow and a sheet that looked like a well-used tablecloth from an Eat at Ma's restaurant. I thanked her warmly. Fifty-four beds were in that sleeper car, but only two other beds were occupied. The train pulled twelve cars in all, and we added and subtracted cars along the way according to some arcane Balkans formula.

It was a warm August night, and the only fresh air in my compartment entered through a trick window. To let the air in, I had to lower the only section of the window that moved and raise the shade. But the dance of the train over the rough rail bed slowly raised the window all the way up and at the same time lowered the shade all the way down, shutting out the air. I figured the window was left over from World War II, and that perhaps I was occupying the torture cabin. I was determined to keep the window down, the shade up and the fresh air coming in, but that proved beyond my tools or technological expertise. I believe, in retrospect I hope, that there was a good reason for not jumping to another cabin, but I don't recall what it was.

All the Macedonians on the train had to leave when we reached the border with Greece two hours and twenty minutes after we left Skopje. Macedonian officials checked passports for visas, grunted and left. The Greeks were more sophisticated. They took the passports to a police post alongside the track and told passengers to pick up their documents in five minutes. They took 10 minutes. It was another 30 minutes before the train continued on its journey. At the border station, fans watched a soccer match on television, a small blue light in the darkness, and drank beer for an added glow on that hot summer night with the crickets hard at work all around but out of sight.

We left the border shortly before 10:30 P.M. Sometime around midnight I gave up juggling the window and shade and finally fell into a restless sleep, eager to reach the Acropolis. We arrived in Athens at exactly 9:22 the next morning, two hours and twenty-two minutes later than scheduled. But we made good time considering that we had left Skopje two hours and fifteen minutes later than the schedule said we would. This kind of reasoning and marking of time is required to live properly and sanely in Eastern Europe and the Mediterranean area.

Dawn is always magical, especially when the first light strays inside a train. And especially around the Mediterranean, where every ray of soft, dusty light shines on history not just on rocks, olive trees and vineyards. Groggy, I went mano-a-mano with the window and shade again and was greeted by a sultry sun glancing off rocky hills and mountains and farms tucked in valleys. Large sprinklers sprayed huge fields of crops, and the ever-present sheep and goats chewed relentlessly against hillsides. When the train chugged to a stop in Athens, I saw two other passengers depart. The train wasn't quite up to the thought, and neither was I really, but I felt a little like one of those European princes of old leaving his private train. But I had no retinue and no one rushed to help with my bags, shortcomings that even now do not dim the memory of the journey.

Next to walking in a foreign city, train travel is my favorite form of transportation. Long train rides usually allow time in spaces small enough to observe and talk with people of many tribes. This is especially true on older trains in poorer countries where people are easier to talk with; less true on modern trains where passengers wearing suits lump strangers with danger. Trains are like villages of strangers on wheels, and no one talks more openly than a stranger on the move. Even if you don't speak the local patois, a dictionary, a map, sign language, eating and drinking together allow for a surprising amount of communication.

Large boats and ships also can be useful for learning from locals and the diaspora. Except for riding on the *Santa Maria* catamaran from Cyprus to Lebanon and back and ships crossing the English Channel, my experience with floating transportation has been confined to rafts propelled by old men or by steel cables pulling me across rivers to escape shouting young men with guns who preferred that I leave town on some vague tribal principle that I didn't always understand but grasped sufficiently to move on. Riding on overloaded rafts pulled by cables across fast-flowing rivers tends, however, to put a crimp in conversation.

Buses are bedlam and should be avoided. Period. With people jammed elbow to Adam's apple and nostrils to armpits, it is impossible to converse in any way beyond useless grunts, which sound much the same regardless of sect, ethnic or language group, although women as a rule make much less noise than men. Taxis and private cars are fine for private conversations, but are too limited for measuring the local culture or political climate. Taxi-drivers are widely esteemed for imparting local folk wisdom, but for every talkative and informed hack there are two who always seem to belong to a religious order where silence is considered the pathway to heaven.

If the airplanes of Central Asia and some parts of the Middle East are dangerous, to me the danger always seemed more abstract than peering over the side of a cliff from the passenger side of a top-heavy vehicle sliding on rocks and gravel. Besides, when people talk at all on planes, conversations usually are limited to one or two people. As for donkeys, horses and camels, my experience is that they usually keep to themselves.

Of the conventional modes of travel on reporting assignments, the automobile is by far the most risky. One reason may be that much of my travel by auto was done crossing deserts, mountains and rivers to report on tribal conflicts. When you consider that most hired vehicles aren't known for reliability in such areas, that many roads were not made for auto travel and that I was traveling to areas where I wasn't always welcome, the reason for the risk becomes all-too evident.

Trails called roads in Somalia, Bosnia, Iraq and Afghanistan were dangers unto themselves, altogether separate from surrounding conflicts and other dangers such as militias, snipers and brigands. Travel in Afghanistan in particular was a test of vertebrae and sanity, and one journey in particular, on a main route at that, offered rare challenges to run a gauntlet thrown up by man and nature, and survive.

Afghanistan's Rough Roads, Rough Lives

Shawfik, a young man who helped to run the house where I rented a room in Kabul, woke me on schedule at 4:15 A.M. Before the day was out, I wished that Shawfik had forgotten to do his job.

Within a half hour, I waved goodby to Shawfik. Then Abdullah, my expert scout and all-around factotum who could tweak grunts and generals; Assaf, my fearless driver who could fix anything mechanical, or get it fixed; Eymal, my clever translator and budding computer expert, and I began a daunting trip: We would take thirteen hours to travel 139 miles north of the Afghan capital on this Saturday, March 30, 2002, merely one leg of the journey that often defied travelers, ancient and modern. An overnight stay in a town and another four hours of fast driving the following day would get us to our destination, the northern city of Mazar-ash-Sharif, dominated by eth-nic–Uzbeks and lying prone on the open steppe like a sprawling outgrowth of a nomad village. The Taliban had slaughtered Uzbeks, Tadjiks and Haz-aras in Mazar and been slaughtered in return so tensions remained high among competing tribal leaders when we pointed our compasses north from Kabul.

Afghan roads, even main roads, overall were the worst that have ever rat-tled my teeth and spine, worse even than those in northern Iraq. Strewn with bomb craters and obscured by mud, snow and rocks, they formed outlines or trails rather than roads themselves. Traveling 10 to 15 miles per hour, how-ever, does offer one envious benefit: ample time to admire Afghanistan's stun-ning scenery, its rugged and rainbow-colored mountains, wide foamy rivers carrying mineral waters of ochre and green, camel-colored steppes and ancient villages hidden in lost valleys where women and men, oblivious to time, hoe side-by-side in somehow-fertile fields.

Afghan highways: A typical road in Afghanistan's mountains. It was common for a 100-mile journey to take ten hours in 2002, when this photograph was taken, after the U.S. invasion to capture or kill Osama bin Laden (photograph by the author, © Cox Newspapers Inc.).

Joining us on the journey was its fearsome reputation, which often convinced travelers to seek other destinations, especially in winter, which March 30 still was in the mountains. A poorly ventilated and usually unplowed tunnel filled with snow, ice, deep ruts, small lakes and cars about 12,000 feet up in the snow-clogged Hindu Kush Mountains made carbon monoxide poisoning a real and present danger. Signs urging motorists to turn off their engines and walk out of the tunnel until stuck or drowning vehicles could be moved have an unfailing way of focusing the mind.

Two-way traffic to the Salang Tunnel and smaller tunnels leading to it was prohibited. Traffic north and south ran on alternate days. This bit of local trickery fooled many a traveler. One weary reporter took three days to reach his destination in the north. On the first day, he headed north from Kabul when only southbound traffic was permitted. Back to Kabul he crawled late that day. A blizzard blocked the road to the tunnel on the second day, forcing him to limp more than a hundred miles back to Kabul for the second time in two days. Strike two for Afghanistan. On the third day, the reporter and his team pulled off a trick of their own: They snuck in against the southbound traffic and squeezed through the tunnel with the arriving darkness. Just north of the tunnel they were forced to sleep in their car overnight because traveling in the darkness offers no advantage, except to brigands, guerrillas and craters in the road.

My team and I left Kabul in a large but old van with enough gear and emergency rations — such as cookies, bottled water, tins of tuna fish and the worst chicken ever canned into dust — to last two weeks at the most, if we didn't eat much.

As it turned out, we cajoled fine breakfasts and sometimes dinners at our Mazar hotel, which we deemed without question the best in the entire country. Thanks to American taxpayers, I resupplied in Mazar by purchasing U.S. military rations, portions of Meals Ready to Eat, from street vendors who claimed the goods in shrubs from parachutes that had missed their marks.

From the house where I was staying in Kabul, we drove through the predawn darkness to the Mustafa Hotel in another part of the city to meet another correspondent and a photographer. Their driver and translator were young and inexperienced, and there was serious doubt that their chains would actually fit the tires on their car. Inexperience and faulty equipment are a quinela that no traveler should bet on when trying to cross the Hindu Kush. It was too late then to find out for sure whether their chains would work, but we learned the regrettable answer hours later in the ice and snow.

Traveling in a two-car caravan was safer than slogging alone. After buying gas from suppliers at the curb and double-checking film supplies, we finally left Kabul shortly before 6 A.M., gazing through foggy eyes and a gauzy dawn at the snowy mountains that ring Kabul. Ready to wrestle with Afghanistan's demons, we were a rather ragged tag team in old cars with fraying fan belts, oil leaks and one set of chains that gave material meaning to missing links.

A city of worker bees, cyclists and hangers-on, Kabul was just beginning to go to work when we left. In a few hours, women wearing blue burqas would fill the streets, shopping, drawing water, a few walking to government jobs. Only the toes of their shoes would be exposed. A woman might round the corner on her way to fetch water from a public well on the street with her face showing, but as soon as she saw a man, especially someone she didn't know, she quickly covered up. Although the Taliban and their gender war had been driven from power a few months earlier, most women were still too afraid to remove their burqas in public. They needed time for their husbands, fathers, brothers and sons, the rule-makers, to accept what might become another counter-revolution.

Women at work or at home met visitors without their burqas. Many older women laughed and said that they were free because men no longer desired them. They defied the weakening rules and refused to wear the head-to-toe coverings that served as personal prison cells. As they do in most restrictive societies, older women try to teach younger women how to manipulate the rules made by men, and sometimes even how to break those rules.

As we saw along the road to Mazar and traveling elsewhere in the country, women in the usually conservative towns eschew public appearances altogether. Publicly, women in those areas didn't exist. In some agricultural areas, where women and men worked together in the fields and were all familiar with each other, women wore scarves but no burqas. When a foreigner drove up, those women would throw a scarf over their heads. In Mazar, where the traditional color is white, not blue as it is in Kabul, women wearing burqas looked like white wraiths levitating along the streets and sidewalks.

Long before we traversed the Salang Pass and reached the treacherous Salang Tunnel, the space called road was better suited to donkeys and horses than motor vehicles. We crossed the Salang River bridge on a shaky one-lane steel structure, a replacement for the old bridge that had been on the wrong side of some battle and been bombed into the water. Rain turned to sleet and slush as we drove higher into the Hindu Kush.

Silent in our concentration on the road and weather, we watched deepening snow and cold transform the road from a slough of mud and slush into icy ruts. Sometimes we were cowed into silence by the deafening groans and creaks of old metal as our van bounced, swayed and shook from crater to crater. Visibility shrunk to the vehicle directly ahead, a rather uncomfortable sensation for those of us accustomed to traveling by sight rather than feel. As we entered one of the smaller tunnels leading to the main Salang opening, a treacherous monument to Soviet engineering, clouds smothered the mountains and a blizzard struck so fiercely that the sky and the peaks in our faces were obliterated by whiteness. Ah, I thought, this is a whiteout. We could be sure only of the ground we stood on, which we could feel more surely than we could see.

Assaf, my driver, switched to four-wheel drive before we entered the chain of small tunnels. In four turns of the wheels we were stuck. Strong and resourceful, Assaf soon attached the chains. We waited as our colleagues, whose car yielded to the snow beyond one of the smaller tunnels, tested their chains. At 9:20 A.M., according to my notes, we lost sight of our colleagues. We crept slowly with the traffic through the snow and ice ruts, but they didn't follow. With no hesitation Eymal, my translator, and I trudged back through the slow-moving traffic searching for the second car. That was the point of traveling together, so we could help each other.

We found our colleagues helpless in the snow, their missing links missing and the remainder too small to cover their tires. Eymal and I helped haul our colleagues' gear more than a half-mile through the heavy snow to our van, which was crunching ahead slowly in the deepening drifts. Our colleagues told their driver and translator to meet us at the hotel we had selected in Mazar. I figured that we might see them by summer. They were as surprised as we were when we met in Mazar a couple of days later, not long after the rest of us had arrived. Sheer luck, I would call it. Fate, an Afghan might say.

Etiquette is not high on the agenda of Afghan drivers. Survival is. The wide entrance to the Salang Tunnel looked like a rugby scrum on wheels. Cars and trucks filled the space in three short lanes and then drivers played chicken to see who would enter first in the one open lane through the tunnel, although trucks weren't supposed to enter until the afternoon. Horns blared in various decibels and crazy rhythms in the blizzard and bedlam while cars and trucks became mired in snow and ice, blocking the sliver-like entrance that drew the crowd.

During a two-hour delay entering the Salang Tunnel, I met warm-blooded Hamid. He wore plastic sandals, no socks, no hat and no coat in the freezing mountain blizzard. He was covered only by a traditional long white garment called a shalwar kamez, which flowed over a shorter white cotton shirt. Hamid, 25, stared at my gloves as if they were foreign objects, which to him they were. "I am not cold," Hamid declared, displaying the hardiness for which Afghans are noted. I figured that Hamid was, indeed, cold, but refused to admit it, which is also part of the Afghan code: If you don't admit to being cold, you'll feel warmer and gain an advantage over those who are cold.

Hamid drove people and goods through the tunnel twice weekly in a seven-passenger Toyota van. He was paid $6 per trip, no matter how long a trip took. One time, Hamid said coolly, he was stuck at the tunnel for three days, sharing walnuts and other food with other drivers. Many times, Hamid said calmly as I looked toward the peaks that I couldn't see, people were killed in avalanches or died from a shortage of food. He didn't mention death from carbon monoxide poisoning, but we knew about that prospect and would learn more shortly when we read the warning signs.

Two hours after we reached its main entrance, we finally crawled into the Salang Tunnel. Almost two hours after that, shortly before 4 P.M. we cleared the tunnel itself with relief but no cheers. At times the road through the tunnel was as rough as a rock quarry. Deep rails of ice raised the wheels of smaller cars off the ground, leaving the vehicles flopping gently from side to side like beached whales flapping their fins. Other cars stalled in the small lakes. Some motorists walked through the tunnel urging drivers to turn off their engines and walk outside to avoid asphyxiation. Two of my colleagues, Abdullah and Assaf, left us to help unplug the passageway of stalled cars. With Eymal, I stayed with the gear and the car, its engine off. I was not trying to play the role of a canary in a mine, but kept a keen eye out for Afghans who might. As they walked deeper into the mire and toward the exit, Abdullah and Assaf helped to free disabled vehicles. When traffic began to move, they returned to drive us slowly from the tunnel.

By 6:15 that night, with the blizzard and tunnel two hours behind us, we entered the village of Pul-i-Khumri, wayfarers begging for a place to eat and sleep. At that time, with no knowledge of road conditions and with the new government of Hamid Karzai in charge of Kabul only, and barely that, it would have been bad form and probably worse to drive in the darkness. An international organization that was expert in removing land mines proved as hospitable as their Afghan hosts and happily put us up at their guest house in Pul-i-Khumri. Another aid organization did the same there on our return trip. On the southern edge of the great Turkestan steppe, we entered a world that floated somewhere in antiquity as we thought of it, where camels and donkeys, latched to wheels and wells, drew water for irrigation.

After a relatively fast four-hour drive the following day, on the best road I ever saw in Afghanistan, we reached Mazar-ash-Sharif. For more than a week, we chased Uzbek leader Gen. Rashid Dostum; we ate lunch in his home, heard his peacocks screech and sped in straight lines and in circles but we never caught up with the man who didn't want to be caught. Rival tribal chiefs told us of slaughters followed by massacres during the civil war of the 1990s. The Taliban emerged from those ashes, but nearly all the tribes had stoked the fires.

A Fish at the Israeli-Jordanian Border

Food is more than a mere symbol of culture and tribe. It is a concrete recipe of welcome, of belonging and acceptance and sometimes it can remove barriers. Late in 1992, I was crossing the Allenby Bridge and the trickling Jordan River from Israel to Jordan. I was on assignment, but my wife, Pat, was taking her sister, Joanne, and brother-in-law, Bill, on a sight-seeing tour of King Hussein's kingdom. Jordanian authorities sneered at Joanne's passport; seems as if an Israel official, despite a request not to, stamped an Israeli visa in her passport when she had landed in Tel Aviv a few days earlier. The whole business of crossing from Israel to Jordan was a diplomatic charade at that time. The Jordanians acted as if travelers were crossing from Cyprus, not Israel, when Israelis and the Israeli border checkpoint were a shout away.

What occurred next was one of those great moments in tourist travel that is frightening to the individual when it happens but unforgettable and humorous forever after.

JORDANIAN OFFICIAL TO JOANNE (pointing to the Israeli visa in Joanne's passport): "What is this?"

JOANNE TO JORDANIAN: Silence. Joanne's mouth moved like that of a fish out of water, but she uttered no words or noises.

JORDANIAN TO JOANNE: "You cannot stay in Jordan with an Israeli visa in your passport."

JOANNE TO JORDANIAN: More silence. Her mouth was still moving but no noise followed.

JORDANIAN TO JOANNE: "You must return. You cannot stay in Jordan. We will take you to the bus terminal, but you will have to turn around and leave."

Joanne had figured a problem awaited her because an Israeli official had told her so at the Israeli checkpoint a few yards away. Still, she was surprised into silence when the questions came. As Joanne wondered whether she would be booted, alone, from Jordan and maybe the region, Pat began to answer the questions for her sister. Pat explained that we were traveling together, that no one else had a passport problem and we weren't about to let Joanne return alone. I remained quiet, hoping that the women would have a better chance of finding sympathy and working through the problem than if a man interfered and aroused the testosterone. But I miscalculated.

When we reached the Jordanian bus terminal on the east bank of the river, officials there insisted that Joanne would have to leave Jordan. Bill, Pat and I could stay because we did not have Israeli visas. That's when I asked to see the police chief in charge of the border area so I could play my tribal card. For about an hour, I drank coffee and tea with the chief. We talked about the great country of Jordan and its leader at the time, King Hussein. For an hour, we discussed all the wonderful Arabic food I ate as a child, my mother's unusual old Arab name which only a tribal member would know; I dropped in several old Arabic words that my grandparents brought with them to America almost a hundred years earlier. While I talked with the police chief, other Jordanians attempted to put Pat, Joanne and Bill on the bus back to Israel. But Pat refused to leave the terminal with Joanne and Bill until I returned.

Drinking tea and coffee and running down the menu of food cooked by my family in America was fun, especially so since the tribal remedy worked. The police chief waved us through to Amman, but warned Joanne to get a new passport at the American embassy as soon as possible and for sure before she left the country. Joanne complied, quickly. More than 17 years later, Joanne can't tell the story without becoming speechless again, but now it's because she can't stop laughing.

EIGHT

Crosses to Bear in Belfast

Near the Syrian-Iraqi border, far from Ireland, Martin Nangle and I were knocking on doors looking for help to reach northern Iraq in March 1991, hours after the end of the first Persian Gulf War. A free-lance photographer, Nangle was on assignment for a wire service's London office. "Where you from?" a Syrian asked. "Ireland," Nangle answered. "Irlanda, Irlanda," the Syrian shouted with hard hand-shaking joy. To the Syrian, Ireland meant the Irish fight against British colonialism and occupation. In the Syrian's eyes, Nangle was a tribal ally because he brought to mind a European version of the Palestinian fight against the Israelis. The official didn't ask whether Nangle was a Catholic or a Protestant, a republican or a unionist, a Christian, Jew or Muslim. To the Syrian, the tribal stimulus that mattered most was the occupation of one ethnic group by another. With Nangle's Ireland as the key, we were offered a phone to call his wife in Ireland and my wife and office in the United States, and given ample food and drink. When we set off for Iraq, Nangle and I left our gear in the safe-keeping of our new friend.

Drained beer bottles shattered on the asphalt, scattering beer cans like pins in a bowling alley for the homeless. Some 50 young men, Catholics and Irish republicans all, maneuvered to charge the marchers but police blocked their way. Stymied on foot, the republicans waved the Irish tricolor and shouted, "Hey, hey, IRA" for the Irish Republican Army. Up went their middle fingers, high and stiff and meant for the marching Protestants who are loyal to the union with Britain.

Unable to swallow the insults, the parading, frustrated Apprentice Boys of Derry and Northern Ireland fired back higher with their own middle fingers, the surest sign of life in the province. When some of the marchers attempted to break ranks and fire fists at their taunting sectarian, ethnic, political and tribal rivals, the local police, the mainly Protestant force called the Royal Ulster Constabulary, swarmed to turn them back.

At the Butcher Gate leading to the Bogside, a staunch Republican

Catholic neighborhood in Derry's medieval walled city, a couple of hundred people gathered without metallic weapons, anger rippling from elbow to elbow. A few held a large sign that said the RUC means "Rotten Unionist Coersive," lest anyone doubt where the Bogsiders stood.

Warmed by a brilliant sun, the day was still a fearsome one. A charming old town whose 1.2 miles of protective walls rose to their pinnacle in 1618, Derry is Northern Ireland's second largest city. For most of the previous 45 years, sectarian, political and cultural conflict had been synonymous with Derry, dulling the city's quaint man-made appeal but not nature's sparkling waters called the River Foyle. It might be said that riots in Derry during a similar march almost three decades years earlier locked in the most recent era of violence in Northern Ireland, a period called, rather modestly as if they were a family spat, The Troubles.

On this day, August 10, 1996, the Apprentice Boys were strutting in Derry, contributing their personal salute and bang of the drum to the divided north's summer marching season. Catholics and Protestants, republicans and unionists, were tiptoeing away from violence at that moment and no one wanted to see Derry dash into another riot. Always a potential fuse and powder keg, the Apprentice Boys' march marks the anniversary of the day in 1689 when the forces of Protestant King William of Orange drove off the yeomen of Catholic King James II and broke the siege of the city. History and hate were no strangers in Northern Ireland.

Typical of Ireland's problems at that time and thereafter, both kings wore English britches. Thirteen Apprentice Boys had slammed shut the gates of Derry late in 1688 against King James' forces and held the walled enclave until the Orangemen came and proved, to Protestants then and for centuries more, which side was right. Three hundred and seven years later, 1689 was just like yesterday. So it was in the six Ulster counties called Northern Ireland. The past was not past.

Irish-Catholic republicans call the little gem of a city Derry; they can't say London except when they cross the Irish Sea. Even then the bone sticks in their gullets. The London part of many road signs that say Londonderry was crossed out. Protestants loyal to Britain and the union shouted Londonderry whenever they had the opportunity. Mostly, the city is called Derry and the county is called Londonderry. Basically, however, the Catholics and Protestants there found it difficult to agree on the name of this place where they live.

About 15,000 Apprentice Boys and their cohorts paraded three and a half miles through Derry on August 10, 1996. With them marched the hearts and souls of their compatriots. Their rivals seethed and watched with angry eyes and flexed muscles. The Boys wore dress suits with maroon sashes angled across their chests. Almost 200 bands marched with them, for three hours. Fifes and drums, flutes, horns, accordions, almost every instrument that makes noise you can hear on a street roared off the stone buildings and walls and into the ears of friends and foes. Marchers wore spit and polished shoes and carried flags, pikes, swords and banners. Their uniforms were of red, white and blue; orange and blue; orange and black; blue and gold and black; red and gold uniforms, too. No green. Almost every color that pleased the marchers angered the spectators on the other side.

The thump, thump, thump of the drums was visceral. Horns screeched in the martial atmosphere. The march was traditional. Stylishly old. As tribal as clans and righteous prayers can be. Very proud. Weirdly happy in triumphant anger.

For every five marchers there was one security officer, either a cop or a British soldier, for backup. After the marchers crossed from the Protestant Waterside area over the Craigavon bridge through the gates into walled Derry, tension and fear paraded with them strut for strut. Palpable, visible. The Protestants said they were marching to defend their rights, not to intimidate their enemies. The Catholics said they were there to protect their neighborhoods and defend their rights, too. Both were fibbing, or at least neither was telling the whole truth. The Boys were marching and shouting and throwing bottles and threatening so they could poke a stick in a republican eye: they said that, too. At the end of that day, violence did not rule for a change, not only because of the heavy security presence, but also because both sides had made temporary territorial compromises that kept the Catholics away from Protestant neighborhoods and Protestants from intruding in Catholic areas. Despite the absence of violence, the barking forces aligned against each other limned the conflict in Northern Ireland.

John Taylor Meldrum, who had ridden his "peace horse" from Cork to Waterford to Derry, was largely ignored by both sides. But he did escape. "You make peace for your children. Now," said the white banner that Meldrum carried. Those who missed the banner might have seen the chalked message on the rump of his horse, Black Beauty: "Time for peace. Now." But Meldrum's message was no one else's rallying cry in Derry's streets that day.

Catholics and Protestants in Northern Ireland usually asked "Where you from?" with a pointed twist. Religion, or sect, topped their tribal list, although tribalism in the province took many other powerful forms as well. What mattered on the street was whether you were a Catholic or a Protestant, or which side you favored. No other denomination, no other sect, mattered. No one asked, "Are you a Baptist, a Methodist, Greek Orthodox, or a Hindu?" The question of whether a person was a Christian, a Jew or a Muslim didn't come up. But if a Protestant in Belfast said he was a Presbyterian, a Catholic would probably have said, "I told you so."

Religion remained a powerful political force on the island, even if the land of St. Patrick celebrates sacraments more these days by hoisting a pint rather than by taking communion and hewing to religious orthodoxy. It's acceptable for Catholics to admit that they have strayed from the pews and the priests, but let a foreign tribesman accuse Catholics of being less than Catholic and you will get a good argument and probably more. Republicans for sure are now more secular Catholic than religious conformers, but that does not weaken the link between republicans and nationalists and Catholicism on the political front.

On the other side of the aisle, Protestantism and unionism were essentially one. With the Rev. Ian Paisley and his flock, there was no line of separation between Presbyterianism, British culture and maintaining the union with Britain, even though Paisley recently has agreed, in a dramatic change, to share local political power with Sinn Fein's republicans.

Northern Ireland's tribal battle has also been pitched on nationality, culture, economic and political power. The British-Protestant culture versus the Irish-Catholic version, no matter that those cultures are no longer what they used to be. The fight for political control is a more public and, therefore, a more obvious conflict, but it only masks the battle over which of the nationalities and cultures will dominate in the north.

Language is an integral part of ethnic and tribal identity. Strip a people of their language and a large part of their identity vanishes. That's the reason dominant tribes move quickly to impose their language over conquered tribes, as the Turks did for so long with the Kurds. Reversing direction, immigrants in Israel are immersed in Hebrew to build their Jewish and Israeli identities.

In Northern Ireland, language is part of the historic conflict, though now mostly sub rosa.

Northern Ireland's Presbyterians migrated from Scotland, and Scottish, like the Irish/Gaelic tongue, is a Celtic language. But with England's rule came the English language and culture throughout the island. Irish republicans are trying to bring back their Gaelic language, but Northern Ireland's unionists were having little if any of that. For most of them, the English language is as much a part of unionism as the Union Jack.

For Irish republican Catholics, however, the story, the language, is different. The Irish or Gaelic tongue is the language of their nationality and identity, the historic language of the island. More than ever, Irish/Gaelic was being taught in some schools, spoken on the radio and in public. Gerry Adams,

Sinn Fein's president, is often quick to switch from English to Gaelic and back again. Adams wants to link the Irish language to the Irish identity as much and as often as possible. The practical and psychological effects are difficult to measure, but they are real.

Northern Ireland gives concrete meaning to the cliche that Christianity would be a great religion if it weren't for the Christians. Of course much the same could be said about other religions and their adherents. People make religions. Their Gods, scriptures and interpreters create their theology.

Visitors to Northern Ireland are to be loved, at least for tourism and business purposes and at least until their sectarian or political sympathies are divined. If the Catholics and Protestants treated each other as they treat visitors, Northern Ireland would be as sweet as it looks. The people admit that, too.

One morning, about 6:30, shortly after the locked parking area was opened at a small hotel in Belfast where I was staying, my rental car was stolen. Horrified at such treatment of a visitor, the hotel management called the constabulary. They were equally troubled. What would I tell the world about Northern Ireland? I was in a rush to get to the airport, so the police offered me a ride, which itself was unusual by standards elsewhere. Their help proved unnecessary because the police soon found the car abandoned on the street, with some light fender damage. Kids, joyriders, probably stole the car and dumped it quickly. Wary about tacking on an extra charge for damages and further tainting Northern Ireland's reputation, the rental agency absorbed the repair bill. I doubt that a local tribesman would have been treated so well.

Catholics and Protestants in Northern Ireland meet so many Americans they can tell one immediately, by dress, walk and manner; never mind the accent. They know where an American is from, generically speaking. Most Protestant Unionists assumed that all Americans favor the nationalist Catholic cause because so much money flowed from Americans to the IRA and Sinn Fein, the IRA's political voice. The day after the Apprentice Boys' march in Derry, I drove to Belfast for a Sinn Fein rally. There I met a lad from Kansas City, family name of Quinn, he told me, who spoke to loud hurrahs when he said, "English out of Ireland. We will not be silent. We will stand in solidarity with the people of Ireland until we have a reunited Ireland."

On another occasion, however, I was lucky enough to spend a long, long night drinking Guinness with a Protestant oil rigger and his two sons, the older of whom was about 22. The younger son had just reached the drinking age and the father was a traveling man whose shoes gathered no bog and who was rarely home. Their night at a local pub in the town of Bangor was a family rite of passage. This father and his sons were distant, but for a pub moment they were together as parent and children, never totally apart no matter how distant they might have been. They were, after all, part of the same basic tribe, the family.

The sectarian-ethnic divide never came up in that Bangor pub, but we were swimming in their culture. I drank half pints to their two pints each. And I couldn't buy a drink. "What's wrong?" the father asked, "You're not drinking as much as we are." I didn't want to admit the obvious, that I couldn't drink as much as they could and stay upright. So I replied, "Oh yes I am. I'm just drinking slower." My reply made little sense but, under the circumstances, it seemed logical to them. For hours I swallowed all I could of their culture and listened to their tongues thicken to the point where I could understand maybe one of every three words they uttered before we all rolled out the door three hours after last call.

That I landed in Bangor at all was, to me, either a leprechaun's trick or a journalist's luck. But to the people of Ireland, north or south, it was an intentional act of hospitality commonly visited upon strangers. All the rooms in all of Belfast's hotels were taken when from London I called the small hotel near Queens University, where I usually found a large room that the clerks and Colin, the persuasive bouncer, matched with a grand welcome. After apologizing profusely because my favorite hotel was fully booked, a clerk offered to call around and find a room for me. If she succeeded, the clerk wondered, would I mind if she gave my credit card number to hold the room. Not at all, I answered. Within 20 minutes, the clerk called back to say that she had booked a room for me at a bed and breakfast, right on the sea, in Bangor. Not before or since has any hotel treated me that well.

—⦿—

In the mid–1990s, the tribal conflict in Northern Ireland was like a fight with concrete pillows when compared with the mass killings in Bosnia, Lebanon, Rwanda, Somalia, Iraq, Afghanistan; the list goes on. But the continued republican rebellion against the British nation-state presence in Northern Ireland was an example that other tribes in similar circumstances looked to and imitated.

Northern Ireland's Catholics and Protestants, republicans and loyalists, were bombing, shooting, wounding and maiming to defend neighborhoods, streets, blocks, even street corners, walls and fences. On a larger tableau, their battle concerned religion, language, culture and traditions, ethnicity, civil rights, colonialism and economic and political power, all of which turned the conflict into a tribal fight over principles as well as turf and patches of sod.

Principles fluttered on the highest masts in Northern Ireland. They were difficult to measure but were routinely waved. Minor slights were turned into major offenses. The territory involved is both physically small and therefore huge in importance, a matter of identity and control, psychologically vital to one's self-respect. In many ways the fight over neighborhoods and streets made the conflict more intense. The smaller the prize, the tougher the fight for morsels. If two rival families are fighting to control one room or one house, the battle can be more vicious because it's more personal than when two nations fight for control of a region. When gods and cultural identity, colonialism, flags and freedom are involved, emotion overwhelms reason. Historical events become hangers on which rivals drape and dramatize triumphs and disasters, to keep them ever visible, memorable and often distorted.

Unionists in the province think of themselves as loyal to all things British, and to little or nothing that is Irish. Ever-loyal unionists say they are fighting to preserve their British traditions, which in part mean Protestantism. Sever Northern Ireland from British control, most unionists believe, and their culture, their traditions, their identity will wither and die. Those fears are probably real in the long run because cultural changes would certainly follow political alterations.

For the republicans, "Brits out of Ireland" remained the cache at the end of their rainbow and at the core of their political campaign. The IRA/Sinn Fein policy morphed into a search for change through political rather than violent means, but the objective of a united Ireland remained. For republicans, Ireland is all one and without a united Ireland there is a wounded Ireland, a violated Ireland, an Ireland as amputee. Isn't that what the Irish tricolor means, unity?

Moderates of all stripes walked both sides of the street in Northern Ireland, but extremists usually drove the causes. Compromise in local politics has gained ground, but historically the center had not proven strong enough to support trust across sectarian and cultural lines. The gap between the demands for a united Ireland and the retention of the union with Britain remained wide. The 2005 election for seats in the British parliament showed the extremes swallowing more of the moderates on both sides. Paisley's Democratic Unionist Party put the traditional, more moderate Ulster Unionist Party into retreat. The nationalist but centrist Social Democratic Labor Party lagged behind Sinn Fein's republicans. All-party government in the province, stymied for a promising decade, was on the burner again as, ironically, Adams and Paisley grew stronger and agreed to share local political power, although their ultimate and conflicting aims remained alive.

As for the British, they have found it difficult to slip from history's grip, but in the end time will shed them. Whenever I visited Ireland I thought of the real estate agent in London who showed me and my wife an apartment that was being renovated. "Irish workers," the realtor said, pointing with disgust to the work still undone, as if the Irish always screwed up everything they touched. "English supervision," I answered as we walked out, ending our last conversation with that realtor or estate agent, as the English call them.

Almost 3,500 people have been killed on Northern Ireland's sectarian, cultural and political battlefield during the past 35 to 40 years. That's a penetrating figure in a sea of only 1.6 million people. The conflict has been grinding, corrosive, but it hasn't affected everyone.

On the blood-red scorecard of international conflicts during that time, the total number of deaths in Northern Ireland ranks near the bottom. But the theory of relativity does not apply when talking with the relatives of the dead, of children without fathers and of innocent bystanders caught in the middle of extremists who see only orange, green or the Union Jack. As small as Northern Ireland is, those deaths touched many families with an intensity that is difficult to feel or understand if you're an outsider. Violence and the threat of violence held whole communities hostage. Battles fought between the English and the Irish 800 years ago were recalled as if they happened last week. Bloody Sunday, that January day in 1972, when British forces killed 13 people in Derry, was recalled as if it happened five minutes ago. A fourteenth person died later, the republicans are quick to point out. It's a matter of responsibility, British responsibility, they insisted. They are right about responsibility, all the way around. History is helpful when it is used for instruction. When used as a bludgeon, history lives to keep on killing.

—⚬⚬⚬—

The ethnic aspect of this tribal conflict, ignited by the intervention of a foreign tribe, began in Ireland in the latter part of the 12th century when an earl of Anglo-Norman roots went to the aid of one Irish king who was at war with an Irish rival. This, indeed, was the Middle Ages, when kings were like gods. Ireland was never the same after that, whether the Anglo-Norman earl imposed himself in a Celtic row or whether he was invited to help an ally.

Like it or not, God was injected into the conflict almost 400 years later when the English King Henry VIII, who split from the Roman church and founded the Anglican Church of England, humbly imposed himself as the King of Ireland. The Irish were Roman Catholics. Henry's English became mostly Anglican Protestants. The Catholic-Protestant split remains, although the religious and secular power and influence of each church has waned in each domain.

English control and exploitation expanded in Ireland after Henry VIII. The English yoke was tightened in 1690, when the Protestant William of Orange defeated the Catholic James II at the Battle of the Boyne, a name that still thunders among the Apprentice Boys. England continued to strip the Irish of rights and possessions in their own land, sucking out economic benefits

Remember, never forget: This Derry monument reminds Northern Ireland's Republican Catholics of Bloody Sunday, when British troops killed 14 people in 1972 (photograph by the author, © Cox Newspapers Inc.).

until all pretense of independence was peeled away in 1801, when England abolished the Irish parliament and created the United Kingdom of Great Britain and Ireland. Only Anglicans had a role in how Ireland was governed: Not Catholics, not Protestants of any other sects, not even Presbyterians, the essential Scotch-Irish who were sent en masse to Ireland in the early 17th century and many of whom still fight to retain Northern Ireland's loyalty to throne and sceptre. "How do you feel about colonialism?" Northern Ireland republicans asked a visitor.

When Britain finally began to let go of most of Ireland, it did so with more malice than generosity. The law giving Ireland self-rule went into effect after World War I, but six counties in Northern Ireland remained part of Britain. Partition ushered in about nine more decades of conflict. In the five days of the Easter Rising against Britain in 1916, more than 400 people were killed, almost as many as were killed in Northern Ireland in 1972, four years into "The Troubles." The 26 counties in the south of Ireland slowly separated from Britain, first becoming a British dominion and then, in 1948, an independent republic. But the north stewed until intermittent violence became more regular and turned into The Troubles in 1968-1969, after the Unionist government's attempt to quash a mainly Catholic civil rights demonstration in Derry had riotous consequences.

All-party participation in Northern Ireland's internal affairs began again in the late 1990s, but that process collapsed in 2002. What was the moderate middle on both sides began shrinking, as Ian Paisley's Democratic Unionists and Gerry Adams' Sinn Fein republicans grew to the point where optimists, and pessimists, may have said that Paisley and Adams no long sit on the extremes. After the IRA disarmed in 2005, and Paisley and Adams further expanded their electoral bases in 2007, on March 26 of that same year the two men sat in the same room for the first time, a strong signal that this tribal conflict has become less deadly though no less real.

The road from Belfast to Coalisland goes from east to west. It also runs, as the names themselves seem to suggest, all downhill. Belfast has felt the effects of the conflict more than most communities, but its wealthier areas have been spared. Areas thick with poorer people of different sects, living next to each other, are spared nothing. Coalisland is predominately poor and predominately Catholic. It has no garden spots that I have seen. The civil rights movement in Ireland's north, patented after the civil rights movement in the United States in the 1960s, began without incident in Coalisland in 1968. Yet from that first peaceful though limited march on August 24, 1968, grew The Troubles.

On December 8, 1994, I drove from Belfast around the southern end of Lough Neagh, the largest lake in Britain and Ireland, then north to Coalisland, County Tyrone, off the lake's western shore to talk with Bernadette McAliskey, Bernadette Devlin McAliskey. The road was easy; the risks few. The British Army bivouacked in its bases. No police roadblocks slowed the way. No one would die in a booby trap or a pub shooting that day. No blizzards blocked the road; no rivers to cross by raft or leaking boat, no masked men kidnapped foreigners.

Lough Neagh's 153 square miles swallow a large chunk of the middle of Northern Ireland. Its sweep reminds me of the way Lake Okeechobee sprawls in a large circle in South Florida. The town of Coalisland had about 4,000 people. Born in Cookstown, not far away, in a rural republican Catholic family, McAliskey leaves the area often, sometimes to knock on the American door when her views, such as opposition to the war in Iraq, make Washington paranoid, petulant and small-minded enough to kick her out or bar her presence. But wherever McAliskey goes, County Tyrone goes with her.

We met at a small restaurant. I had called to discuss her opposition to Sinn Fein's efforts to engage in all-party talks that would again allow the people of Northern Ireland to govern themselves, within the British fold, of course. To McAliskey, all-party local government alone merely stuck ribbons and bows on an empty box. She didn't believe that unionism and republicanism could live together under the same roof unless Britain pledged to leave Ireland.

McAliskey carried more scars of the conflict than most living nationalists, republicans, unionists or loyalists. Only the dead, it might be said, carried more. It's impossible to mention McAliskey without recalling the wounds and triumphs of her decades-long career at the core and edges of the conflict. A fundamentalist Irish republican, she is also a socialist because she cares more than most about equity in jobs, wages, housing, schools and how people live. As an unyielding republican socialist, she had evolved into more of a lone wolf as she aged and socialism, even in Britain and Ireland, had withered. Intellectually, however, her howl was as loud as ever, even if few people were listening.

In her years as a student of French, Celtic and psychology at Queens University in Belfast, when she was Bernadette Devlin, McAliskey was a leader in the student campaign for civil rights. She was a star whose megawatt glow pierced the political darkness way beyond her orbit. When it comes to politics, the right uppermost in her mind when we met was Ireland's right to be united. She was in many respects the republican Catholic bookend to the Presbyterian unionist, the Rev. Ian Paisley, although she was and remained a secular Catholic while Paisley remained then a fire and brimstone preacher of the here and hereafter.

McAliskey is surely no minister and carried none of the moral responsibilities that come with words and emotions shouted from a pulpit. As an intellectual and political provocateur who ardently believed in the philosophical underpinnings of her actions, McAliskey had few equals. She, like Paisley, refused to compromise her principles although he profited far more in every respect from his position than she did from hers. McAliskey used the political system as a lever to advance her causes. But she was an anti-politician and remained so when we met. McAliskey was no gradualist, no compromiser. Her days in the political sunshine were long past, but the consistency and logic of her beliefs remain as bright as ever. And she may be right, even if few others will admit publicly that unionism and republicanism might not be able to live side by side with Britain providing interminable cover.

Imprisoned once herself, McAliskey has fought for the rights of other political prisoners and was nearly murdered for her troubles. Single-minded and unbending, she grappled as much with Sinn Fein and the provisional IRA and with those she earlier called comfortable middle-class Hibernians as she has with loyalist fighters, unionist politicians and British power. In time and space, McAliskey seemed a minor, even quaint, figure. But in her shining moment she reopened the festering wounds of the British occupation that turned into decades of tribal bleeding before today's peace and threshold of promise were reached.

McAliskey was a student firebrand when fire engulfed Northern Ireland and the world watched and listened. The early years of her public life track the early years of The Troubles. After the first civil rights march went off peacefully, if incompletely, in Coalisland on August 24, 1968, the next march, planned in Derry for October 5, was banned by the Unionist government. When some of the would-be protesters showed up to defy the ban, police pummelled them. This use of force raised the stakes, expanded the protest movement and led to a large demonstration in Derry on November 16 of that year.

Wherever there was a civil rights demonstration in 1968, McAliskey was there or thereabouts. She helped to lead a march of more than 70 miles from Belfast to Derry on January 1, 1969. In that same year, Bernadette Devlin, woman, student, aged 21, was elected to the British parliament from her hometown area. She was the youngest woman ever elected to Westminster and the youngest MP, period, in 200 years.

Civil rights protests were spreading and soon Derry was again a flashpoint. When several thousand Apprentice Boys held their annual march in Derry on August 12, 1969, the marchers and the police spilled over into the Catholic Bogside area. The war was on. Britain's Labor government sent troops to quell the violence, and there they stayed. That same year, Bernadette

Devlin was arrested for her role, allegedly inciting a riot, in what is known as The Battle of the Bogside. Devlin knew all about rights and wrongs and she could articulate them better than most. Her long black hair, mini-skirts and beauty did not hurt Devlin's role as a crowd-pleaser and a media magnet. On April 17 of that same year, six days before she turned 22, Devlin was elected to the British Parliament. She was, the British Broadcasting Corp. reported at the time, the third youngest person ever elected to that body. She was sworn in on her 22nd birthday. Devlin's maiden speech, delivered an hour after she took her seat, was acclaimed by both Labor and Tory MPs. The next year, in 1970, while still an MP, she served four months of a six-month sentence for her role in the Bogside riots.

Bernie, as she was sometimes called, punched and scratched the British Home Secretary Reginald Maudling in the House of Commons in January 1972, after she accused him of lying about the killings in Derry on Bloody Sunday a few days earlier. That was undoubtedly another first for Devlin-McAliskey; the first time a female MP ever punched a male MP in parliament. Since then there have probably been more such fisticuffs, but not in parliament. Devlin lashed out after she was barred from speaking to counter Maudling, although reports at the time said that she had the right to speak under parliamentary rules.

Re-elected to parliament once, McAliskey lost in 1975, when she and a more mainstream Catholic split the Catholic vote in her district. She also lost in attempts to win a seat in the European Parliament from the Republic of Ireland. McAliskey helped to found the Irish Republican Socialist Party, the political branch of a radical republican paramilitary group that had split from the IRA. Later, she left that party to launch the Independent Socialist Party, which better suited her independence of mind, character and politics.

In the late 1970s, by then married to elementary school teacher Michael McAliskey, she was a member of the National H Blocks/Armagh Committee. The group campaigned to have the political prisoners in the H-Block of Long Kesh prison and in the Armagh women's prison declared political prisoners rather than common criminals so they would be recognized for what they were and thus would be entitled to better treatment. After three committee members and a sympathizer were murdered, McAliskey became the next target.

The attempt on her life, and on her husband's, came at their rural home near Coalisland in January 1981. With the McAliskeys' two-year-old son at home, three loyalist gunmen, later convicted of the crime, broke into the house with an ax and pumped eight bullets into Bernadette Devlin McAliskey's back, a lung, both arms and a leg. Her husband was shot four times in the head, shoulder and right arm and was close to death but survived. The gunmen did not intend to fail in their mission. But they did. Bernadette McAliskey has only one vocal cord and walked with a limp, but when we met she still talked with the fervor of years past.

Less than two months after McAliskey was shot, Bobby Sands, one of the H-Block prisoners, went on a hunger strike. If the world hadn't turned toward Northern Ireland before, democrats, socialists, communists, capitalists, republicans and all those in between the world over were standing at attention after the hunger strikes began. Before he died in prison on May 5, 1981, Sands was elected to the British parliament. Nine other prisoners who had joined with Sands in the hunger strike followed him to the grave.

Although largely forgotten now, Bernadette Devlin McAliskey's role in Northern Ireland's troubled history can never be expunged.

When McAliskey and I met, I didn't want to count bullet wounds or review her life, although her past and her personality dictated her present, and my interest. I wanted to see whether she had changed, perhaps mellowed, to assess her intellectual tenacity and determine why she opposed the Sinn Fein peace effort.

McAliskey had changed, but only physically. Her husband hadn't been able to work since he was nearly killed. She aches and limps and leans, and the family was living in public housing in Coalisland instead of in their own house in the countryside. Graying, plump and looking more like a grandmother than like the student activist she was, McAliskey would be easy to misjudge. Her friends and foes in Northern Ireland know better. A loner more than ever, she remained a strong and able exponent of her hardened republican and socialist views, consistent throughout, like them or not.

McAliskey's problem was not that she hadn't altered her hardline views about a united Ireland and how to get there, it was that those around her had. This shift weakened McAliskey's hand considerably, basically took her out of the game. At that time, Ian Paisley hadn't altered his unwavering opposition to a united Ireland, but those around him hadn't changed either. This strengthened Paisley's hand, but that didn't bother the woman who had shaken Westminster in the fire of her youth.

"Honesty with me is not a virtue; it's an affliction. I was born with it," McAliskey said, with no apologies given. "I'm a disaffected, isolated individual. I'm not a member of any party. Fundamentally my ideology hasn't changed. I was fortunate to have the right instincts from the start. This is my own opinion." If her strength is also her weakness, that isn't a flaw that bothers McAliskey.

More like a local political philosopher than a politician, McAliskey reminded me of Adem Demaci, the ethnic–Albanian from Kosovo who spent about 28 years in Yugoslav prisons because he contested Serb oppression in a province that was more than 90 percent Albanian. Demaci said that Kosovo was as much a prison as the tiny dungeons where he had survived for almost three decades. Speaking of her wounds and the oppressive conditions in Northern Ireland, McAliskey told journalist Katie Donovan in a 1992 interview, "In relation to coping with this communal weight of sorrow, having a pain in my leg is nothing."

When McAliskey and I talked, almost everyone except loyalist and unionist hardliners and some republican extremists favored the peace process that was plodding along. With American help, the governments of Britain and Ireland were attempting to bring republican Sinn Fein into all-party talks among Unionists and the more moderate Catholic nationalists. The goal was to restart all-party self-government in Northern Ireland under Britain's hegemony. Many would call McAliskey's view extremist because she said the process was burdened with dishonesty and would fail. She shunned the gradualist approach behind the talks, not because she opposed peace but because she believed that gradualism in the end would bring more frustration and no peace. Ian Paisley and his hardcore band, at that time, understood the game for what it was and wanted no part in it either, she told me. Time and Paisley have proven her wrong on that point.

As McAliskey saw the theoretical game, after a few decades, maybe 30 years, of all parties governing Northern Ireland under London's wing, the British would pull out and a united Ireland would evolve. If her view was accurate, McAliskey said, the British, the Irish and Sinn Fein should say so from the beginning and put the plan for a united Ireland on the table from the start. Short of this approach, she said, the game was all wishful thinking, groping in the shadows, and would eventually fail.

McAliskey said, without convincing me, that she was not opposed to taking the gradualist approach, because even the absence of war was worth seeking. But, she contended, the differences were so fundamental they would not be resolved without confronting them directly. "I want to be wrong about this whole process," she told me, "but the facts don't lead me to believe I'm wrong. They talk about faith, hope and momentum, and I say no to faith, hope and charity; give me facts. And no one will give me facts. So what if we postpone the war for 15 or 20 years; then what?"

McAliskey may not live to see the "then what?" of her mind. The road is open to a better result than she envisioned, but certainty is not written on any of the road signs ahead. For the moment a political peace is in place. If good fortune holds, Belfast, Dublin and London will reach the point where "then what?" becomes a question they all must answer.

McAliskey disliked and distrusted the British government probably more than she disliked and distrusted the Protestant loyalists and unionists. She won't get much of an argument on that, if for different reasons, anywhere in the north or south, not from Catholics or Protestants, republicans or loyalists, nationalists or unionists.

Traditionally clannish and tribal to begin with, Ireland was easy for an invader to divide, turn on itself, conquer and exploit. Centuries of foreign intervention intensified all aspects of the tribal conflict in Ireland. From this Irish-English-British stew, Northern Ireland's politics boiled down to a sectarian, quasi-military and partisan soup. If a political party or paramilitary group weren't splintered, it didn't exist. Some of the splinters were splintered. Even the republican and loyalist paramilitary groups and gangs were divided and subdivided. Some Catholics crossed sectarian-political divides for political reasons as did some Protestants. Mainstream unionists varied in intensity and a large number differed from Ian Paisley's sticky and powerful evangelical blend of church and unionist state. Socialists coexisted with

Walled in, walled out: One of the many sectarian/paramilitary murals that decorated Northern Ireland. This one, seen in 1994, was painted by the Ulster Volunteer Force, the most lethal of the Protestant/Unionist paramilitary groups that countered the IRA before it renounced violence in 2007 (photograph by the author, © Cox Newspapers Inc.).

women's political groups and with reasonable political ecumenists who often seemed adrift in the constant ideological tempests.

The Irish Republican Army of most recent vintage was one of the most tightly controlled revolutionary groups that I have encountered. Solid information about its leaders, plans and operations was just about impossible to uncover. The closest a foreign correspondent could get to the IRA was Sinn Fein, the IRA's political voice. Listen closely to a republican say I R A and all you'll hear is R A. The "I" for Irish is implicit; it's run together so fast it's not said but it's surely understood. The leaders of Sinn Fein, which in the Irish language means "Ourselves alone," were doubtless active in the IRA, but after they shifted full-time to Sinn Fein the lines back to the mother ship were impossible to detect.

After many hours on several occasions talking and drinking with Sinn Fein members at a republican social club in Belfast during the mid-to-late 1990s, all I learned was that Sinn Fein's gradualist political approach to a united Ireland was not universally embraced in republican ranks. The rest was old news: During the day, the lads could throw down two pints to my half then ask whether something was wrong with me. At night the drinking would stop hours after last call when the multi-colored strobe lights still flashed against the glass ball that twirled over the dance floor. From the back of many rooms and the front of many podiums I watched Sinn Fein leaders Gerry Adams and Martin McGuinness match wits and lies with the power of British officials and institutions and, all alone, more than hold their own. Except when Adams spoke in what he usually calls Irish rather than Gaelic, I didn't need a translator.

One of ten children born in Belfast to a construction laborer and a linen-factory worker, Adams comes from a background of rich-green republicanism to whom the insides of British-unionist prisons are alien but were not unused. Inside and outside of prison, Adams has read, thought and etched himself into a formidable political leader.

An admitted IRA leader from Derry in the 1970s, the street-schooled McGuinness learned his politics on the job, from day-to-day, smoothing his rough edges as he scraped through political battles in alleys, on sidewalks and in recent years from behind podiums. McGuinness still has tough street-kid eyes glaring from middle-aged flesh. He and Adams are trusted partners.

The IRA is considered responsible for almost half of the roughly 3,500 conflict-related deaths in Northern Ireland since 1968, although almost 300 more Catholics have been killed than Protestants during that period, according to published figures. As the IRA's political arm, Sinn Fein can't get away with playing Pontius Pilate to the IRA's killings, although it tries. Loyalist gangs, who came later to the fray, are responsible for between one-quarter and one-third of all the murders. For years British forces played secret roles in backing loyalist gangs in their combined attempts to punish or destroy the IRA. No sect, gang or nation-state has a corner on responsiblity for The Troubles; no one's hands are clean.

Criminal activity spewed from the bowels of the conflict on all sides of the tribal walls. Even British forces engaged in what should properly be called criminal activity in their state-sanctioned violent attempts to counter violence, although nation-states often escape responsibility for such actions because they carry the legitimacy of statehood. That gangsterism thrives in the midst of tribal conflicts is more common than rare. So it happened as well in Sarajevo, Beirut, Mogadishu, Algiers and Baghdad. Violence begets violence, whatever the motivation.

Adams, McGuinness and the IRA in July 2005 gave unionist hardliners what they wanted in order to resume all-party government in the province: an announced end to the IRA's campaign of violence, and disarmament. But part two of that announcement said the IRA would use peaceful political means to unite Ireland. The conflict seemed to have entered a new, less violent phase, but it probably will go on in a distinctly tribal manner.

―――

McAliskey, who says that she opposes violence but is not a pacifist, denies that she is a hardline republican bookend to Ian Paisley's hardline unionism. Intellectually she is, I would say, but politically she is not.

Paisley is a voracious political animal; McAliskey used politics for a short time but generally disdains the process. As much as McAliskey espouses a united Ireland, Paisley probably would be willing to die to prevent one. McAliskey rose to prominence with the civil rights movement in 1968. Every march McAliskey helped to organize Paisley opposed, building his fundamentalist church and political party on the opposite side of the barricades. Using the pulpit and the street corner as bullhorns, Paisley did as much as any individual, and more than almost any other, to create The Troubles and keep the cauldron boiling.

The civil rights movement attempted to bring together Catholic and Protestant workers, both of whom had suffered under the province's political and economic system. Paisley broke up that alliance and on the rubble he built a united hardline church and allied political party. Paisley kept his Zoroastrian-like world simple: Life in Northern Ireland is a contest between good and evil. Popish Catholicism was evil and most Catholics were devils. A united Ireland is a Catholic conspiracy, which is bad. Only his brand of Protestantism is good, and absolute loyalty to the Union Jack is essential.

Whether they are sober or have had one-too-many full English breakfasts — which some London East-Enders define jokingly as a pint of Guinness — the English like to joke about the dour Scots. But the only place I ever met a dour Scot was in Northern Ireland. And many of them were in Paisley's church.

To his followers, Paisley, now in his early 80s, is a fascinating and remarkable fellow, able to rule the hardline unionist street and nave for almost 40 years. Politically he appears stronger than ever. Paisley's party won nine seats, a gain of four, in the May 2005 elections to the British parliament. His party leads the way in Northern Ireland's assembly, going from 30 to 36 seats in the March 8, 2007 elections. But Paisley is aging, and his world was built on fear and hate, which should detract somewhat from the achievements of a Christian evangelical preacher. His decision to sit at the same table with Adams indicates at least a change in tactics and strategy at this late point in his life. If redemption exists in Northern Ireland's pantheon of religious blessings, Paisley will require more than his share to redeem his past.

Paisley always said that he opposed violence, but his words and actions provoked it. In March 1998, when Paisley was boycotting talks that included Sinn Fein, he carried a yellow sign that said, "Bloody and deceitful men will not live out their days." The preacher is transparent but lucky; he can say that he eschews violence and lay the blame on the Bible for the blood-red line that connects inflammatory words to deadly acts. That he is not alone in using religion to obtain political power and exploit popular emotions to create conflict says as much about sectarian tribalism and his breed in general as it does about Paisley in particular.

The Protestant or Presbyterian pope, as Ian Richard Kyle Paisley has been called, however ironically, comes by his life's work genetically. His father was a Baptist preacher of the steaming pulpit variety. Born in Northern Ireland, Paisley was a Presbyterian rebel almost from his first breath. He founded the Free Presbyterian Church of Ulster in 1951. In his early years, Paisley remained on the edges of unionist politics, not by choice but because more mainstream unionists controlled Northern Ireland. His hysteria and provocations at first attracted few ears.

With the civil rights marches came The Troubles, which Paisley did his best to ignite. Next came his forced merger of religion with politics. First he founded the Martyrs Memorial Free Presbyterian Church in Belfast in 1969. On that base, he launched the Democratic Unionist Party in 1971, and went on to serve lengthy terms in Northern Ireland's provincial government and in the British parliament. Only lately did he bow out of the European Parliament after serving for 25 years. Like McAliskey, he was convicted of a crime related to his political activity during the civil rights protests. Paisley served three months in prison for unlawful assembly in 1966.

The term "bully pulpit" should have been coined for Paisley and his lectern, as much as for the U.S. presidency. The Bible, his religion and his church were whips he used to keep his flock in line at the ballot box. His pulpit was the rock from which he called his opponents evil, sinners and devils, lest anyone miss the points he made on the street. The cord between Paisley's church and his politics is unbroken.

When I traveled to Northern Ireland from my London base during five years in the mid–1990s, which was often, I made a point to attend Paisley's Sunday services. I sought not religious enlightenment but clues to his constituency and the source of his power. When Paisley was not stirring anti–Catholic and anti–Irish hatred with his voice, he was passing out religious literature mixed with political fear and loathing that kept his followers in line and stiff with paranoia. His voice still boomed and with his bulk Paisley retained some of his old bullying, intimidating presence. Even then he was stooped, his hellfire fading.

Paisley's Martyrs Memorial church is an attractive modern building of wood and white brick in a quiet area of East Belfast. He held morning and evening services each Sunday. Most of his parishioners always appeared to be 50 years or older. The children and young people who attended usually did so in the evenings. The church is large and most of the time when I've been there the evening service was much better attended than the morning sermon. Every Sunday was like Easter Sunday; women wore large hats and their Sunday-best dresses, while most of the men wore suits and ties. Paisley's parishioners were accustomed to visitors coming to hear their messiah. I always sat in the last pew so I could scan the entire congregation. Minus the modern building, Paisley's services have the strong whiff of American Gothic with an accent. Whenever Paisley surprised me with a calm demeanor, he was only taking a deep breath before firing off another tirade. Invariably, he would open with a few political comments about the threats to the union before he flowed into a fundamentalist biblical speech.

In his opening remarks on December 11, 1994, Paisley said that church was a place to put aside temporal concerns. But before he began his religious sermon, Paisley told his flock that it was "a dark day, a sad day" of "apostasy" in Northern Ireland because Britain and the mainstream unionists were surrendering to the enemies of unionism, the IRA. His biblical sermon that morning was cut short because the building's heating system had broken down. The church was no more than half full, and Paisley made the usual pitch for manna, tithings and offerings, and the basket was passed for contributions.

Anyone who dozed during his sermon could have picked up the gist of his remarks by reading *The Revivalist*, "the official organ" of Paisley's church.

The front page of the November issue of the brochure, which was available when I attended services in December, began with the words "In the evil day," a biblical reference that was printed in large red capital letters. Beneath the "evil" reference was an item titled, "A look at the present situation in Ulster by the editor," who happened to be Paisley. He never missed an opportunity to link his God and his Bible to Northern Ireland's politics and the righteousness of his political views. The link between Paisley's opponents and evil was direct. He warned his constituents that the British "were callously taking steps to undermine, betray and sell-out the Union" by allowing Sinn Fein to participate in all-party talks before the IRA had disarmed.

May 19, 1996, was another somber Sunday in Paisley's church. An election was pending and Paisley vowed to win, with the help of his God and of his believers. "The situation grows more serious by the hour. I'd gladly take up the gauntlet and stop the movement toward a united Ireland," he said, as if he hadn't done just that 25 years before. He continued to oppose Sinn Fein's participation in all-party talks and predicted, predictably, that "We're going to get a glorious victory, but we must be humble before God." Humility was not a Paisley virtue. And there was God again, being called upon to take one side with no regard for what the other side's God was doing. Paisley began the evening service that same day by saying, "We pray tonight God save Ulster." "Amen," said the 250 people in Paisley's church. Ulster happens to include nine counties, only six of which make up Northern Ireland; the remaining three are in the republic.

But amen and any one tribe's God are not enough to save Northern Ireland for the Protestants, the Catholics or the British and Irish governments and traditions. It's easy to find Catholics and Protestants, republicans and unionists, who live separately but close together throughout the province, speak sincerely of peace, justice, political cooperation and economic parity. Fear and the violent activities of extremists blocked their way forward for years. In the short term, cooperation and power-sharing are essential to drain the conflict of its negative energy. In the long run, which is probably years off, Westminster's hand will have to be withdrawn or the core of the conflict will remain.

Tribalism in many forms had driven the bloody conflict, and will continue to do so in more moderate ways even as all sides see their interests best served by talking and positioning themselves for subsequent political and diplomatic phases in deciding Northern Ireland's future. Four people from Northern Ireland — two Catholics, one Protestant and one whose mother was Catholic and whose father was Protestant — have been awarded the Nobel Prize for Peace in the past 30 years or so. They were honored for their efforts to bring peace to the province and in the hope that the awards themselves would help to end the violence. The two most recent Nobel winners from Northern Ireland, John Hume and David Trimble, won the international prize but lost the local war, at least temporarily. Hume, of the mainly Catholic, nationalist and moderate Social Democratic and Labor Party, left provincial politics for health reasons. David Trimble of the conciliatory Ulster Unionist Party lost his seat in the May 2005 elections to the British Parliament. Trimble then resigned as leader of the UUP. Despite their pattern of good work in the past decade to pacify Northern Ireland, the time is past for any political figure from Dublin or London to win a Nobel for efforts to pacify Northern Ireland.

NINE

Somalia, Land of the Walking Dead

Cause: "Sometimes I think the devil lives in this country. We can't improve anything. No one wants it. They fear it will benefit another clan or hurt themselves, so why take the risk." — Official of the rump state called Somaliland speaking in the northern Somali city of Hargeisa on August 11, 1992.

Effect: "I just couldn't imagine human beings could live such a low existence and survive," said an American aid worker I interviewed on August 6, 1992, at a small hospital in the south-central Somali town of Baidoa. The aid worker spoke as she and others pulled maggots from under the rotting teeth of a little girl, and treated a young boy whose right ear and face were rotting away after an untreated ear infection had "exploded." At that moment the hospital had hired two more men to bury the daily dead —14 on August 1, 1992, 11 on August 2, eight on August 3, 14 on August 4...

A U.N. official warned us not to take one step outside the agency's compound without armed guards. The panorama of destruction from the battered airport to the center of the barricaded and divided Somali capital of Mogadishu offered a valuable clue that this was not an empty admonition.

Too many guns, too much robbing and killing, too many clans and subclans fighting for power and territory, for fetid water, scraps of camel and goat hide that served as entrees, and for life. Too many people dying from drought, famine and a tribal war stoked by weapons that nation-states left behind after they had quit the Cold War cold turkey.

Naked ethnic-tribal enmities, old and new, had been unleashed a year earlier. Children, women and old men across the tribal divides — the easiest of prey — covered the parched wasteland with their dead bodies. In August 1992, Somalia was filled with the dead and the living stumbling to their graves on a scale I had not seen before.

Here was tribalism in the raw: Families, clans and tribes circling around their own and fighting to inflate their own power and to punish other families, clans and tribes with no visible concern for broader values. In an even larger circle, men and women, the armed and the unarmed, squared off in a contest which proved only that men have enough muscle to gather the food and strength necessary to squeeze a trigger while women crumble in the dirt trying to save the children of women and men.

"There are no good guys here," a U.N. official said 30 months before the warring clans and their leaders drove all U.N. forces from Somalia on the heels of the departing U.S. troops. His assessment was no joke and I took his travel advice, hoping to find a few Somalis who would be good guys while I counted their dead and tried to tell the world of their ruination.

With U.N. guidance, I and a couple of other journalists who had entered the country on a flight from Kenya hired entire families every time we left the U.N. compound, the only safe place to sleep in Somalia's bleached-white but bloodied capital.

Once a small gem, at least superficially and from a distance, the capital was now a decaying victim of another society gone haywire.

My choice was stark and simple: Hire whole families to help me or hire no one and go nowhere. Whenever I left the compound, whether to travel around the city or venture 150 miles into the bush country, I hired a driver, guides, protectors, translators and gawkers along for the ride, among them three or four armed guards who rode inside and on top of our cars or trucks. When I left a vehicle, the guards went with me. Where the air reeked of death and disease, where order, routine services and all organization had been vaporized by tribal conflict, drought and famine, and where hot rifle barrels resting in the nervous hands of testosterone-pumped young men were the law, only paid protection provided the safety and the ability to report on Somalia's slow death.

Whether you hire an entire family or only a driver, translator or someone who knew the local landscape and could help arrange interviews, a journalist has little choice but to put complete trust in those local masters. For a Westerner or any outsider to think that he knows more than a local person is to display an arrogance that without fail will purchase a ticket to trouble.

Weapons were never part of my journalistic tool kit, but on more than one occasion in Somalia I was happy to have gunmen along for the ride. I traveled as light as possible. In Somalia I carried a small bag about two feet square and six inches deep. In it I brought a few clothes, a self-created first-aid kit, toothbrush and other personal hygiene items, background papers, pens, pencils and notebooks. On my right arm I protected a small Tandy 200 computer. I filed stories from Mogadishu by borrowing a satellite phone wher-

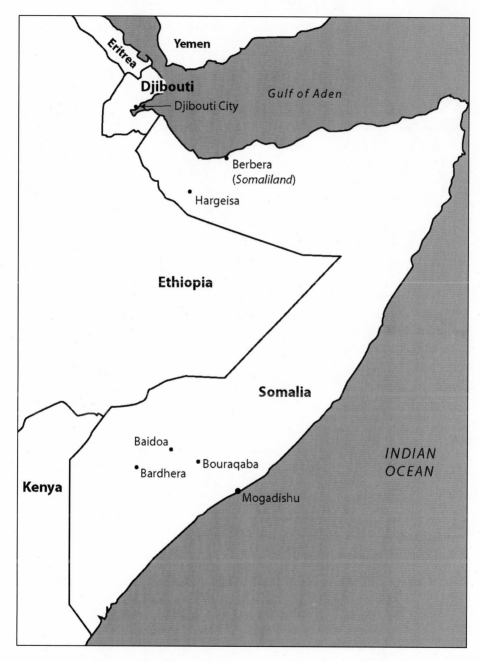

From the coast to the bush country, on the trail of Somalia's dead and dying.

ever I could find one, usually at the office of a foreign humanitarian agency. An antique by today's standard, the Tandy never failed and would operate as long as I could keep throwing in four double A batteries. Once, to my great surprise, I filed a story from a lonely public phone on the Iraqi-Turkish border.

In Somalia, journalists and aide workers rode in vehicles that locals called "technicals" because they had machineguns mounted on their roofs. Technicals burned gold; it cost $110 to fill one with gasoline and have enough left over for emergencies in the barren bush country. Gasoline was pumped to the engine from a large plastic container under the hood of the vehicles. Something told me this wouldn't pass safety regulations in a country that had any. One day the technical might be a pickup truck; another day an old Toyota Land Cruiser, both of which my drivers had to hot-wire to start.

On the outgoing leg of a 300-mile round trip from Mogadishu to Baidoa, we drove near the village of Bouraqaba, which was filled with starving, desperate people. We turned off the road into an opening in the middle of a monolith, a huge rock that was split in two. I wanted to gauge the level of misery and starvation. Within minutes, maybe seconds, the villagers, many of them naked and most of them literally dying for something to eat or the means to get it, descended on us, shouting and waving, if they could raise their hands.

My "family" recognized the danger of being robbed, overrun or worse, immediately, before I did. Guns raised, my Somali protectors threw fistfuls of almost useless Somali money into the air. I added to the monetary cascade as we sped, the guns of my protectors up and ready and with dirt and dust flying, from the village before the mass could reach our "technical." If my guards hadn't reacted so quickly, we might have encountered more trouble than four armed guards could have handled and I probably would not have left the village alive.

In the famished bush-country town of Baidoa, guards or not, I was warned not to take photos of armed men at a hospital. If I defied the warning, I was told, I would be shot. I had difficulty grasping the logic of this argument, but it was persuasive. I surveyed the situation with the astuteness of someone about to be dropped down a well filled with rats, vermin, reptiles and spiders and decided the best course was to hide my camera deep in my bag and to make absolutely sure the person who gave me the warning saw me do so.

From the coast into the bush country, Somalia's changing landscape was deceptive. A few scrawny camels, goats and cows stood within sight of the road leading from Mogadishu. That might be expected. But in stretches closer to the city the land was green and rich-looking, its soil dark. Then the trees thinned to shrubs in the bush country where a few and only the fittest wild pigs scampered across the hard red clay and the weakest Somalis lived and died in beehive-shaped thatched huts. Prosperity, always a relative term, never visited this land. Survival was the best hope.

Somalia is the only place where I ever wept while reporting. A child, with his distended stomach signaling starvation, defecating and vomiting in the dust as his mother held on helplessly should always melt a lens' hardness.

The Somalia story was anything but another routine journalistic moment. What was happening was not in dispute: The sickening evidence of the dead and dying was in front of my face, in my nasal passages, my ears, mouth and throat; it was all around and inescapable. Sultry winds bore the stench of death along with the dust. The responsibility was broad and well-known and didn't make much difference anyway because the number of people who were falling daily and whom only food and security could save was so large. Bombarded by drought, famine and war, Somalia was a human disaster of biblical proportions in a world where human senses and sensitivities were fast being hardened or eroded by repetition on 24-hour news cycles and advances in communication that seemed to exaggerate events or make few distinctions among them.

Every time I peered into the camera lens to capture the blank face of a dying child or talked to old women and men creeping toward their graves with already-dead eyes, I had to toss my head to shake away the tears and pretend that my eyes were merely polished glass.

Humor had worked before as a means to break down language and cultural barriers — but humor was homeless in Somalia.

At a private home in Syria, for example, the family patriarch, the boss, announced that he was going to find a new wife because his present wife was getting too old. His joke drew only forced laughs. Then I remarked that the man's comment was odd because his wife told me the same thing about him when I walked in, that he was too old and she was looking. The whole room exploded in laughter at the twist at the husband's expense and the rather absurd notion that an elderly Arab woman would be looking to replace her husband. It's never a good idea to embarrass the man of the house in that region, but in this case the joke broke a barrier. The husband was forced to laugh with everyone else.

With a camera and notebook, a visitor always draws a crowd, especially of children. For children in Afghanistan, for example, I winked with one eye, then the other, then blinked both, and the kids in Mazar-ash-Sharif roared with laughter and ran off to find their friends and parents so they, too, could see the strange show. As I winked and the crowd grew to more than a hundred children and adults, I showed the children the hand game. It's simple:

open palms placed on top of open palms, and the hands on the bottom then try to smack the hands on top before the hands on top can be moved away. A child's game, it requires no equipment except hands, eyes and awareness — which in some war zones is more than kids have. But, like the winking, the hand game is something the kids had never seen. I had to stop entertaining because the crowd grew too large and unruly as kids and adults shouted and elbowed their way in for a closer view.

But Somalia was no place for the slightest bit of humor. The numbers of dead and dying were shocking, and the way the people were dying — slowly, from starvation and disease — was wrenching. Violence and killing, especially in civil wars, only bring more violence and killing in a worsening cycle. The tribal engines that power civil wars are easy to start but difficult to stop. No one really wins. Exhaustion alone stops the killing, and by then only a few people who remain standing can recall what the carnage was all about.

People everywhere say that war is terrible and that their neighbors or mysterious tribes far from them are crazy to kill and be killed. But everywhere it's the same: Let a general shake his medals in the sun, or a smartly dressed politician wave an oversized flag high enough and shout about an axis of evil, or a praying man in tie, smock or turban raise a holy book and suddenly war becomes an act of loyalty and sound logic.

Of the wars that I have seen, the worst are tribal civil wars, Lebanon, Bosnia, Algeria, Somalia. But to describe even those conflicts simply as civil wars is to describe them incompletely.

A seeming conspiracy of human and natural forces sent Somalia hurtling into a tribal hell during the late 1980s and early 1990s. Somali clans and subclans, elsewhere usually called tribes and clans, fighting to avenge old grievances and for crumbs in Mogadishu and the barren semi-desert countryside caused the final explosion that sent Somalia into the abyss.

At least six major tribes, referred to as clans in Somalia, warred with each other. Those clans included a total of about 30 major subclans, or subtribes, which fanned the civil war throughout the country.* Try to follow the Somali

---

*Seifulaziz Milas, a UNICEF consultant from Madagascar, seemed to know more about the civil war, famine and drought than Somalis themselves. In a report prepared for UNICEF in June 1992, Milas listed six major clans: Dir, Issaq, Hawiye, Darod, Rahanweyn and Dighil. He also listed the indigenous Banadir coastal people and ethnic Bantus as non–clan-based political organizations. The six major clans or tribes included the following sub-clans, according to Milas: Dir Tribe; Issa, Samaroon, Bimaal, Gadabursi and Gadsan. Issaq Tribe: Habr-Younis, Habr-Ja'alo, Habr-Awal, Idagale. Hawiye Tribe: Habar-Gadir, which is divided into small subgroups called Ayr, Saad, Suleiman, Surur; other major clans of the Hawiye tribe are Abgal, Hawadley, Murursade, Sheikhal, Ajoran and Gurreh. The fourth major clan or tribe is the Darod, which is divided into the following subgroups or sub clans: Mijerteen, Ogaden, Marehan, Awrtableh, Lalkasse, Dholbahante and Warsangeli. The Rahanweyn Tribe is divided into the Sagaal and Siyyed clans, while the Dighil Tribe or clan has no meaningful subgroups.

conflict without a large wall chart and you will be lost hopelessly in a maze of meaningless names.

Civil war in Somalia was not rooted in religion or language differences unless those elements were a faceless part of clan and subclan cultures. Most Somalis practice a mild-mannered form of Sunni Islam. There are more than a dozen languages spoken in the country, but Somali is by far the dominant one.

A combination of nature being mean and tribes fighting for crumbs destroyed Somalia's pastoral economy and piled death upon grief. Drought and famine, nature's way of telling humans who or what rules, and war, humanity's way of competing with nature for making misery, bludgeoned Somalia's weakest targets. In their civil war, the Somali tribes fought for power and territory; food was power and even dried up bush country was territory worth grasping.

Nation-states — foreign tribes — supplied the ammo that fueled the civil war. Instead of lances and spears, the Somalis could now fling bullets from automatic rifles and machine guns. Somalia, its position on the Horn of Africa being strategically important as a guardian of the Gulf of Aden, the Red Sea and the Persian Gulf, was a Cold War battleground. It wasn't worth occupying, but Somalia was a perfect place for your side to destroy so your enemy couldn't control it by default.

The Soviet Union, the United States, Germany, Italy, Britain, China, Pakistan and other countries supplied the weapons for the Somali government and all of its tribal opponents during the Cold War. The Somali people, most of whom were civilians, paid with their lives for the weapons when the Cold War ended and the cold warriors skated away. Then the civil war began and none of the Cold War combatants or the arms dealers cared much about the havoc their weapons brought to Somalia.

An official with a British company that was removing thousands of land mines from the earth in northern Somalia figured that there were enough weapons in that region to fight a war for 18 months without having to resupply.

Following up their arming of Somalia to offset the old Eastern bloc's weapons, American and Western European taxpayers were splitting the cost of clearing land mines, but only land mines, from northern Somalia. I wondered how that deal squared on financial terms, let alone human values, with the arms shipments that put the land mines in the ground to begin with.

Somalia's suffering was also raised on a foundation of British and Italian colonialism and a 21-year local dictatorship that followed independence from Italy and Britain in 1960. In 30 years, Somalia's feuding nomadic tribes assisted by international tribes playing proxy power games on alien soil destroyed what was at best a fragile nation-state. This was the Somalia I found in August 1992.

Most Somalis are Muslims, nominally at least. I never saw anyone pray, not even once. If the people I saw had kneeled, they probably would not have been able to get up again. Somalis speak many dialects of the same Cushitic language, but the ethnic makeup of the tribes and subtribes varies widely. The tribes were fighting over old and new grievances, for the spoils of power in a land where traditionally the amount of animals a family owns or the amount of land it tills determines its wealth. In the end, Somalis were crawling and begging for scraps of rotten food and drops of putrid water to live another day.

The massive and slow deaths of civilians made Somalia's condition the worst I had seen anywhere. Children, old women and old men, mothers without milk or other means to save their babies, could not escape. Nomads from the bush country migrated to towns that had no food. Somalis gathered insects and tiny scraps of food from the ground or boiled camel and goat skin trying to survive. Mothers ate lice picked from their children's hair then fed some to their children. Men, women and children ate maggots from camel carcasses that lined roads.

People from the towns migrated to Modgadishu to eat thin gruel before they were buried on the street a few feet from where they had died in food kitchens built to save them. U.N. workers and others with nongovernmental relief organizations risked their lives attempting to build the only lifeline Somalia's civilians had. To reach the civilians with life-saving nourishment and medicine, relief workers had to fight off warrior-thugs who used food as levers of power.

Desperation was so deep in the bush country that relief workers said a little food was worse than none at all. Bringing in a little food would attract too many people from the surrounding countryside who couldn't be fed. But if herdsmen stayed in their own territory, they might be able to scrape by.

Young children, famished and naked, were hours from death as their mothers, with no milk to give and themselves slipping toward death, ate rawhide in hopes of surviving until dawn. Tears filled my eyes as I squinted into a camera to record a child vomiting, defecating and dying at the feet of his helpless mother.

In a blur of self-doubt I questioned my role as an observer and chronicler. What I was doing was pointless, I thought. Help the kid, get food for the mother. But I was helpless. This is all I have, eyes, ears, feelings, a camera, a pen, a notebook. A memory. Ah, the papers won't publish the photos anyway; too hard to swallow over oatmeal, fresh juice, an omelette in the comfortable nooks of newspaper-reading America, I thought, imagining the reaction back home. The foreign editor will ask for 600 words, if I'm lucky, and the papers will trim the story to an item in the World Briefs column: "Thousands dying in Somalia." These are Africans; they're black and "uncivilized." Who cares? Besides, there are no American troops here; but just wait.

All of these thoughts flitted through my mind as I shook tears from my eyes, centered and filled the frame with the swollen abdomen of a dying child. My final thought was that reporting the disaster might help prevent further deaths by enlightening an unknowing and callous world. The old horse pulls the fire wagon and the dog barks. Always. Click.

Officially, a tribal truce was in place in Somalia when I landed in Mogadishu on August 5, 1992, on a U.N. flight from Nairobi. But skirmishes and threats prevailed on almost every street corner in Somalia's shredded power center. A shantytown filled with starving Somalis and framed by battered stoves, refrigerators and other appliances rimmed the cratered landing strip. A paved road ran along high ground into Mogadishu, but for safety reasons we took a less exposed lower road that was paved with dirt. The vehicles in our small caravan bristled with machine guns and armed guards. Officially, the truce was holding. In reality man and nature were dismembering the fragile Somali nation-state.

One tribe controlled the barely functioning airport; another controlled the seaport. Food brought in by the U.N. and other relief agencies often was stolen by tribal gunmen at Mogadishu's port or at its airport and never reached the starving civilians.

Relief agencies were forced to hire armed guards to transport food to distribution centers or into the bush country on roads where warriors sought booty for the privilege of passing through their tribal territory. The big question at that moment was whether U.N. troops should be brought into Somalia to protect food shipments from tribal chiefs and warriors who used food as a power tool.

The effects of all the forces that had devastated Somalia were visible throughout the country. Everywhere, it was the weakest who were dying, in stupifying numbers, of starvation. Who was responsible for the deaths? Nature to be sure. But just as surely it was the tribal leaders and the young men with weapons, and all the countries that provided those weapons.

The International Committee of the Red Cross provided the food at Kitchen Number 51 in Mogadishu: white rice and oil in the morning; beans and white rice in the afternoon. The bones of the near-dead were kept in place only by skin draped more loosely over their bodies with each passing day. On the day I visited, August 5, 1992, seven people had died by 4:30 P.M. on the grounds of Kitchen Number 51, which was pitched at an old petroleum compound. Every day 10 to 12 people died of starvation and disease in a place where relief workers strained to save the living from the inevitable. All of the dead were removed from their primitive plastic-covered tree-branch tents and buried, sometimes one on top of another, in the swale beside the dirt road outside the compound.

Daily the trail of death hardened under foot as more people died and were buried on a city street a few yards from where their relatives struggled to stay alive. The picture was so graphic it seemed unnecessary to talk with anyone.

Ahmed, 63, a farmer driven by famine and war from his home in Baidoa, watched his three children dying. Sitting in the dirt was one of those children, Abdi, 7, being feasted on by flies. Drained by diarrhea and vomiting, the boy could have passed for three or four. He stared blankly straight ahead, too frail to raise his hand to brush away the flies that were feeding on his face. Still a beautiful boy, with curly black hair, his skin taut over protruding bones, Abdi had plenty of sad company. Those that starvation didn't kill disease did.

About 150 miles from Mogadishu lay Baidoa, a city of about 80,000. The population fluctuated as starving people left in search of food in Mogadishu, others died, and more came from deeper in the bush country in search of morsels.

On the way to Baidoa, we expected to be stopped at a tribal boundary and we were. I held a document that was supposed to permit passage to Baidoa, provided that I paid $75 at a border outpost. The warrior at the checkpoint was offended by the $75 offer. "Sorry," I said, "that's what your boss in Mogadishu said I would have to pay, and that's all I'm paying." He insisted that I pay $150. We argued and my team explained the deal we had made in the capital. The warrior discussed this with cohorts and then still insisted on the higher figure. I continued to resist, on principle. Then I gave him $80 and told him that he had won. This warrior at the checkpoint wasn't thrilled with a $5 tip, but he let us pass.

What I did was risky, I realized later, because I was at the mercy of the warriors who held all the power. I probably should have paid the higher amount. Sure, I had armed guards, but the warriors had more and could have robbed us or worse. On similar occasions, such as at the airport in Mogadishu, I stood on principles that people anywhere could understand, no matter what their culture or tongue: A deal is a deal; common sense is understood in any language; a person's word is all you need.

When I left Mogadishu on a U.N. flight to northern Somalia via the dismal country called Djibouti, a gunman at the airfield wanted $25, just because his tribe claimed the territory. The airport had just been reopened but no one and nothing functioned. I looked around at the gigantic craters in the tarmac and at the crumbling terminal and said that I wasn't paying anything to fly out of such a useless place. The gunman shrugged and left. Later, I thought that I had taken an unnecessary risk. But my reaction was spontaneous, human and easy to understand. I was happy that the gunman got the point.

After I arrived in Baidoa on August 6, 1992, a U.N. worker took me to a large cave. You can sleep here, he said, as scores of women, children and old men looked on hungrily at the mouth of the cave. You'll be fine if you sleep way in the back, he said. The other people will sleep in the front. That might be a five-star cave, I thought, but no thanks.

You must have a chair in your office, I said to the U.N. worker, a very helpful black man who lived in New York. I'll sit in the chair tonight and try to sleep. But my new friend found an extra cot and I slept in a room with him. I was lucky. Somalis were not. When I walked into the compound where my friend and workers for other relief agencies were staying, I strolled into a simmering dispute that appeared racial in nature, a form of tribal dissension with a New World hue.

Some of the others in the compound were kind enough to invite me to dinner that night, but they didn't invite my U.N. friend. I declined the invitation and stuck with the man who was helping me, although he tried to persuade me to stay at the compound where I would eat a better meal. But I refused his offer to satisfy my hunger while violating the loyalty that I felt towards him. Instead, my friend and I went to a large open soup kitchen for dinner. I declined to eat the broth because I knew that local water would cause great pain, probably right away. The next day I ate breakfast at the compound with my friend and the relief workers. I was offered a shower, which I took, by walking behind a small curtain and pulling a rope that tipped a small bucket which I had filled with water. The arrangement, while not top drawer, was one of my best moments in Somalia and surely beat the prospect of sleeping in the cave.

Baidoa was one large food kitchen, but not nearly large enough to feed the thousands of famished pastoral tribesmen drawn there. Routine public services didn't exist. The deeper into the bush one traveled, the more penetrating was the starvation. "This place makes Mogadishu look like Nairobi. You've got bones wrapped in skin," my U.N. friend said, affirming again the truism that all things are relative, even the speed with which dying people die.

I watched as boys and girls, women and old men, searched the ground for scraps of food or seeds to collect in black cups or in the rags they wore, hoping to gather what they might call a meal. Relief workers begged for a massive airlift of food comparable in size to the buildup for the first Gulf war or the U.S. bombing of North Vietnam and Cambodia. At this moment in history the world's ear was tuned more to Bosnia than to Somalia.

Faces of famine: A Somali mother feeds her children what little was available in Baidoa during the devastating civil war, famine and drought of 1992 (photograph by the author, © Cox Newspapers Inc.).

Relief workers are today's heroes wherever natural disasters, tragedies or wars assault people, usually poor people. The greater the need, the greater their heroism. When most of the rest of the world was deaf to Somalia's dying, relief workers brought some food, medical care and comfort at great risk, which they ignored, to themselves.

Anita had spent 11 of her 33 years in one rescue effort after another working for the Irish relief agency Concern. For a week to ten days after she arrived in Baidoa, Anita and others like her had to deal with countless numbers of people who were lying on the sides of the roads, dead. She brought children to the hospital immediately and began feeding as many other people as supplies permitted. By early August 1992, Irish Concern was feeding 8,000 a day in Baidoa and still 20 people were dying daily at the agency's four feeding centers, and were buried just outside those compounds. No one could count the number of people dying elsewhere in Baidoa every day, and the number succumbing in the desert wasteland was beyond measure.

Anita, other workers and I watched as old men and women boiled and ate goat and camel skins because nothing else remotely edible was available. One worker with the relief agency CARE said he saw 20 to 30 people die in 30 minutes in Baidoa. "Every shanty had dead bodies. People are dying like flies," the CARE worker said.

The coordinator of all UNICEF activities in the Baidoa area said he spent the first several days burying the dead after he arrived in the city on June 5, 1992. Neither he nor other hospital workers, including several Americans, talked of being overworked because there was no other standard.

Dead children were wrapped in empty food bags because no animal skins were left to serve as burial shrouds. The animal skins had been eaten or already buried with dead people. Children too weak to cry were brought to the hospitals with faces being eaten away by maggots because ear or other infections had not been treated.

One hospital worker who thought she had seen it all described the food kitchens as "a Friday night horror movie with skeletons walking around. I just couldn't imagine human beings could live such a low existence and survive." The scale of the human tragedy was numbing, but the relief workers kept their sanity and their focus on trying to ease the throbbing misery and sadness.

Food, animals, guns — anything that could be eaten, bartered or used to control others — was valuable in Somalia. In Bardhera, a dusty bush town spilling over with displaced shepherds 240 almost-inaccessible miles from Mogadishu, there was nothing at all of material value. Serious looting of the thatched-hut homes had taken place a couple of years earlier when the civil war was blood-red hot. There was nothing left to loot now. Even the little food being brought in to prevent wholesale starvation was too little to merit thievery.

Habiba, 70, and her seven-year-old granddaughter dined on camel skin, grass and leaves from trees and bushes. "This is worse than anything I've ever seen, and I worked in Ethiopia in 1984 and the Sudan. This is a lot worse," said a worker with the U.N. agency that aids displaced persons.

It was impossible to know how many Somalis had been displaced and were refugees in their own land searching for food. But one estimate put the figure at four million in a country with a population of absolutely no more than nine million. U.N. officials in Bardhera said the remote town had the potential to be a worse disaster zone than Baidoa, which at least was connected to Mogadishu by an asphalt road. From what I could see, with 2,000 famished refugees reaching town daily, Bardhera was as bad as, if not worse than, Baidoa.

When I flew to Bardhera with an Italian senator who was trying to negotiate for further U.N. help, we landed on a level area of desert dirt that should not be called an airstrip. The senator met with Gen. Mohammed Farah Aideed, who led the United Somali Congress and the Habar-Gadir sub clan of the Hawiye clan in central Somalia.

Aideed was instrumental in bringing down the Siad Barre regime after 21 years in absolute power, and was one of the principal contenders for control of the country. He was, by any accounting, one of several clan chiefs behind the fighting. When I interviewed him, Aideed made it clear that he opposed any foreign troops on Somali soil, no matter what the reason. It is easy to underestimate people in poor, distressed countries because the Western measuring stick is essentially material. That is always a mistake.

A handsome man with typically fine Somali features, Aideed carried a silver-topped black cane when we talked, and he pleaded for U.N. help to train a 6,000-man Somali police force to provide security and protect emergency food supplies. At the same time, Aideed strongly opposed U.N. troops themselves attempting to impose security in order to protect the supply and distribution of food. "We don't want incidents with bandits shooting at U.N. troops," he told me. Aideed said nothing about the prospects of his own militia and U.N. troops killing each other.

Less than a year later, Aideed's clan killed 24 Pakistani U.N. troops who were backing the agency's attempt to shut down Aideed's radio station. Not long after that, fighters loyal to Aideed killed 18 American soldiers, wounded about 80 others and shot down three U.S. helicopters. Aideed, who never stopped opposing U.N. military intervention in Somalia, had then been the target of a U.N.–backed manhunt, which was quickly abandoned. He escaped that net, but was killed during continuing clan warfare in the summer of 1996.

The best and maybe the only way to reach northwest Somalia, which then was called Somaliland and which was formerly British Somaliland, was to hitch a ride on a U.N. cargo flight from Mogadishu. The ravages in the north were supposed to be less severe. I wanted to see for myself the extent of the killing and dying there. The U.N. flight stopped overnight in Djibouti then took off before sunrise the next day headed to a landing strip in the bush country outside the town of Hargeisa.

We landed in Djibouti in the early afternoon, ready to enjoy the best a former French colony has to offer. My stay in Djibouti was short and I found nothing there to entice my return.

Sorry, I was told at the airport, you must leave your passport here because we don't have transit visas now. Take a taxi to a hotel, return in two hours and we will have a visa for you. I argued against this plan, but without success.

It is a gross understatement to say that it's a bad idea to be anywhere in this part of the world without one's passport or even to risk losing one's paper identity. Perhaps I could have slept inside the airport, but that didn't tempt me. My taxi sped into town, where I checked into a hotel before returning to the airport within two hours. By that time, the friendly folks at Djibouti international with a lower case "i" were deep into their stash of Qat, also spelled Chat or Kat, a narcotic leaf widely chewed in the Horn of Africa and the Arabian Peninsula. And I was in deeper trouble.

I had seen Qat, which has effects similar to marijuana or hashish, at work a couple of days earlier in the bush country outside of Mogadishu. Half of my family team of driver, translator, armed guards and gawkers was in a stupor and the other half was bouncing up into the roof of our Toyota Land Cruiser, or jumping on top of the roof itself, when our vehicle struck a goat on the way back to Mogadishu. My hired hands were all high, or low, on Qat. The goat was dead. We paid a thick wad of Somali money to quiet the goat's owner. A tire, fender, headlight and part of the bumper and grille also died in the crash.

Daily, around 2 P.M., many people in the Horn of Africa get high or low with Qat in their bodies and smothering their minds. They usually remain in that condition for the rest of the day, sometimes for days or weeks. When this condition prevails no one and nothing works.

Sorry, I was told when I returned to the airport to reclaim my passport, we don't have any transit visas. You must buy a regular visa, which will cost $36 instead of $18. No problem, I answered, I'll pay the baksheesh. Please give me the visa and my passport. Too bad, the two men said, laughing and swivelling in their creaking chairs, their eyes pointing to Qat heaven. We don't have any regular visas now. You must come back tomorrow. You will get your visa and your passport then. I was angry and getting angrier. I began to argue loudly, saying the plane would be leaving before dawn and they wouldn't be at the airport then to return my passport. The more I argued, the more they laughed. Their Qat was potent. It was evident that Qat would win and I would lose.

As I paid for the regular visa, I continued to argue when one of the men hit me with that old trick question: "Where you from?" he asked. I began my New England routine. But, quickly, he zeroed in: "Where's your grandfather from?" "Syria," I answered, eager to cut short our argument, leave the joint and return to my hotel. With that the entire office, three men by now, burst into laughter. "Syria, that explains why you're acting so crazy," one of the men said. That was very funny, I thought to myself. But I refused to give them the satisfaction of laughing out loud.

I slept lightly that night so I would return to the airport in plenty of time to find my passport and make the U.N. flight. When I returned to the airport about 4 A.M., workmen were demolishing the little passport office. Holy shit, I thought, what now? The passport officials, of course, weren't around. They were sleeping off the effects of the Qat or still chewing it. Amid the mounting rubble I located the desk behind which the men had laughed. In the top drawer on the right hand side I found my passport with a regular visa inside, not that the visa mattered any longer. I grabbed the passport and took off with the U.N to Hargeisa to see old Chinese MIGs rusting on the ground and weapons being dug from the earth, land mines and mine-laying machines from the Cold War era, and some explosives in boxes dating to 1945 that showed the Stars and Stripes and two hands locked in a hand shake to indicate friendship. How and exactly when those explosives reached Hargeisa was a puzzle no living Somalis would or could answer.

Not much changed in half a century: Large tribes that call themselves nation-states fighting each other for control of foreign lands morphing into fights among local tribes able to be more effective killers because of weapons inherited from their powerful but departed visitors. Local control, I guess. Maybe that is progress of a sort. Local tribes usually don't need any stimulus to war against each other. But they usually get it in the form of foreign powers that seek to divide and conquer or control in their own national interests.

In Somalia's far northwest, a rump government was in place in the main city of Hargeisa, well outside of Mogadishu's sphere of influence and the battles being fought there. When our U.N. cargo plane flew from Djibouti to a rough landing area outside of Hargeisa on August 10, 1992, I saw a region that had largely escaped the famine and drought which elsewhere in the country had formed two-thirds of a lethal trifecta with the civil war completing the losing bet.

Somalis in the north had it relatively easy: all they had to overcome were the brutal effects of the war and the massive number of weapons dumped there by the supposedly more sophisticated international tribes during the Cold War. Anywhere from 80,000 to 120,000 people were killed in this area during the tribal civil war, a U.N. official said.

Hargeisa was calm when I visited. An estimated 80 percent of all buildings in the city had been destroyed during the fighting. So many people had been killed or had fled that the city's population was sliced by almost half, from 750,000 to 350,000.

Land mines designed to maim or kill people and disable tanks, those silent killer ghosts of the Cold War and the civil war that followed, filled the earth in northern Somalia. Short of chemical, biological or nuclear arms, almost every weapon imaginable had been stashed in the region, the gifts of foreign tribes that had used Somalia as a proxy in their global war.

Pure and simple, the area was a garbage dump for military hardware. Atop the dump were Chinese-built MiG's, about 250 surface to air missiles, tens of thousands of small and deadly U.S.– and Pakistani-made anti-personnel mines and about 50 sophisticated wire-guided anti-tank missiles, made by Britain, France and Italy, and used by NATO. I walked the minefields with local workers who kneeled and probed the earth with long icepick-like devices trying to find and remove an estimated 300,000 anti-personnel and anti-tank land mines in the region. It's a dangerous job, but one that earned a local worker a normal year's salary, about $130, in a month. Risks are relative, and so are salaries.

No records or plans existed to show where the mines had been laid. Some of the workers who were searching for the mines actually had laid them in the mid-to-late 1980s, so they had a general idea of where to look. But by and large the search was like groping in the dark on a moonless night, knowing that a wrong move would take a hand, an eye or your life.

More than 100 people had been killed and many more badly injured trying to remove the mines in the months before the British company Rimfire arrived in November of 1991, to train workers and manage the demining program. With the better training, only three workers had been killed removing land mines, although many others had been injured, in an eight-month period.

Thousands of people cheered the U.N. crew as we prepared to leave the dirt airstrip at Buroa east of Hargeisa on August 12, 1992. I couldn't imagine where all the people came from, although it appeared the masses had emerged from somewhere beneath the earth. The people treated the faceless U.N. officials as rescuers or conquering heroes. My mouth agape, I watched the thousands of people who cheered the bare U.N. logo on the cargo plane and wondered whether all those poor Somalis thought the U.N. would drive the other tribal devils from their midst.

We had brought nothing with us, and U.N. officials made no promises that I could detect or that the people could understand. But to the Somali people, if not to their tribal chiefs, the U.N. logo was a visible symbol of hope, at least, a sign that someone at last was paying attention. Hope was all the people had. In their way, the Somalis were saying thanks for paying attention and please return, with more people and real help. They might have added, in typical tribal fashion, come back and help us, but don't tell us how to live and don't stick around.

One man stood out in the huge crowd near the nose of the aircraft before we took off. He waved his elbows, what was left of his arms. His hands and his forearms were missing, probably blown away during the fighting.

I flew back to Mogadishu on my way to Nairobi. I left Somalia behind but, like their brethren in the ground, the walking dead could not.

TEN

Desert Anarchy, Algerian Style

"I am inclined to believe that government death squads exist just as I am inclined to believe that many countries have death squads. In some countries, democracies for example, they simply take longer to kick in. In dictatorships they're almost always present."—A Western diplomat talking in Algiers in 1997, about the Algerian government's alleged use of death squads against Islamic fundamentalists and people in the villages where fundamentalists lived.

Sliding his thumb across his throat, a universal sign of slaughter, Rashid began to tell his story of terror and civil war in Algeria. With other journalists on a state-sponsored tour of villages that shared a deadly experience — massacres — I listened, watched and questioned. This was one time when it was better to arrive late than to be an eyewitness, I thought, as Rashid spoke through a translator. On a typically warm night in late August 1997, about 200 killers entered the town of Reiss and within one hour made the earth warmer with the blood of roughly 250 local residents, including 24 members of Rashid's extended family.

"They took Nadia from me and they cut her throat with a knife," said Rashid, demonstrating the fatal gesture to a small group of foreign correspondents as our gendarme guardians watched from a distance. Nadia, Rashid's daughter, was two years old.

Rashid said he survived by leaping from a second-story window and hiding until the killers fled. That's when he found Nadia's body, along with those of his wife, another daughter, his father, mother, two sisters and the other family members. A six-month-old cousin of Rashid's, and a 70-year-old aunt, were among those slaughtered. Only Rashid and two of his brothers remained in the family to tell the tale for the dead.

Religious extremism, cultural, language and ethnic tribalism so tangled as to be inseparable roiled Algeria when I arrived in late October 1997. A military dictatorship determined to crush all opposition, especially the Islamists, and hold total political and economic power added a modern twist to recurrent tribal conflicts.

Rashid and other villagers were still stunned by the slaughter when they told their stories. They spoke without anger, grief or other emotions, as if the killings had occurred elsewhere. Their eyes were blank. Villagers said that some, but not all, of the killers were Islamic extremists widely referred to as "Afghanis." These true-believers had traveled with Islamic fundamentalists from other countries to fight in Afghanistan in their holy war against the Soviet Union during the 1980s. They wore what may loosely be called the Afghan uniform: full beards, long shirts that were slit on the sides and reached to the knees, and full billowing pants. Those "Afghanis," like many other fighters from the Islamic world, were trained or armed by the Central Intelligence Agency, or by others whom the CIA aided, to help the real Afghan tribes defeat the Soviets in Afghanistan during the 1980s.

The killers in Reiss, some of whom were from the neighborhood, entered the town of almost 10,000 people about 15 miles south of Algiers at midnight on August 28, 1997. By the time they left in the face of a sluggish Algerian army reaction, the killers had decapitated about 100 people with knifes and axes and shot at least another 150. Some bodies were burned. Most of the dead were said to be women and children. Villagers said the killers also stole jewelry, gold and cash. One woman said that she fled with her two children when the killing began. When she returned at daybreak, the woman said, she saw bodies piled in the street leading to the village. "I don't know who did it," the woman said. Then, she added, it was "the terrorists."

Massacres such as the one at Reiss were numerous, and the military junta routinely employed a tight news blackout to conceal the extent of the killings, the identities of the killers and the junta's response. Local journalists and human rights advocates were forced to scour cemeteries and villages in the countryside outside of Algiers in an attempt to count the dead, measure the scale of the killings and maybe identify the killers.

Few Algerians were positive of the killers' political identities. Were they all religious extremists seeking to make Algeria an Islamic state or were some tribes simply fighting back against military efforts to wipe them out? Were some of the massacres triggered by army provocateurs inserted into radical religious ranks to stoke the war, the terror and the confusion? Were some of the killers death squads organized by the military junta to continue the killing and justify further military rule and repression? Were some of the killers vengeful villagers armed by the military junta to retaliate against religious extremists who had murdered first?

The town of Reiss is slowly being sucked into the orbit of sprawling Algiers, a capital overflowing with countless migrants from rural areas seeking jobs that don't exist and who live half-lives on the city's expanding edges in buildings that look half-built or half-destroyed. Most of the houses in Reiss are made of concrete blocks and stucco. Many are built villa-like within high walls around which are orchards of fruit trees and gardens laden with eggplant and other vegetables.

We reached the village on October 22, almost two months after the massacre, in a convoy of eight military vehicles. The soldiers said their job was to protect us from possible attack by fundamentalists seeking foreign scalps. But we knew that the soldiers had another role: To ensure that we saw and heard only what the ruling junta wanted us to see and hear. Light filtering through the junta's pinched lens showed only the brutality of the Islamic fundamentalists in a civil war that the generals said they were forced to fight to prevent an Islamist takeover of the country. But the army's view was too simplistic for many civilians, for the few practicing human rights lawyers in Algeria, for muzzled local journalists and for international human rights organizations that believed the junta was as responsible for the lingering civil strife as were the religious fundamentalists. During five years of civil war, according to many local and international estimates, 80,000 to 120,000 Algerians were believed to have been killed, and the fighting was still raging.

The army wanted us to see the site of a massacre by the Islamists, and without a doubt there had been mass killing in Reiss. But the attack was more complex than the army wanted us or anyone else to believe. Soldiers were based less than a mile from where the killers struck, and there was much confusion during the attack. But why, villagers asked, did it take the army almost an hour to intervene? By the time we reached Reiss, the people there had become "Patriots," civilians armed by the military junta to retaliate slaughter for slaughter against the "Afghanis." As defensive a measure as these militias might have been, they spread revenge killings from village to village and introduced raw criminal activity into the war.

From Reiss we drove six miles to the farming village of Ben Telha, the site of another massacre barely a month before our arrival. Villagers in Ben Telha described the roughly 30 killers as a mixture of "Afghanis" and people wearing shorts, the latter a rather strange outfit for Islamic fundamentalists. The army's role in Ben Telha was highly questionable, raising the real possibility that soldiers either participated in the attack or allowed it to happen. Secret provocation by the military would help to justify the junta's repression of political and human rights and its war against the religious fundamentalists. In Ben Telha, the reasons for the continuing war became more murky and questions raised by international human rights groups about the junta's role in perpetuating the fighting seemed more valid.

Villagers estimated that between 250 to 320 people were killed in Ben

Telha from 11 P.M. until almost 4 A.M. on September 23, while the army, based a little more than a mile away, did nothing. With villagers leading the way, I toured houses where the fading blood from wholesale massacres was still visible on walls, doors and floors. Sixty people fled to one house, where they were all slaughtered with axes and knives. On a street where I stood interviewing people, villagers said that 44 people had been killed. Most of the dead had their throats slit, and about half were women and children. "The army was here," one man said, "The army came 15 minutes after the killing began, the army was very close, but the army stopped in the center because they feared mines." It was those same mines, Algerian human rights lawyers said, that never seemed to explode.

Lethal weapon: Villagers said that this hand scythe was used to kill several people in a house in Ben Telha, Algeria, before the room was torched (photograph by the author, 1997. © Cox Newspapers Inc.).

Ben Telha's villagers told horrific stories. Aboub, then in his early 20s, said that 23 members of one family had been murdered. Nine people, including five children, were slaughtered in one house after the killers blasted their way through doors and killed slowly, carefully, sometimes using small hand scythes.

A few days later, I left Algiers with other journalists in two army vehicles before we shifted to five vehicles and added many more gendarmes as we entered the Blida district. If there was a front in the amorphous civil war, it was in Blida, where security forces had found nothing but war, and many villagers and Islamic guerrillas met death. Security was a great concern here, although the military said the region was calm. A string of villages about 30 miles southwest of Algiers near the forested foothills of the Atlas Mountains, Blida sheltered wolves and wild hogs and remnants of religious radicals.

A region of farmers and shepherds, with some textile and plastics factories, the district was once a stronghold for Islamic radicals who imposed strict religious conduct on the people. After more than four years of religious rule and support for the radicals, many of the villages rebelled and drove out their masters and were now armed by the military. "We could not smoke. We could not do what we want," said Ahmed, who headed a 150-man local force of so-called "patriots" armed by the military. "We are not Islamists," another man said, "We do our prayers, that's all."

These villages were in the line of fire, first from the military which had attacked the religious radicals hiding there. After villagers gave the radicals the boot, the Islamists returned for vengeance. And because the villagers had first harbored the fundamentalists, the gendarmes and the soldiers had little sympathy when the radicals struck back at the villagers. As with civilians throughout much of the country, those villagers were targeted by both warring camps. By arming civilians, the military pit village against village in a way that fueled revenge killings, criminal activity and land-grabbing, and kept the cycle of war spinning.

In late September 1997, barely two months before I visited the Blida region, the village of Ben Ali had been attacked by about 40 to 50 men, some dressed as soldiers, others as ordinary civilians. Villagers said the attackers killed about 40 people, "cutting off their heads completely with knives and axes." The villagers of Ben Ali were convinced that the killers were militant Islamists, the armed wing of a banned Islamic political organization.

From village to village in the Blida region, the stories were similar: Islamic radicals attacked villages where they once had support but which had turned against their religious extremism. The army did not warm to those villages because of their earlier support for the fundamentalists. In Blida and other regions, the war was confusing to nearly everyone except the fundamentalists and the military apparatus. Most confused of all were ordinary civilians, who were the war's chief victims.

After our security teams had finished showing the Algeria they wanted us to see, a British reporter with one of London's largest broadsheets rose to make his contribution to the great moments in journalism. Government forces and the Islamic fundamentalists were both responsible for the killing, the reporter said. To protect himself against the competition, he wanted to be sure we all shared that view and wrote essentially the same story. None of the other reporters said a word in response. The truth seemed obvious. Who needs a consensus anyway? I thought. What's wrong with different interpretations based on further reporting to disperse some of the haze? At that moment I thought that I had been transferred to the pages of *Scoop*, Evelyn Waugh's wonderful novel about British foreign correspondents reporting on an African war most were unable to find.

Later, Muhammed, a young member of the main Berber political party, put his finger on a large truth behind the violence: "Yes, we are afraid in all of Algeria," he said. "The state doesn't preserve the security of the state. We are afraid from terrorism. Yes, we are afraid of the government, too. The government was established by force so the government uses force to stay in power."

The Algeria that I saw in frontline villages, in Algiers and in a large oil town about 500 miles deep into the great Sahara was in the grip of complex tribal warfare. The tribal branches were sectarian and also related to gender, ethnicity, language, nation-state, and the overarching conflict of three cultures with the usual foreign intervention — in this case 132 years of oppressive and ruinous French colonialism and its poisonous aftertaste — thrown into the volatile native mix. In more mundane and more modern tribal terms, control of political power and of Algeria's large and expanding oil and gas supplies were the top prizes.

When Algeria had beckoned, I reached for my passport and began plotting ways to obtain a visa. A journalist friend from Canada had called me in London with an alluring notion: The second largest country in Africa was staging local elections to show the world Algerian democracy at work. Therefore, the chances were good that the Algerian junta would grant visas to foreign correspondents. These were the same generals who in 1992 voided one round and cancelled a second round of parliamentary elections when it appeared that Islamists would win power. The military takeover triggered the civil war that five years later continued to spread death and terror across large swaths of the country, brought condemnation from international human rights organizations and silence from other nation-states that have an affinity for oil and gas but only blank stares for raging tribal conflicts.

For three weeks, I traveled periodically between London, where I was based, and Paris, the most likely place where an Algerian embassy would stamp a visa in my thick blue U.S. passport. Sometimes flying, other times taking the new train tunnel under the English Channel, and sometimes staying in Paris for a few days at a time, I kept visiting the Algerian embassy at 50 Rue de Lisbonne. The respect and courtesy I showed each time I knocked probably had nothing to do with it, but visa officials finally decided to open the door to Algiers' mysterious casbah and beyond. The door opened, but never too far, and the rooms beyond were filled with smoke and mirrors on the outside but windows on the inside.

Along with other journalists, I was forced to stay in the El Aurassi Hotel. There, my bags and computer were searched in my room while, guarded and watched by gendarmes and secret police, I was off touring what I called the massacre villages. State security could protect, and watch, us better if we were all in the same hotel. I did manage to sneak out of the hotel alone in a pre-arranged deal with a driver/translator so I could see Algiers without the hovering presence of one or more layers of the security forces. From the hotel overlooking the city, the view of the waterfront was spectacular. From a distance, but only from a distance, Algiers looked like a shining jewel on the Mediterranean, shimmering in the blinding white sunshine, like Nice, or

Another face of Algeria: The distant beauty of Algiers belied the murderous violence beyond the country's shimmering Mediterranean capital (photograph by the author, 1997. © Cox Newspapers Inc.).

Beirut before the fall. But up close the capital was worn, torn and peeling, the neglected, bedraggled orphan of occupation, revolution and tribal wars.

With their dark glasses and menacing presence, the secret police weren't so secret. They instantly chilled conversations with Algerians in shops and on the street. When we left for the countryside, we did so in convoys guarded by soldiers and gendarmes. On trips into the center of Algiers to talk with people about the local elections, we were heavily guarded and watched, and not by hotel maids. Six plainclothes security officers accompanied me on an afternoon foray into the alleys, narrow streets, jammed living quarters and breezy roofs of the casbah where women and girls smiled as they prepared couscous while overlooking the Mediterranean. On the streets below, jobless young men stuck like stucco to buildings.

Two representatives of Algeria's national oil company flew with me deep into the Sahara and stayed at my elbow, along with reinforcements, the entire time I was in the oil fields of Hassi Messaoud. Two other bored security officers tagged along after I reached Algiers on a flight from Hassi Messaoud until I boarded a plane back to Paris. I grew itchy and uncomfortable being so warmly embraced by Algerian security. With more breathing room, I might have found fewer Algerians who waved me off because they knew that I was being watched, as were they.

Algeria's civil war erupted after the army in 1992 scrapped parliamentary elections when it appeared certain that the Islamic fundamentalists would win. Generals — called the High Council of State — took over after the army bounced President Chadli Benjedid. The junta slowly erased political and human rights in order to save them from destruction by the fundamentalists. Their salvific act confused most Algerians, if not immediately then later. When the generals took power, Afghanistan's civil war was raging, the Taliban were on Kabul's doorstep and Tehran remained in the unyielding grip of Khomeini's heirs. That map surely didn't encourage Algeria's generals, although Iran and Afghanistan differ vastly from Algeria and all aspects of its tribal conflict, even its religious side.

Before the aborted 1991-1992 elections, Islamist political power had been expanding slowly in the 1980s, due largely to the absolute dominance of the National Liberation Front. The NLF had ruled Algeria since independence. Over time the NLF power grid became more like that of the all-grasping French colonial elite than like a new force of Algerians eager to bring freedom to their own people. Triumphant revolutionaries adopting the ways of their oppressors is more common than not. As difficult as revolution can be, the art of governing can be even more taxing. Barred from power and patronage, poor Algerians in rural areas joined with urban poor and educated but jobless young people in turning to the mosques for political direction and social and economic aid. This is an old story in human history and is not restricted to the Middle East or Muslim countries: Social and political upheaval erupts from the minds and stomachs of deprived, frustrated and discriminated masses. What differs from people to people is how the power structures react to the conflicts. In Algeria the generals took control and went to war against nearly everyone.

Democracy is fragile and relative, as Algerians would attest. It is not a form of government that should, by its own definition, be scrapped when the outcome of elections does not suit the ruling party or the power behind the throne. That is, in fact, the opposite of how a democracy should work. Independent institutions — presidential, legislative, judicial — are essential in a democracy, but even democratic institutions will function only as well as the people who control them allow. When people become corrupt, their institutions will follow.

In Algeria the facts on the political ground created the widespread and somewhat realistic fear that a triumphant Islamic party would replace a secular government with a religious state, the likes of which existed in other Muslim countries. In this context, the Algerian military showed what can happen when power is threatened, especially by what rulers consider to be someone else's extremists. The army itself became extremist, rigging elections by banning parties, turning moderate Muslims into radicals, creating death squads to fight its antagonists, fueling and dragging out the war to justify military control. In an irony familiar in countries where destructive occupiers are finally defeated after long wars, the Algerian army became like the country's old oppressors, the brutal French colonizers whom Algerians finally ousted in 1962. The choice in Algeria may well have been between a religious state and a military dictatorship. But by voiding the 1991-92 elections and taking power, the military regime — fundamentalists of a different stripe — allowed only one choice and exposed the hypocrisy of would-be democrats who like elections only when they like the results.

Algeria is huge, Africa's second largest country after Sudan, more than one and a half times the size of Alaska. About 32 million people live in the country, most of those in a narrow band along the Mediterranean coast. The great Sahara swallows most of the country. Only about three percent of the land, along the coast, is arable.

Berbers are the original inhabitants of Algeria, and most of the present population are, by ethnicity, Berbers, not Arabs. But only about one-fourth of the population clings to its Berber cultural identity and language called Tamazight. Most of the remaining Algerians identify themselves as Arabs, although they, too, are surely Berber by ethnicity. They call themselves Arabs because they have totally adopted the Arabic language and culture brought to Algeria by relatively small invading Arab armies from the eighth to the 11th centuries. Most of the Algerian Arabs are orthodox Sunni Muslims. Algerians who cling to Berber traditions are also Muslims, but many lean toward Sufism's mystical and tolerant side and worship Islamic saints and icons. The Berbers are not religious fundamentalists, not even orthodox Muslims, although many of them who call themselves Arabs are.

Without question Algeria is a Muslim country, although there are divisions even on religious grounds. While divided along Arabic and Berber cultural and linguistic lines, lingering French cultural and language influences add to the tribal potpourri. After national independence the one-party government controlled by the National Liberation Front slowly began to Arabize the country and pull it from the French cultural and linguistic orbit. That move encouraged the Muslim fundamentalists among the Arab population. It also antagonized those who identified themselves as Berbers and helped to inflate Berber identity, language and culture. In 2002, to pacify Berber nationalism, the government made the Berber language a national language, too, but not an official one.

As evidence of their divided cultural and language personalities, many Algerians speak a language that is both familiar and strange: it sounds like French and Arabic and is actually a combination of both. In some circles, Berber is thrown into the mix. It seems fair to say that most Algerians are now in many respects Francophobes, although the human, cultural, political and commercial ties between Algiers and Paris remain. At the same time, many of the more educated Algerians remain Francophiles, although the official government policy is to return to Algeria's Berber and Arabic roots.

Algeria's recent history is that of a stepchild of colonialism, French colonialism, a 132-year-old era when one people took the land, resources and wealth of another while trying brutally to impose an alien culture, language and way of life. The French conquerors of 1830 and those who solidified the conquest thought only of their own designs, never of their victims and never of the inevitable revolutionary consequences that would follow in Algeria or in France. No one can come close to measuring the number of people killed during the long French occupation, although the level of subjugation and violence is deep and well-known. French generosity delivered Algerian dead right to the end. During the eight-year war for independence alone, from 1954 to 1962, estimates of the number of people killed range from 300,000 to well over a million.

In what echoes like recent American policy toward Iraq and Afghanistan, the French said that they were going to civilize Algeria, free its women from the constraints of Islam, bring France's superior democratic institutions to the country and accrete non pareil French culture and customs to inferior Arabic and Berber traditions and practices. What the French really wanted was a conquest and Algeria's land, its human and natural resources to serve the colonialists and their masters in Provence and Paris, and to build French wealth. The land grab so close to home proved to be easy. The claims of political and cultural uplifting were rationalizations, sweeteners, crafted to pacify opposition at home and in other capitals. Algeria's wealth was enhanced considerably by the discovery of substantial oil and gas reserves in the Sahara during the mid–1950s. But that came largely too late for the French. An American oilman working in the Sahara during my visit described Algeria as "one of the last frontiers for oil exploration. We're just scratching the surface. There's still a lot to be discovered."

Under siege themselves, Algerian human rights lawyers estimated that 12,000 people had "disappeared" from 1992 to 1997. How many had been killed and how many more were locked away in remote prisons no one knew except possibly the army, various police forces, intelligence services, and the High Council of State itself. By the end of the 20th century and the beginning of the new one, as the violence slowly subsided, estimates of the number killed since the army cancelled the 1992 elections reached as high as 200,000. On the lighter side of martial law, Algerians had the opportunity to vote in several elections later in the 1990s and early in the 21st century, but few trusted the integrity of the ballot.

Before he asked me to leave, his eye on the not-so-secret plainclothes officer standing at the door, a store owner in Algiers vowed not to vote in the imminent municipal elections. "Always the results are the same since independence," he said. "The ones in power always win."

That was a common view in the capital at the time. And Algiers was surely the safest place in the entire country. Since independence in 1962, Algeria had been ruled by political figures or generals linked to the war for independence. When the National Liberation Front didn't put a man in office as president, the generals did it for the NLF or ripped off the facade and took over entirely as the junta did in 1992. Elections, especially real and honest ones, are highly irregular occurrences in most of Africa and the Middle East. Algeria has had its share of presidential, parliamentary and municipal elections in recent years, but most have been marked by conditions which assure that the ruling party and the controlling generals stay on top.

Elections were supposed to be Algeria's ticket to global acceptance. Instead, they highlighted the country's numerous tribal conflicts. Foremost among the army's stated objectives was its desire to block the rise to power of Islamic fundamentalists. So if the fundamentalists can't run, they can't win.

And those who run the country control not only its political system, but its expanding oil and gas resources which form the bulk of Algeria's wealth.

—⚬⚬⚬—

Muhammed was one of a handful of Algeria's human rights lawyers whose doors remained open in 1997. A client was one of countless hundreds, maybe thousands, of Algerians imprisoned and tortured in the name of the junta's campaign to keep its vise-like grip on power against Islamic pressure.

I met Muhammed alone in his small Algiers office. Papered with documents and files on desks, cabinets, chairs and the floor, his tiny space was typical of an overworked criminal defense lawyer who screams unheard for secretarial help. Later, Muhammed's client walked in, slowly, to tell me about how his testicles had been cut off in prison. I didn't ask for proof. "I was put on a table, lying on my back. They put a bottle up my behind, like a soda bottle. They pushed it up until it cut and exploded my organs. Then they cut my testicles off," the former prisoner said. When security forces came to take him from prison to execute him in 1994, they backed off because they thought he had to be crazy to survive that kind of torture in four different prisons during 14 years, Muhammed, the lawyer, said.

A short, stocky man but not big by any means, the tortured man said that he was the principal of a regular high school, not an Islamic school, when he was arrested, tried and imprisoned in 1979 for alleged ties to Islamic organizations. "They arrested me because I am in a dictatorship, not because I have extremist religious views because I don't," the man said. The government presented no evidence that he had ties to radical Islamists, said the former prisoner, who was 55 when we talked. From 1979 until 1988, when he was released, the man was locked away in Saida prison far from Algiers, an area he called "the door of the desert."

At first, the man said, he was tortured in Saidi prison, but that was nothing like the brutality that followed after he was arrested again in September 1992. That arrest came nine months after the military junta took control and Algeria had descended into civil war. For almost five years, the man said, he was imprisoned and brutalized. It was during this period that he was dismembered. "I was years alone in Serkaji prison. I could not see the light," he said.

After his arrest in 1992, the military at first accused the former high school principal of being part of a group that planted a bomb in the Algiers airport. Nine people were killed in the explosion. During interrogation the man denied planting the bomb. When he was imprisoned and tortured, the man said, his jailers never mentioned the airport bombing. They accused him of meeting with an "Islamic terrorist."

Muhammed, the man's lawyer, said all human and legal rights protections were washed away in 1995, when the junta eliminated courts established solely to hear security and terrorism cases. "Before that prisoners went to court and their families could see them, and they had a lawyer," Muhammed said. "Now they disappear totally. They can't see a lawyer or their families." The special security and terrorism courts were harsh, but at least lawyers and families knew where they could find the prisoners. By mixing political prisoners with all others in common criminal courts, the political prisoners disappeared; neither lawyers nor families could find them. When we spoke, Muhammed said, there were so many political prisoners there was no room for criminals, many of whom received short sentences for major crimes.

In the whiplash of killings by Islamic radicals, government security forces, civilians armed by the military and criminals taking advantage of the mayhem, the number of dead, disappeared and imprisoned varied wildly. Most international human rights organizations use conservative figures. Muhammed did not. In a February 1998 report, Human Rights Watch said that more than 1,000 Algerians had disappeared at the hands of security forces. Its findings were based only on eye-witness accounts. Muhammed counted four lawyers among the 12,000 Algerians who had disappeared, 65 journalists known to have been killed during the war, while two journalists simply vanished. About 20 Muslim journalists were also in prison. A 1996 U.S. government human rights report said that at least 59 journalists had been killed in "terrorist attacks" since 1993. The killings, torture and disappearances crossed military, sectarian and civilian lines. Muhammed's estimate of the dead since 1992: 400,000 to 500,000, if everybody is counted, the military, police, Islamists, men, women and children. Some countries noted the savagery in dry official reports, as if they were recording the minutes of government meetings. The effect was that most nations ignored the violence, except to shut down airline service to Algiers, close or pare down embassies and give diplomats who remained 25 percent combat-pay bonuses. Other nation-states looked the other way because the victims were mostly Algerians. Of all those killed in the conflict, more than 120 were foreigners, according to a U.S. report on human rights in Algeria, and none was an American.

It wasn't easy, but I caught up to Salima Ghozali in Algiers in late October 1997, a couple of months before she received the European Parliament's Sakharov Prize for freedom of thought. It's no exaggeration to say that Ghozali was on the run from all those who profited from the civil war because she fought them all. With her newspaper, *La Nation*, and as a leader of Algeria's women's movement, Ghozali never missed an edition or a podium from which to charge that Islamic and military criminals used the veil and religion to keep the flames of war burning. This was a religious war, all right, the kind of war that served both the principles of the religious fundamentalists and of the military regime that, in Ghozali's mind, fueled the killing to keep its own lock on the country and its growing oil industry, and to protect the national elite.

As a woman, a leader of Algeria's women's rights movement and a journalist seeking information against a regime trying to hide it, Ghozali wore three bull's-eyes on her back. She suffered personally from the war, as did many thousands of other women. And in Ghozali's mind, all Algerians suffered either indirectly or directly. The government had shut down her newspaper 11 months earlier because the paper circumvented government censorship by visiting cemeteries and counting the dead to show the extent of the violence and to uncover its hydra-headed sources. A 1994 military decree ordered that security information printed by private newspapers was to come only from official bulletins published by the Algerian Press Service. On security issues, the independence of independent newspapers was erased. The official reason that Ghozali's newspaper was shuttered was that the paper owed the government printing office, which monopolized newspaper printing, $100,000. The government wanted payment at once. Editors who wanted to amortize the payment over months need not knock on the official door. That financial demand effectively closed the paper, demonstrating how a government can destroy a free press without shooting all journalists or blowing up a newspaper plant. For propaganda purposes, the interior minister tried to justify its pressure on *La Nation*, which had been the country's only independent paper when it shut down, by telling the public that the paper was aiding the terrorists and endangering Algeria by developing a file on human rights violations and pointing out the dangers of arming civilians. While the junta was busy bringing newspapers to their knees, radio and television stations were already there: They were government controlled to begin with.

Despite the personal risks, Ghozali never backed off. The regime "thinks it can manage chaos. I think they need a certain level of chaos to manage social fragmentation and political incompetence and hopelessness. Chaos and violence go together," she said. Her words should not be limited to Algeria at that moment. They can be applied to any government anywhere that is aggressive in erasing political, legal and civil rights in the name of security and in promoting fear to manipulate public opinion.

In 1994, Ghozali abandoned her home where she had lived for ten years with her two daughters. Between then and the time we talked, she had relocated four times to different towns. She wasn't literally dodging bullets, but she was skipping away from implicit threats that told her to keep quiet, stop digging, avoid foreign human rights organizations, stop calling for an international investigation of the killing. With the Sakharov Prize, her public shield thickened. To protect her two teenage daughters, Ghozali sent them to live with her sister far from Algiers. She visited her family at most once a month. "The only real protection is a rational one; I didn't do anything wrong," she said. "The generals are afraid of people like me, a little person. So that is some consolation."

Whether long-resisting the French occupation, playing leading roles in the open war for independence, straining against religious and tribal restraints or being used and punished by all sides in the civil war of the 1990s, women have been central figures in Algeria's recent history. By itself the role of women in Algeria's war against the French is high drama in an Islamic country. Their role was also a great irony because the French had labored to convince themselves and everyone else that they were liberating Algeria's women from cultural and religious bondage. After independence the government did a radical two-step on women's rights. In the mid–1970s, a new national charter declared Islam the state religion while also guaranteeing women full rights in Algerian society. But less than a decade later, in the face of rising pressure from Islamists and Algeria's deep-rooted patriarchal tribal and clan structure, the government approved a Family Code that stripped women of most of the rights they were granted in the national charter. Women became, in effect, minors under control of their husbands, fathers or other male relatives.

Because of this history, it was not so surprising to find women such as Ghozali and Louiza Hanoun continuing to fight for the freedom of women and of their country. In a society where men ruled without question, few men are comfortable with women pointing fingers at Islamic fundamentalists, generals and patriarchs. Hanoun led the Algerian Workers' Party and was at the time the only woman to head a political party in the Arab world.

In prisons, in cemeteries mourning family members, with or without the veil and seeking an international inquiry into the violence, women struggled through the civil war, fought it and tried to stop it. To the extent that the conflict was tribal in its many forms, which it was, one aspect concerned gender.

Algerian human rights lawyers believed that at least 500 women were killed in the fighting, just because they were women, although that figure is no more than a guess. Hundreds more, another guess because the military kept the names and numbers secret, were believed to be in prison. Only when families sought help, Hanoun told me, did she learn about imprisoned women. Some women gave birth in prison, Hanoun said. All the women in prison were there because they were married to Islamists, she said.

Early in the war, some Islamic radicals promised to kill women who didn't wear the veil. Security extremists responded by saying they would kill ten veiled women for every woman killed who did not wear the veil. With friends like that, women were surrounded by enemies. Patriarchal family, clan and tribal customs were at work here as much as religion. Those threats did nothing to protect any women. From that moment, women were injected front and center into the civil conflict accenting its religious nature, which was only part of the gender war. Islamic radicals kidnapped and raped women, but the veil was a false front for the conflict, Ghozali said: "The veil is used by criminals on all sides to justify the continued violence," said Ghozali, who pointed out that some women were forced to wear the veil by family members while others wore it for protection. After villagers were slaughtered by Islamic radicals, military forces or civilians armed by the military, both veiled and unveiled women were seen mourning at cemeteries, said Ghozali, whose newspaper tracked the killings by following women wailing.

To illustrate how religion was used to explain the killings, Hanoun said, the first woman murdered in the fighting wore a veil. But her husband worked for the security forces. The first woman security officer who died in the war was killed by her fiance, who killed her because she broke off their relationship. But the military blamed Islamic extremists for the woman's death, Hanoun said.

Massacres were so widespread and their causes so serpentine and tangled that no one knew with absolute certainty who was behind them. The suspects had been narrowed: Islamic fundamentalists, the army, the gendarmes, the national police, military-backed civilian militias that numbered about 230,000, and common criminals seeking their own slice of profit from the chaos. When Algerians called for an international inquiry to determine who was behind the killings, the junta stood tall in opposition. Every Algerian knew that much.

Hassi Messaoud, Algeria, October 27, 1997 — Almost 500 miles southeast of Algiers and the Mediterranean coast, the vast, forbidding Sahara disorients the littoral-minded. The wells of Hassi Messaoud, which oil engineers described as "a world class field," were blazing like mammoth torches against the midnight desert sky when my plane landed at the jewel among Algeria's oil and natural gas oases. When the sun rose to reheat the desert a few hours later, I saw the brilliance of the oasis spring to life with bougainvilleas, hibiscus, date palms, eucalyptus and pine trees. On another night, beer cans and whiskey bottles suddenly appeared from the hands of faceless people who reached through windows from the darkness. It was acceptable to sneak in alcohol, but not to be seen touching it.

Foreigners were allowed to breach the oil zones, but not alone and only under protective and watchful eyes. The tribal wars threatened Algeria's valuable and vulnerable oil fields hundreds of miles from Algiers and the thin ribbon of arable land where most Algerians live.

Sahara burning: Desert dunes rose like sawed-off sentries around the smoking oil and gas fields of Hassi Messaoud, hundreds of miles from the Mediterranean (photograph by the author, 1997. © Cox Newspapers Inc.).

I was accompanied and gently kept on a leash by two representatives, a young woman and an older man, of Sonatrach, Algeria's national oil company. I was required to stay in Sonatrach's crisp well-watered compound near the town of Hassi Messaoud, which had about 65,000 people and, for security reasons, an 8 o'clock nightly curfew. When I left that compound, I was always accompanied by several guards who transported me to other secure compounds belonging to American and other foreign oil companies that were heavily guarded by legions of Algerians. The Sonatrach village, where guests and some company workers were required to bivouac, was a collection of long metal buildings that reminded me of a new college that was using temporary buildings during its early stages of construction.

To reach Hassi Messaoud, which means Messaoud's well, I was required to obtain an internal Algerian passport called a *laissez-passer*, which I obtained after several days of prodding. Hassi Messaoud lies within a secure area that has a radius of nine miles. That area lies within a much larger exclusion zone, where no one, not foreigners or Algerians, was allowed without that special passport and where travelers were required to have armed guards. The exclusion zone, which is so huge it is almost boundless, was established by the military junta in 1993, after Islamic radicals vowed to kill all foreigners in the country and the civil war hit its stride. Algeria's ticket to greater wealth, corruption and a widening gap between rich and poor was punched in 1954, when oil was first discovered, where else but in Hassi Messaoud. The country's oil and gas wealth was barely being tapped, American oil engineers told me in Hassi Messaoud in late October 1997, when about one-fourth of Algeria's national income and 95 percent of its exports came from its petro industry.

No editor was badgering me for a story about American oil interests in Algeria. But where there was oil I knew there would be Americans. And that was a story, especially so with the civil war raging. I was also as curious about the Sahara as I was about the lives of American prospectors working the vast petro reserves.

When we touched down on the desert airstrip, I felt the embrace of a powerful alien landscape. Its strength sprung from the desert's vastness not from the fiery wells. Fire shoots from gas wells in the Caspian Sea on the doorstep of Baku in Azerbaijan, looking like flaming geysers leaping incongruously from the water. But water is more familiar than alien, and the Caspian is a large inland lake or sea. The mysterious Sahara swallows the land and appears unending in its dunes, mountains and valleys. It is also familiar by name, which makes it more enticing: The Sahara is rich in its history of camel caravans, roaming native tribesmen and World War II battles. In our mind's eye, we can see the Sahara on a map galloping across broadest Africa. The desert covers North Africa as the United States sweeps over North America, from sea to sea. We know where the Sahara is, but most of us know little about it. Stars over the desert form a spectacular roof that twinkles from horizon to horizon and diminishes the night. Wispy white clouds race across its bluest of blue skies during the day, every day. The blazing sun can be a mortal enemy in the desert; frigid nights are not necessarily a friend. Day or night, the limitless sands are awesome, couriers of solitude and almost absolute silence.

I was greeted in Hassi Messaoud by Dick Cheney. Remember him, the former chairman and chief executive officer of Halliburton, which was going gung-ho in Algeria at this time? Cheney's typically thin smile gazed at me from a photo inside a Halliburton brochure that I picked up in Hassi Messaoud. "Thanks to a lot of hard work and company-wide commitment to adding shareholder value, we are entering a period of significant growth and opportunity," Cheney wrote. That was before Cheney the oil man became Cheney the vice president. And that was before all those wonderful opportunities happened to open up for Halliburton in Iraq.

Like all the other 30 or so foreign companies drilling, pumping and constructing pipelines in Algeria, Halliburton's exploration and production experts operated from a huge, heavily guarded, fort-like compound. Engineers and contractors from Halliburton's Brown & Root wing were on the desert floor as well. I counted nine other American companies engaged in work related to the Hassi Messaoud field. One official of a U.S. company estimated that 4,500 Americans were working in Algeria's oil industry. Americans, like all the foreigners in the industry, worked 28 days before they took 28 days off. Most of the workers earned 40 percent bonuses for living every other month in the desert's isolation. They lived as if they were working on an oil rig in the North Sea.

New oil and gas discoveries were being made regularly. Pipelines criss-crossed the desert floor and looked like railroad tracks run amok, mocking nomads and camels alike as the petroleum industry powered the country. Gas pipelines stretched across the desert and under the Mediterranean to fuel Europe. Petro wealth supported the military and what passed as the civilian government, which would be better called the bureaucracy or, as Algerians called them, the *nomenklatura*. But even in good times, precious few of those petro dollars reached rural Algerians, educated Algerians who couldn't find jobs and others who instead relied on religious leaders in mosques to provide financial and social support. When oil prices plunged in the mid–1980s, the national economy went down with them, inflating popular discontent and strengthening Islam's radical wing.

Every foreign company that operated in Algeria did so under a joint venture with Sonatrach, the national oil company that was not known for efficiency or a strait-laced operation. In every joint venture, Sonatrach held a majority of the shares. Secrecy and security were the passwords in the desert. Most foreign workers refused to give their names or divulge the number of workers in their compounds. When officials said there was no reason to be in the town of Hassi Messaoud after 8 P.M., they meant that no one was permitted there after that hour. The rules of the secure area called for anyone who heard a gunshot, an explosion or a siren to move quickly indoors, secure windows and doors, turn off the lights and "avoid being an easy target. Delay the attacker from achieving his goal."

American policy often follows the logos of American companies, so it was no surprise that the Clinton administration's policy toward Algeria was one of careful neutrality. Business is business, and the oil business is big business. Algeria had also helped to handle the release of the American embassy hostages from Iran in 1981. Gratitude was due for Algeria's role, and it was duly given. Americans weren't being harmed in Algeria either, and the civil war remained just that, mainly an Algerian affair. When the violence occasionally spit bombs and bullets at France, well that was, predictably, an Algerian-French affair.

The United States did criticize the Algerian junta and the religious radicals it called "terrorists," for a variety of human rights abuses. But that criticism was stated in a matter of fact cover your ass way, without emotion or cries for an international inquiry to pull the veil from the dark recesses of the war. Algerian Islamic fundamentalists, once happy to take money from the Saudi royal family, severed ties with Saudi Arabia because the Saudis allowed U.S. troops on Islam's holiest ground during the first Persian Gulf War in 1991, and thereafter. On that score, the Algerian fundamentalists were in loose league with Osama bin Laden and his al Qaida network. The split between Algerian fundamentalists and the Saudis certainly did nothing to push the U.S. government away from the dictatorial military junta in Algiers.

After I had left the dining room in the Sonatrach village with my two minders one evening, we walked through a shaded open area where tribal music was blaring from loudspeakers. The music blocked any chance of conversation, even private thoughts.

Scores of the Algerian workers were seated on short concrete walls in the quadrangle-like area. The men were silent. I decided to have a little fun, to take a chance with the Algerian sense of humor and see what happened. My female minder had a sharp sense of humor, so I wasn't much concerned about her reaction. The workers were the X factor. I took a large white dinner napkin from my pocket and started to dance in a circle around my female minder. She smiled but did not respond with a step of her own. To do so in such a public place, I thought, would probably have been too risque and arousing for all those men watching, their personas hidden behind culturally enforced silence. Then the men, all of them, started clapping, loudly, but not wildly. But no one joined me on the dance floor. They knew better, I guess. The men clapped as long as I kept dancing, which wasn't long because, with no real partner, my limitations were soon exposed. When I stopped dancing, the men stopped clapping. The music blared on. This was Algeria in the midst of tribal war, even in desert isolation. Background music there was, but few people were smiling and fewer still were dancing.

ELEVEN

Bosnian Test: Who's Your God?

War is mob rule that silences individuals when it doesn't kill them.

Munib Jusufovic was the Muslim mayor in exile of the Bosnian city of Brcko. Before the Balkan wars, 50 percent of Brcko's 41,000 residents were Muslim, seventeen percent were Christian Orthodox Serb and seven percent were Catholic Croat. The rest were of mixed religious heritage. Better armed and backed by Yugoslav federal troops, who were mainly from Serbia, the Bosnian Serbs cleansed Brcko of Muslims and Croats and claimed the city for their version of Christian Orthodoxy, and for Slobodan Milosevic's Greater Serbia.

After the Serbs expelled the Croats and Muslims, 30,000 Serbs from other towns moved to Brcko to hold it for Serbia. A refugee in his own country, Jusufovic recalled that before the war he was good friends with the then-new Serb mayor of Brcko, Miodrag Pajic. Yet when I spoke with Jusufovic, he and Pajic were forced to work through intermediaries just to meet again. "We were very good friends," said Jusufovic in December 1995. "We worked together. We went out together. He would come to my house. In his house, I felt as if I was in my own house. We both tried to calm things before the war. I cannot hate him, and I don't think he would be able to hate me. I don't blame the mayor for what happened."

A British lieutenant colonel in Sarajevo etched the brutal Bosnian wars in these words: Croats beheaded Muslims, removed the dead persons' bowels and put the heads in the bowels. The Bosnian Serbs used machineguns and bulldozers to expel, starve and imprison the Bosnian Muslims and Croats whom they didn't kill.

Roman Catholic Croats, Christian Orthodox Serbs. Bosnian Muslims. All God-loving, God-fearing people, by their own admission; all members of self-righteous sectarian tribes. "No one is guiltless in this country," said the lieutenant colonel. But Croats and Serbs, who started the wars, were more guilty than others while the Muslims fought for survival.

Once all those terrible genies were out of their bottles, the Bosnian Croats and Bosnian Serbs needed only the continued military and political direction from their super-nationalist tribal leaders in neighboring Zagreb and Belgrade to continue killing Bosnian Muslims and each other. Zagreb and Belgrade had triggered the fighting and were bursting with zeal to kill to win.

In raw numbers, Bosnia didn't sink to the level of Rwanda or Somalia, but it was no less brutal. And it was a supreme embarrassment to the West because it is white and it is in the loins of Europe rather than in what the West perceives as a sinkhole in black Africa. The aggressors were Christians, too, not "infidels." With ethnic-cleansing at its core, the Bosnian conflicts also revived the memories of Hitler's Naziism and Germany's Aryan Nation only 50 years earlier.

My journey on the peace trail to Bosnia began in Northern Ireland, then another hoary tribal battlefield.

In Belfast the Clinton administration was sprinkling peace seeds that since have sprouted in ground hardened by centuries of religious, ethnic, cultural, political, language and colonial conflict. At that same moment, American soldiers were preparing to enter Bosnia for the first time — officially.

For a few days at the end of November and early December 1995, Bill Clinton quieted Catholics and Protestants, British unionists and Irish republicans, even stolid British colonialists, long enough for them to consider what a peaceful silence might be like. Huge crowds greeted Clinton in the Northern Ireland cities of Belfast and Derry. Even more excited, the Republic of Ireland to the south declared Clinton's visit a national holiday.

Amid all the street noise and minced political verbiage, the most dramatic moment for me was in the heart of Dublin, closer to the heart of the matter. On a gorgeous day, I walked around a corner into a large square filled with enough people to exceed an exaggerated police estimate and was greeted by one man singing, a cappella, "Danny Boy." At that moment, I felt that the clarity and strength of the man's voice couldn't be matched in any great music hall anywhere.

Despite the crush of people, that lone singer might as well have been as alone as his voice was in that square; not one cough, not one scrape of a foot on the pavement, not one contrarian could be heard. If at that moment in that place the hair on your neck and arms didn't stand straight up and salute the blue sky, you weren't alive.

Moments like this would not even be deemed worthy of a parenthetical note in a newspaper story. But they stick in the mind and heart for all time, much more than do couched comments by queens and princesses, presidents and prime ministers; interviews with diplomats who cough and clear their

The Balkans wars of the 1990s, when tribes, history and gods dictated the fire this time.

throats more than they talk, or background briefings with high officials who are permitted to lie because under the rules of obfuscation they can't be named. Maybe singing is the answer, I thought, although there again it depends on whose tribal song is being sung and where. "Danny Boy" just might raise the hackles of a few Protestant unionists in the north.

After his Irish lullaby, Clinton was whisked to Germany where, on December 2, he praised and encouraged 4,300 troops of the U.S. Army's 1st Armored Division. Those troops, based in Baumholder, were among the 20,000 U.S. soldiers bound for a peacekeeping role in Bosnia. The soldiers practiced shouting that old infantry cheer, Hooah! Hooah! Hooah!, so as good soldiers they could welcome the commander-in-chief and his wife, although it was clear they would have preferred Ike and Mamie because of Clinton's aversion to the draft and the Vietnam War. The soldiers ate better — roast beef, baked chicken and roast turkey with 19 side dishes and desserts — than they would in freezing and muddy Bosnia during the holidays less than a month away.

The Dayton Peace Accords (the Bosnia peace treaty) would be officially signed in Paris on December 14. On that day and for weeks to follow, U.S. troops and forces from other NATO countries were to pour into Bosnia in an effort to keep Orthodox Serbs, Catholic Croats and Bosnian Muslims from continuing the latest outbreak of their ritual killings.

My assignment was to check strategic points on the overland route that American troops would take from Germany to Hungary, Croatia and down to the main U.S. base at Tuzla, Bosnia. I would find out whether bases in Hungary were being equipped to handle the load, whether key bridges were being constructed and roads paved to bear the soldiers and equipment. That done I was to arrive in Tuzla on or just before December 14, blizzards or no blizzards, war or no war, the day the peace treaty was to be signed and the first American soldiers were due to arrive as part of an officially recognized force. A few days after reaching Tuzla, I talked with a U.S. Army special forces soldier who had been in Bosnia for months. And he hadn't been alone.

After I flew from Ireland to the Ramstein-Baumholder area of Germany on the White House press plane, I was on my own. I hitched a ride with some soldiers to Heidelberg, a beautiful university town that was dressed up special for the Christmas season. American troops had been training for Bosnia duty at bases in Grafenwohr and Hohenfels nearby, but those activities were winding down and the soldiers were preparing to move on, which I took as a signal that I should do the same.

In Heidelberg I enjoyed a warming grog-like beverage, bought cold weather gear and tried to plot a backup emergency plan to reach Tuzla on deadline. Talk of helicopter and cargo flights taking off from Germany at just the right moment seemed more fantastic than dependable. I couldn't count on them.

So I flew to Budapest to chart the Hungarian leg of the troop route, and decided that there was no turning back: I would leg it to Tuzla anyway I could and arrive by December 14. Hungary was eager to cooperate because the door was opening to NATO and Western Europe after the Communist house collapsed.

When I reached Budapest on December 5, I rented a car, hired a translator and drove through a postcard-perfect snowstorm 120 miles southwest to the Taszar air base near the city of Kaposvar. Snow obliterated the road signs and an English language radio station was playing, "Let it snow, let it snow, let it snow. Oh, the fire is so delightful." I smiled, might as well get lost in Hungary. This was wintry Bosnia without the snipers, land mines and vengeful tribes.

From Kaposvar to the air base to the hotels in between, signs of the American presence were scattered across the landscape. But the preparations were behind schedule, although the troops were being readied to keep the peace, not make war, and maybe they had more time than the calendar showed or the politicians said.

The Taszar air base, which previously housed Scud missiles, was to be a main rear support staging area for American troops going to and from Bosnia by air, rail and road convoy. Some 50 to 100 U.S. troops had visited the base a month earlier, analyzed facilities and troop needs and left. No more than 10 American military planners were at the base when I arrived. They proclaimed the base perfectly suitable, with its typical red and white watertower, concrete walls ready to accept barbed wire that was nowhere in sight, one active and one inactive air strip, and enough space for a soldiers' tent city.

Fresh asphalt patches healed the road leading to the base, but much more work remained to be done to accommodate the troops and equipment. I couldn't wait around to watch. A small force of American soldiers, many of whom could be seen studying Hungarian, had taken over the Panorama Resort Hotel not far from the base. From 2,500 to 2,800 U.S. troops were already billeted in Hungarian army bases in the area.

In Kaposvar, a lovely, industrious enclave with many 17th and 18th century buildings, residents eagerly awaited the invasion of the American tribesmen. "We have been waiting for the United States since the Second (World) War. Instead, we got the Russians," one resident joked. Discos and a strip joint were being readied, and waitresses were practicing their English: "Enjoy your meal," "Good afternoon," "Good evening," "May I help you?" they repeated with the humor of people expecting a free-spending liberating force, foreigners though they would be. The Americans would be easy to accept because some would be spending money in Hungary while others patrolled in Bosnia.

Americans were in Hungary, to be sure, and thousands more would follow. But I was not impressed with the level of preparations a week before the Bosnian peace treaty was to be signed.

After a few days in Hungary, I flew to Zagreb, Croatia's capital, on December 10. With my deadline closing in, I met with a NATO officer who said that U.S. and other NATO forces would build a pontoon bridge at Zupanja on the Croatian side of the Sava River to the east. A bridge 320 yards long was being assembled by the Army's 40th Engineer Battalion in Hanau, Germany, the NATO officer said. The structure would link Zupanja with the town of Orasje across the Sava in Bosnia. From Orasje the road was open to the U.S. base at Tuzla. But it would be weeks before the road leading to the bridge at Zupanja and the bridge itself would be ready for use.

With a translator from Zagreb, a city I like for its museums, old buildings and because it invites walking, I sped east across the disputed Croat-

Memorial: To peace or war? Almost 14,000 red and gray bricks were stacked outside the United Nations peace mission in Zagreb, Croatia, in memory of Croatians who were killed or missing during the Croatian-Serbian war in the early 1990s. The memorial was moved to Zagreb's Mirogoj Cemetery in 2005 (photograph by the author, 1995. © Cox Newspapers Inc.).

Serb area of Slavonia to Zupanja to see for myself where the bridge would be erected and the state of preparations there. Flat and fertile, Slavonia had been the frontline periodically during the five-year Croat-Serb conflict for control of the region. Only six months before the peace treaty was to be signed, after heavy fighting, the Croats regained control of Western Slavonia from local Serbs.

About 15,000 people lived in war-battered Zupanja and the adjacent village of Gunja. Often on the bloody edge of the Croat-Serb battles, the area was later in the crosshairs of cross-border shelling by Croats, Serbs and Bosnian Muslims. The last shell had hit the town on October 12, but two months later Zupanja still looked like a city under siege.

First-floor windows of buildings were boarded up with logs, lumber and bricks to protect residents against artillery and mortar fire. About 20 American and Croatian soldiers had been in the area 10 days earlier to examine the terrain with an eye toward building the vital bridge there. The American surveyors came from the Army's 1st Armored Division, local officials said. But if other preparations were being made, they were invisible.

The slow pace of U.S. and NATO preparations along the road to Bosnia exposed once more the wide gulf between the propaganda that officials spout for home consumption and the harder-to-digest truths on the ground.

Before the war, two bridges, one exclusively for railroad use, crossed the Sava River nearby. But both were knocked out during the fighting. Zupanja's city administrator told me that in four years of fighting, sirens summoned local farmers, factory workers and their families to bomb shelters on 1,237 days of the 1,460 days during that period. With the peace treaty, sighs of relief would reach the town before the new bridge did.

At that moment, the functioning "bridge" across the Sava to Orasje in Bosnia was actually a motorized raft steered and towed by a tugboat and guided from bank to bank by steel cables. As makeshift as this arrangement was, it was several notches up the technological ladder from the rope-guided raft that ferried me across a river in northern Iraq three-and-a-half years earlier.

Four inches of fresh snow covered the earth and a blinding fog filled the air when I drove up the muddy, cratered road to the river with other motorists to catch the raft. Ducks swimming to Orasje traveled about as fast as the raft. It took us six minutes to make the crossing that I figured measured about 250 yards.

A rural area where farmers raised tobacco, chickens and pigs and worked in chemical factories before the war, Croat-controlled Orasje was quiet at that moment. Only 10 percent of the area's 40,000 residents had jobs, but residents weren't clamoring to lynch local officials over the unemployment rate.

The town had been battered during the war, logs remained piled against buildings for protection, and I could hear shells exploding across the woods and fields in the city of Brcko, where Bosnian Muslims and Serbs were still battling for control.

Orasje's mayor told me that he hadn't seen any Americans, period, although he had heard rumors a new bridge would be built. He welcomed the gossip, as if it were a real bridge. I thought my luck had worsened when the raft broke down and couldn't make the return trip to Zupanja. But a small boat with a putt-putt engine and no sides that looked like a poor man's Chinese junk was offered in the raft's place and we crossed back to Zupanja in only two minutes.

Official talk of a bridge between Zupanja and Orasje seemed more a diversion than a plan. So I drove immediately to another location, the village of Gunja, which was also being discussed as a possible location for a bridge. But Gunja was right on the confrontation line, across the Sava River from Brcko. The road beyond Brcko didn't lead to Tuzla, which made this an unlikely spot for a new bridge to ferry U.S. troops. Peppered with land mines, the nearby woods added to potential problems. Don't look for a bridge anywhere across the Sava by December 14, I reported confidently when we returned to Zagreb, which we reached in what I would guess was record time for a foreign tribesman.

Zagreb was not my home for long. The next day I left Croatia's capital and drove to Split, a small Croatian city on the Adriatic Sea where the Roman Emperor Diocletian built a palace fit for an emperor at the end of the third century A.D. The palace remains a centerpiece of Split's core. A hefty section of the drive runs along the beautiful Dalmatian coast, with the Adriatic Sea on the right and steep mountains rising straight up opposite. I arrived in Split on December 13, and immediately found a Croatian at the airport who agreed to drive me from Split to Tuzla, a long and dangerous haul in wartime winter. Antun, who worked for the Croatian government, also inadvertently welcomed me to Bosnia's tripartite godhead, although I never felt blessed.

A monster blizzard the day before had obliterated our planned mountain route. Better weather lay ahead, we believed, so we planned to head for Tuzla before dawn the next morning, December 14, armistice day for Bosnia, and my deadline for reaching the American base at Tuzla.

With another American reporter, I spent the night at Antun's home. A tall, lanky Croat, Antun reminded me physically and temperamentally of Goran Ivanisevic, the big-serving and talented Croatian tennis player. By staying at Antun's apartment, we would be able to wake together and leave before dawn in order to reach Tuzla before dark and danger arrived.

Driving at night in Bosnia was recommended only for killers, victims and fools. Eventually, we joined the category of fools, although I never used that word in front of Antun. Radio reports before dawn said the mountain roads remained blocked by snow piled higher than cars and by vehicles that became stuck trying to plow or slide around broken down cars and trucks.

Nervous, Antun refused to leave his home in Split. We got on well together, Antun and I, but I was growing more unhappy by the minute as he dallied and his fear grew. The other reporter decided against making the risky trip on any terms, which weakened my hand with Antun. I kept hounding and reassuring Antun that all would be well if we just left immediately. Antun was to drive a friend's car, with Martin, his friend, coming along to protect his investment and offer moral support. Martin, in other words, was supposed to ride shotgun without a weapon.

Our car was a standard rear-wheel drive and Antun was convinced we would be doomed in anything but a large four-wheel-drive vehicle. I had tried to find other transportation to Tuzla without success, so I kept harassing Antun, pestering him with strategically unsound arguments in which he had no faith.

I had raised my offer from $600 to $800, but Antun remained stuck in the blizzard of his fear as the hour grew later. I didn't think that he was trying to squeeze more money from me. He seemed genuinely afraid, not only of the awful road conditions, but of the war and the fact that he was a Catholic Croat believer heading into Bosnian Muslim territory where the war dial remained set on high. At that moment, tribalism, in the form of sectarianism, became personal rather than abstract.

The longer we waited to leave, the later and darker it would be when we reached Tuzla, if indeed we would be able to drive that far. Finally, Antun weakened, or got what he wanted, after I raised my offer to $1,000. A couple of hundred extra dollars didn't dissolve all of Antun's fear, but it sure made his gamble more worthwhile.

Antun's next move was to make sure that his chains would fit the car's tires. Then we topped off the gas tank, bought extra oil, antifreeze and drinking water, cheese and bread for the trip that would take a little more than 14 hours, more than double the normal time. "What, no restaurants along the way?" I asked Antun with a smile. He didn't smile back.

It was 10 A.M. on Thursday, December 14, 1995, when we finally pulled out of Split, five hours after our original take-off time and way too late for safety's sake, a point I kept to myself.

Only 24 hours before our departure a vicious blizzard with near hurricane-force winds had dumped more than three feet of snow along our mountain route. The drifts dwarfed cars and large trucks. The day we left was sunny and bright in Split, maybe a good omen, and the low, easy road north of Livna was clear. That Antun was a Croatian government employee in Split didn't hurt when we reached the Croatian-Bosnian border checkpoint at Kaminsko.

Croatian customs and police waved us through. Bosnian officials were nowhere in sight, having taken the prudent route to a safer haven. Outside a mountain tunnel at Kupres, we stopped to put on chains. Without chains we would have been stuck for days in the higher elevations. The road beyond the tunnel was packed with snow while marooned cars and trucks blocked traffic.

To keep moving, we weaved around vehicles locked in the snow until we could weave no more. Then we joined others trying to shovel, push and pull the unmoving cars and trucks to clear the road. We did this every quarter mile or so for many miles, and we kept moving.

At one point two large trucks that had been traveling in opposite directions blocked the mountain road. A third truck crawled up the hill, attached ropes to the truck that was trying to descend the hill and after a lot of pulling finally freed the descending truck and opened the road. Hundreds of trucks and cars were trying, and most were failing, to negotiate the narrow path called a road. It was like playing bumper cars at an outdoor winter carnival, only the cars were larger and the trucks were, well, trucks.

At several points I counted 100 trucks stuck on the road, many crunched against others in hard metal embrace and always blocking our path. Only cooperative pulling, tugging and shoveling, often with hands only, kept us moving. A lone U.N. snowplow did its best, but it wasn't made to plow vehicles.

A sign in a place called Borgoino warned that police used radar to patrol the road. Even Antun laughed at the absurdity of that warning under present conditions.

High in the mountains we were traveling in the middle of the narrow road opening, the only place where we could keep moving, when a large U.N. supply truck, also in the middle of the road and speeding in the opposite direction, slid around the corner in front of us and came straight at our ordinary little car.

Antun stopped our car dead center in the road and leaped ass-first, his legs dangling near the accelerator and brake pedals, into the lap of his friend to escape the truck that was headed right at him. Antun's contortion was Olympian, for he had to leap around the gear shift and great pain while not going through the roof and land, like a high-jumper, in the pit of his friend's lap. With our driver no longer driving and the truck bearing down on us, I could detect immediately from my perch in the back seat the approaching doom. Eyes locked wide beyond their sockets, I braced for the collision when

I should have ducked. The truck driver leaned just enough to miss us and continued rolling out of control down the hill. Antun wasn't impressed when I reminded him of my prediction that we had nothing to fear.

The image of six-foot-four-inch Antun leaping halfway across the car into the passenger side of the front seat provided comic relief after our thin escape. But the comedy was absent when it looked as if we would be buried in the truck's radiator.

After we cleared the mountain snows, the war became our next obstacle. Another wave of fear swept over us, and Antun wanted to stop and spend the night at or near British military headquarters in Gornji Vakuf. Not I. At military checkpoints, we began hearing rumors of Muslims and Serbs battling along the last long stretch of road leading to Tuzla. It was already dark, a particularly bad time to run a gauntlet of snipers and hostile armies. I had learned long ago to doubt rumors and to see for myself. Usually, the rumors are only rumors.

The Balkan wars were nationalistic and sectarian tribal conflicts rooted in historical flesh-eating hatreds that were resurrected by political figures who sought more land and power for their tribes and to etch their names for all time into tribal monuments. Antun was a Catholic Croat, and proud of it. He was also nervous about continuing on into Muslim territory at night. He finally agreed to go as far as we could, but he also needed some religious reinforcement and protection.

Pointing to rosary beads strung from the rear-view mirror, Antun turned to me and, with a mixture of fear, doubt and determined faith, said rapidly as if his speed of speech would be all-convincing, "This is my God. I am not going to take them off. Do you have a God?" "Yes," I answered simply but firmly, figuring that this was no time for philosophical or spiritual nuance. He didn't press further and I volunteered nothing.

Antun really wanted to know my religion and hence my tribe, my origins, my blood, in order to learn, in his mind, which side I was on. My answer was sufficient only because Antun was too courteous with a visitor to press the issue and ask, "Who's your God?" But his simple question elevated the moment to the sectarian, cultural, political and ethnic level where he and most Croats, Muslims and Serbs in the region instinctively believed the conflict resided.

Gods are important in the Balkans. The God of the Catholic Croats, the God of the Christian Orthodox Serbs, the God of the Muslims were an integral part of life, and death, in the Balkans wars. Even if the people didn't know or accept it, godlessness was present, too, in the attitudes and behavior of the people and in the atmosphere where the conflicts festered and exploded.

Outside the town of Trevink, melting snow, mild temperatures and heavy ground fog, for which that area of Bosnia is notorious in winter, slowed our pace. After our ordeal in the mountains, it would have been the height of ignominy to disappear into a bomb crater that had been turned into a pond. By then I felt that Tuzla, and success, would be ours.

We reached the U.S. base at Tuzla shortly before midnight. Given the six-hour time difference between Bosnia and the United States, I had time to file a story and meet my peace-treaty deadline.

At the front gate of the base, a U.S. airman told me that the bad weather had kept the number of U.S. troops there down to approximately 65. If American troops couldn't be flown in, I knew for sure that none could reach the base by rail or land. By another bit of luck, CNN, the cable television network, had rented an entire house a few steps from the entrance to the base. I went looking for a phone and found one at the CNN office, a line so clear that it seemed as if I were calling Washington from Maryland.

The CNN house was comfortable and the staff happy to offer professional courtesies common with people in that organization. I wrote the story and filed it from the CNN house in time for the next day's paper. That same night I took 10 $100 bills from their handy hiding place and gave them to Antun and his pal, Martin, $1,000 as we had agreed. I could read Antun's mind: Does he always keep $1,000 in cash within such easy reach? No, I said to myself. We shook hands, they gave me a receipt and the deal was done. Antun and Martin smiled. So did I.

All three of us slept at the CNN house that night. We enjoyed a full breakfast there the following morning, after which Antun and Martin left for Split. I never saw them again, but I'm sure that their return trip was easier than the journey to Tuzla.

With two weeks to go until Christmas, when I ate a hamburger for Christmas dinner at the Tuzla air base, I had a lot of reporting left to do about the burgeoning American presence and the Serbs, Muslims and Croats, who were still threatening to shred the peace treaty.

Several more weeks, way behind the originally announced schedule, would pass before the full complement of American soldiers arrived at Tuzla.

—◦◦◦—

My base in Tuzla was a small apartment that I rented from a Muslim family. The woman of the house and her teen-age kids needed the money; I needed shelter. With running water and electricity, unseen luxuries in many parts of Bosnia, I felt as if I were in Croatia. A small shop on the street sold oranges and a few other provisions, another bonus. With a translator who had a car, I kept a close eye on the Americans at the air base and roamed northern Bosnia. When I pulled out of Bosnia several weeks later, my translator gave me a warm and beautiful locally made scarf in gratitude for what I had paid him, which was money he had well-earned. He affirmed what I found to be a universal human trait: Those who have the least give the most.

A walk late at night from a downtown hotel, where I filed stories using phones in the Associated Press office, to my apartment was almost as adventurous as the drive from Split to Tuzla, The roads, sidewalks and bridges were mottled with deep water-filled craters, the result of shells and bombs that pulverized the asphalt and the earth below. There were no lights on the street except for sky light filtered through dense, almost impenetrable, fog.

Due to the fog that blinds, I could barely see the pavement at my feet. It was very difficult to detect the craters because the water in them looked like a black glaze that blended evenly with the dirt and remaining asphalt chunks. As I am unable to swim, I laughed to myself that it would be possible to fall into one of those craters late at night and not be discovered until morning when I bobbed to the surface. When I trudged back to the apartment around midnight each day, I did so very carefully, worried more about the craters than about possible snipers in the shadows. I knew the craters were there; I wasn't sure about the snipers. But I was blind to both.

By Christmas of that year, 1995, Bosnia and its sectarian tribes were free of an official state of war for the first time since the spring of 1992. At the U.S. base in Tuzla, an Army private from Mississippi volunteered to play Santa Claus for about 100 local children. Most of the children were Muslims who didn't know Santa from the Easter Bunny or Allah, and many were orphans.

When the soldier needed to bulk up and look more like Santa, I lent him my heavy green coat to wear under his Santa suit. I found a white plastic bag to hang under his chin and around his neck to resemble a beard. "Ho, ho, ho," said the soldier, the only Santa words he knew. All the kids, oblivious to what adults might call cultural and religious transgressions, sang and danced, ate cookies and candy, drank cocoa and soda and received stuffed animals, toy trucks, fire engines and teddy bears. Children usually know little or nothing about tribal differences and tribal wars, varying gods and cultural icons. But if adults have anything to say about it, the children will learn, the cycle will continue and the wars will go on.

Almost all Bosnian Muslims and thousands of Croats and Serbs opposed the efforts of supra-nationalist Croats and Serbs to carve exclusive ethnic, religious and political enclaves in Bosnia-Herzegovina. Bosnian Muslims — mostly tolerant secularists rather than religious fundamentalists, strong believ-

ers in the separation of religion and state and proud of Bosnia's pre-war plu-
ralism — were the main targets of Serbs and Croats and they bled the most.

Shunned, even murdered, by their own tribes, the Bosnian Croats and
Bosnian Serbs who opposed the revival of old hatreds were too small in number to prevent the religious-nationalistic march. All were overwhelmed by
tribal vitriol rooted in religious, cultural and nationalistic differences and by
the power-hungry politicians in Belgrade and Zagreb who used their contemporary political and military advantages to resuscitate history as a weapon
of terror and mass murder.

This steamroller effect of the masses over the fringes is not unusual. War
is a steamroller, no matter what the causes, because killing perpetuates killing
and revenge spins in all directions. War imprisons reasonable people, if it
doesn't kill them first. All Romans weren't decadent. But when the institutions and the people who controlled them became corrupt and the manipulated masses did not or could not resist the decline, the conclusion was
inevitable no matter how many individuals shouted in opposition from the
forum.

Unbounded rage in the Balkans resulted in at least 300,000 casualties,
some 1.35 million refugees in Europe and other countries, and 1.3 million displaced persons in Bosnia itself, refugees in their own country, according to
the U.N. High Commissioner For Refugees and the International Crisis Group
that was working in Bosnia.

From 1991 to 1995, after the splintering of Yugoslavia, Bosnia was trapped
in wars ignited by related tribesmen from beyond Bosnia's borders. Here was
another example of opportunistic outsiders taking advantage of endemic internal stress to create new conflict.

Tribal differences in the Balkans can be traced back hundreds of years
to the Catholic conversion of the Croats, the Orthodox conversion of the
Serbs and more recently to the Ottoman Turk conquest of the region in the
14th and 15th centuries and the subsequent conversion to Islam of those related
Slavs who are now called Bosnian Muslims.

In this sense, the wars were another version of East-West conflicts. Once
it started, the fighting also could be viewed as a local continuation of World
War II. During the early 1940s, Croat, Serb and Bosnian Muslim alliances
with and in opposition to Nazis and Communists were so tangled and shifting as to defy understanding except, perhaps, by the participants at specific
moments during that war.

Most Western peoples preferred to view the latest Balkans wars as simply an extension of the historic regional conflicts. "They've been killing each
other forever" is one way this New-World view is often expressed. By seeing
the war in that smug, oversimplified way, Westerners could more easily ignore

or exploit it. From this perspective, outsiders could more easily shun attempts to understand the historical complexities and the contemporary triggers to determine who was most responsible for the current conflict and to act appropriately on that knowledge.

Despite their religious differences, Bosnian Muslims, Orthodox Serbs and Catholic Croats are all Slavs and speak essentially the same language, Serbo-Croatian. They know each other well, too well perhaps, but deep down they don't care to know each other well enough.

Separate but entwined conflicts, the Croat-Serb, Croat-Muslim, Serb-Muslim and Serb-Croat-Muslim wars, used thoroughly modern political tactics and weapons that were deliberately tipped with revived religious and cultural poisons from the past. The original Serb and Croat provocateurs employed propaganda and unspeakable brutality to conceal wars for land and power in a civil war shroud. That proved easy because the old blood feuds were simple to revive, making the cycles of retaliation inevitable.

Instigated by Belgrade, the conflict between Serbs and ethnic–Albanians in the once-autonomous Yugoslav area of Kosovo added to the fervor among Serbs for a Greater Serbia that peaked in Bosnia.

The conflicts in Croatia, Bosnia and Kosovo were brewed in the minds of Croatian leader Franjo Tudjman and Serbian boss Slobodan Milosevic during the late 1980s. Tudjman is dead now. So is Milosevic, who died while on trial as a war criminal in The Hague. The nationalistic demons in Milosevic and Tudjman came to life with the death of communism in what had been Marshal Tito's post–World War II Yugoslavia. By the time the Balkans wars engulfed the region, only Serbia and Montenegro remained of Tito's Yugoslavia.

Tudjman desired to cleanse Croatia of Serbs. Once the Croatian tribal flag was unfurled, Croats wanted to add Croatian dominated areas of Bosnia to Croatia and to create Croatian enclaves in other parts of Bosnia.

Milosevic pursued his ideal of a Greater Serbia, reviving that long-dead but not forgotten medieval tribal enterprise. To create Greater Serbia meant gluing Serb-dominated areas of Bosnia to Serbia after Muslims and Croats were expelled, and destroying Bosnia as a separate state. If Milosevic could kill enough Muslims and Croats and help provoke them to kill each other as well, all three parties just might agree to carve up Bosnia into separate enclaves, with Muslims, of course, getting the runt's share, if anything, and Bosnia evaporating as a separate entity.

When first Slovenia and later Macedonia, both essentially Slavic, split from Yugoslavia after the fall of communism, there were no wars because those republics had no ambitions to grab other territories. Croatia and Serbia also lacked any desire to absorb parts of Macedonia or Slovenia, where neither Serbs nor Croats figured significantly in the tribal mix. U.N. and U.S. troops in Macedonia helped to check any designs Milosevic might have had on stitching parts of Macedonia to Kosovo and therefore to Serbia.

Kosovo, about 90 percent ethnic–Albanian, had been an autonomous region in Yugoslavia under Tito. Milosevic stripped the region of that status in 1990, which meant that he and Serbia had self-proclaimed legal cover to do as they pleased against the Albanians in Kosovo. Neighboring Bosnia was different from Macedonia and Slovenia. Croats and Serbs lived, with Muslims, in Bosnia, and Milosevic and Tudjman wanted pieces of that rugged land to expand their little empires. Ethnic cleansing, sometimes called genocide, was one result of their war games.

At their core, the Balkans wars were Hitlerian. Milosevic might just as well have touted the ethnic and genetic purity of Serbs and their rights to more breathing space in an expanded Serbian Fatherland when he gave new voice to the notion of a Greater Serbia. His methods, applied in Bosnia by henchmen Radovan Karadzic and Gen. Ratko Mladic, came straight out of bad European history, West and East. The expulsion, detention, rape and murder of non–Serbs to create exclusive ethnic-religious enclaves for Serbs was, in its broadest sense, racist. Short of gender warfare, that's as broadly tribal and offensive as tribalism can get.

Once the swords were unsheathed, the vicious personal nature of the fighting offered further evidence that the wars were tribal.

On a later trip to Bosnia, a man I was interviewing in the Serbian stronghold of Banya Luka kissed a photo of Karadzic that he pulled proudly from his wallet. He criticized the United States for brokering the Dayton Peace Accords and keeping the Serbs from total victory.

At first the angry man refused to give his name. "If I give you my name, everyone will know I'm a war criminal," he said in a way that made me uncomfortable wondering how many he had killed and how. His logic was a bit fractured, I thought, although there was no doubt what he meant. Then the man gave me his name and I moved on, facing him as I backed up and said so long.

Plunder, pillage and rape are the currency of war on the battlefield and behind the lines. It matters not whether the armies are mechanized or travel on foot, by donkey or camel. War brings out the worst in human nature, and the worn out suits that send boys, girls, men and women to plunder, kill and die know that truth.

Serbian fighters in Bosnia, armed and aided by the Serbian-controlled Yugoslav federal army, imprisoned, starved and massacred able-bodied Muslim men. Civilians were easier targets. Serb snipers in Sarajevo targeted women, old men and children — anything that moved — in an attempt to break Muslim resistance in Bosnia's heart and soul and therefore in Bosnia itself. Ethnic cleansing became synonymous with Bosnia. Lies about Muslim threats and conduct were the tools used to justify the Serb attacks and block outside intervention by nation-states and organizations that were reluctant to get involved to begin with in what they preferred to see as more of the same old civil wars.

Open warfare began in Croatia in the summer of 1991, after Croatia had trumpeted its religious-nationalistic identity and became independent. Croatian forces attacked Serbs in Croatia after the Serbs had usurped control of an area along the border with Bosnia. The Croat-Serb war spread to eastern Croatia, in an area called Slavonia, which was devastated during the fighting.

Within a short time, Milosevic and his henchmen, led by a thug named Zeljko Raznjatovic, aka Arkan, took terror and murder to predominately Muslim towns along the border with Serbia. The Muslims who weren't killed were driven off. Until the wars wound down in 1995, Croats fought Serbs and Muslims separately, Croats and Muslims combined for a period to fight Serbs, and Muslims fought for survival against Serbs. War crimes were common because civilians often were targeted for expulsion from towns and cities, and countless numbers were detained, tortured and killed.

Milosevic, Karadzic and Mladic were indicted by the International Criminal Tribunal for the Former Yugoslavia in the The Hague. Milosevic was charged with genocide and with instigating, planning, ordering and committing crimes against Albanian civilians in Kosovo. He was found dead of natural causes in prison on March 11, 2006, depriving the world of a verdict concerning his role in war crimes. Karadzic, looking like a mad monk who had been on a thirteen-year diet, was finally seized in July 2008. Mladic remains at large.

Eight months after my long trek that began in Northern Ireland and ended plowing through the snows from Split to Tuzla, I returned to Bosnia twice for several weeks in a two-month period to report on elections in the country and on conditions a year after the Dayton Peace Accords were signed.

On each trip, I drove alone from Split, Croatia, to Sarajevo, Bosnia's capital, which I used as a base for travel throughout the country. In Sarajevo I rented a room in an apartment a ten-minute walk from downtown. The apartment was owned by a Serbian woman, whose twelve-year-old daughter surrendered her room so the family could make a little extra money. A poster of the Spice Girls, the hot young English singers of the moment, stared at me from the wall of the room. Cross-cultural pollination, I thought, maybe some progress in the next generation. Then I had, as the English say, a rethink: It all depends on a person's definition of culture.

Tens of thousands of Muslims throughout Bosnia were in a daze long after the killing stopped. Some Bosnian Serbs and Croats walked that same dizzying path. All were refugees in their own land, and there was little confidence that the fighting was really over.

Post-war Bosnia brought innocent civilians from each tribe together in ways that created new conflicts over squatters' rights and building ownership. Homes in various regions that had belonged to Croats, Serbs or Muslims before the war often were occupied by tribal enemies after the fighting ceased.

Housing conditions were so poor in and around Sarajevo that destitute Muslims, Croats and Serbs from other towns shared squatters' quarters because they had no other shelter. But they were living in houses that others would claim. There was no shortage of poignant stories that highlighted the horrors of the fighting, how it was ignited and inflamed and the absurdity of war itself. Those stories pour out after the killing stops, always when it stops, but sel-

Bosnian blueprint: One of countless architectural skeletons drafted by war, in and around Bosnia's capital of Sarajevo (photograph by the author, 1996. © Cox Newspapers Inc.).

dom when the hot blood is flowing. Each generation, it seems, has to learn for itself the pain and futility of war.

Munib, then 62, and his wife Almasa, stood in front of their home that was now a shell of a few walls and a floor in their old neighborhood near the Sarajevo airport. They laughed out loud, silly, like teenagers, their behavior perhaps a substitute for weeping, at the absurdity of their situation. Munib, a Muslim, built the house himself in 1960 and now, at their age, they talked of rebuilding and starting over.

An elderly Serbian woman shared squatter space with a Muslim family of five in a house near Sarajevo. Before the war, the house belonged to other Serbs. None in the group worked or had money. The family, which included three children and a man who was bed-ridden with the effects of a stroke, had been driven like animals from two northern cities before they could stop with relative impunity near the capital.

Radmila, a Serb, held firm in the Grbavica area of Sarajevo throughout the war. Born in the battered town of Brcko in the north, Radmila lived in Sarajevo for 40 years. She blamed Milosevic and other politicians for the war. Her husband was a Croat, her sister married a Muslim, her daughter-in-law was a Muslim, her granddaughter was then married to a Frenchman and her brother's wife was a Croat, she said proudly. "I'm Serbian by religion, but Bosnian Serb by nationality, not Belgrade Serb," she said, taking a swipe at Milosevic and his role in causing the war. But few Serbs or Croats I met made the distinction between religion and nationality.

The old and beautiful city of Mostar, near the Croatian-Bosnian border, was split in two between Croats and Muslims. This was an angry place, where young Croats and young Muslims were prohibited from crossing to each other's zone. Here I met Salih, 74, a former professor of history and art who might be called Mostar's historian. Salih rode his bike back and forth from the Muslim to the Croatian zones to show that he, an old man, at least was free. It was in Mostar where Croats, out of the explosive meanness of war, destroyed a magnificent stone bridge over the Neretva River that dated to early Ottoman times. When I crossed the Neretva, I stepped gingerly on a flimsy, swaying suspension bridge, further evidence that war and progress are enemies, a reality that, unfortunately, each generation must see for itself.

On a return trip from Mostar to Sarajevo one night, I pulled out to pass a couple of cars that were motoring along like lawnmowers. As I drove past the first car, I was struck in the rear, by the car that I was then passing which had pulled out to go by another car that I was about to pass. This was a very unusual collision. The driver who hit me should have been able to see me clearly because I was in front of and just about past him when he pulled out. With my translator, we drove a short distance and pulled over with the other driver following. We had a civil argument, complete with graphics which I drew, as the damage to both cars was slight. The other driver said that I had struck his car, which was impossible.

After a long argument that ended in no decision, we both drove off. A couple of miles closer to Sarajevo, a car with a flashing light urged me to pull over. I was amused: a highway patrolman in Bosnia. I stopped. The man said he was indeed a police officer — for what side he didn't say and I didn't ask. The officer grilled me and my translator about the bumper touching.

Apparently the driver who hit me had already told the officer his version of the collision. We explained our version to the officer, who, quite naturally, was confused by the conflicting stories. It seemed as if he wanted to take some action against us, but couldn't figure out what charge would fit the supposed violation. My translator and I kept talking and pointing out the absurdity of the other driver's claim. This added to the confusion, which is always a good strategy in a foreign land.

Eventually, the officer threw up his hands and drove off. We left without protest. As a member of a foreign tribe, in lands where people often want desperately to be liked and respected, I was always treated better than were local residents, a principle I came to rely on often.

When I was working on a story in southeastern Turkey several months later, my rental car went missing as I was making telephone calls at the post office in Antakya (the ancient town of Antioch). Figuring that the car didn't drive itself off, I thought theft. But locals, who earlier had assured me that the car would be safe in front of the post office, told me the police had ordered the car towed for illegal parking. My faith in Antakyans was restored immediately.

Towed in Antakya. I laughed at the notion. When police in the nearby traffic kiosk learned that they had towed a foreigner's rather than a local's car, they were mortified and apologized profusely. It was as if they were pleading with me not to report Antakya to the international tourism police. So they were pleased and probably confused when I smiled and wasn't angry. The police waived the fine, which was $3.68. I smiled again at the amount. But they couldn't waive the towing fee, which upset them further, because the towing company was private. When I picked up my car an hour later, I paid the towing charge, which was another $3.68. I smiled again and drove off, imagining what the fine and towing charge would have been in an American or European city.

Before the Balkans wars, about 18,500 people lived in the town of Stolac southeast of Mostar and even closer to the Croatian border. About 43.5 percent were Muslims, 33 percent Serbs, 21 percent Croats, while the remainder was mixed. Until, that is, the local Bosnian Croat militia, backed by the Croatian Army, went knocking on doors. At 5 A.M. on July 3, 1993, as Adela remembered it when we met in Mostar in October 1996, Croatian soldiers rapped on her door in Stolac and gave her, her mother and sister 15 minutes to pack and get out, ordering them to leave the key in the lock as they pulled out.

Nearly all of the 8,000 Muslims who lived in Stolac were expelled from the town, which overnight became a Croatian and Serbian enclave. Adela said that her father and almost all of the Muslim men were hauled off to detention camps. All the Muslim men were tortured and most were executed, according to a study of the cleansing of Stolac. But, Adela said, her father was released from a detention camp after three months.

After the Croatian soldiers came calling, Adela recalled three years later. "I brushed my teeth, I washed my face, and I left," taking only a few personal effects in a small bag. With other Muslims from Stolac, Adela said, she and her family were taken to an iron factory, where the invaders stole all the money and gold they could find. From the factory, the group was taken in a truck used to transport animals to a town where everyone was forced to discard their bags. Then they walked about two miles to the Bosnian Muslim army lines and on to a safe town where 35 villagers from Stolac lived in one room for a year. Related families settled in the four corners of the room and called it home, Bosnia style.

Living with Madmen

The road to Slobodan Milosevic's Greater Serbia and ethnic cleansing in Bosnia began with a minor political coup in Kosovo. Milosevic's power trip essentially ended in Kosovo as well, after a war with NATO and the West.

For most outside tribesmen, especially for journalists seeking to determine the level of friction between minority Serbs and majority ethnic–Albanians, Kosovo's gates were hard to penetrate.

After a two-hour taxi ride from Skopje, Macedonia's capital, to the Blace border crossing with Kosovo, my translator and I reviewed our intricate plan, synchronized our strides so that I always walked a step behind him, and put our simple scheme into action.

My translator was to knock on the window of the border post, explain that I was an American journalist and that we wanted visas to enter Kosovo, where ethnic–Albanians were choking under the heel of Milosevic's shrunken Yugoslavia and his ambitions for a Greater Serbia. My complex role was to smile and nod while standing at my translator's elbow to coach him should unexpected questions be raised. Not a hitch came our way. It wouldn't have been easier if Milosevic himself had called ahead with orders to let us in.

The border police were a bit unsure of what to do when they opened the window. But after a few minutes of shrugging and widening their eyes, they gave us two Yugoslav visas, good for seven days, to travel anywhere in Yugoslavia, which then meant only Serbia, including Kosovo, and Montenegro. The visas were free; no charges. I was amazed, but acted as if we expected nothing less.

Our next move was to get out of sight of the border post without delay, nonchalantly and without running. Once we had moved away, it would be unlikely that a suddenly empowered soldier would point a gun at us and shout "stop." We walked a half-mile or so before we began flagging cars headed for Pristina, Kosovo's capital. A taxi stopped. A little more than an hour's drive later and $30 lighter and we were in Pristina.

Despite many attempts, I was never able to get a Yugoslav visa through normal embassy channels in London, Washington or Paris. Nothing personal. Milosevic didn't want too many foreign journalists roaming around and learning what was being done to other Balkan peoples in the name of his ego and a Greater Serbia. The only other time I received a Yugoslav visa was in February 1997, when I paid $100 to a middleman in Sofia, Bulgaria.

When I left Skopje, Macedonia, with a translator that May of 1994, I had decided on the direct approach, a simple trick that is often forgotten when higher intrigue seems in order: Push on the border post door and see what happens. It is surprising how many closed doors open when nudged.

To reach the Blace border post my translator and I walked confidently from our taxi past long lines of trucks and cars, and international customs and police officials, directly to the Yugoslav post itself. The trucks and cars could take hours, even days, to cross the border. We crossed in minutes. Perhaps the border police figured that we must have known what we were doing. Otherwise why were we there? This is another assumption that is often made, wrongly.

Conditions were relatively calm in Pristina because Serbian authorities were in total, suffocating, control. The ethnic–Albanian armed rebellion didn't break the surface until 1996 and 1997, after weapons from sacked military bases in Albania were smuggled into Kosovo, before most of the world realized that Milosevic was forcing reluctant Serbs from Croatia and Bosnia-Herzegovina into Kosovo to squeeze out ethnic–Albanians, and before the world's deaf capitals noticed that Serbian police in Kosovo were punishing the local Albanian population. We entered Kosovo five years before NATO launched its first-ever military action to halt Milosevic's military and police offensive against the ethnic–Albanians there.

Milosevic's idea of creating a Greater Serbia began to take shape in Kosovo in September 1989, when Yugoslavia stripped the region of its status as an autonomous province. After that came the Croat and Serb wars against each other and later against the Bosnian Muslims.

Kosovo was a raw and ripe sectarian and ethnic battleground where Milosevic blended history, ego and empire-building to arouse and deepen the evident tribal fissures. Some of the charges brought against Milosevic in the Hague concerned crimes against the ethnic–Albanians in Kosovo.

Tribalism in Kosovo was as visible as the satellite dishes dangling incongruously from Pristina's crumbling apartment buildings. Serbs are Slavs and Orthodox Christians who speak the Serbo-Croatian language. Once split between Roman Catholicism and Eastern Orthodoxy, most Albanians converted to Islam during the Turkish occupation. But they are not Slavs. Their Indo-European language descends from the Illyrians who settled in the Balkans about 3,000 years ago.

As did many of the Slavs in Bosnia, perhaps 70 percent of Albanians converted to Islam after the Ottomon Turks conquered the area. In a decisive battle at Kosovo Polje, which means the field of blackbirds, in 1389, the Turks brought down the medieval Serbian empire, a humiliating defeat forever lodged in Serbian throats. Milosevic relied on the belief that Serbian Orthodoxy and nationalism, a ready mix, would rally around Kosovo. The Albanians, as substitute Turks, would be made to pay for his visions of grandeur. When Milosevic was bursting his suit swallowing the powerful potion of a Greater Serbia, Kosovo must have seemed like an appetizer.

Another passenger shared the taxi with us on the ride through rural Kosovo to Pristina. We bounced along from the mountains near the border with Macedonia past small farms that were worked slowly as if to reflect their age and the age of the farmers. A few horses and water buffalo labored and grazed in the fields. The land flattened as we neared Pristina, a mish-mash of typical Soviet-style concrete slabs thrown up and called apartment buildings. Along with laundry drying and bicycles leaning on crumbling porches were small satellite dishes, strung like round white pendants scattered on long necklaces that stretched from floor to floor and building to building. I found the satellite dishes remarkable given the harsh conditions under which the Albanians lived.

Ethnic-Albanians were more than 90 percent of Kosovo's two million people, but had zero influence over government agencies. Young men were fleeing the area to avoid being forced to join the Yugoslav army and die in

Bosnia. Their secondary schools and universities had been closed, Albanian writers couldn't get their books published; if they somehow managed to find a printer, they weren't allowed to distribute the books. Yet there were all these satellite dishes, sort of like small circuses for individual families.

All of the Albanians I spoke with in Kosovo were deeply depressed. The Serbs, they said, were crushing them, trying to drive them out to Albania or to Macedonia, which had tribal differences with its own ethnic–Albanian population. If that didn't work, the local Albanians said, the Serbs wouldn't mind provoking an armed uprising, an invitation to a slaughter. A worker with Mother Teresa's humanitarian organization in Pristina called the Serb strategy "silent ethnic-cleansing," a variation on a phrase that later received more bloody and less muted prominence in Bosnia.

Milosevic would have loved a full fight with Kosovo's Albanians then because the Albanians had few weapons. In a few years, the arms balance would not be so one-sided; Kosovo would be in open revolt, NATO would bomb the Serbs and an uneasy truce would result after the Albanian Kosovars accepted autonomy within Yugoslavia for a limited time. When the tide turned toward the Albanians and against the Serbs, *voila*, the Albanians would claim that Kosovo was for Albanians only.

Prospects of a full-blown conflict in Kosovo raised European and U.S. fears that the Balkans wars would spin out of control from Kosovo south to Macedonia and even Greece, a NATO ally and Christian Orthodox nation, and then east to Bulgaria. Maybe even Turkey, another NATO ally, would be drawn in. Restless ethnic–Albanians in Macedonia were demanding more rights from the Slav-dominated government there while Milosevic armed Serbs along the border with Macedonia.

An economic and political disaster under decades of closed, paranoid and super-repressive Communist rule, Albania itself, the poor man of Europe, was ripe for an upheaval that might have fed Albanian nationalism throughout the Balkans.

Slowly, Albania was being turned into a U.S. listening post with all ears on Bosnia. U.S. spy planes, drones, operated from Albanian bases. American soldiers, 515 of them, were stationed nearby on Macedonia's frontier with Serbia under a U.N. mandate to monitor conditions in Macedonia and to make Milosevic think three times before making trouble there. The U.S. soldiers were almost half the U.N. force in Macedonia; the American presence alongside the U.N. and operating for the first time under U.N. command was so sensitive as to be almost top-secret everywhere except on the ground.

Kosovo itself was a simmering brew of Serb suppression and Albanian misery and unbridled anger, only a few guns away from open revolt when I met with Adem Demaci, a man rightfully referred to as the Albanian Nelson

Mandela. Demaci paid for his political principles by spending, at this point, almost half of his life in prison cells with madmen and violent criminals.

A small, wiry and dapper man with thinning white hair who looked older than his 58 years, Demaci was fiercely uncompromising in his campaign for Kosovo's independence. Yet, like Mandela, he spoke through a thick shield of tranquility, wry, sometimes dark, humor and serene confidence that derived from personal knowledge that some people can be imprisoned and tortured but not broken. After what he had been through, Demaci said, nothing could hurt him, not torture; not even death. Prison and torture made Demaci a free man.

Demaci was imprisoned for nearly 28 years, five-and-a-half of them in solitary confinement. "Prison for one

Face of dignity: Free at last, Adem Demaci at his home in Pristina, Kosovo. Known as the Albanian Mandela, Demaci spent almost 28 years in prison because he campaigned for Kosovo's independence (photograph by the author, 1994. © Cox Newspapers Inc.).

person is nothing when you compare it to prison for a whole people," said Demaci, echoing others in battle zones elsewhere. A writer of Romance novels, Demaci's views of Kosovo's independence were more real than romantic to Milosovic and his henchmen. Life in Kosovo was similar to life in prison, Demaci said: there were no rights, no freedoms in either place.

Steely, dignified and confident, Demaci wore a dark gray suit and a white shirt when we spoke in his home. In a sense, he was the old man of the Albanian Kosovars' battle for freedom and independence. In another sense, he was not old at all and probably never would be.

Demaci's first prison stint was an even three years from November 19, 1958 to November 18, 1961. His second term was from June 8, 1964 to June

8, 1974. Some weird jailer, a stickler for watching the calendar, kept precise time for him. Before long Demaci was back in prison. His longest term, 15 years, was from October 6, 1975, until April 21, 1990. His release came six months before his scheduled term was up. International pressure sprung him early, Demaci said, "The Serbs wanted to impress the world."

All of his offenses, Demaci said, were for pacifist protests against the government that denied Kosovo's Albanians the same rights as the ruling Serb minority. "All I did was write graffiti and wave an Albanian flag in public places and speak nationalistic slogans in public," Demaci said. "I was not such an important man." Ah, but he was persistent, and dangerous to authority. The charges against him, Demaci said, were of the usual generic kind: attempting to destroy Yugoslavia's Communist system.

If Demaci was strong in mind when he went to prison, he seemed to strengthen with each sentence. "Somehow," he said, "my years all alone in prison were the easiest ones. It was cold, dark, wet and dirty. Still, you can organize and control your life as you want to." Outside of solitary confinement, almost all the prisoners with him, Demaci said, "were either crazy or criminals of the most hardened kind. When you live with madmen and criminals, you need a lot of will to preserve yourself from those characters."

Instead of being in his late fifties, Demaci said with a smile shorn of anger but not of confidence, he thought of himself as being in his late thirties. He preferred not to count his time in the dungeons. Throughout the open conflict that was to come, Demaci insisted on an independent Kosovo, not on one tied to Serbia.

In the mid–1990s, Demaci was president of Kosovo's human rights council and editor of the *Forum* magazine, which couldn't be published because it had no money. He described the human rights council as a group that merely "cried over the situation because there was nothing they could do about it but collect information about police actions against Albanians."

Albanians in Kosovo received verbal and moral support from the outside world, Demaci said, but nothing more. Outside advisors said Kosovo should remain part of Serbia, accept wider autonomy, advice Demaci found impossible to accept. At that moment, Demaci recognized that a peaceful solution was the only answer because the alternative would be a massacre. By and large the Serb police left him alone, but they harassed the human rights council, raided the council's office, confiscated documents and gave one man what Demaci called "a savage beating."

"The Serbs are getting tougher all the time," Demaci told me; "By bothering the people they are bothering me. The object is to drive out the Albanians. The Serb policy is to eliminate the Albanians. The rest is detail."

When the Blind Shoot from the Hip

A teenager waved a Kalashnikov and fired wildly overhead. I drew close to him to make sure that I avoided the bullets that would fall around us. Then I started laughing at this Third World comedy. He was a funny sight, although no one else saw the humor. The gunman's eyeglasses were so thick I doubted that he could hit the Adriatic from the crest of its waves. Unsure of whether he could see me, I kept talking to him, hoping that his hearing was better than his vision. The weapon was an alien in his young hands. Yet he was giddy with a power that he didn't understand and couldn't direct.

It was March 1997, and I was in southern Albania, the mother country to ethnic–Albanians in Kosovo, Macedonia, Greece, elsewhere in the Balkans, and in Italy, too. At heart these were all the same people from roughly the same ethnic, cultural, linguistic and sectarian tribe. They were all Albanians, even if time and the cities where they lived had made them different on the fringes.

A chaotic dime-store revolution was rollicking along Albania's rough roads, ripping through military bases and police stations in town after town. The popular uprising would soon topple Albania's first democratically elected but corrupt government, funnel guns and ammo to the ethnic–Albanian rebels in Kosovo and ultimately compel NATO to intervene between the Albanians in Kosovo and Milosevic's Serb/Yugoslav army.

What are fellow tribesmen for? The Albanians in Kosovo were about to find out.

Albania's revolt crawled along on knees made of bullets and rifles to the doorstep of the Western powers. Anywhere from half a million to a million weapons, mostly submachine guns, assault rifles and smaller arms, along with plenty of ammunition, were plundered during the upheaval, and most of those were smuggled to Albanian cousins in Kosovo. NATO's attacks against Serbian forces in Kosovo marked the defense organization's first military action in its 50-year history. That alone makes the tribal war in Kosovo worth far more than an historical footnote, at least in Western eyes.

Sympathetic soldiers and police abandoned their posts throughout southern Albania; some joined the rebellion. Anyone who wanted assault rifles or handguns and trunks of ammunition to go with them, maybe even a lame tank or anti-aircraft gun, could walk right in and haul them away. That's what the blind man with the Kalashnikov did, and he wasn't alone. The rebels won every fight I saw, even when a few government mercenaries and secret police resisted. There was some killing at this time, but not much, unless you were one of the dead. Near the city of Gjirocaster, rebels captured 15 government mercenaries, took their weapons, stripped them of clothing and released them naked into the mountains.

Off to the side of a road near Gjirocaster, a man showed a woman how to use a handgun. A young girl was wounded in the garden of her home by aimless gunfire which prompted her father to say, "We're making war without enemies. We are shooting ourselves." His complaint was not isolated. By the time the government of President Sali Berisha was ousted that summer and the upheaval had spread, more than 1,500 people were reported killed in seven months.

Unorganized but effective, the rebellion swept from Kakavile on the Greek border north through Himera, Saranda, Delvine, Permet, Kulcyre, Tepelene, Vlore, Grajice all the way to Berat where a kid with swelling testosterone and a new weapon fired away at random, saying, "Everybody here has a gun. I never had a gun before. It's fun to shoot." Whoopee!

Newly armed kids aboard donkeys, bicycles and motor scooters hauled boxes of ammunition from Permet. Their wild firing echoed off the snow-capped mountains that rimmed the town. They would sort the ammunition later. At the looted Poshnje civil guard base, a World War II–era complex in Berat, a smiling boy said, "Nobody says no, so we're taking everything." Guns, ammo, auto and truck parts.

In Grajice, a boy used a rope to sling the wood and metal of his fresh Kalashnikov over his shoulder. In a nearby field, three women and a man were hoeing. Surrounded by rolling hills and snowy mountains, Berat is one of the prettiest towns in Albania. The cultural and historical heritage of its Old Quarter is protected by UNESCO, and the Osumi River cuts through the valley that beautifies Berat.

Civil upheaval piled atop an economy that was too nonexistent to collapse. Albania's new political structure stole votes and money and produced a nation made for the theater of the absurd, not one that could thrive or even survive on the competitive street. Only smuggling brought relief, and chaos crippled smuggling, too.

Between Saranda and Vlore, telephone wires were strung on broken tree limbs stuck in the ground. The limbs looked like scarecrows on the horizon or like the arms and legs of a skeleton spread akimbo a few feet above the ground. Dead horses fed the ravens along the road from Vlore to Fier. Donkey carts, kitchen sinks, trash bins, car mufflers, tubs, trees and burned trucks served as makeshift checkpoints. One newly armed kid laughed as he asked me for $10 to cross a checkpoint. He was in on his own joke.

The upheaval was an Albanian affair, internal, clannish and tribal to the core. Albania had its share of broader sectarian, political and other tribal conflicts. Sali Berisha, a cardiologist who was elected in 1992, after about 50 years of Communist rule, was the target of popular wrath.

Berisha was accused of buying votes in the 1996 election to keep his party in power and of profiting from 10 failed pyramid schemes that promised investors a 300 percent profit in three months. Instead, the money disappeared into the hands of the pyramid schemers and Berisha's political party. Having seen enough of their heart doctor, Albanians sought a second opinion.

For a desperately poor people, the Albanians somehow found millions of dollars to invest collectively. Much of that cash probably came from relatives who lived abroad. Like the poor everywhere, Albanians sought a quick exit from poverty, but entered even deeper poverty and bought new anger. I talked with Albanians who said that they had invested as much as $40,000, and lost it all. In a short time, Berisha was forced to grant amnesty to the rebels and to call elections, which he lost. Albanians lost their money but not their new democracy.

The revolt in southern Albania had internal tribal overtones indirectly involving language. The Tosk dialect is spoken in the south, while the Kheg dialect dominates in the north. Berisha was a northerner, further reason for the south to grant him no quarter.

To reach southern Albania, I flew to Athens and then to Ioannina, a nice town on the Greek side of the border where I kept a hotel room as I traveled back and forth to Albania. I stayed in Albania for a couple of days before returning to Ioannina to file stories, a routine that I maintained for several days. The border, 35 miles from Ioannina, was a sieve. The first day I crossed, a border guard checked my passport. After that the border guards had checked out. The border was wide open; enter Albania at your own risk. Most of the Greeks who lived in Albania near the border took the cue and fled with Albanians, about 300,000 in all, to Greece.

Mired in poverty and choking under political repression for most of the 20th century, Albania in revolt was even worse off. No one and nothing worked. At "The Gloria" restaurant in Vlore, a center of the rebellion and a smugglers' paradise, on the Adriatic shore, there were no fish. There was no water or electricity either. The only food left there were morsels of cold spaghetti, bread, lettuce and olives. Whiskey, vodka and a half-bottle of bad white wine were available to slake one's thirst. No one was working in the town. Although the sea lapped at the door of "The Gloria," a fish restaurant, no one fished for food. They stole guns instead.

This is what happens when a country descends into an economic and political freefall. Routine business doesn't get done because it doesn't exist. Albania didn't have far to fall. For almost 50 years, under Enver Hoxha's paranoid, personal brand of communism, Albania befriended then rejected Tito and his loosely bound tribes in Yugoslavia, was allied with and then mocked the Soviet empire and its many tribes that spanned Eurasia, embraced and jilted Mao and his multi-layered Chinese Communist tribe.

Concrete paranoia: Albanian dictator Enver Hoxha ordered the construction of 750,000 of these small concrete bunkers in his tiny country. The bunkers created fear among Albanians and made it easier for Hoxha to control Albania for decades (photograph by the author, 1997. © Cox Newspapers Inc.).

Exhausted from fighting his Communist cohorts, Hoxha rejected the world. Hoxha was so bizarre that he made mountainous, backward Albania even more isolated by constructing three-quarters of a million small concrete pillbox bunkers for civil defense against possible invasion, as if any other tribe would waste time traipsing to Albania or that medieval defenses could stop them if they did. The bunkers look like oversized concrete versions of World War I soldiers' helmets.

The collapse of tiny Albania and the effects of civil conflict show the extent to which poverty and repression in one country can affect other tribes nearby. Upheaval in Albania eventually helped to force NATO's intervention in Kosovo, and could have caused a civil war between ethnic–Albanians and Macedonians. If NATO had failed to stop the Serbs in Kosovo, the results probably would have been a larger war there, complete with more Balkan-style tribal slaughters.

Kosovo's Albanian majority declared independence in February 2008, a reality that seemed a distinct impossibility a decade earlier. Europe's newest nation-state continues its search for wider political and monetary recognition.

Back in the Albanian mother ship, memories faded. Sali Berisha's party scored again in 2005 elections and named Berisha Albania's prime minister.

TWELVE

Soul-Searching in Central Asia

With the dissolution of the Soviet empire came the revival of Islam in Central Asia and the Caucasus Mountains region. Saudis, Kuwaitis and Iranians led the charge to reconvert the peoples of the steppes and mountains to their own brands of Islam.

At Friday prayers in a mosque in Tashkent, Uzbekistan, in November 1992, a guest speaker told the gathering that he was from "Arabistan," the land of the Arabs. One of the newly converted translated for those around him: "That's Saudi Arabia."

While this competition heated up to bring the newly religious people into the fold of Sunni or Shiite Islam on their own grounds, Israel at the same time was working quietly to ferry long-forgotten and isolated Jews in the region to Tel Aviv.

"Our first priority is to absorb Jews from all of the old Soviet Union," an official of the Jewish Agency told me in Baku, Azerbaijan's capital. "We can't let the opportunity slide to bring all Jews from here to Israel. Because of the turmoil, the opportunity is here now."

He looked like a businessman, not an agent of the dying KGB. In his suit, shirt and tie, Yevgeny could have been in the vanguard of the new Russian entrepreneurs angling for a joint business venture with a Western company. But there he was, a spy by trade, warning that it could be fatal for me to ask the questions in Central Asia that I was asking him in the Soviet capital. The Soviet man in Moscow looked and acted nothing like a descendant of Stalin's intelligence network that 60 years earlier had sealed Central Asia from foreign eyes.

In the early 1990s, its Communist Revolution spent, the Soviet Union was a dying Soviet and a fraying union. Tribalism in its most literal sense was riding and roaring again in the ancestral mountains and open spaces of the Turkic and Mongol peoples and among the many fractious peoples who lived in the valleys and on the slopes of the Caucasus Mountains. In the East as well as the West of the former Soviet empire new states were sprouting from its still-warm ashes. In Central Asia Uzbeks, Kazakhs, Turkmen, Tadjiks and Kyrgyz were rising again in new expressions of tribal identity. Empires they had been, or been a part of, in centuries past, but never before had they been the rough nation-states that they were becoming. And this time there was no way to keep foreigners from their sweeping steppes, majestic mountains, wild valleys, broad deserts, rivers and seas. So Yevgeny warned me about the visceral tribal competitions ready to blow in the vast region, the ethnic, language, religious and cultural conflicts in Central Asia and to the west in the Caucasus region between the Black and Caspian seas.

The potential for endemic tribal clashes was real enough. And, as usual, outsiders added to the danger: Iranians, Saudis, Kuwaitis and Turks, and Russians who were left behind in the tribal regions and along their borders with the huge new and largely self-contained Russian state. All were bidding in various degrees for souls, political power and influence, money, land and oil. Always oil. Americans and Israelis were in the region, too, the Americans sniffing Caspian Sea oil and gas and checking the intentions of the new Russia; the Israelis working with great success to build a people pipeline to Tel Aviv for the region's Jews and to use the emigration connections to knit technological, political, security and other ties with the fresh, mostly Muslim, nations.

"This isn't America. You must be careful," Yevgeny whispered. "Over here you could be killed asking questions like this. The problems in Central Asia are very serious and very dangerous."

The sun was high and cast no shadows on that beautiful day in May 1990. Only Yevgeny's words darkened the skies, over Central Asia as well as in Moscow. Yevgeny had my attention. And I had his. We looked each other over carefully, trying to make it appear that we weren't doing so at all. We passed each other's test. Sometimes standing, other times sitting on a bench, in a park not far from the Kremlin, with no one else in sight, Yevgeny and I talked for an hour. Unlike many American agents and diplomats who clear their throats before they speak and say nothing, Yevgeny was direct. I recall one American diplomat in the Middle East who said *sui generis* in every other sentence for an hour, but who said nothing else worth noting. That diplomat was one of his kind, and not a very interesting one either. But Yevgeny was helpful; the closest he came to clearing his throat was his warning to me. He added details to what I already had been told about foreign interventions in Central Asia.

"How did you find me?" That was Yevgeny's first question. The answer was a secret that I would never reveal. I figured that Yevgeny had some ideas about how I found him, but he didn't let on and neither did I. Instead, I mumbled something about being a journalist and that's what journalists do, find

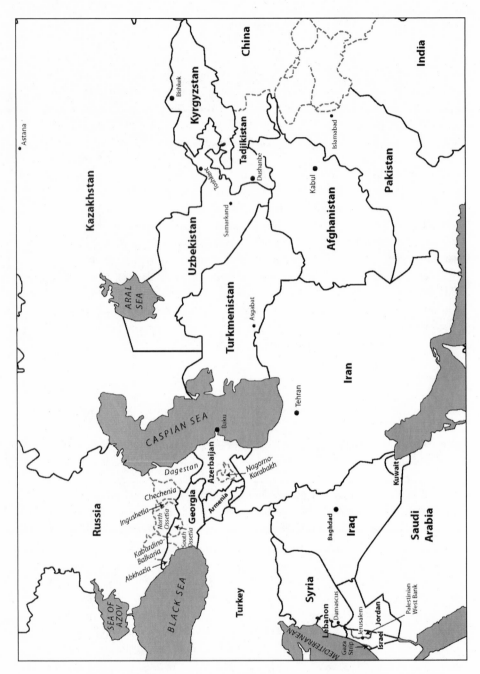

After the collapse of the Soviet Union, Middle Eastern tribes dashed in to convert or reconvert Jews and Muslims in the tribal states that emerged in Central Asia and the Caucasus mountains region between the Black and Caspian seas.

people with information. At that moment, I thought of an old friend's joke, which always comes to mind when I hear the word journalist and which the younger generation finds harder and harder to grasp: What's the difference between a reporter and a journalist? A journalist is a reporter with two suits. I didn't share the joke with Yevgeny, figuring that it would lose too much in translation.

I acknowledged Yevgeny's concern for my safety, took it seriously. His warning wouldn't change my plans, but I thought he was serious and wasn't being melodramatic or trying to scare me off the story. Through banks in Moscow and through newly established Islamic cultural and religious institutions in Moscow and Central Asia, Yevgeny said, the Saudis and Kuwaitis were pouring millions of dollars into the tribal regions. Their objective: to swing the reborn Muslims to the mainstream Sunni sect of Islam, which is centered in Saudi Arabia, although few would call the Saudi royal family mainstream. Newly recharged Sunni Muslims and a wider network of religious and cultural institutions linked to Kuwait and Saudi Arabia would hand those two Arab kingdoms sweeping influence in Central Asia. In case anyone missed the point of their zeal, the Saudis and Kuwaitis were shipping millions of free Korans into the region.

If there's a single flip side to Saudi Sunni Islam, it's Shiite Iran. The Iranians are an Indo-European people who speak Farsi; they are not Arabs and are not a Semitic people, but they are Shiite Muslims, sectarian rivals of the Saudis and Sunni Muslims. A regional neighbor, Iran's fundamentalist Shiite Islamic regime was also doling out millions of its Korans and seeking to inflate its religious, cultural, economic and political influence in the region. Iran's long borders worked to its great advantage. Its northern border binds Armenia and Azerbaijan in the South Caucasus, the Caspian Sea and Turkmenistan in Central Asia, to say nothing of an eastern border with chaotic Afghanistan, then in the disabling pre–Taliban throes of a devastating civil war that was leveling what little was left standing after the Afghan war against the Soviet invaders during the 1980s.

Sunni and Shiite numbers, in terms of money and religious followers, would be favored to win their share of hearts and minds in the new nation-states. Although Islam in those states was originally rooted in more tolerant Sufi practices, decades of Communist control had watered down sectarian influence of any kind. Thus, Saudi Arabia, Kuwait and Iran spied new opportunities for conversions.

No one with specific information about the amount of money the Saudis and Kuwaitis were pouring into Central Asia would talk about it without being paid, Yevgeny said. Even at that, he said, there is no guarantee that anyone who talked would tell the truth.

The huge amounts of money and the power and influence that the money was intended to buy were the reasons Yevgeny warned me about probing the struggle for dominance in Central Asia. I wasn't asking about a local struggle; this was global. The stakes were high by any terms, and anyone or anything that might upset the program would be dealt with in a fashion more painful than comfortable.

All the activity that Yevgeny described was taking place as the Soviet Union was falling apart, in anticipation of the formation of new countries where the officially atheistic Soviet republics had stood for about 70 years. Saudi, Kuwaiti and Iranian money and religious and diplomatic activity in the region would increase even more dramatically within months, after the five Central Asian nations along with Azerbaijan, Armenia and Georgia in the soon-to-be roiling Caucasus region were formed. Turkey, a Muslim country but a secular state and an old imperial power in the region, was also spreading its diplomatic and economic tentacles in Georgia, Azerbaijan and Central Asia, as I would see on a later trip to those regions.

Yevgeny's personal concern was the fate of ethnic–Russians in Central Asia and the Caucasus. As Slavs and ethnic and imperial occupiers in those areas, Russians there were feeling uncomfortable as the Soviet security blanket unraveled. And the new Russia, seeking to retain political influence and access to natural resources in the area and to protect its southern flank, was doing its own share of tribal meddling. It would not be long before Russia itself felt the results of the tribal revolutions, first in Chechenia and Dagestan in the North and East Caucasus, where Islam was a factor, and later throughout the volatile Caucasus mountain region. By meddling in Georgia and Abkhazia, Nagorno Karabakh, Armenia and Azerbaijan, and in Tadjikistan, Russia added its own powder to the local tribal kegs.

Yevgeny and I never discussed Afghanistan, which is in South Asia, when we met in May 1990. If that was in his thinking, it was not in mine. Later I realized that what he was saying about the struggle for power in Central Asia reached south into viscerally tribal Afghanistan, through Pakistan to the Arabian Sea, a critical channel for natural gas and oil pipelines from the Caspian region and beyond. In Afghanistan, U.S. arms fought the Soviet Union in the 1980s through Saudi, Pakistani and Afghan surrogates before the Soviets quit in defeat in 1989, and the Americans left the Afghans to kill each other with Pakistani help. During and after the Afghan civil war, the Saudi Sunni fundamentalists and their Sunni counterparts in the Pakistani intelligence services built up the Taliban, the Students of Islam. There, on the horizon, sat Osama bin Laden and his Al Qaida cohorts who became allies of the Taliban against the Western outsiders. And from that came September 11, 2001. An ally, directly or indirectly, with the United States, Saudi Arabia, Pakistan and of the Afghan mujahedin fighters against the Soviets during the 1980s, bin Laden easily morphed into an enemy of the Saudi royal family and its American allies, whose forces massed and stayed in the Islamic holy land, soiling it in his fundamentalist eyes, during and after the Persian Gulf War in 1991.

A good post for gathering tales of global intrigue, Paris is where I first learned about the Saudi-Iranian war for souls in Central Asia. After pinning it down more in Moscow, with a Central Asian expert from the West as well as with Yevgeny, a couple of years later I pursued the story further in the region itself. In Tashkent, the capital of Uzbekistan, I heard stories of rival Sunni and Shiite clerics preaching at the same new mosques, pitching for support like retailers selling dry goods to the same customers. In one year alone and in Uzbekistan only, one Tashkent-based Western intelligence agent told me, the Saudis had shipped in one million Korans. Figure one Koran per family and maybe five to 10 people per family and the Saudis alone reached a high percentage of people in a country of what was then about 23 million.

Foreign embassies were new, few and usually ignored in the new backwater capitals of Central Asia in 1992. They drew no crowds and were distinctly minor league when compared with embassies in London, Paris, Cairo and Moscow. When I walked into one of the new embassies in Tashkent in November 1992, I was greeted as a rescuer from boredom. Finally, there was someone to tell about the explosion of new mosques that had been constructed in so short a time. Central Asians had been Muslims for centuries, but in most cases strongly influenced by the Sufi style rather than by fundamentalist Sunni or Shiite zealotry as practiced among Iranian mullahs and some Arabs in the Middle East. From the early 1920s, when Soviet rule began in the region, until their liberation almost 70 years later, the tribes were forced to be official atheists. Uzbekistan had about 26,000 mosques in 1924, but by the mid–1980s, working mosques had plummeted to 84. The figure had risen to about 300 just before the Soviet demise. By the end of 1992, a little more than a year after Uzbekistan became a separate country, the number of mosques there had soared to about 4,500, with scores more under construction. The Saudis, the people from the place that Uzbeks and their neighbors called Arabistan, or land of the Arabs, were probably more responsible for the boom and budding of radical Islam than was Iran.

One Western diplomat in the region put it this way: "Islam is alive and well and definitely enjoying a rebirth in Uzbekistan." For most of the time since then, the repressive Uzbek government has been trying to suppress Islam's religious, political and cultural appeal.

As Muslim missionaries moved into the region seeking specific converts, the Israelis also moved in, to take Jews out of the region and to open friendly lines between Tel Aviv and the new capitals. The result was a weird and awkward juxtaposition of interests that conflicted but did not intersect. But it went on, with little apparent notice at the time. Like the Saudis, Iranians, Turks and even Russians, the Israelis were also seeking to plant diplomatic, commercial, technological and political roots in the Caucasus and in Central Asia. Anytime Israel sees an opportunity to develop ties with non–Arab Muslim states, it does so with zest. Israelis call it playing their Muslim card, which means splitting non–Arab Muslims from the Arab states. Israel had good relations with Turkey, which the Israelis wanted to build on with other Muslims.

Quietly and with considerable success, Israelis were teaching Hebrew, Judaism and Jewish history to the forgotten Jews of Uzbekistan, Tadjikistan, Kazakhstan, Azerbaijan, Georgia and the Caucasus region of Russia such as Dagestan. The number of different ethnic and language groups in the Caucasus alone is almost countless. The words Caucasus and tribal are synonymous, and when it comes to a linguistic ragout, the Caucasus is a modern Babylon.

"Youth is the future of Fatherland," said a banner strung across a street in Tashkent, Uzbekistan's capital. The Soviet Union was dead but Communist-style slogans clung to life back in November 1992, when I read that proclamation in the ancient city that in three generations had been converted from an exotic Oriental town to a bland mound of Soviet concrete. Not being politically correct, the Uzbeks were still stuck on fathers and fatherland and knew nothing about founders and homeland security.

Tamar, 60 at the time, was no youth, but he had a future in Uzbekistan. And in a small way he had a role in the new global arena that was emerging. A feisty little man with Soviet army and police credentials, Tamar worked with the Jewish Agency that was helping Jews flee wars and economic uncertainty in Central Asia for Tel Aviv and Jerusalem. About 135,000 Jews lived in the five new Central Asian nations at that time. Roughly 85,000 of those were in Uzbekistan, more than half of whom lived in Tashkent; Tamar was one of those.

A son of World War II refugees, Tamar was living on the fringes of new wars and in the midst of new waves of refugees and displaced persons. No human activity puts people to flight more quickly and in larger numbers than war, and Tamar could vouch for that. As a boy during World War II, Tamar had fled with his family from Minsk in what is now Belarus. They headed east into the vast Eurasian land mass to escape Hitler's invading forces. Tamar and his family stopped running when they reached safety in Siberia. Without checking a weather map, Tamar's father quickly realized that there must be a warmer place to raise a family. To Tashkent the family went and that's where I found Tamar, then retired for five years from the Soviet army, living on a pension and using his military and police skills to water his Jewish roots.

War in neighboring Tadjikistan, a mixture of civil conflict leavened by Russian meddling, sent people fleeing from city to city and across the fresh and tender national borders. From Tashkent and Samarkand in Uzbekistan and from Dushanbe and Leninabad (now Khudjand) in neighboring Tadjikistan, the Jewish Agency taught local Jews Hebrew and Jewish history and helped them board planes for Tel Aviv. Ethnic-Armenians, Russians, Ukrainians, Uzbeks, Tadjiks and others fled the fighting, uncertainty and possible retribution of war. Russians, who could call the Soviet empire their own, felt in great jeopardy after the local tribes, the Uzbeks and Tadjiks, became nations.

A tank mechanic in the Soviet army, Tamar drove his tan souped-up Moskvich sedan as if he were leading the NASCAR circuit. He provided further proof that fast, reliable wheels in war zones and along wild frontiers are more important than cheese and crackers. With his military mentality and a car that he tailored to all but fly, Tamar left all other vehicles sucking his exhaust fumes, shouting warnings as he zoomed by.

His mechanic's garage was Tamar's home. It reminded me of the fix-anything-shop where I used to take my 1950 Ford. A small refrigerator, a television, heater, sink, telephone and a picture of Jerusalem added color to the simplicity of a home-alone man and his essential tools. Tamar's lifestyle offered further evidence that resourcefulness exists where 60-inch televisions do not. Tamar was not a dull man and work wasn't everything to him. To put the finishing touches on the garage and its image, Tamar displayed several pictures of nude women. Quickly, he assured me that the pictures were art, "erotica" he called them, rather than evidence of sexual desire that people in that part of the world prefer to keep private. "I understand perfectly," I told him, smiling. "Either way it's fine with me," I added. He laughed.

Then we sped from Tashkent, first to the old imperial city of Samarkand and later to warring Tadjikistan. Tamar was serious about himself and his job, but there also was a comic aura about him. Short, wiry and fit, Tamar wore his old still-spiffy olive green army uniform with the pride of a general. Two stars radiated from the epaulets. He wore a shirt and tie below a large hat that was decorated with a red band, gold-colored braids and a black visor with a large star front and center above the visor. His pension said that Tamar had earned the right to wear the uniform as long as he lived. In Tamar's mind, that meant whether the Soviet Union was dead or alive, and all the Uzbeks who crossed his path had better grasp that powerful meaning.

Tamar's car and equipment alone might be labeled a police action if not an act of war. Inside the car were a flashing red light, which he pulled out and placed on the dashboard when he zoomed through traffic; a siren he sounded to make other cars pull over and let him pass, and a loudspeaker he used to scold motorists who ignored his sound and light show. When necessary he also flashed the smile of knowing authority as he carefully adjusted his oversized cap.

In case of emergencies, Tamar also carried a handgun and a hand grenade that rolled around under his seat. We preferred no emergencies, no gun play. We insisted that Tamar corral the shiny grenade that was wrapped in a dirty white towel and clattered around under the front seat. He got the point. Festooned with radio antennas, Tamar's car was royalty on the rough roads between Tashkent, Samarkand, Leninabad and back to Tashkent. A sticker on the car said, "Rolex the Best in Israel." Inside, we rocked along to a tape of "Hernando's Hideaway," "Mack the Knife," "Arriverderci Roma," "Matilda," "The Lady Is a Tramp," and "It Had to Be You," all instrumentals. No words. It was just like home, except for the checkpoints, the refugees and the beautiful imperial and religious monuments of Samarkand.

Better than he knew English, Tamar knew the broad plains, valleys and rough hill country as would a local farmer or shepherd.

Trust in Tamar we did as he roared past nearly every vehicle on the road, triggering his gerry-rigged electronic warning system and shouting man-to-man for good measure at stubborn drivers who didn't acknowledge his authority and pull over to let him pass. He barely missed colliding with cars, cows, people and sheep, but he did miss. On one occasion, a Mercedes whizzed by us. We didn't stay in second place for long. Up went the light, on went the siren and the loudspeaker and to the floor went the accelerator. Tamar screamed at the offending motorist as we took over first place, and stayed there.

Our gerneralissimo's sound and light show kicked in each time we reached a tribal checkpoint. Some of the soldiers and police of the infant nations were not impressed with our old boy and his old uniform, but they didn't impress Tamar either. Agitated and angry, Tamar shouted at the soldiers before dismissing them with a wave of his hand and roaring off through checkpoints. Pierre Rousselin, the Middle East correspondent for *Le Figaro* in Paris, and I laughed through all of this. Our man was a good driver, we made good time and didn't crash. Tamar was serious about his old soldier's life and authority. But to us Tamar was more of a comic interlude on the fringe of real drama.

Side by side, the Saudi, Iranian, Kuwaiti, Turkish, Russian, Israeli and American tribes pursued their separate and often conflicting interests in the newly minted countries. Local tribes did the same. When regional fighting did break out, such as in Tadjikistan, in Nagorno Karabakh between Armenia and Azerbaijan, and in the Georgian province of Abkhazia between local mountain peoples and the new nation of Georgia, the hands of meddling outsiders played in the shadows. Russia, Iran, Turkey and the Saudis all played roles in stirring up some of the fighting in the region to promote their own interests and keep their rivals off balance.

That Israel was laying its own tracks in the alien region along with those of Iran and Saudi Arabia was most intriguing. Israel focused first on flying Jews to safety in Tel Aviv, where they would add to the Jewish state's population weight and directly or indirectly add settlers to the West Bank and Gaza. To that effort Israel piggybacked important programs to build a range of commercial and diplomatic ties with the new states.

Aware of the U.S.–Israeli alliance, the new tribal nations believed that by cooperating with Israel they would receive favorable treatment from the United States and a wider opening to the West. The United States and Israel also cooperated on agricultural and commercial projects in the region, which gave Israel easier entree to the new governments and to Central Asian resources. From these new connections Israel also received another bonus: wider global acceptance and neutrality, at least, from more Muslim lands. Israel had no trouble getting Jews out of Tadjikistan, Uzbekistan, Azerbaijan, Georgia and Kazakhstan, for example.

Shadowy alliances in the region made for unusual allies. Turkey and Israel, for example, were on good terms with each other and with Azerbaijan, which was at war with Armenia, a Christian country that welcomed Iranian aid. This was an alliance web that Israel did not advertise because there is a substantial Armenian population in Jerusalem and because the Armenians and Jews had both been victims of genocide. The Turks had slaughtered at least one million Armenians during an eight-year period that began in 1915, a disaster comparable in kind if not in scope to the Nazi Holocaust. A Turkic people, the Azeris are predominately Shiite Muslims like the Iranians, although Sufi practices and beliefs remain strong among Azeris, who may even have been Sufism's first practitioners. But the Azeris feared and resisted the Iranians and their fundamentalist brand of Shiism, which opened a door for Israel. At the same time, the Azeris welcomed the secular, less fundamentalist, brand of Islam practiced in Turkey.

The Orthodox Christian Georgians wove another braid into the complex regional tribal alliances. They welcomed good terms with Israel. Yet the Georgians were on opposite sides from Israel in the Armenian-Azerbaijan conflict over the disputed territory of Nagorno-Karabakh: The Georgians were allies of Armenia, also an Orthodox Christian country, which was fighting Azerbaijan. Georgia distrusted Iran, but the Shiite Iranians were aiding Armenia, as was Georgia, against the secular Muslim Azeris. Iran was trying to counter Turkish influence in Azerbaijan and the region. In another twist, Georgia rejected Turkey's overtures because the Georgians feared a revival of Turkish imperial power. Call it Balkanization, Byzantine, Venetian or just plain modern international politics and duplicity, but these alliances required a wall chart to follow.

—⊗∞—

Tashkent was the main exit door for Jews who lived in Uzbekistan, Turkmenistan, Kazakhstan and Kyrgyzstan. That pool, at most 125,000 Jews in all, was large enough for the Jewish Agency to move in and work without obstruction from Uzbek authorities and to ferry as many Jews as were willing in Israel's direction. Jews from Tadjikistan, about 13,000, were being flown hurriedly from Dushanbe, the capital, where war hastened their exit.

I expected Tashkent to be as exotic, beautifully Oriental and historic as I knew that Old Samarkand was. I was disappointed. For centuries a major trading and cultural center on an old silk route, much of historic Tashkent was leveled after the 1917 Communist Revolution. Most of what was left standing was destroyed by a massive earthquake in 1966. High-rise Soviet-style concrete buildings front broad avenues in the post–1917 part of the city. This modern appearance is drab, lifeless and superficial, totally devoid of classical Uzbek history and culture, as the Soviets were intent on creating a uniform Soviet tribal culture throughout the union. The Old City still wears an Oriental skirt, but its historic buildings are few. What was left in November 1992 was crumbling and decaying; lots of tin shacks, mud huts and Mongol-style tents around which sheep and goats grazed; a maze of narrow streets with much more dust than the noise of commerce. The atmosphere was more one of poverty than of mystery.

The roughly 85,000 Jews in Uzbekistan were under no direct threat, but war on the country's borders and political and economic uncertainty within them offered Israel an opportunity to rescue more members of the Jewish tribes from possible harm. Uzbekistan was healthier economically than most of the rest of the old Soviet Union. But to avoid trouble in the street and maybe another revolution, the new government was subsidizing bread, selling a kilogram (2.2 pounds) for three-and-a-half times less than it cost to make it. One might call that failing economics but survival politics.

A generally tolerant land, Uzbekistan was the fruit bowl of the old Soviet Union. Uzbekistan also produces grapes that make a dry, sweet wine. About 18.5 million Uzbeks, who comprise the vast majority of the nation's population, live within its borders, and 70 million or more Uzbeks live throughout Central Asia, Afghanistan and even China. Russians, Tadjiks, Kazakhs and Tatars also live in Uzbekistan. Uzbeks are a Turkic ethnic group, and speak a Turkic language that is closely related to Turkish itself. For most Uzbeks, Islam means the milder Sufi brand.

Uzbek police and soldiers hugged the road on the three-and-a-half-hour drive from Tashkent to Samarkand, but they didn't impress Tamar. He waved, whistled, tooted and blared his way past uniforms and civilians alike. His uniform was like a magic carpet. Armies and police forces are always among the principal employers in new and poor countries. It's a way to keep restless young men occupied and fed, thwarting possible revolutions. In the West, the big money goes to defense contractors for weapons and weapons systems; in most other regions, army rifles and ragged uniforms mean jobs and security against possible social unrest.

Frost glistened on golden fields but was barely noticeable on others that were blanketed in white by dots of cotton balls ready to be picked. Women in colorful dresses, scarves and pants were doing just that in the early morning, picking cotton fist over fist. When we stopped to pick a few balls of cotton as souvenirs, which I still have, I lost my scarf to the wind and the coming Uzbekistan winter. Ground fog hung low above the broad fields along the

Cotton harvest: A quick stop at a field off the main road from Tashkent to Samarkand netted our driver and me a handful of fresh cotton balls as one memory of Uzbekistan. I still have the cotton (photograph by the author, 1992. © Cox Newspapers Inc.).

four-lane road southwest of Tashkent. Leaves were changing color to bright yellow, orange and red, but they had vanished completely as we drove into higher, colder country to the south. Farmers on horseback fed cows to welcome the day in that land of deserts and fertile river valleys. The road changed from asphalt to rougher concrete as we sped toward Samarkand.

A farmer stood alone on the road selling fruit. We bought apples and brightened his day. As foreigners Pierre Rousselin and I belonged to tribes he didn't recognize and so the farmer stared, and stared, but said nothing. Tamar almost hit a cow as we raced, like Michael Jordan splitting the defense, between two of the animals wobbling along like drunks in the road. Tamar never took his foot off the accelerator as we swerved. He drove fast and flawlessly all the way to Samarkand, on to Leninabad and back to Tashkent.

In Samarkand we drove straight into another dizzying tribal irony: About 6,000 Jews lived, prayed and learned Hebrew in that soft-core but reawakening Muslim city. Most of the remaining Jews lived in the Old City, and many were preparing to move to Israel; others were weighing the risks of going to the distant, ancestral and foreign home they didn't know versus the risks of staying in a land where they were born but remained outsiders. Uzbeks, Tadjiks, Kazakhs, Armenians, Russians, Ukrainians and members of other tribes were also pacing and preparing to flee from Samarkand. Another in Central Asia's great migrations was building. The angst of all the tribes was driven by the death of the Soviet Union and the economic collapse that followed, the fear that the war in Tadjikistan to the east would spread their way, as might the civil unrest in Afghanistan to the south, where large numbers of ethnic–Uzbeks and ethnic–Tadjiks lived.

Known for its tolerance and grandeur, Samarkand remains a beautiful if decaying city that was once the seat of a mammoth Mongol empire and one of the world's great centers of Islamic culture, science and learning. Colorful architectural gems, such as schools, mausoleums, mosques and public buildings, all giant mosaics of bygone imperial wealth, remain as spectacular witnesses to Samarkand's greatness.

Almost 3,000 years old, Samarkand reached its peak under Timur the Lame, or Tamerlane, the Mongol conqueror who ruled the region in the late 14th and early 15th centuries. What Tamerlane didn't build, when he was off conquering India, his grandson, Ulegbek, did. Tamerlane's Registan, the Old City's main square, is rimmed with buildings of great domes, archways and minarets, decorated with colorful blue, green, gold and orange mosaics that retain their beauty despite their age, decay and disrepair.

By the time hardline Soviet communism filtered from Moscow to remote Samarkand, the red star had lost its luster and muscle. The Soviet yoke was looser in Samarkand than in most cities in the old union. The Jews of

Imperial beauty: The magnificent Shir Dor Madrassah (Islamic school) in Samarkand's Registan Square. Built between 1619 and 1636, Shir Dor is one of several stunning Islamic monuments in the Registan, which for centuries was the center of this imperial city, now second to Uzbekistan's capital of Tashkent (photograph by the author, 1992. © Cox Newspapers Inc.).

Samarkand, which is heavily populated by ethnic–Tadjiks, worked freely and without threat in all trades and professions. They also worshipped, if they wished, in two synagogues, one in the Old City and one in the new. Samarkand-born Rabbi Immanuel, 35, who had studied in the United States, operated the Hebrew school where about 100 students were learning a new language. If the Jews of Samarkand wanted to leave for new lives with the other Jewish tribes in Israel, they would know some Hebrew when they arrived. But the decision to stay or leave was not always as easy or as certain as it might have appeared.

A large poster of Arnold Schwarzenegger fondling a mega-weapon was hanging in the outdoor kitchen of Tzipora's house in Samarkand's Old City. Tzipora, her husband and their three children were conflicted about their future. Even if Schwarzenegger had been the governor of California then, he couldn't have helped them. The family was poor, too poor to leave, Tzipora said, and her parents, who lived nearby, didn't want to leave the place they considered home. Only 37, Tzipora was different. "I feel that Israel is my home," she said. "If I could, I would leave right now."

Tzipora's 14-year-old daughter Gila was learning Hebrew from Rachel, a Tadjik-speaker who was sent by the Jewish Agency from Ramat Gan, Israel, to teach Hebrew and biblical history. The teenager had been studying Hebrew for two years. She was primed to leave, but she couldn't go alone. We interviewed several people like Tzipora, in various stages of deciding whether to stay or leave for Israel. Rousselin and I also spoke with many people from other tribes who were intent on fleeing the unrest approaching from the east.

Rachel was a tribal messenger sent by the tribal chiefs in Israel. Her job was to cajole Samarkand's Jews to move to Israel by preparing them to live there. Tzipora was not religious; she visited the synagogue once a year, she said, on Yom Kippur. Her husband was more observant. He attended synagogue on the Sabbath and the high holy days. But with the proper coaching, the Israelis believed, the potential immigrants would become more religious and more tribal. A small picture of the Lubavitcher Rebbe hung in the family living room, and a beautiful Bukharan carpet decorated a wall. Tzipora said that she and her family were followers of the Lubavitcher Rebbe, which some might find odd in the land of Central Asia's Bukharan Jews. A messianic figure, at least in death, Menachem Mendel Schneerson was the last Lubavitcher Rebbe. Schneerson was born in Russia and died in the United States in 1994. He led the Lubavitcher Chabad movement, which originated in Eastern Europe and is an Hasidic sect of Judaism.

Moshe, who made ornate gold-covered wood chests, feared that the war in Tadjikistan would spread to Samarkand. In that he was not alone. But his wife said she feared nothing in Samarkand. She wanted to leave anyway, not because of the dangers where she lived, but because she was drawn to Israel.

Young Assaf, Rachel's son, was playing a baseball video game on a television he brought from Israel when I walked into his house in Samarkand's Old City. Baseball, not a game invented or widely played in Israel, was being played, sort of, on a video in Samarkand, which is not known for sheltering a field of dreams. Video baseball was enough to raise an eyebrow on anyone who recognized the game. Assaf playing baseball, even on a video, reminded me of the baseball glove I brought to Israel as an inside joke to catch rocks thrown by Palestinians. Later, I brought a baseball, a couple of gloves and a bat to a puzzled family in the West Bank. That's a funny looking little soccer ball, they must have thought, but they went along. Let the game begin, I said, after a few lessons, and then I promptly drove a ball through a window of the family's house. That's all part of the game, I joked, but the family didn't get that either. Game called after a half-inning, never to resume.

Assaf, his younger sister Dana and their father, Yaacov, then 42, went along for the ride when Rachel, their mother and wife respectively, contracted with the Jewish Agency to work in Samarkand. Then 33, Rachel was hired to teach Hebrew to adults and children and to instruct children in Judaism. A nurse by profession, Yaacov said he was a house-husband in Samarkand. If Yaacov was actively engaged in work for the Jewish Agency, he wasn't telling. Three or four times a year, for two weeks each time, the family returned to Israel for a vacation. At the time, the Jewish Agency spent $60,000 to $65,000 per year for each Israeli family it sent to other countries to bring Jews to Tel Aviv.

The movement of Jews to Israel from around the world is a fascinating tale of tribal bonding and often of human rescue operations. Many Jews in Israel who were not born there, so many families, have different but equally wondrous stories, and most of them remain fresh. Rachel said her father and her father's mother spoke Tadjik, a Farsi-related language, and her mother spoke Farsi. Rachel's father, a Bukharan Jew, was born in Tashkent and reached Israel in 1950, by traveling through Pakistan and India. Some relatives on her father's side moved to Israel in 1992, Rachel said, while others remained in Tashkent. "I will search for them," she told me. Yaacov said his father went to Israel from Yugoslavia, while his mother was originally from Libya. Without Israel, Yaacov's parents probably would never have met and he would never have existed.

A strong wind blew Tamar's old army hat off his graying hair and down a hill after we had stopped at railroad tracks to tighten the rattling license plate on Tamar's car. We're doomed if we don't get that hat back, I thought, as we headed from Samarkand to Leninabad, Tadjikistan. In full army uniform, but without the hat, Tamar would have looked like an old phony and no one would have bowed, scraped and pulled over no matter how many sirens or lights he set off. But Tamar was quicker than the wind; he retrieved his oversized cap and three hours after we had left Samarkand we whizzed across the Uzbek border, through a long and empty neutral zone where high tension wires crackled and buzzed, and past the Tadjik border post without being stopped or even gearing down. Tamar's full uniform worked, along with his siren, flashing light, loudspeaker and an authoritative wave of his left hand. He knew the value of first impressions.

The earth was covered with large melons and vegetables. Farmers picked cotton by hand. Animals grazed in sweeping meadows. The range and farmland were unfenced. Hills and valleys, rivers and mountains and deserts are much the same anywhere you go, never exactly, but very similar. It's the people who are different. Even then the human condition and human reactions are remarkably uniform once you go beyond the obvious cultural differences.

Fifty minutes after we crossed the Uzbek-Tadjik border we reached Leninabad, now called Khudjand, in northwest Tadjikistan, far from the fighting to the south in Dushanbe. As we entered the city, wedded bliss struck us head-on. A car draped in colorful ribbons passed. On the car's grille was the large doll-like figure of a bride in a white wedding gown. Inside the car the bride and groom smiled, apparently ready to stay with their tribe and increase its numbers. Just like rural life anywhere, I thought, as I recalled getting caught in a joyful wedding motorcade on a country road in Normandy behind a gaily decorated tractor that was carrying a bride and groom in full finery. A wonderful Normandy moment that was, as I joined others in waving, smiling and leaning on the horn as if I belonged. I didn't belong to the local tribe or town, but I did belong to the human tribe, any member of which would have reveled in those moments.

Panic spoke through the eyes and whispers of the people in Leninabad. The Jews of Dushanbe to the south, where the Islamic revival was strongest and the rumblings of war audible, had already fled, some to Leninabad, others to Tashkent, still others to Israel or the United States. Leninabad's Jews, at the most 1,500 and so far spared the bloodshed but not the fear of war, were packing to leave for the United States, Israel or wherever else the door opened. Tamar showed business cards for one of Israel's leading industrial companies and another for a leading communications company indicating that Israel was doing business in the region as well as helping people leave.

"The people are afraid of everything, of being killed, of hunger. There is enough food now, but there is fear for the future, that Leninabad might be cut off from Dushanbe and the rest of the country," said Marina, our translator. The road to Dushanbe had already been cut, but a railroad line remained open. Soldiers, armed but not really organized, strutted without purpose in the streets of Leninabad, hometown of the former Communist president of Tadjikistan who two months earlier was ousted by the Islamic Renaissance Party and now feared for his life. Marina knew more than Hebrew; she knew the people.

Resurgent militant Islam was no threat in northern Tadjikistan. Many villages and towns had working mosques, almost all of which were in small, simple buildings. Women covered their heads, more against the wind and cold than for religious reasons. I saw no women wearing veils. After independence the government made Tadjik the official language, creating ego problems, at least, for Uzbek and Russian speakers. Russians in particular, representatives of the old Communist regime, felt enough fear of ethnic retaliation to flee.

Jews from the Polish, Russian and Bukharan sub-tribes, few of them observant or even close, feared talking openly and drawing attention to themselves. To do so might block their exits. In a few days, a bus filled with Jews would leave for Tashkent: People going to the United States would fly through Moscow; those going to Israel would fly directly to Tel Aviv from Tashkent.

One by one, in the quiet of their small homes, the Jews of Leninabad whispered about leaving. An extended family of nine led by Mordechai and Tatiana had papers to leave for New York in two months. One of the group, Elozor, had two brothers in Israel and two other brothers and two sisters in the United States, and he had chosen America as his new home. Elozor said it took two years for his documents to be approved. Entrance to the United States was difficult to obtain, but this group was lucky. Edgy about the widening conflict, Asher and Svetlana kept trying to enter the United States, so far without luck. They would go to Israel if the dangers continued to mount.

In Central Asia, an easy trip does not exist. Any journey of more than an hour is usually an adventure. Pierre Rousselin and I were bound for Baku, Azerbaijan, when we went to the Tashkent airport early in the afternoon of November 8, 1992. But we couldn't fly directly to Baku; instead, we were forced to fly all the way to Moscow and then back to Baku, a huge diversion in miles and time but not money. Our flight to Moscow was scheduled to leave at 6:50 that night, after we fought with a mob for seats and then kneed and elbowed our way through a mass of people, who hoped to make the flight, in order to pay a $10 airport exit fee. We knew the plane wouldn't leave on time, but we didn't think that it would leave as late as it did.

When we finally took off, it was 4 A.M. on November 9, a delay of more than nine hours. During that time, someone stole my wallet — I think it was one of the gendarmes — in the waiting room while Pierre and I, along with everyone else, tried to stay in position to dash for a seat on the plane when the time came. Open seating meant just that, no seat assignments and a scrum to beat the locals to a cushion.

We picked up a couple of hours flying west and arrived in Moscow about 7:30 A.M. Then we had to figure out how to fly back to Baku in Azerbaijan. The answer lay in the help provided by a Moscow-based colleague of Pierre's at *Le Figaro*. Breaking every rule in the conventional airport book, we walked across the wide tarmac, around and between planes, to a building where passengers were not invited. Inside, we found a woman who sat behind a small window; from our view she was collecting foreign cash. Pierre and I each paid the woman 20 U.S. dollars for tickets. Dollars beat rubles every time. The woman would give the money directly to the pilot and the pilot would bump some poor local travelers who would have to wait hours, maybe days, for another flight.

Never certain when the flight would leave for Baku, we hung around the

Moscow airport for hours and returned to *Le Figaro*'s office a couple of times before we dashed back to the airport for a 2:30 P.M. flight, which was cancelled. The next flight time was 7:55 P.M.; the one after that was 10:30. Just before midnight, we dashed aboard a plane bound for Baku, fought our way to a couple of seats that had broken backs before we finally soared from Moscow with luggage and a few caged animals squirreled away in the aisle. Traveling east on this occasion we lost time, arriving in Baku at 5 A.M. on November 10. Eerie in the torch-like light of blazing natural gas wells just offshore in the Caspian Sea, Baku's eclectic buildings stood like tribal sentinels casting long but losing shadows against the coming day. A couple of hours after our arrival, we were lucky enough to find a room in the Hotel Azerbaijan, and to sleep, almost two days after we had set out for the airport in Tashkent.

A few days later, we took a much shorter flight on a small plane from Baku across the Caucasus Mountains to Tblisi, the capital of Georgia. Because of the personal connections that we had made, Pierre and I paid $25 each for tickets that usually cost $81. We paid the money — the mundane commercial tribe that speaks a universal language — to the pilot through a third party, and the pilot bumped other passengers to make room for us.

—∞—

Akzabidi Refugee Camp, Azerbaijan, November 12, 1992 — An old woman lay dying in the ooze of a mud hut, half-buried in the soaked soil. No one I spoke with knew her name. She looked 85, but may have been 45. So it is with refugees. They are blanks on the human landscape, a tribe apart, united only by rags, hunger, homelessness and often early death, whether they are Afghans, Bosnian Muslims, Somalis, Sudanese, Hutus or Tutsis, Palestinians or Kurds. This was the volatile Caucasus region, between the Caspian and Black seas where the numbers of tribes and language groups are almost countless. The refugees in this camp were Azeris. Most were simple farmers or shepherds. They make nothing and have nothing so no one wants them. If they survive, usually international aid saves them.

Animal waste soaked up the mud at the entrance to the long hut. Lying on a thin straw mattress, the woman moaned as water and mud dripped to the cold earth around her. A couple of cows defecated in a nearby section of the hut; next to the cows were the sheep. It was raining and raw and getting colder as winter approached. Outside, a four-wheel drive vehicle was stuck in the thick mud. Refugees who didn't live in the huts, lived in caves or tents. Drinking water was trucked in, when trucks could get through the mud. A year-old boy ate pomegranate seeds in front of a little stove burning scraps of wood gathered from a largely barren land. Refugees said two children died on arrival at the camp, and three others later died in the cold and rain.

Fruits of war: Chickens pecked to the right of the entrance of this dugout abode at the Akzabidi Refugee Camp in Azerbaijan. Underground, elderly refugees lay dying (photograph by the author, 1992. © Cox Newspapers Inc.).

"All we want is our land back," said one old man. "They don't need gold or silver, only to get back to the graveyards of their ancestors," said Ahundof, who ran the refugee camp. That is a tribal magnet unlike many others: "The graveyards of their ancestors."

Far from those graveyards, about 1,000 families shivered in the immediate area, a five-and-a-half-hour spine-shrinking drive from Baku. Another 30,000 refugee families squatted in squalor in the wider area outside the nearby Azeri town of Agdam. Many of the refugees left everything they owned except the clothes they wore and walked for ten days to reach the Akzabidi camp and its dugout huts, just to stay alive. Maybe.

The refugees had fled the war between Armenia, an Orthodox Christian country, and Azerbaijan, a country of moderate Muslims, over the disputed territory of Nagorno-Karabakh. Most of the people in the territory are Armenians, and they were winning. We were less than 20 miles from the Nagorno Karabakh frontier. Estimates of the total number of refugees from the war varied wildly: An American diplomat in Baku put the figure at anywhere between 200,000 and 400,000. A representative of Doctors Without Borders estimated that 120,000 Azeris were refugees.

Azeri officials in Baku insisted that this was not a sectarian war, but rather a fight over land. Religion was only an incidental part of the fighting. From what I could see, I thought that was correct, but the Armenians didn't buy it and neither did the Georgians, also Orthodox Christians, who were engaged in their own war in Abkhazia in the northwest Caucasus. Nevertheless, these were ethnic-wars in which tribe mattered. This is also certain: Because they were regional conflicts with little effect on global interests, like so many other regional conflagrations in the world, they received little international attention. At the same time, powers inside and outside the region backed the combatants directly or indirectly to advance their own tribal interests.

Northwest of Nagorno-Karabakh, in the west Caucasus area called Abkhazia, a separate tribal war was sending about 80,000 refugees to flight, some 60,000 of them Georgians. Under the Soviet umbrella, Abkhazia was an autonomous republic within the Republic of Georgia; the Abkhazians and Georgians are different tribes with different languages and histories. When the Soviet Union collapsed, the Abkhazians struck for total independence, which Georgia opposed, sending about 1,000 people, many of them teenagers, to die in the fighting.

The Caucasus region, a large chunk of which lies in Russia, remains as tribal as any place in the world. Each valley and mountain is home to different tribes each with a language different from its neighbors. Rival religions, Christian Orthodoxy and Islam of varying sects and intensities, are sometimes thrown into the mix. But resurgent nationalism in the post–Soviet era seemed the main reason for the eruption of fighting in the Caucasus. In Russia's Dagestan region alone, for example, just outside of Georgia and Azerbaijan, almost 40 tribal groups live among a population of slightly more than two million people.

Similar numbers of tribes live throughout most of the Caucasus. As many as 50 tribes live in some areas, all divided by language, geography, culture, ethnicity and sometimes religion. Some were often in conflict with the big bear in the region, Russia, and sometimes among themselves. When the Soviet Union broke apart, tribes in the north Caucasus region of Russia rose against what the tribes called their Russian occupiers. Rebellions, some of which continue, flared among the so-called Confederation of Mountain Peoples, which included Chechenia, Ossetia, Ingushettia and Dagestan. Islamic at least in name, the rising Confederation of Mountain Peoples aroused great fear among Orthodox Christian tribes to the south.

———— ∞∞∞ ————

Exit doors swung open for Jews in Azerbaijan, Georgia and Russian areas of the Caucasus in the early 1990s. Uncertainty of all kinds topped by spreading rebellions gave Israel an opportunity to prepare Jews in the region to leave and to fly them out when they decided to go. Anti-Semitism was never a problem during this period, but the fear of its revival provided an opportunity for Israel to convince Jews to leave, and many did. In Azerbaijan a draft of men 17 and over to fight the war in Nagorno-Karabakh also convinced many Jewish families to leave while they could. Indeed, it was widely believed that a couple of dozen Jews from Azerbaijan were fighting in Nagorno-Karabakh at the time.

About 45,000 Jews lived in Azerbaijan at that moment, most of them in Baku, a fascinating blend of Caucasus, Turkic/Central Asian and Eastern European culture. So-called Mountain Jews or Tat, lived in northern Azerbaijan and adjacent Dagestan. From Baku and the northern cities of Quba, Ogus and Genja, the Jewish Agency had, as it was doing in Tashkent, been teaching Jews Hebrew and Jewish history and preparing the minimal paper work required for them to make new homes in Israel. The government in Baku, where two synagogues functioned without obstruction, greased the exit rails for Israel, and multiplied the satisfaction for Tel Aviv by agreeing to establish a range of relationships with the Jewish state. Jewish Agency officials had no trouble meeting any time with Azeri officials from then-President Adulfaz Elchibey on down.

By cooperating with Israel, the Azeris believed and certainly hoped that the West would help Baku. For their part, American oil interests — a powerful financial tribe unto themselves — lusted for access to Azerbaijan's rich oil and natural gas fields in the Caspian. When I was there, the oilmen had no trouble moving in to replace Azerbaijan's antiquated equipment and to remove its wealth. Israel, which has no oil, was also seeking access to Azeri petroleum resources.

From Baku Jewish Agency workers flowed north into Derbent in Dagestan, teaching Jewish history and Hebrew and offering Jews a way to revive their tribal roots by moving to Israel, From Tblisi, Georgia, well to the northwest of Baku, Israelis entered Abkhazia and, with apparent help from Tblisi, rescued about 150 Jews from around the Black Sea port of Sukhumi under what Georgia's prime minister described as "hot conditions." No one was targeting the Jews in Abkhazia, but the fighting offered them a chance to flee and for Israel to take them.

The Mountain Jews speak a Farsi-related language called Tat, and have lived in the Caucasus for centuries. Lost in the mists of long-ago migrations that no doubt resulted in blends with other tribes, their origins are murky. But they probably moved north from Persia long before it was called Iran. An ancient people not readily seen even in Azerbaijan or Dagestan, a large number of them moved to Israel in the early 1990s, although they were not persecuted or under threat at the time. They are not related to another people in the region called Tatim, who are Muslims. Whatever their religious ardor in 1992, a large number of Mountain Jews were expected to embrace Judaism quickly after they reached Israel.

Georgia also welcomed Israeli efforts to bring Jews to Tel Aviv. Georgian officials met frequently with Jewish Agency workers in Baku. An Israeli plane carrying relief supplies was the first to reach Tblisi after an earthquake a year earlier, generosity the Georgians had not forgotten. Yearning for help from the West, Georgia believed that close relations with Israel would accelerate that process.

Tblisi at the time was a Wild East town. Criminal gangs ran the city. Visitors were asked to check their guns when they entered a large Western-style hotel that attracted local gangsters like a high-stakes poker game draws card sharks. Darkness frightened visitors and locals from Tblisi's streets. Food and gasoline were difficult to find. Newly independent and mired in a war that sapped its meager financial resources and brought death to about 1,000 Georgians, the country's economy was as weak as its security.

As with most people in the Caucasus, Central Asia, the Middle East and Africa, Georgians want the material and technological advantages of the West without allowing Western culture and values to destroy their own. A Tblisi filmmaker might have been speaking for other tribes as well as Georgians when he told me, "Western culture is a threat to the rest of the world. The people want Western materials and goods and progress, but they don't want to be overwhelmed by all Western values, some of which they reject."

I heard words like those from members of many tribes throughout less developed areas of the world. In Asia the message was one and indivisible: The people want new technologies, more opportunities, education and wealth, but they want to acquire them at their own pace; they don't want the West to swallow their culture and values, their way of life, or to steal their resources. Fear is hidden in those words. It is the fear that change may also bring tribal losses too grave to accept without a fight. This ambivalence for and against change pivots on whether the older more tribal societies can draw the line against the cultural incursions that come with the trinkets because history shows that the pendulum never stops in the middle. Despite the internal and external conflicts that swirl around it, change is synonomous with inevitability. Only the pace of change and who will control and benefit from it are in question.

THIRTEEN

In Syria, My Name Is Not My Name

Long Wolf, a Lakota sub-chief, was twice-removed from his native tribe when he died of pneumonia in London in June 1892, while performing with Buffalo Bill's Wild West Show. Leagues from his native South Dakota hills and prairies even when he rode with other warriors and with Buffalo Bill Cody in America's cities, Long Wolf was even more distant from his tribal home when he gazed about the strange land of kings and queens.

The old chief expressed no desire to be buried in London's Brompton Cemetery. Neither did he want to be buried at sea, as forbidding a place to him as any in the white man's world. Long Wolf wanted to be returned to his tribal homeland, which was impossible at the time of his death. For 105 years, Long Wolf lay beneath Brompton's dark emerald and shaded grass, until 1997, when his descendants came to fulfill his wishes and take Long Wolf home.

Martha and Mary Ann Black Feather, Long Wolf's great-granddaughters, sang and played the guitar in London's St. Luke's Church of Prayer for All Nations during a simple but riveting funeral ceremony. Wrapped in fresh buffalo hides, Long Wolf's remains and personal artifacts rested in a zinc-lined coffin that was placed in an aisle of the church. An American flag, representing still another tribe, and a red and white flag decorated with geometric figures that represented the Oglala Sioux Reservation at Pine Ridge, South Dakota, covered the coffin.

Four English singers further tried to bridge the cultural and language tribal gap by banging an Oglala drum slowly and chanting in their native language a lengthy memorial song. One moment they sang softly, the next they emitted sharp whistle-like sounds.

The funeral service crossed several cultures, touched several tribes. And the circle would finally be completed: Long Wolf was returning to his tribal homeland.

Mariam sobbed and trembled. When the ship steamed from port, horn wailing and stacks belching, she stared back toward land. Mariam wasn't wav-

Tribal trail: In 1997, 105 years late, an Oglala tribal flag and an American tribal flag draped the coffin that carried the remains of Long Wolf from London to his tribal land in South Dakota (photograph by the author, 1997. © Cox Newspapers Inc.).

ing to the crowd; the city and its people were strangers to her. Through a teary haze, Mariam gazed at the eastern horizon, beyond Beirut, over mountains and Lebanon's stately cedars to the small village twenty miles or so north and a bit east of Damascus and the old house where her flesh and blood would grow without her touch and tactile love, out of sight forever but never out of her mournful heart and mind.

The tribal village was home, or had been until that moment more than 100 years ago. The village they called Maarrat-Saidnaya was also where Mariam Shaheen Monsour and her husband, Hanna Lyos Monsour, had left their only child, a two-year-old daughter named Khaleyeh. Hanna and Mariam never saw their daughter again. They never saw her grow up, become a teen-age bride though barely a teenager, bear six children and die of cancer at age 45, while they, her elderly parents, still breathed in their new country. Their daughter never saw her parents struggle to collect pieces of coal, cloth and anything else they could acquire and sell to earn pennies with the forlorn hope of bringing their first-born from Syria to America. Khaleyeh never saw the American side of her family. America became their home, but never hers.

The Monsour tribe was split, yet parents and daughter were inseparable in their mutual and muffled sorrow and longing, a family — the smallest of tribes — separated by time and distance but organically tethered by blood and flesh. Letters and gifts alone did not keep the bond from unraveling: The diamond-hard umbilical cord between parents and child, strengthened by tribal traditions, did.

From their old stone and mud-brick home in the oasis-like village tucked among small mountains, Mariam and Hanna Monsour were westward bound in the lowest of the low holds of a strange vessel on strange seas, headed first for France and then New York and a new life in what to them would be a linguistic and cultural, if not an economic, desert. They were also at the start of decades — some 57 years for Mariam; 48 years for Hanna — of unrelenting sadness that ended only with their deaths cultural eons from their native village and Khaleyeh's children, their own grandchildren.

The departure scene described above is imaginary in detail, but the story is real. Mariam (Mary) and Hanna (John) Monsour were my mother's parents, my maternal grandparents. Khaleyeh was an aunt I never knew, a girl and a woman who never saw the rest of her immediate family — her American-born sisters and brothers, the oldest of whom was my mother, Rose Monsour Salome. Khaleyeh belonged to my tribe. She was the blank, dark space in Monsour family photos, the apparition only her parents could see. In her parents' minds, she was always two years old. If they had another picture of her, it was imaginary. To her sisters and brothers — seven in all — in America, Khalayeh represented the land and people their parents had left behind: She was like an agnostic's view of God; she existed, was part of the family, but they couldn't know her.

In her village, Khaleyeh (which means creation in Arabic) and later her children tracked the lives of their American relatives, learned from her parents about who had been born and who died. Khaleyeh was slow to pick up the pieces of her American family because travel between America and Maarrat-Saidnaya was ticker-tape tardy and irregular. Postal service was no better. On the American side of the family, her parents' separation from their daughter was a stain deemed so embarrassing and hurtful that what talk there was remained submerged in the unlighted recesses of the immediate and older family members. Even then my grandparents talked through tears of sadness, pain and regret. Most of the time, Mary and John Monsour seldom spoke, except to each other, of the child they left behind. They locked away their loss in hearts that swelled with shame and sorrow as the years passed, their love and duty blunted by time, space and a family that grew in America, their deprivation eased only by their own deaths.

Family members in Maarrat-Saidnaya and in Woonsocket, Rhode Island, where my grandparents settled, tell the same story: Khaleyeh's maternal grand-

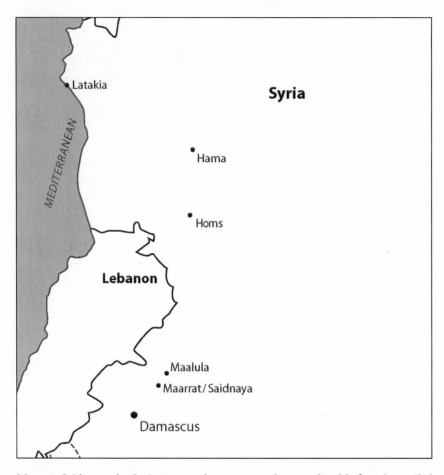

Maarrat-Saidnaya, the Syrian town where my grandparents lived before they sailed to America and where my maternal grandparents left a two-year-old child. The town is sometimes referred to as Maarrat-A-Sham, Sham being the Arabic name for Damascus, to indicate its proximity to Syria's capital.

mother — Fareida Gibron Shaheen Lattash — refused to let the little girl leave for America with her parents. By keeping her in the village, her grandmother sought to ensure that Khaleyeh's parents would return to Syria. If the parents did not return, at least their daughter would remain in the village, and the family, as Khaleyeh's grandmother knew it, would not be severed entirely from its tribal roots, or from its matriarch.

Whether the grasping grandmother was right in her reasoning depends on perspective, but she succeeded in her objective: Khaleyeh lived and died in Maarrat-Saidnaya. Three of her six children still live in the village, one died there while two others, ironically, moved away, to Europe. Most of Khaleyeh's grandchildren and great-grandchildren live in the village. Of Khaleyeh's seven American-born siblings, all of whom have died, not one ever visited Maarrat-Saidnaya. They all lived in a different village in a tribe that was reshaped in a different space with descendants of people who came from different continents as well as from different tribes.

In Arab families, the elders rule, especially the strongest personalities, woman or man. In this case, Khaleyeh's grandmother and her tribal rules trumped.

It's possible that my grandparents themselves had balked at taking a young child on such a long voyage under difficult conditions. They may have intended from the outset to save money in America and return for their daughter. But Khaleyeh's grandmother, one of my great-grandmothers, had other plans. Family members said that by the time my grandparents had enough money to bring Khaleyeh to America, she was fourteen or fifteen years old and married, according to church records in Maarrat-Saidnaya. Khaleyeh's grandmother supposedly arranged the marriage as further insurance to keep her granddaughter in the village and within her arc of the family circle. Because of her youth and her parents' absence, a bishop in Damascus probably had to give permission for Khaleyeh to marry.

John Monsour came to America on a test run with his brother-in-law just after the turn of the 20th century. When America passed the test after a year or two of hardscrabble living and earning travel money, John Monsour returned to Maarrat-Saidnaya, where Khaleyeh was born a year or two after his return and later left behind when her parents returned to America for good. One of Khaleyeh's daughters still weeps when she recalls how Khaleyeh blamed her grandmother for the family separation. Her children recall that Khaleyeh herself wept every time she received clothing or other items from her parents in America. She wept at the reminder that her parents had vanished physically from her life. She wept because her parents' continuous communication reminded her of what might have been. Khaleyeh also wept in unrelenting anger at her grandmother for strapping her to the matriarch's bosom and keeping her from the growing Monsour family in America.

Mary and John Monsour could have moved back to the tribal village with their American-born children. But their family was increasing rapidly in America, and their return to Syria would have defeated the purpose — to escape poverty and seek a better life — which had led to their departure. With one child in the village and six children already in America by the time Khaleyeh married in 1918, the weight of numbers alone would have kept the Monsour family in America.

The pioneers: My maternal grandparents, John and Mary (Shaheen) Monsour. This photograph was taken about 1950, in Woonsocket, Rhode Island, when John was in his 90s. Mary was about 18 years younger. Always with a twinkle in his eye and an urge to ramble, John regularly fled from his family's watchful eyes to walk the neighborhood.

On my first visit to Maarrat-Saidnaya, in 1989, while I was on a reporting assignment in Syria, I learned a secret that was unknown to any surviving member of the Salome family in the United States: My name is not my name.

When I reached the village — now a villa-filled town more than a village and called simply Maarra or Maarrat Al-Sham to show its proximity to Sham, or Damascus — I began searching for the Salome family, or Beit Salome as villagers would say it. The first few people I stopped appeared puzzled and unaware. They had never heard the name Salome. Then I knocked on the door of a man who explained the puzzle: Salome is an anglicized form of Salim, the first name of the family patriarch, Salim Assaf, who had died many years earlier. Only within the immediate family did the name Salim or Salome have meaning. Elsewhere in Maarra, the family was known by the name of Assaf or Beit Assaf, which meant nothing to family descendants in the United States.

My paternal grandfather, known as Louis Salome in America but as Lyos (Louis or Elias) Salim Assaf in Maarra before he reached New York, was Salim Assaf's second oldest child. My grandfather died in 1966, when he was about 74. It's impossible now to know for sure how my grandfather's name was changed, but it's easy to guess what probably happened. When my grandfather landed in New York as a teenager in 1908, an immigration worker probably asked the name of my grandfather's father. As would have been customary in the village, my grandfather probably answered by giving his father's first name, Salim, not his surname of Assaf. Salim quickly became the more recognizable Salome from the Bible. Salome then became my paternal grandfather's last name while his real last name of Assaf vanished in America. Another possibility is that immigration officials simply lopped Assaf from my grandfather's name, and turned Salim into the more familiar Salome.

Similar name confusion confronted my mother, who was born in Woonsocket, rather imprecisely, "when the leaves were falling" in 1907. When my mother entered the first grade, a teacher asked the name of her father. Being a child and following tribal custom, my mother gave her father's first name, John, not Monsour, the family's surname. For three years, until the name confusion was straightened out more or less by accident, my mother's name in school was Rose John, not Rose Monsour.

If you wish to trigger a rousing conversation among a group of people, ask how their lives would have been changed if they had grown up with different last names, say with an Irish, rather than an Italian, name in a predominately Irish neighborhood, or with an old New England Yankee, rather than a French-Canadian, name in a traditional New England town.

In my experience observing behavior in the Middle East, Central and

South Asia, Europe and parts of Africa, my tribal story is typical. Change the religion, the place, the language, the culture or the ethnic group and my family story could fit in any traditional tribal society. The similarities would also hold if the characteristics and behavior of my tribe were applied to a wider circle that encompassed region or nation-state rather than village; different ethnic and sectarian groups in a much larger place rather than in a small Arab Christian village in Syria.

The road from Damascus to Maarra weaves through several towns that have grown to become true suburbs of the Syrian capital in the twenty years since I first wandered into the family village unannounced. My driver on that first trip was a young Jordanian, whom I hired at the Hotel Meridien in Damascus, where I usually stayed. His was the common yet special name of Muhammad and he spoke the Levantine Arabic dialect of Lebanon, Jordan, Palestine and Syria. Because he drove a car that operated from the hotel rather than his own car, I figured his primary job was to alert the government to any political inquiries I might make or unusual interests that I might express.

Road to prosperity: New houses reflect the prosperity that has grown in Maarrat-Saidnaya during the past half century. The view is from a new resort hotel on a hill overlooking the town (photograph by the author, 2005).

I was searching for the family village and relatives, so I didn't care if the secret police steered the car, braked, accelerated, watched and listened. My visit offered an opportunity to show the police, if indeed they were watching, that I was harmless, which might lead them to drop their guard later when I was doing political reporting. Besides, I might learn more from a hotel driver than I could from a driver hired on the street.

We were heading to Christian territory, into a religious culture that was foreign to my Muslim driver. Christians and Muslims in the region generally share everything except religion and religious traditions and customs, although this exception is critical because it periodically leads to conflicts. During Ottoman Turkish rule, waves of religious persecution swept through the empire from time to time, causing minority peoples to flee. When a boy reached the age of sixteen, he was liable to be conscripted into the Turkish army and never heard from again. My paternal grandfather, Louis Salome, was about sixteen when he left Syria with his thirteen-year-old wife in 1908. One reason he left may have been because he feared the Turkish draft, although he told authorities in New York that he was twenty, giving his birth date as 1888, a story he stuck to throughout his life. I know that because his declaration of intention to become a U.S. citizen says he was born in 1888; he was built like a wrestler and could have easily passed for twenty. His wife, my paternal grandmother, never became a U.S. citizen, so I am uncertain of the age she gave when she arrived in New York, although I believe she added three years to her real age of thirteen. The reason my grandfather lied is understandable: If he told authorities that he was sixteen and his wife was thirteen (and that he and his wife were first cousins besides, but more on that later), they might have been sent back to Syria, or worse.

My maternal grandparents, Mary and John Monsour, arrived in America a few years earlier and were much older than my paternal grandparents. They left to escape poverty and for a better life. As mature adults, the Monsours were probably waved through immigration along with millions of other immigrants who had no contagious or terminal illnesses and no visible criminal records.

Religious differences can be major factors in determining whether there is peace or warfare, as they have been in Bosnia and Lebanon and are in Iraq, for example, but by themselves they do not always cause conflict. Other circumstances also play a role. In Syria the ruling Assad family belongs to the minority Alawite sect of Islam. The Alawites are closer to the Shiite than to the Sunni sect of Islam, although Sunnis comprise the religious majority in Syria as they do throughout Islam as a whole. Christian sects in Syria generally support the Assad regime because they consider it to be the protector of all minority sects and ethnic groups in the country. It's also safer that way.

Alawites comprise 12–14 percent of Syria's 18 million people, while Christians are about the same. Sunni Muslims, however, are more than 70 percent of Syria's population.

Political circumstances among the Palestinians are different, and so is the result: Without a hiccup, Christian minorities as well as the majority Muslims among the Palestinians have joined hands, violently as well as vocally, in opposition to Israel's occupation of Palestinian lands.

Before entering Maarra, which is to the right of the main road north and slightly east of Damascus, Muhammad and I took a hard left and went directly to the larger town of Saidnaya, which could be considered Maarra's biological and historical parent. If we had not turned and instead continued northeast about 25 miles, as I did on another occasion, we would have reached the town of Ma'alula, where the ancient Aramaic language, along with modern Arabic, is still spoken on the streets. When it comes to tradition, few villages trump Ma'alula: Ancient Aramaic, which sounds like a ritual mixture of Arabic and Hebrew, was widely spoken in the region 2,000 years ago. Ma'alula is still known for baking the best Syrian bread in an area where food is a leading identifier of culture, tribe and village. Along with religion, language and other shared transcendant traits, food ranks high in the cultural identification signs of tribes everywhere.

A mere discussion of tribal food, to say nothing of sharing it, can create a bond strong enough to lift a traveler out of trouble. On a trip to Syria's northern reaches, for example, I was held up routinely at the airport in Aleppo as I waited to board a plane to Damascus. A security officer had asked for my currency declaration, which under the circumstances was a trick question. According to Syrian law, foreigners were required to declare the amount of money they brought into the country and obtain receipts when they exchanged foreign currency for Syrian pounds. Each currency exchange is supposed to be recorded on the currency declaration form. When a person left the country, the theory is that the amount of money exchanged plus the remaining foreign currency are supposed to equal the total amount of money a person brought into the country. Although I wasn't leaving the country, I was a foreigner and the officer was checking whether I had been complying with the law by recording currency exchanges in the declaration and retaining the exchange receipts.

My conversation with the security officer went like this:

OFFICER: Where is your currency declaration?

ME (as I rummaged through my shoulder bag and pockets searching for the declaration): What's your favorite Arabic meal?

OFFICER: You must carry your currency form at all times.

ME (still searching): When I was growing up in America, we used to eat Arabic food all the time.

OFFICER: You must find your currency form or you will not be allowed to board the plane.

ME: When was the last time you ate shooshbarak (dumplings stuffed with ground lamb, cooked in a seasoned yoghurt sauce and served over rice)?

OFFICER: Let me look through your bag. Maybe I can find the currency declaration.

ME: That's OK. I'll look again. Do you like sfeha (open meat pies, a bit like pizza; also called meat and dough)?

OFFICER: Did you eat all that food in America?

ME: Sure, that and much more. All the food you eat here we eat in America.

OFFICER, smiling: Never mind the currency declaration, you can go.

ME: Thanks and I'll think of you the next time I eat sfeha (lamb and dough pies).

Our chat in a small waiting room at the Aleppo airport lasted less than an hour. Gliding from one dish to another, I kept the conversation focused on tribal food and culture and away from the currency declaration. I didn't come close to exhausting stories about food cooked by my parents, aunts and grandmothers. Our friendly talk strengthened the link between me, the officer and tribal culture that had crossed the seas and pried me from a pickle.

An old Christian town, Saidnaya, across the road from Maarrat-Saidnaya, is home to three large monasteries/convents, the oldest of which reputedly dates to the sixth century. In Saidnaya, Muhammad and I visited a grotto filled with icons of Christian saints and holy people and candles that burn like flickering stars in the clear desert sky. As usual in such grottoes, the ceiling is blackened with the soot of centuries of lighted candles. Muhammad, my driver, had never seen such a place; icons and other pictures or images of saints are largely alien to Islam. To any person unfamiliar with the religious tradition, the grotto would have seemed more weird than iconic. For what seemed like two hours, my Muslim driver stared in the grotto, awed by the candles and the painted faces of ancient holy people. I was awed by my driver's awe and his attention span at what to me was a more familiar sight. Perspective, however, brings a flood of light or a shroud of darkness. When I enter a mosque, I usually gawk. I try to be inconspicuous and casually observant, but I still gawk, almost as much as Muhammad did in the Christian grotto.

Translated from the ancient Aramaic language, Maarrat-Saidnaya means the caves of Saidnaya. Taken alone the name Saidnaya does not have a literal translation; the meaning of the name comes from two versions of the town's origin and is rooted in secular legend and religious belief. Some in the town

say the word comes from ancient Aramaic and means Our Lady. Far from
that, however, is another meaning: deer hunting, which relates to the legend
of the Byzantine Emperor Justinian hunting deer in the region when he
founded the Convent of Our Lady in Saidnaya.

Until early in the 19th century, some of the older villagers say, the land
that Maarra now occupies was loosely a part of the municipality of Saidnaya
and was tended by farmers and shepherds who lived in the fields. The caves
undoubtedly provided shelter for the people who farmed the land and cared
for the animals, and for the animals themselves. Tired of being the rough
equivalent of subservient tenants, the farmers and shepherds across the road
from Saidnaya's center broke away and formed the new and much smaller village. Time and construction have buried the caves of Saidnaya, but a few
remain visible in the hills that ascend from the bowl bottom that forms
Maarra's center.

With the passing years, Christians from similar villages to the west in
what is now Lebanon and from the south in northern Palestine migrated to
Maarra. From the time my grandparents left about a hundred years ago until
the 1970s, the village grew only slightly and changed little.

Then came what would qualify locally as a revolution. Due in part to
drought, many villagers sold their farm and grazing lands to buy large trucks
to haul produce and other goods across the wider Middle East. Business and
wealth boomed with the advent of refrigerator trucks, leading to the construction of large and expensive villas, some of which are so lavish they consume
sizable plots. More money from the elite of Damascus flowed in for the construction of large houses used mainly in the summer months, when Maarra's
cooler air offers relief from Damascus' edge-of-the-desert heat.

Change visits tribal villages like Maarra in small doses over long periods. But change does come, in the form now of video games, cell phones, less
traditional clothing, ornate houses and large trucks that bring wealth and
sometimes contraband and then trouble. It also comes in the form of new
bread machines and preservatives that water down the thickness and taste of
delicious flat Syrian bread in the interest of delaying spoilage. When I complained about the bread at the new resort hotel on a hill overlooking the town
center, the kitchen made, special for me alone, some of the thicker more traditional bread. When I complained about the new bread another time, partly
in jest to test the reaction, at a party thrown by my Assaf family cousins, they
laughed at me. One of them, a baker, was supremely confident that if I made
the old-style bread and he offered the new bread that stayed fresh longer, villagers would buy his bread and not mine. Never focused on marketing, I
joked that quality mattered more than sales, but I convinced no one.

Some villagers still cultivate vineyards, others plant wheat and grow a variety of fruits and vegetables; fewer still raise goats and sheep. Maarra lies in a semi-arid region, where winter rains provide enough moisture to water large coniferous trees that surround houses and delineate property lines and fields. From a hilltop vantage point, the village looks rich and green because of the trees, but a closer look reveals that there is no grass; sand and rocks cover the earth. What goods and supplies villagers can't provide for themselves, they bring from Damascus, Saidnaya and neighboring towns. Fifty years ago, water for household use was carried mainly from a now-stagnant spring in the village center. Today, water is rationed and comes from a series of artesian wells that villagers use to fill tanks on top of their houses a couple of times a week.

The people of Maarra are traditional and tough, conservative and fundamentally religious, which in this case means Christian, although they are not all of the same Christian denomination. They are united by family, faith and village, or place, a sturdy tripod that supports traditional lifestyles among tribes in the Middle East and elsewhere. Other principal aspects of tribalism as I observed them, such as a common language, ethnicity and culture, along with signature social rules such as patriarchy, are built into this same tripod.

On all of my visits to Maarra, both sides of my family welcomed me warmly, although they knew little or nothing of me personally. Older family members knew the names of my parents, aunts and uncles — the first generation of their cousins born in America — but I knew nothing of my cousins in Maarra. First and second cousins and people related through marriage greeted me with elaborate feasts for their entire families. I dare say that their American cousins would be stretched to do the same for them in this country. Even strangers on the street were friendly when I introduced myself. Everyone knew someone in my extended families. One man in his 90s showed me the site of the Monsour family house which, in a bow to modernization years ago, was leveled to allow construction of a road in the village's eastern sector.

One of my father's first cousins in Maarra recalled that he postponed his wedding early in 1964 out of respect for my father who died in late December 1963. When the wedding of my father's cousin, who is my second cousin, was held later in 1964, the reception was small and muted, held in the family home rather than in a restaurant or hall. This was a family-cultural decision, made out of respect for my father and my grandfather, who was still alive then. It did not matter that my father and his cousin had never met, that they lived very different lives in different countries: Their fathers were brothers and from the perspective of age and hierarchy, village and family, they all belonged to the same tribe.

My own wedding was scheduled for July 4, 1964. Despite family efforts,

led by my paternal grandfather, to force a postponement because of my father's
death six months earlier, I refused to comply. Several relatives then refused
to attend my wedding. The cultural bond and tribal pressure, though still
present, were much weaker and less ingrained in my time and place than they
were for my second cousin in Maarra.

Because I grew up around all of my grandparents, especially my paternal grandfather, Louis Salome, and my maternal grandmother, Mary Shaheen Monsour, I never had the impression that Maarra was governed by
timidity. A waiter in Damascus enlightened me further in the early 1990s,
after I told him that my grandparents had emigrated from Maarra to America almost a hundred years earlier. Let me tell you a story about the Maar-
rawiyeh (the people of Maarra), the waiter said, with a mischievous smile:
Two men were standing on a balcony overlooking a large crowd. One man,
a stranger, told the other man, who was from Maarra, to, "Shoot George."
The man from Maarra balked at first, saying, "But I don't know who George
is." When the other man insisted, "Just shoot George," the man from Maarra
fired randomly into the crowd and watched a man fall. "I guess that's George,"
the man from Maarra said, grinning down at his unknown victim.

Several years later, I asked a man from Maarra whether this story accurately reflected the character and personalites of the villagers. The man said
he never heard the "Kill George" story, but he quickly repeated a saying that
reflects the tough tribal cohesiveness of the town and its people: "If a lion
comes into Maarra looking for trouble, it will leave without its skin." In other
words, villagers, no matter what their internal divisions and external rivalries, will always unite against an outsider. That simple saying is as good a
definition of tribalism as I ever heard.

Older villagers recall a raid on Maarra that dates to about 1925, when
the French controlled Syria and what is now Lebanon under a League of
Nations mandate. Muslims from neighboring villages, believing that Christians supported French rule on the grounds that the French were also Christians — an allegation that villagers to this day say was not only untrue but
defamatory because they would never support foreigners — attacked Maarra,
killing, pillaging and taking prisoners. The people of Maarra and neighboring Saidnaya soon banded together and gave chase, finding the corpse of my
aunt Khaleyeh's father-in-law, who had been taken prisoner, by the main road
south of Maarra. The force from Maarra and Saidnaya caught up with the
attackers and killed their leader, cut off his head, stuck it on the end of a long
pole and paraded around Maarra in triumph. That happened a long time ago
and relations among neighbors are peaceful now, but the incident is an example of tribalism — rooted in religion, politics, family and village — that turns
violent. It is not far removed, either, from recent tribal conflicts in Lebanon,

Bosnia, Somalia and now in Iraq and Afghanistan, right down to the foreign intervention.

Families from my ancestral village will quarrel within and among each other and sometimes go years without communicating because of some slight, large or small. But they will usually come together when threatened as a group or as a sect; the village itself, no matter what familial or sectarian divisions are simmering, will unite when threatened from the outside by an enemy common to all.

My paternal grandparents, Louis Salome and Mary Ghazale Salome, were first cousins. The marriage of first cousins was customary in order to strengthen the family by increasing its numbers. The larger the family, the stronger it would be, in church matters, local politics and financially. Chil-

An American original: This Salome family photograph, a classic of the immigrant genre, was taken about 1935 in Woonsocket, Rhode Island. *Front row, from left:* Louis, Charles, William, the unmistakeable partriarch Louis and his wife Mary (Ghazale) Salome; Mary, who was the youngest child; Anne and George. *Second row, from left:* Joseph, John, Abraham, my father, who was the oldest; Michael and James. Only my uncle Louis survives.

dren are considered members of the father's, not the mother's, family. So if first cousins marry, their children will add to the united, extended families of both parents. But if a man and woman of different families marry, the woman's family essentially loses her children to her husband's side and her own family is thus diminished.

The tribal custom of first cousins marrying continues in Maarra, and throughout the region, despite its genetic risks, but the custom is not as strong in Maarra as it was 100 or even 50 years ago. Another tribal custom in Maarra, that of parents arranging the marriages of their children, is also weakening somewhat, but it continues as well. The first generation of children born in America of immigrants from Maarra, such as my parents, usually did not marry first cousins. But the oldest among the first generation of children born in America usually had marriages that were arranged by their parents. That was the case with my parents, Abraham Louis Salome and Rose Monsour Salome. When we were children and according to custom, my sisters and I always were pushed more in the direction of the paternal Salome side of the family than toward the maternal Monsour side. But my seniority-wielding maternal grandmother, Mary Shaheen Monsour, did not let go without a fight and without piling heavy guilt on my mother, who then transferred it to my sisters and me, if for any reason we failed to visit on a Sunday or holiday.

Tribal families still protect each other if one parent dies and leaves young children. If it's the mother who dies, her sister may marry the widower to raise and protect the children, and the newly married couple may even have children of their own. If it's the father who dies, his brother may marry the dead man's widow to keep the family in the family. It has not been uncommon for a man and a woman who have each lost a spouse to marry each other, to end up raising three families, all of whom are related, and then for a half-sister to marry a half-brother — all in the interest of protecting and enlarging the family and ultimately the village as tribe.

In the village of Maarra itself, the question of individual family size and strength may be moot because the village seems to be one large family that is divided only by names rather than by blood. On my most recent visit to Maarra, during January 2005, I joked that if DNA tests were taken of all the villagers, the results would show that everyone is related and villagers belong not to the family of Assaf, Alam, Srour, Khoury, Shaheen, Ghazale or any others, but to the family of Maarra. Their smiles conceded the point.

The tribe is the village; the village is the tribe. There are splits and divisions, the most serious on religious matters concerning turf, control and influence, but those are strongest at hierarchical levels rather than in the village itself.

In practical matters, family members care for each other in everyday ways, such as providing food and shelter for members who may need help. Parents commonly build houses that are reinforced on the ground floors to accommodate additional floors later for adult sons and their families. When sons marry and have their own families, they often move into apartments in their parents' large houses. Reinforced floors are added according to the number of sons in the family. It is common throughout the region to see iron rods sticking above a completed floor of a house in preparation for adding another floor.

Religion, faith, is a powerful leg of the tribal tripod in Maarra. Allah — God — is a critical figure among Christians there as well as among the 90 or so Muslims who live year-round in the town of about 3,500, which swells to 7,000 or more during the summer.

God is everywhere in the language and lives of the people of Maarra. May God give you peace. May God go with you. May God keep you. God willing. May God have mercy on his/her soul. When things go badly, God may be invoked to damn your religion or your family.

Those who are less observant tend to worship gambling and manna. Many appreciate Maarra's other secular activities, such as enjoying a few beers or arak, the local clear anise-flavored brew distilled from fermented grape juice, without diminishing the sincere homage they pay to God and God's leading local acolyte, St. Elias. When God isn't asked for help, St. Elias is.

Members of Maarra's religious sects get on well with each other, but there are limits. Marriage between a Christian and a Muslim, for example, is grounds for family exile and maybe worse. The village mosque was built during the mid–1960s, when local Muslims swapped property with members of the majority Christian denomination. In return for the house that Muslims gave to adjacent St. Elias' Melkite Greek Catholic Church, the church gave Maarra's Muslims land a little farther away on which Muslims built the mosque that stands there today. Before the mosque was built, the Muslims, at the time probably no more than 50, worshipped in a room at the house they later turned over to St. Elias' Melkite Greek Catholic Church. Maarra's first Muslims, members of the Khidr Shaheen family, had been Christians before they left their church for Islam decades ago after a patriarch refused Khidr Shaheen a divorce. Many of Maarra's Muslims, who are probably also my distant relatives, greeted me warmly as a descendant of families from the village, further evidence of the magnetic oneness of family, village and tribe.

Maarra's patron saint is surely Elias, known as Elijah in the Old Testament. Stories about St. Elias performing miracles are legion in the village. Both the Antiochian Greek Orthodox Church and the Melkite (which means royalist in the old Aramaic language) Greek Catholic Church are named for

Soulful: The mountaintop Sanctuary of St. Elias, the patron saint of Maarrat-Said-naya (photograph by the author, 2005).

St. Elias, and a shrine or sanctuary on a mountain high above the village is dedicated to St. Elias. Dutch archeologists working in the 1980s and 1990s uncovered religious frescoes in the shrine that date to the 13th century. It takes little prompting for a villager to show a visitor hoofprints of a horse embedded in rocks high inside the St. Elias shrine. To the people of Maarra, the hoofprints symbolize the biblical version of Elijah's ascent to heaven in a horse-drawn fiery chariot some 3,000 years ago.

John Monsour, my maternal grandfather, was a devout believer in St. Elias. The first stained-glass window on the right side facing the altar of St. Elias' Melkite Greek Catholic Church in Woonsocket, Rhode Island, bears the name John Monsour and Family. John Monsour, I believe, was one of the first, if not the first, persons to emigrate from Maarra to Woonsocket. The second stained-glass window on that same side of St. Elias' church bears the name Louis Salome and Family, my paternal grandfather, who donated the land for the church and paid most of the bills in the early years of that parish.

One day, in the mountains outside the village, as John Monsour told the story 60 years ago, he was guiding a donkey loaded with chairs to St. Elias' shrine when the animal and its cargo became wedged in a mountain pass. My grandfather was stuck, too, but he knew the way out: He prayed to St. Elias.

I would have removed chairs from the donkey to lighten and thin the load. But John Monsour, who was born in Maarra in the mid–nineteenth century, prayed to St. Elias. The answer came, my grandfather proclaimed without putting his hand on a Bible, when the mountain pass widened, allowing him, the donkey and the chairs to pass. John Monsour's belief was not unique then among the people of Maarra, and it is not now.

Paternal grandfathers carry the most weight in Arab families and Louis Salome, my father's father, was not close to an exception. He worshipped power and influence, inside and outside of church. Money was his religion, and he made large contributions to local priests and to the church in Woonsocket. He represented the hard, tough side of his ancestral village. Big Louie, as he was known in Woonsocket and in nearby Millville, Massachusetts, where he moved with his large family in the mid–1930s, was a bookie who had also operated a jitney service. With a wife who served his every wish and died at age 53, he supported 11 children, bankrolled the church he helped to build, sometimes supported the rival Orthodox church in a neighboring city and helped a large number of people along the way. Twice he sent money back to Maarra to help a younger brother who had pleaded self-defense in the killing of two men in separate fights.

When my grandfather, Louis Salome, was a very young man working in a Woonsocket factory, he knocked out another man during a fight, and thought the man was dead. My paternal grandfather didn't pray to St. Elias or anyone else to revive the unconscious man. Instead, he opened the window, which was on an upper floor, picked up the man with a neat clean and jerk move and was preparing to throw him out the window, to destroy the evidence I suppose, when the man woke to find himself in a precarious position above Big Louie's head. According to my father, who told me this story, the happily revived man made a fast and permanent peace with my grandfather.

Louis Salome, my grandfather, didn't tell stories about St. Elias performing miracles, although he praised Allah every time he finished a fine Maarra meal prepared by his wife or older daughter. Roughly defined, my paternal grandfather was a budding rural scientist, not a religious man of the old school. A story he liked to tell concerned the balmy night he slept outdoors with his mouth wide open. After he awoke, feeling a bit peculiar, he realized that a snake had crawled into his mouth and down his esophagus. Perhaps this was common when a boy slept outside with his mouth open in Maarra. Instead of praying to St. Elias, Big Louie prepared a more secular solution: He placed his face, mouth open, over eggs frying in a pan on an open fire so the fumes and odors would lure the snake from his body. That worked, too, according to my paternal grandfather.

Maarra is oval-shaped, with a circular road that originally formed a rough boundary that has been broken by the construction of large houses and new roads. A main road cuts through the middle of the oval and forms the village center. Smaller streets flare off from the main road and the circular road. It is easy to walk the village, although if a woman, especially a young woman, desires to stroll alone around town without a specific purpose such as going to church or a store, she will probably be stopped by adult males inquiring about her purpose and safety and suggesting that she pace inside her house instead. This interference is so common and intimidating that few young women walk simply for exercise, to smell the flowers and trees or to listen to the hammers pounding out the new houses.

In Maarra's families, women and men have well-defined roles. When women marry, it is customary for them to be considerably younger, as much as fifteen years, than their husbands. This usually means that women will bear many children to enlarge the tribe and their husbands will be well cared for in old age. The oldest son's role is to serve the father, too, and to follow the father in the family business or trade. The youngest son is usually protected and favored. Daughters are supposed to do as they are told, and no less. Any modifications in these roles are usually the result of the intervention of a strong mother. Slowly, the rules and roles are changing. More women, for example, are attending Damascus University than ever before, to become doctors, teachers and other professionals.

The walk between St. Elias Antiochian Orthodox Church and St. Elias Melkite Greek Catholic Church is easy. So are relations among parishioners of the two Christian churches. Priests from the churches participate in each other's ceremonies, such as baptisms, weddings and funerals, which are major events in Maarra because they bind families and the village itself. Both churches share a common liturgy and rituals, but not a common hierarchy. St. Elias Orthodox Church is an Eastern rite Christian church that comes under the authority of a patriarch based in Damascus; this church does not recognize the authority of the pope. It is not a Western, or Latin, church. But St. Elias Melkite Greek Catholic Church does recognize the authority of the pope. It is an Eastern rite Catholic church in union with Rome, although it uses the same Eastern liturgy and rituals as St. Elias Orthodox Church. Priests in both churches are allowed to marry.

At the village level, relations among the two churches are cooperative, not merely cordial and courteous. But higher up the hierachy, among bishops, for example, relations are not always as harmonious. At the higher level, power, influence, control and turf come into play and cooperation diminishes as often happens among rival sects and churches. When, for example, an Orthodox bishop went to a village service that was heavily attended by

Melkite Greek Catholics, who widely outnumber Orthodox parishioners in Maarra, the bishop ignored the Greek Catholics and focused on the Orthodox believers. This angered the Greek Catholics who said they would walk out of the service if the bishop ever repeated his conduct.

My paternal grandfather, Louis Salome, moved between the local Melkite Greek Catholic and Orthodox churches in the Woonsocket, Rhode Island, and Pawtucket, Rhode Island, area, both of which were attended by people from Maarra. He helped priests in both parishes, gravitating toward the church and priest where he could exercise more power and influence and perhaps playing it safe in religious terms, like a wealthy person who contributes to both Democratic and Republican presidential candidates in the same election. One day my paternal grandfather received a letter from one of his brothers in Maarra urging my grandfather not to give money to an Orthodox priest from Maarra who was in Rhode Island. The priest was a thief, my grandfather's brother claimed, a sure indication that the two men had had a serious falling out. Although he had a street doctorate in Arabic numerals, my grandfather was illiterate. Without knowing what the letter said, my grandfather brought it to the accused priest who laughed like hell, along with my grandfather, when he translated the missive. This story still brings great laughter in Maarra.

Religion is a powerful force for Maarra's permanent population of about 3,500. On a plateau high above the village center, the Damascus-based Syrian (or Syriac) Orthodox Patriarchate in the past decade constructed a large complex that includes a seminary and monastery, convent, education center, home for elderly priests and crypts for ancestral patriarchs. The Syrian Orthodox Church is separate from the other two Christian denominations in the village, has its own hierarchy, rituals and liturgical language, and joins with other Orthodox sects in not recognizing the authority of the pope.

—— ∞ ——

Never have family members in Maarra asked where I was from, where my grandfather came from, whether I had a God, "What's your blood?" or where I was from "originally," as a young Latvian woman working at a London hotel did in 2004. The people in Maarra instinctively knew, or thought they knew, the answers. Tribal traditions, family names, old-fashioned Arabic words that I spoke, knowledge of family members in America and my taste in cuisine told them, in their minds, the answers to those questions. But they also know that I am from a different place, that I look like them but act differently and have different expectations. We share some, but not all, cultural traits, mainly those I ingested as a boy.

One of my Maarra cousins wondered why I was asking so many questions about my grandparents, but was saying very little about my parents. The

The first generation: In their 1937 wedding photo taken in Woonsocket, Rhode Island, my mother, Rose, is seated in front of my father, Abraham. Laura, one of my mother's younger sisters, was the maid-of-honor. John, one of my father's younger brothers, was best man.

question and the answer were helpful to them and to me: If I was ever to learn more about my own past, I had to learn it through my grandparents and their closest and oldest relatives in Maarra and through the village itself. My parents had no identifiable past in Maarra, except through their parents. What Abraham Louis Salome and Rose Monsour Salome knew about their lost tribes in Maarra they learned through their parents and as far as I could decipher, they were consciously aware of very little because they were on the single, narrow path toward Americanization and blending in. My grandparents lived in America, but they weren't from America. My parents were born in America and were Americans; what they knew or felt about Maarra came, filtered and watered down, through the elders in the family circle.

Few of my remaining older relatives in America know anything about the tribes in Maarra, and still fewer care. All their memories tell them is that their relatives in the village were poor and wanted money. What was true in 1905 and 1950, when my paternal grandfather visited Maarra, is no longer accurate.

Tribal threads remain strong in Maarra, however, where most family members live and stick together, sharing in weddings, births and deaths. Families — indeed the village itself— change, but tradition holds change in check. Maarra has grown dramatically in the past 30 to 40 years. In the past 100 years, villagers emigrated to America, Argentina, Europe and the United Arab Emirates; local officials estimate that Maarra's current permanent population of about 3,500 is matched by the number of people who have left the village for foreign lands.

But in America, cousins don't know cousins and many probably couldn't locate Syria on a map, let alone identify the name of the village which was the wellspring of the original immigrants. The original tribes melt quickly in America, but later generations of those forgotten tribes don't really vanish; they take new form as members of other tribes that are peculiar to America. Surviving relatives, uncles, brothers, sisters and cousins spread out to join varied tribes in neighborhoods, towns and cities, in different churches, political parties, professions, clubs of all kinds. The tribes in America, where individualism is prized above family and community, differ dramatically from the family tribes in Maarra, but they are still tribes because all people need to call some land, group or intellectual pursuit home. No one can be entirely from nowhere.

Soon my family tribes in Maarra will also lose memory of their families in America, despite the grip that tribal traditions have on traditional peoples. But those tribes will remain much as they are. This disappearance of immigrant names and faces has already happened in the United States, the inevitable consequence of time and change. Even the older people of Maarra remem-

All in my family: Ibrahim Shahedeh Alam is my first cousin. He is a son of my aunt, Khaleyeh, my mother's oldest sister, who was born in Syria and never left. His late wife, Laurice, the daughter of one of my grandfather Louis Salome's brothers, was my second cousin. In 1955, when Ibrahim and Laurice married, Ibrahim sent this photograph to our grandmother, Mary (Shaheen) Monsour, in Woonsocket, Rhode Island.

ber little or nothing of Louis Salim Assaf and Mary Ghazale Salome, and John Monsour and Mary Shaheen Monsour; soon no one in the village will know those names. The Monsour family has already vanished from Maarra, gone to Argentina and America where it has faded and morphed into new tribes.

On a visit to Maarra in 1999 with my daughter, Mary, and son, Andrew, older sister Lois, youngest sister Mary Lou and Mary Lou's daughters Laura and Rachel, Mary Lou and I looked at each other and declared with broad smiles of discovery that Noor, our Aunt Khaleyeh's youngest daughter and our first cousin, "even smells like Ma Hanna," our name for our maternal grandmother who, despite her dominating presence, we knew by the link to her husband John, or Hanna. Noor, with whom I and my sisters share Monsour grandparents and Shaheen great-grandparents, looks more like Mary Shaheen Monsour — her grandmother and ours — than did my mother or any of the other Monsour children who were born in the United States.

Why shouldn't Noor smell like her grandmother and dance like her grandmother, despite the passage of time? They come from the same family, from the same place; they ate the same food and had the same roots, and in a sense time never changed for either of them, and so the distance between them wasn't as great as it would seem. Noor stayed in the same line from grandmother to mother to granddaughter in the same place, living the same culture, which none of Mary and John Monsour's American-born children can claim. All because Khaleyeh's grandmother wouldn't let her leave with her parents for America.

On the day I left Maarra for the United States after my most recent visit, I did not sleep. Before I left the hotel at 2:30 A.M. bound for the airport in Damascus, I went from house to house, cousin to cousin, to say goodbye. It would have been an insult to leave without saying a special farewell to each family. I thanked them all for their hospitality and promised to visit them all again when I returned.

In conventional American terms, I was a total stranger to most relatives in the village. So were my deceased parents and grandparents who, despite their closer chronological links, were long separated by lives lived elsewhere. But in tribal terms, I was part of the family and would always be. When next I visit Maarra, I will be welcomed by surviving family members, no matter how young they might be or whether they remember me at all. My face, my name, my family, the words and names I use will ensure another warm welcome because that's how tribe and tradition work.

Index

Page numbers in **_bold italic_** indicate illustrations.